FAUQUIER COUNTY, VIRGINIA DEEDS 1759 – 1778

Compiled By

John K. Gott

HERITAGE BOOKS, INC.

Published 1988 By

HERITAGE BOOKS, INC.
1540E Pointer Ridge Place, Bowie, Maryland 20716
(301)-390-7709

ISBN 1-55613-102-X

A Complete Catalog Listing Hundreds Of Titles On
Genealogy, History, And Americana
Available Free Upon Request

DEDICATED

TO

T. TRIPLETT RUSSELL

Friend and helper,
Historian and Genealogist
<u>par</u> <u>exellence</u>

TABLE OF CONTENTS

INTRODUCTION

Fauquier County was established by Act of the General Assembly of Virginia on 1 May 1759. The Act had been passed 22 February of that year. The first instruments recorded in the Deed Books were the Bonds of Joseph Blackwell as Sheriff and Thomas Marshall as Surveyor, on 24 May 1759.

Fauquier County is fortunate in being one of those Virginia counties in which all of the deed books from its establishment to the present day are extant. The abstracts in the present volume covers the first six deed books, including every entry contained therein, i. e., deeds, leases, bonds, contracts of sale, mortgages, agreements, etc. The first Court in which an instrument was ordered recorded was 24 May 1759 and the last, covered by the abstracts, 28 September 1778.

Each abstract is meant to cover the original recorded instrument as fully as possible; giving the names of every individual mentioned, besides the grantor(s) and grantee(s), any geographical feature mentioned. When a slave has been named this, too, has been added.

Every attempt has been made to include enough of the recorded document to be in itself complete, the metes and bounds of any tract of land excepted. The exact page references are given in case a researcher should wish to order a photocopy from the Clerk of the Court, Warrenton, Virginia 22186. There are few, if any, original deeds kept among the records in the Clerk's Office. Unlike wills, marriage bonds, etc., deeds, after being recorded, were returned ("delivered", as the marginal note often states) to one of the parties, usually the grantee.

This project has been completed to 1800 and, it is hoped, will be published in a companion volume.

John K. Gott
Glencairn
Marshall, Virginia

ABBREVIATIONS

ack.	acknowledged
B & S	bargain and sale
beg.	beginning
cert.	certificate
cor.	corner
Culp. Co.	Culpeper County
dau.	daughter
exor(s)	executor(s)
Fx. Co.	Fairfax County
Fauq. Co.	Fauquier County
F'rick Co.	Frederick County
Ham. Par.	Hamilton Parish
h. w.	his wife
K. G. Co.	King George County
Lan. Co.	Lancaster County
nat.	natural
Loud. Co.	Loudoun County
N'land Co.	Northumberland County
o.	oath
OR	ordered recorded
par.	parish
Prop.	Proprietor
prov.	proved
purch.	purchased
rec.	recorded
Staff. Co.	Stafford County
W'land Co.	Westmoreland County
wit(s)	Witness(es)

DEED BOOK 1

1759 - 1763

Page 1. 24 May 1759. Bond of **Joseph Blackwell**, Sheriff to collect and receive monies under Act of Assembly to raise Ł20,000 for the better protection of the inhabitants on the frontier of this Colony. For Ł10,000. *Securities*: **William Blackwell** and **William Eustace**, Gent. *Rec*: 24 May 1759.

Pages 1-2. 24 May 1759. Bond of **Thomas Marshall** as Surveyor of Fauquier County. For Ł500. *Securities*: **James Keith** and **Cuthbert Bullitt**, Gent. *Rec*: 24 May 1759.

Pages 2-3. 4 May 1759. **William Eustace**, Gent., to **George Crump**, Gent. Thirty-one acres, part of a tract of land the said Eustace now liveth on .. dividing line between the said Eustace and Crump .. On Elk Run .. in exchange for 30 acres .. part of tract the said George Crump now lives on .. same granted to Wm. Eustace in 1758, recorded in Prince William Co. *Wit*: **Jeremiah Darnall, Martin Pickett, Mat'w. Harrison.** *Rec*: 24 May 1759.

Pages 3-7. 19 June 1759. **Richard Henry Lee** and **Anne Lee**, his wife, of County of Westmoreland to **William Edmonds**, of Fauquier. Lease and release, for Ł230. 514 acres 2 roods 14 poles, near the main road that goes to Winchester .. near Capt. Elias Edmonds's plantation .. paying therefore the rent of one Ear of Indian corn, if demanded. *Wit*: **Willoughby Newton, Thomas Lawson, William Jett, Jun'r.** *Rec*: 28 June 1759

Pages 7-8. 30 June 1759. Certificate verifying to examination of **Ann Lee** who cannot conveniently travel to our County Court .. examination by **Willoughby Newton, Samuel Oldham** and **Richard Lee**, Gent. .. that she freely and willingly does consent (without the persuasion or threats of her husband) to the conveyance of the above mentioned land. *Rec*: 28 June 1759.

Pages 8-9. 20 June 1759. Bond from **Richard Henry Lee** to **William Edmonds**. For Ł1,000. *Securities*: **Gawin Corbin** and **Francis Lightfoot Lee.** For the performance of the lease and release of the above land and agreements. *Wit*: **John Stewart, William Lee, Geo. Cook.** *Rec*: 28 June 1759.

Pages 9-13. 1759. **William Fitzgerald** and **Kitty**, his wife, of Fauquier to **Henry Churchill**, Esq. For 5 shillings. All that tract of land granted by patent, 5 Jan 1741, to **John Higgins** .. 110 acres. Corner to the land of **Benjamin Newton** .. line of **Colo. Carter** .. cor. to a certain tract of 900 acres surveyed by Mr. **John Warner** for **Lord Fairfax** .. cor. to the aforesd. Benj. Newton .. crossing a small branch of the Walnut branch .. Also all that other tract granted, 5 Aug 1747, to **James Genn** .. cor. to John Higgins' tract in the late Secretary Carter's Line .. cor. to Lord Fairfax .. near Rogues road .. to Falmouth road .. to Quantico road .. cor. to Higgins and Benj. Newton .. Spanish oak on the Walnut Branch .. cor. to said Newton, **Thomas Stamps** and **Timothy Dorgan**. *Signed*: **William (+) Fitzgerald**. *Wit*: **Thos. McClanahan, John Duncan, Henry Martin**. *Rec*: 28 June 1759.

Pages 13-16. 26 June 1759. **Joseph Deleny** to **Charles Deleny**. For 5 shillings. Lease and release. 352 acres, being part of a larger tract purchased by Joseph Deleny of **Edw'd. Twentyman** & acknowledged in Prince William Co. Court, 26 Feb 1744. Cor. to **Peter Hedgman** .. along Hedgman's line .. crossing **Field**'s rolling road .. *Signed*: **Joseph Delaney**. *Wit*: **G. Hume, And'w. Barbe**. *Rec*: 28 June 1759.

Pages 17-20. 26-27 June 1759. **Joseph Deleny** to **Joseph Deleny, Jun'r**. For 5 shillings. Lease and release. 362 acres, being part of a larger tract purchased of **Edw'd. Twentyman**, 26 Feb 1744 .. cor. to **Peter Hedgman** .. *Signed*: **Joseph Delaney**. *Wit*: **G. Hume, And'w. Barbe**. *Rec*: 28 June 1759.

Pages 20-23. 24 August 1759. **John Bell** and **Frankey**, his wife, of Parish of Hamilton, to **Thomas Porter**, of same. For 5 shillings. Lease & release. 120 acres .. near the mouth of the North Fork of Cedar Run cor. to the **Reverend Mr. Scott**'s land in the line of the land of **Mann Page**, Esq. .. cor. to **William Russell & Rich'd. Grubs** .. cor. to Grubs and **Mr. Barber** .. along Barbers line .. *Wit*: James **Bell, William Edmonds, Jafery Johnson**. *Rec*: 23 August 1759.

Page 24. No date. Report on motion by **James Slaughter** to lay off one acre belonging to **Peter Rout** for the use of a water mill. Jury of 12 lawful men (**Joseph Hudnall, Wm. Morgan, Wm. Settle, Bushrode Doggett, Vincent Garner, Thomas Garner, Sen'r., Thos. Garner, Jun'r., Thos. Mitchell, John Stone, Parish Garner, Robert Hinson & David Welsh** (signed **Welch**) sworn before **Thomas Marshall**, Gent. .. one acre is of the value of 20 shillings. *Rec*: 23 August 1759.

Pages 24-26. 13 Jan 1759. Articles of agreement and Bond between **Thos. Colson & Margret**, his wife, of the parish of Frederick, county of Frederick and **Jeffrey Johnson** and **Moses Johnson**, of Parish of Hamilton .. Thos. Colson who is now intermarried with Margret, the widow of Jeffrey Johnson, late of Prince William County, dec'd., who bequeathed unto his said wife, **M a r g e t**, all his estate, real and personal, during her natural life and after her decease to be equally divided between two sons, Jeffrey and Moses. Whereas Thos. Colson has enough for plentiful support and maintenance for himself and his wife .. do hereby relinquish unto said sons all rights, etc., except two feather beds & furniture, one large trunk and all the pewter that

2

belonged to the said Estate, one Lin'n wheel and one gray horse .. Jeffrey and Moses agreed to pay Thomas Colson and Marg't, his wife, 100 gals. of cyder and 10 gals. brandy .. yearly and every year during the said Margaret's life if it be a fruitful year with the said orchards on the premises. *Signed*: **Thomas Colson, Margaret (X) Colson, Jeffrey (X) Johnson, Moses Johnson.** *Wit*: **Laz's. Taylor, Simon Morgan.** *Rec*: 23 August 1759

Pages 26-27. 23 August 1759. **Thomas Dodson** to **Joseph Dodson.** For natural love and affection .. for my well-beloved son. 150 acres on ridge between Thomas Dodson and **Timothy Stamps** .. cor. in Carter's line .. Cor. in **Debut's** line .. along ridge between Thomas and Joseph Dodson. *Rec*: 23 August 1759

Pages 27-29. 23 August 1759. **John Gardner, Sen'r.** and **Jane**, his wife, to **John Gardner, Jun'r.** For natural love and affection for their son. 232 acres on Tin Pot run in his actual possession .. part where John Gardner, Sr. now lives .. on the south east side of Tin Pot .. line that divides the said land from the land given by the said John Gardner, Sr. to his son Thomas Gardner, Jr. .. box oak on the Lick branch. *Signed*: **John Gardner, Jeane Gardner.** *Wit*: **John Ashby, Joseph Oder, Thos. Marshall.** *Rec*: 23 August 1759.

Pages 29-30. 23 August 1759. Deed of Gift. **John Gardner, Sr.** and **Jane**, his wife, to **Thomas Gardner, Jun'r.** For natural love and affection for their son .. 232 acres beg. where the road crosses Tin Pot Run at the Bridge .. east side of the Lick Branch and cor. to the land given to **John Gardner, Jr.** John Gardner reserves right of taking timber off the said land for his proper use. *Signed*: **John Gardner** and **Jeane Gardner.** *Wit*: **John Ashby, Joseph Oder, Thos. Marshall.** *Rec*: 23 August 1759.

Pages 30-31. 22 August 1759. Bond of **Joseph Blackwell** as Sheriff of Fauquier County. *Securities*: **William Blackwell** and **William Eustace**, Gent. *Rec*: 23 August 1759.

Pages 31-34. 24 September 1759. Lease. **Thomas Lord Fairfax** to **William Corder.** Two hundred acres, in Manor of Leeds, cor. to **Joseph Williams'** lot .. by the side of the Hedgman river. For his natural life and the natural lives of **J o h n** and William Corder, his two sons. Yearly rent, 40 shillings, sterling, due on 25 December. *Wit*: **Thomas Carter, George Neavill, G. Johnston.** *Rec*: 27 September 1759.

Pages 34-37. 24 September 1759. **Thomas Lord Fairfax** to **John B l a c k m o r e.** Lease of 200 acres, in Manor of Leeds, for his natural life and the nat. lives of John Blackmore, his son and **Ann Blackmore**, his wife. Yearly rent, 40 shillings due on 25 December. *Wit*: **Thomas Carter, George Neavill, G. Johnston.** *Rec*: 27 September 1759.

Pages 38-41. 1759. **Thomas Lord Fairfax** to **Valentine Flynn**, lease of 200 acres, in Manor of Leeds, cor. to the Rev'd. **James Scott's** land, **Col. Fairfax's** and **Walter Anderson,** dec'd .. sapline near a large Branch of Carter's Run .. with the line of Col. Fairfax. For his natural life and the natural lives of **Hannah,** his wife and **Michael Flynn,** his son. Yearly rent, 40 shillings sterling, due 20 days after 25 December. *Wit*: **Thomas Carter, George Neavill, G. Johnston.** *Rec*: 27 September 1759.

Pages 41-44. 24 September 1759. Lease. **Thomas Lord Fairfax** to **Joseph Williams.** Lease of 200 acres in Manor of Leeds .. north side of the Hedgman River and on a branch thereof. For his natural life and lives of **Mary Williams,** his daughter and **Joseph Robinson,** his grandson. Yearly rent, 40 shillings sterling due on 25 December. *Wit*: **George Neavill, Thomas Carter, G. Johnston.** *Rec*: 27 September 1759.

Pages 44-47. 24 September 1759. Lease. **Thomas Lord Fairfax** to **Elias Wood,** 150 acres in Manor of Leeds .. crossing Crooked Run .. during Wood's natural life and during the natural lives of **Catharine,** his wife, and **Nathaniel Wood,** his son. Yearly rent of 40 shillings sterling. *Wit*: **George Neavill, Thomas Carter, G. Johnston.** *Signed*: **Fairfax.** *Rec*: 27 September 1759.

Pages 47-50. 24 September 1759. Lease. **Thomas Lord Fairfax** to **David Barton.** 150 acres .. in the county of Prince William .. part of that tract known by the name of the Manor of Leeds .. oak in the line of Col. **James Ball** .. north east side of Carter's Run .. crossing the main road ... during his natural life and that of his wife **Ruth Barton** and **Elizabeth,** his daughter. Yearly rent of 40 shillings sterling. *Signed*: **Fairfax.** *Wit*: **Thomas Carter, George Neavill, G. Johnston.** *Rec*: 27 September 1759.

Pages 50-52. 20 August 1759. **Matthew Moss** and **Sarah,** his wife, of the county of Prince William to **John Willoughby** of Fauquier Co. .. 5 shillings, current money of Virginia .. parcel containing 100 acres or thereabouts .. part of a greater tract belonging to **John Glascock** .. in the Parish of Hamilton on the west side of a branch of Broad Run above the mountains known by the name of Fornication Branch in the County of Fauquier ... *Signed*: **Matthew (X) Moss, Sarah (M) Moss.** *Wit*: **William Wyatt, Daniel (X) Makantish, Evan Griffiths.** *Rec*: 28 February 1760.

Pages 52-54. Release of above.

Pages 54-59. 20 February 1760. Lease and release. **Joseph Settle** and **Mary,** his wife, to **George Settle** .. ₤29.9s.6d. .. 153 acres part of a patent formerly granted to **Isaac Settle** .. 30 July 1742 .. oak on north branch of Rappahannock River .. cor. to **Mordock** .. thence with Mordock line .. cor. of **William Settle** .. to a stump near Joseph Settle's plantation. *Signed*: **Joseph Settle, Mary (X) Settle.** *Wit*: **William Settle, Thomas Blakemore.** *Rec*: 28 February 1760. Mary privily examined as the law directs. Receipt recorded.

Pages 59-60. Bond. **John Darnell**, of Prince William Co. & Hamilton Parish, planter, bound unto **Morgan Darnell** of said County and parish, planter. £100 sterling money of Great Britain .. 5 February 1750/1 .. Condition being that **John Darnal** doth stand abide and allow to the Dividing Line made by the said John Darnal and **Morgan Darnal** of a tract of land left them by Morgan Darnal their Father, dec'd. .. two red oak saplins near the Main Road in **Corbin's** line .. crossing of Ratclifs Run .. to the Horse Pen Run .. to the mouth of Smith's Spring Branch .. laid off by **John Marr**. *Signed*: **John Darnall**. *Wit*: **Henry Bramlet, Waugh Darnall**. *Rec*: 28 February 1760.

Pages 60-61. 28 February 1760. Bond of **Joseph Blackwell**, to receive from the Tithable Persons their County levies. For: 1,264 lbs. of tobacco. *Securities*: **William Grant** and **William Blackwell**. *Rec*: 28 February 1760.

Pages 61-62. 18 Oct. 1759. Bond of **Howsen Kenner**, of Fauquier unto **John Grant** of King George County. For £100 current money. Whereas John Grant in March 1758 by Deed of Feofment in the County of Prince William, dated 27 March .. conveyed to Howsen Kenner the fee simple estate of 541 acres and whereas by survey by **Bertrand Ewell**, Surveyor of the County of Prince William .. 10 Oct 1758 .. doth not hold 541 acres by 113 acres .. John Grant to pay Howsen Kenner £ 15.. which is received .. *Signed*: **Howsen Kenner**. *Wit*: **Wm. Blackwell, Jeremiah Darnall, Martin Pickett, Chas. Morgan, Jun'r**. *Rec*: 29 February 1760.

Pages 62-65. 23-24 March 1760. Lease and release. Between **William Ransdale** and **Mary**, his wife, and **Robert Ashby** .. £70.. 200 acres, being part of a larger tract purchased by **Wharton Ransdell** from the Exors. of **Mr. Burgess** of Lancaster County, dec'd. *Signed*: **William Ransdell, Mary Ransdell**. *Rec*: 27 March 1760, ack. by William and Mary, who was privily examined.

Pages 65-67. 24 September 1759. Lease. From **James Scott** of Dettingen Parish, Prince William Co., Clerk, to **Thomas Stamps** of Hamilton Parish, Fauquier Co. .. 150 acres being part of a greater tract belonging to the said James Scott .. cor. between the Lott surveyed for Mr. **James Stewart** .. to the west side of the Mill Run .. to a white oak on Cedar Run .. to Thomas Stamps, **Mary**, his wife, and **William**, his son, or the longest liver of them or either of them .. for 500 lbs. of food, legal and merchantable Tobacco and Cask .. or 530 lbs of good neat Tobacco to be rolled or otherwise to the next convenient Landing at the proper Risque and charge of the said Thomas Stamps .. *Signed*: **Thomas (X) Stamps, James Scott**. *Wit*: **James Mercer, Timothy Stamps, William Wright, Evan William**. *Rec*: 27 March 1760, prov. by oaths of wits.

Pages 68-70. 22 November 1759. Bargain and Sale. Between **William Beach** of Co. of Hallifax, Colony of Va. and **Peter Beach** of Fauquier .. £34 .. 200 acres on the branches of Deep Run it being the lower part lying on the east side of Deep Run of a Tract belonging to

Alexander Beach .. which was deeded to his son, William Beach, by deed of gift in the County Court of Prince William beginning at the lower end of the said land of Alex. Beach across to the Green Branch. *Signed*: **William (X) Beach**. *Wit*: **Wm. Blackwell, Wm. Eustace, Wm. Kesterson, Rodham Tullos, Daniel Bradford**. Memorandum and receipt rec. *Rec*: 28 March 1760.

Pages 70-75. 21-22 May 1760. Lease and release. Between **Thomas Colson**, of Frederick Co., and **Jeffry Johnson**, of Hamilton Parish, Prince William Co. .. Ł40.. 264 acres in the county of Prince William on the branches of Great Run of Rappahannock River .. survey by **James Thomas the Younger** .. beginning at .. head of a spring branch cor. to the land of **Walter Anderson** .. to a white oak in a bottom in the line of **John Hudnal** .. crossing the main branch of Great Run .. *Signed*: **Thomas Colson**. *Wit*: **Benj'a (X) Johnson, Moses Johnson, Rich'd. Mynatt**. *Rec*: 22 May 1760.

Pages 75-77. 26 June 1760. B & S. Between **Henry Kamper** and **Lettice**, his wife, and **John Martin** .. Ł15 .. 60 acres beginning at a Spanish oak on the side of Licking Run, thence along **John Kamper's** line to a red oak in **Colo. Carter's** line .. cor. of **Joseph Martin**. *Signed*: **Henry Kamper, Lettice (X) Kamper**. *Rec*: 26 June 1760, Lettice being privily examined.

Pages 77-78. 26 June 1760. Between **Daniel Bradford** and **Alexander Bradford**, brother of said Daniel .. for natural love and affection .. 148 acres on a branch of Rappahannock called Marrs Run and on the south side of the said Run .. cor. to the land of **Marr** and Daniel Bradford .. cor. to the said Marr and Barns .. *Signed*: **Daniel Bradford**. *Wit*: **Original Young, William Jennings, Benjanin Bradford**. *Rec*: 26 June 1760

Pages 78-82. 19 November 1759. Lease & release. Between **Benjamin Ashby** and **Hannah**, his wife, and **Robert Ashby**, Gent. .. in consideration of a certain tract of land lying in Culpeper County .. 50 acres near the Cobler Mountains and on the Branch of Goose Creek .. beginning .. by Main Road .. cor. to land of **Turner**, dec'd. .. Tree of Mr. **William Ransdell's** .. being part of a tract granted to **Thomas Ashby** by Patent .. 4 August 1742. *Signed*: **Benjamin (B) Ashby, Hannah Ashby**. *Wit*: **Nimrod Ashby, John Moffet, John (IB) Brown**. *Rec*: 22 May 1760.

Pages 82-85. 26 June 1760. B & S. Between **Isaac Judd** and **Lettis**, his wife, and **Morias Hansbrough**, of Stafford Co., Carpenter .. Ł20 .. 105 acres, part of 825 acres, granted to Isaac Judd by the Proprietor of the Northern Neck .. beginning on the south side of Cannons Run .. to the Road .. to a pine in **Joseph Wood's** line .. *Signed*: **Isaac Judd, Lettis (N) Judd**. *Wit*: **Peter (B) Beach, Nehemiah (HH) Ferguson, William (X) Ballerter**. *Rec*: 26 June 1760.

Pages 85-90. 19-20 June 1760. Lease & release. Between **William Eustace**, Gent. and **Anne**, his wife, and **Mark Hardin** .. Ł10.. 100

acres .. being all the land that lies between **John Macbees** land and **Mary Turner's** and the said **Hardin's** .. *Signed*: **Wm. Eustace** and **Ann Eustace.** *Wit*: **W. Grant, Geo. Crump, John Crump.** *Rec*: 27 June 1760, with receipt and cert. of examination of Ann Eustace who "cannot conveniently travel to our County Court of Fauquier." *Signed*: **Humphrey Brooke,** Clerk of Court. *Wit*: **Wm. Blackwell, W. Grant, John Crump.**

Pages 91-93. 27 August 1760. B & S. Between **John Henry** and **Mary,** his wife, and **Thomas Toms** .. Ł5 .. 50 acres (surveyed by **George Hume**). *Signed*: **John (X) Henery, Mary (X) Henery.** *Wit*: **G. Wheatley, Joseph Sebastin, Wm. Sturdy.** *Rec*: 28 August 1760.

Pages 93-96. 28 August 1760. B & S. Between **William Wood** and **Catharine,** his wife, and **Joseph Sebastian** ... Ł7.10 .. 265 acres on the lower side of a branch of Rappahannock River called Rocky Run .. Cor. of **John Courtney** .. Cor. of **Capt. Skinker's** land .. which the said William Wood purchased of **Howsen Kenner** .. *Signed*: **William (W) Wood, Cathe Wood.** *Wit*: **George Wheatley, John Henery, John Duncan.** *Rec*: 28 August 1760, with receipt and memorandum, Catharine privily examined.

Pages 96-99. 29 August 1760. B & S. Between: **John Henry** and **Mary,** his wife, and **Joseph Sebastian** .. Ł6 .. 50 acres .. tract of land taken up by **Owen Grinnen** for which he obtained a patent .. and by Owen Grinnen conveyed by Deed unto **Jesper Billings** .. by Billings .. unto **George Henry** .. by George Henry, by Deed of Gift, to his son, John Henry, recorded in the Clerks Office of the county of Prince William. *Signed*: **John (X) Henry, Mary (X) Henry.** *Wit*: **George Wheatley, Thos. Allin, John Duncan.** *Rec*: 28 August 1760, with memorandum and receipt.

Pages 99-103. 27 August 1760. Lease & release. Between **John Bell,** Gent. of Hamilton Parish and **Frankey,** his wife, and **George Lamkin,** of same .. 100 acres .. *Signed*: **John Bell.** *Rec*: 28 August 1760, Frankey being first privily examined.

Pages 103-107. 27/28 August 1760. Lease & release. Between **Jeffry Johnson** and **William Johnson** .. Ł22 .. 200 acres .. on the Branches of Carters Run .. part of a tract taken up by **Walter Anderson** .. *Signed*: **Jeffry (I) Johnson.** *Wit*: **George Wheatley, Wm. Keirnes, Edmond Basye.** *Rec*: 28 August 1760.

Page 108. 29 August 1760. Bond. **John Bell** has this day in open Court undertaken to build a courthouse for the use of the county .. shall truly perform build and finish the said courthouse in a Workmanlike manner and agreeable to the order of Court .. For Ł700 current money of Virginia. *Securities*: **Yelverton Peyton, Thomas McClanaham,** and **William Edmonds.** *Rec*: 29 August 1760.

Pages 109-112. 25 September 1760. Lease. Between **Thomas Lord Fairfax** and **Daniel Rector** .. 200 acres in Manor of Leeds .. Beginning

7

.. red oak in a line of the Reverend Mr. **James Scott's** land on Carters Run .. crossing Carters Run .. for said Daniel Rector's natural life and the nat. lives of **Ann Rector,** his wife, and **Henry Rector, Jun'r.** .. *Signed*: **Fairfax**. *Wit*: **Will Chilton, John Moffett, Jeremiah Darnall.** *Rec*: 25 September 1760.

Pages 112-116. 25 September 1760. Lease. Between **Thomas Lord Fairfax** and **Thomas James** .. 250 acres .. in Manor of Leeds .. on east side of Carters Run .. also a small tract adjacent thereto ..for his natural life and lives of **Hannah,** his wife, and **Elizabeth James,** his daughter .. *Wit*: **John Moffett, Sam'l. Harriss, Will Chilton**. *Rec*: 25 September 1760.

Pages 116-119. 18 September 1760. Lease & release. Between **Charles Delany** and **Joseph Williams** .. £50 .. 140 acres .. by **Field's** road .. *Signed*: **Charles Dulany**. *Wit*: **Benjamin Crump, Rich'd Covington, Thos. Brooks**. *Rec*: 25 September 1760.

Pages 119-120. 3 September 1760. B & S. Between **Bertrand Ewell** of Prince William Co., Gent. and **Frances,** his wife, and **Nimrod Ashby** of Fauquier Co. .. 5 s. .. parcel near Goose Creek .. in the line of the said Bertrand Ewell, Gent's. land and Corner to the land of **Ball** .. crossing the road that leads from Manasses Run Gap to Falmouth .. 100 acres .. being part of a larger tract granted to **Charles Burgess** Gent. by Patent .. for 1176 acres .. 17 June 1730 and was conveyed to **James & Jesse Ball** by **Edwin Conway** and James Ball, Exors. of Charles Burgess, Gent., dec'd .. 11 April 1740 and then conveyed to Bertrand Ewell by **James Ball, Jr.** .. 10 March 1753. *Signed*: **Bertrand Ewell**. *Wit*: **Francis Dade, Wm. Seale, John Moffett**. *Rec*: 25 September 1760 with receipt.

Pages 120-123. 24 September 1760. Release of above .. 1.0 .. Release of Dower rights .. *Rec*: 25 September 1760.

Pages 123-126. 11 September 1760. Trust. **John Crump** to **Thomas Harrison** and **Cuthbert Harrison** .. whereas Thomas Harrison of Fauquier Co., Cuthbert Harrison of Prince William Co., and **Benjamin Grayson,** late of Prince William Co., became securities for John Crump to **Lord Fairfax** for his due and faithful collection of the Quit rents .. from the inhabitants or landholders in Prince William Co. .. for two years .. 1751 and 1752 .. John Crump promised to convey to securities his real and personal estate in bond .. and whereas the said John Crump hath not made such Collection as by the said Bond he ought to have done .. and hath not well & truly paid the several sums by him actually received .. hath been altogether deficient in the promises .. and the securities are likely to become considerable sufferers .. Now this Indenture .. John Crump to Thomas Harrison, Cuthbert Harrison .. tract in Hambleton Parish .. which he is seized of .. slaves .. stock .. household goods .. in trust .. for his payment .. *Signed*: **John Crump**. *Wit*: **Edward Humston, Martin Hardin, Edward Humston, Jr.** *Rec*: 25 September 1760, with receipt.

Pages 126-127. 18 September 1760. B & S. Between **Charles Delaney** and **William Delaney** .. Ł10 .. 100 acres surveyed by Mr. **George Hume** .. pine on south side of Fields road .. by **Crumps** path .. *Signed*: **Charles Dulany**. *Wit*: **Thos. Brooks, Benjamin Crump, Rich'd Covington**. *Rec*: 25 September 1760, with receipt.

Pages 128-129. 24 September 1760. B & S. Between **John Ferguison** and **Martha**, his wife, .. planter, and **John Brahan** of Westmoreland Co., planter .. Ł50 .. 140 acres in Counties of Fauquier and Stafford on the branches of Acquia, commonly called Cannon's run .. Beginning red oak in a Poison field corner to **John Savage** .. Robinson's line .. saplin in Col. **William Robinson's** line being corner to the land of John Savage dec'd .. which said land was taken up and a patent obtained .. 17 Jan 1727/8 by **Robert Jones**, dec'd. and purchased of his Exors., **Robert Thomas & William Jones** .. 14 Nov 1752, by the said John Ferguison.. *Signed*: **John Ferguison, Martha (X) Ferguison**. *Wit*: **William Hammett, Wm. Durham, Wm. Underwood**.

Pages 129-131. 25 September 1760. Lease. Between Rt. Hon. **Thomas Lord Fairfax** and **Francis Jett** of Fauquier Co. .. 200 acres in the Manor of Leeds .. on bank of a large branch of Thum Run .. during natural life of him and for & during the natural lives of **Daniel Jett** and **Francis Jett, Jr**. *Signed*: **Fairfax**. *Wit*: **Will Chilton, John Moffett, Jeremiah Darnall**. *Rec*: 25 September 1760.

Pages 134-136. 25 September 1760. Lease. Between **Thomas Lord Fairfax** and **William Day** of Fauquier Co. .. 200 acres in Manor of Leeds .. white oak on the bank of the Hedgman River just below the mouth of a small branch .. opposite a small Island .. for his natural life and the natural lives of .. (blank) .. yearly rent of 40s. sterling .. *Signed*: **Fairfax**. *Wit*: **Will Chilton, John Moffett, Jeremiah Darnall**. *Rec*: 25 September 1760.

Pages 136-138. 25 September 1760. Lease. Between **Thomas Lord Fairfax** and **John Smith** of Fauquier Co. .. 200 acres in Manor of Leeds .. for & during the life of **John Smith, Jr.** and during the natural lives of **Joseph** and **Delany Smith** .. *Signed*: **Fairfax**. *Wit*: **Will Chilton, John Moffett, Jeremiah Darnall**. *Rec*: 25 September 1760.

Pages 139-141. 25 September 1760. Lease. Between **Thomas Lord Fairfax** and **Benjamin Neale** of Fauquier Co. .. 200 acres in Manor of Leeds .. near Thumb Run .. for his natural life and the natural lives of **Mary Ann Neale** his wife & **James Neale** his son .. *Signed*: **Fairfax**. *Wit*: **Will Chilton, John Moffett, Jeremiah Darnall**. *Rec*: 25 September 1760.

Pages 141-143. 25 September 1760. Lease. Between **Thomas Lord Fairfax** and **Benjamin Neale, Jun'r**, of Fauquier Co. .. 200 acres in Manor of Leeds .. Corner to **Benjamin Neale's** Lott .. near Thum Run .. during his natural life and natural lives of **Elizabeth Neale**, his wife and **Matthew Neale** .. *Signed*: **Fairfax**. *Wit*: (as above). *Rec*: 25 September 1760.

9

Pages 143-146. 25 September 1760. Lease. Between **Thomas Lord Fairfax** and **Morgan Darnal, Jun'r.** of Fauquier Co. .. 200 acres in Manor of Leeds .. Beginning .. Cor. to **Charles Jones'** lot .. for his natural life and the natural lives of **Mary**, his wife and **Raughley Darnal**, his son .. *Signed*: **Fairfax**. *Wit*: (as above). *Rec*: 25 September 1760.

Pages 146-148. 25 September 1760. Lease. Between **Thomas Lord Fairfax** and **James Corder** .. two tenements .. in Manor of Leeds .. Beginning .. Corner to Mr. **Wm. Pickett's** lott .. the other lott being some distance .. by a branch side .. 100 acres in each lot .. during his natural life & natural lives of **Elizabeth**, his wife, & **William Corder**, his son. *Signed*: **Fairfax**. *Wit*: (as above).

Pages 148-150. 25 September 1760. Lease. Between **Thomas Lord Fairfax** and **Charles Jones** .. 200 acres in Manor of Leeds .. for his natural life and natural lives of **Elizabeth**, his wife, & **Henry Jones**, his son .. *Signed*: **Fairfax**. *Wit*: (as above). *Rec*: 25 September 1760.

Pages 150-153. 25 September 1760. Lease. Between **Thomas Lord Fairfax** and **William Neavill** of Fauquier Co. .. Beginning .. Corner to the land of Colo. **Thos. Turner**, dec'd. .. with the line of Mr. **John Blackmore's** lott .. 200 acres in Manor of Leeds .. for his natural life and natural lives of **Winifred**, his wife and **Jesse Neavill**, his son. *Signed*: **Fairfax**. *Wit*: (as above). *Rec*: 25 September 1760.

Pages 153-155. 25 September 1760. Lease. Between **Thomas Lord Fairfax** and **William Hammett** .. 200 acres in Manor of Leeds .. by the side Rappahannock River .. to **David Darnals** corner at the mouth of a branch then leaving the river .. during his natural life and the natural lives of **Rosanna Hammett**, his wife, and **Nathaniel Jones Hammett** .. *Signed*: **Fairfax**. *Wit*: **Will Chilton, John Moffett, Jeremiah Darnall**. *Rec*: 25 September 1760.

Pages 155-157. 25 September 1760. Lease. Between **Thomas Lord Fairfax** and **Thomas George** .. 200 acres in Manor of Leeds .. Beginning .. on a point on the East side of Thum Run .. for his natural life and natural lives of **Moses George & Susanna George** .. *Signed*: **Fairfax**. *Wit*: **John Moffett, Sam'l. Harris, Jeremiah Darnal, Will Chilton**. *Rec*: 25 September 1760.

Pages 157-159. 25 September 1760. Lease. Between **Thomas Lord Fairfax** and **John Hopper, Jun'r.** .. 200 acres in Manor of Leeds .. for his natural life and natural lives of **Mary**, his wife, and **Elizabeth**, his daughter .. *Signed*: **Fairfax**. *Wit*: **Will Chilton, John Moffett, Jeremiah Darnall**. *Rec*: 25 September 1760.

Pages 160-161. 25 September 1760. Lease. Between **Thomas Lord Fairfax** and **John Crimm** .. 200 acres in Manor of Leeds .. Beginning

corner to lott of **John Robinson** .. for his natural life and lives of ..
(blank) .. *Signed*: **Fairfax**. *Wit*: (as above). *Rec*: 25 September 1760

Pages 162-165. 25 September 1760. Lease. Between **Thomas Lord
Fairfax** and **Gabriel Murphew** .. 200 acres in Manor of Leeds ..
Beginning .. Corner to **John Robinson**'s lott .. saplin in a great Poison
field .. crossing Thumb Run .. for his natural life and natural lives of
Ann, his wife, and **Mary Anne**, his daughter .. *Signed*: **Fairfax**. *Wit*:
(as above). *Rec*: 25 September 1760.

Pages 165-168. 25 September 1760. Lease. Between **Thomas Lord
Fairfax** and **William Wright** .. 200 acres in Manor of Leeds .. on side
of the Poley Mountain and in the line of **T u r n e r** 's dec'd Land .. with
J o h n S m i t h 's Lott line .. during his natural life and natural lives of
Mary Wright, his wife, and **John Wright**, his son .. *Signed*: **Fairfax**.
Wit: **Will Chilton, John Moffett, Jeremiah Darnall**. *Rec*: 25 Sep-
tember 1760.

Pages 168-171. 25 September 1760. Lease. Between **Thomas Lord
Fairfax** and **William Pickett** .. 275 acres in Manor of Leeds. For his
natural life and natural lives of .. (blank) .. Yearly rent of 55s. sterling. *Signed*: **Fairfax**. *Wit*: (as above). *Rec*: 25 September 1760.

Pages 171-176. 25 November 1760. Lease. Between **George Crump**,
Gent. and **Richard Luttrell**, Planter .. 5s. .. on the Branches of Negro
Run .. 240 a. which was granted by Deed from the Prop. Office .. unto
John Crump dec'd. .. 29 July 1745 .. Beginning in the line of **James
Peters** or near the said line of Peters's 240 a. tract and the beg. tree
of Peters's 161 a. tract on the north side of Negro Run .. to the line of
Joseph Wood .. to the Land granted to **John Forsyth** dec'd .. to the
line of the land granted to **Michael Dermon** dec'd .. to his corner and
corner of James Peters .. *Signed*: **Geo. Crump**. *Wit*: **Henry Smith,
Rich'd Luttrell, Jun'r., John Luttrell**. *Rec*: 27 November 1760.

Pages 173-176. 26 November 1760. Release of above, with receipt
for Ł16 current money. *Rec*: 27 November 1760.

Pages 176-177. 26 November 1760. Deed of Gift. Between **Richard
Luttrell, Sen'r.** to son, **Samuel Luttrel** .. parcel of land .. on the
Branches of Town Run .. 70 a. .. being part of 350 acres granted to
Richard Luttrel by deed from the Proprietor's Office .. Beginning at
mouth of the Cabin Branch .. to the line of the land granted to **Michael
Dermon** .. to Town Run .. *Signed*: **Richard R. Luttrell, Henry Smith,
Richard Luttrell, Jun'r., John Luttrell**. *Rec*: 27 November 1760.

Pages 177-178. 27 November 1760. Deed of Gift. Between **M o r g a n
Darnall** .. Planter .. and sons **Waugh Darnall**, Morgan Darnall and
John Darnall .. to Waugh, 150 acres whereon I now live to begin at
William's corner ..including the Plantation .. son, Morgan Darnall,
150 acres to begin on the Branch going at the Plantation whereon
Waugh Darnall now lives .. son John Darnall all the remainder of the

11

said tract. *Signed*: **Morgan (MD) Darnall**. *Wit*: **Will'm Sturdy, James Arnold**. *Rec*: 27 November 1760.

Pages 178–180. 4 June 1760. B & S. Between **James Bell**, of county of Lancaster, and **John Blackemore**, of Fauquier .. ₤250 .. tract .. from the Prop. Office to James Ball, Gent., father of the aforesaid James Ball .. 6 May 1732 .. 871 acres .. (no description) .. *Signed*: **James Ball**. *Wit*: **Duff Green, John Churchill, Wm. Eustace, Wm. Edmonds, Wm. Pickett, Martin Pickett**. *Rec*: 27 November 1760.

Pages 180–181. 25 March 1761. Between **Thomas Bell and Elisabeth**, his wife, .. and **William Norriss** .. ₤53 .. 550 acres .. near Skinker's Rouling Road .. hiccory marked IB corner to **McGuire** .. Scott's Corner. *Signed*: **Thomas Bell, Elisabeth Bell**. *Rec*: 26 March 1761.

Pagos 181–183. 26 March 1761. Release of above ..

Pages 183–188. 26 March 1761. Lease & release. Between **Thomas Dagg**, of Parish of Dettingen, Co. of Prince William and **Benjamin Ball** of Fauquier Co. .. ₤70.. being part of tract granted to **Joseph Chambers** by Patent .. 15 Nov 1725 .. and conveyed by him to **John Dagg**, Dec'd and by his death descended to Thomas Dagg as heir at law .. 175 acres .. and whereon said Benj. Ball now resides .. 50 acres hereby sold was Patented to John Dagg Dec'd as surplus land within his said Patent purchased of the sd. Joseph Chambers dec'd .. Beginning at a Gum on the banks of Carters Run .. to two elms upon the side of the aforesd. run but properly called Butterwood .. line of **John Barker**'s land laid off by the sd. John Dagg, dec'd. for **Arthur Harris**'s lot .. land of **Thomas Stone** .. *Signed*: **Thomas Dagg**. *Wit*: **Edward Ball, Thomas Porter, William Dulin**. *Rec*: 26 March 1761.

Pages 188–193. 25/26 March 1761. Lease & release. Between **Thomas Porter** and **Sarah**, his wife, and **William Hunton** .. 120 acres .. mouth of North fork of Cedar Run, cor. to the **Rev'd. Mr. Scott**'s land in the line of the land of **Man Page**, Esq'r .. cor. to sd. Page and **William Russell** .. Cor. to Russell and **Richard Grubbs** .. cor. to Grubbs and **Mr. Barber** .. *Signed*: **Thomas Porter, Sarah Porter**. *Wits*: **Samuel Simpson, John Duncan, Samuel Porter**. *Rec*: 26 March 1761.

Pages 193–195. 26 March 1761. B & S. Between **Samuel Porter** and **Eve**, his wife, and **William Hunton** .. ₤100 .. 100 acres, more or less .. bounded by lands of **Tilman Weaver**, Dec'd, **Willian Russell, Martin Russell** and **Armistead Churchhill**, Esq. .. purchased of **John Jones** and **Mary**, his wife .. 23 & 24 April 1758 .. *Signed*: **Samuel Porter, Eve Porter**. *Wits*: **Thomas Porter, Samuel Simpson, John Duncan**. *Rec*: 26 March 1761.

Pages 195–197. 26 March 1761. B & S. Between **William Grinnen**, of Stafford County and **George Williams** of Parish of Hamilton .. ₤172 .. 220 acres (est.) .. adjoining lands of **Peter Hedgman** and **Hancock Lee**, Gent. *Signed*: **William Grinnen**. *Rec*: 26 March 1761.

Pages 197-199. 24 November 1760. Lease. Between **Allan Mac** of the Town of Dumfries, Prince William Co., Merchant and **J o h Frogg**, of Fauquier Co., Gent. and **Humphrey Brooke**, of Fauquier Co. .. unto said Humphrey Brooke the following tracts .. one granted by Patent .. to John Frogg .. 30 March 1740 .. 386 acres. The other, by Patent .. to **John Morehead** .. 10 Sept. 1742 .. 167 acres. One other .. 15 acres (est) purchased by John Frogg of John Morehead .. 29 April 1746 .. all in Fauquier County. *Signed*: **Allan Macrae, John Frogg.** *Wit*: **Cuthbert Bullitt, James Scott, Jun'r.**, Richard Graham, Wm. Blackwell, Wm. Eustace, John Ashby. *Rec*: 27 February 1761.

Pages 199-202. 25 November 1760. Release. Between **Allan Macrae** and **Elizabeth**, his wife, and **John Frogg**, Gent. and Elizabeth, his wife, and **Humphrey Brooke** .. whereas John Frogg by his certain Indentures of Lease and release .. 2 & 3 May 1759 .. ack. & rec. in the General Court of this Colony among other tracts .. did sell .. to Allan Macrae .. two tracts of Land .. Plantation whereon sd. John Frogg then dwelt .. 200 a. .. another tract adj. sd. tract ..400 acres .. Elizabeth now relinquishes right of dower .. £250 .. *Signed*: **Allan Macrae, Elizabeth Macrae, John Frogg, Elizabeth Frogg.** *Wit*: **Cuthbert Bullett, William Pickett, Jun'r.**, James Scott, Jun'r., Richard Graham, William Blackwell, William Eustace, John Ashby. *Rec*: 27 February 1761.

Pages 203-205. Certificate of examination of **Elizabeth Macrae** by **John Baylis, Richard Graham**, and **William Carr**, Gent. .. same for **Elizabeth Frogg** by **William Blackwell, William Eustace** and **William Grant**, Gent.

Pages 205-207. 26 February 1761. Apprentice Bond. **William Carter** apprentices himself to **Charles Hume**, Carpenter .. to learn the art trade or Mistery after the manner of an apprentice .. to serve him five years .. shall serve his Master Faithfully .. serve his secrets, keep his lawful commands gladly, everywhere obey he shall do no Damage to his said Master, nor see it to be done by others .. shall not waste his Masters goods nor lend them unlawfully, nor Contract matrimony within the said term. He shall not absent himself from his Masters Service day or night without his leave .. Master shall teach him the trade or Mistery he now followeth .. procure and provide him sufficient meat, drink & apparel, lodging and washing fitting for an Apprentice .. *Signed*: **William Carter, Charles Hume.** *Rec*: 26 February 1761.

Page 207. 26 February 1761. Apprentice Bond. Same as above for Apprentice **William Henry**. *Signed*: **William ( ) Henry, Charles Hume.** *Rec*: 26 February 1761.

Pages 208-213. 13 October 1760. Lease & release. Between **Francis Jett** and **Elizabeth**, his wife, of Parish of Hanover, Co. of King George and **Thomas Bronaugh**, of Parish of St. Paul, Co. of Stafford .. £150 .. tract in Fauquier .. 300 a. (est.) .. sd. tract descended to **Catherine**, wife of sd. Francis Jett from her father, **Jeremiah Bronaugh** dec'd.

alf of a tract formerly belonging to Jeremiah Bronaugh the
Signed: Francis Jett, Jun'r. Wit: Francis Bronaugh,
gh, Joseph Stewart. Rec: 26 March 1761. Cert. of ex-
Elizabeth, signed by John Tripplett and William Robin-

Pages 213-215. 27 May 1761. Lease. Between Samuel Earle and
John Mercer, of Stafford Co., Gent. .. 5 s. ster. .. tract .. on Hungar
Run, in Co. of Prince William now Loudon Co. .. westward side of the
branches of Hungar Run cor. to the land surveyed for Bur Barton ..
binding on land of Joseph Gibson .. 386 acres, more or less .. Signed:
Samuel Earle. Rec: 28 May 1761.

Pages 215-219. 28 May 1761. Release. Between Samuel Earle of
Fauquier Co. and Elizabeth, his wife, and John Mercer .. 1590 lbs.
tobacco and £10 .. which said land was purchased by John Dalton of
Samuel Harril & Mary, his wife .. 26 March 1748 .. rec. in Prince
William Co. .. and to Samuel Earle from John Dalton & Catherine, his
wife .. 16 & 17 March 1749 .. rec. in Prince William Co. Signed:
Samuel Earle. Rec: 28 May 1761.

Pages 219-223. 13 March 1761. Between Robert Jones, Exor. of last
will & testament of Col. Robert Jones, dec'd. of Parish of Cumberland, Lunenburgh Co. and Bereton Jones, of Fauquier Co. .. £45 ..
tract containing 230 a., more or less, being the reversion of a certain
tract .. obtained by Robert Jones, dec'd by Patent .. 26 Sept 1743 ..
containing 363 a. .. 132 a. of sd. tract was by Deed .. 25 April 1746,
given to Bereton Jones by his father, the sd. Robert Jones, dec'd ..
230 a. being the reversion of the tract of 363 a. Signed: Robert Jones.
Wit: Jos'h. Blackwell, Rodham Tullos, John Edge, David Williams.
Rec: 26 March 1761.

Pages 223-225. 8 May 1761. Deed of Gift. Between Thomas Dodson,
Sen'r of Parish of Hamilton, and George Dodson, son of sd. Thomas ..
for natural love & affection .. in his actual possession .. being part of
a tract of land purchased by the said Thos. Dodson of Thomas Falkner
.. corner to Joseph Dodson .. near Carter's line .. east side of a fountain .. near the top of the said fountain .. down southeast end of said
fountain to the south br. of Barkers Branch .. 100 a. Signed: T h o m a s
Dodson, dec'd. Wit: Thomas Marshall, Thos. Dodson, Wm. Dodson.
Rec: 28 May 1761.

Pages 225-227. 8 May 1761. Deed of Gift. Between Thomas Dodson,
Sen'r. and Thomas Dodson, Jun'r., son to the above .. natural love &
affection .. parcel in his actual possession .. part of two tracts .. on
the Mine Branch in Steward's Line .. in Falkner's line .. 150 acres.
Signed: Thomas Dodson, Sen'r. Wit: Thos. Marshall, Geo'e. Dodson,
William Dodson. Rec: 28 May 1761.

Pages 227-230. 28 May 1761. B & S. Between George Wheatly and
Dianah, his wife, and John Duncan .. £80 .. in his actual possession ..
part of the tract of land whereon the said George Wheatley now lives ..

14

Beginning at an oak in a glade near the line that divides the said land from the land of **Daniel Marr**, dec'd .. land now held by **Sturdie** in right of his wife .. 128 acres. *Signed*: **George Wheatley, Dianah (+) Darnall** (sic). *Wit*: **Wm. Sturdie, Wm. Settle, Jos. Blackwell.** *Rec*: 28 May 1761.

Pages 230-235. 28 May 1761. Lease and release. Between **John Hopper** and **Ann**, his wife, and **Humphrey Brooke** .. Ł15.. 30 acres .. stake in line of Brooke and Hopper .. near Sawpit Branch, corner to Brooke and Hopper .. *Signed*: **John Hopper, Ann (X) Hopper.** *Rec*: 28 May 1761.

Pages 235-237. 28 May 1761. Apprentice Bond. **James Williams** of Fauquier Co. .. doth voluntarily and of his own free will and accord put himself apprentice to **James Beshaw** .. to learn his art trade or mistery .. *Signed*: **James (X) Williams, James Bashaw.** *Wit*: **Dan'l. Bradford, Thos. Keith, Wm. Oldham.** *Rec*: 28 May 1761.

Pages 237-238. 28 May 1761. Bond. **John Bell**, Sheriff, .. to the King .. for Ł500 ... *Sec*: **William Blackwell, Joseph Hudnall, Jeremiah Darnall.** *Rec*: 28 May 1761.

Pages 238-239: (Same as above).

Pages 240-245. 2 June 1761. Lease & release. Between **Leonard Helm** of Parish of Dittingen, Prince William Co. and **Moses Copage** of Hambleton Parish .. 5s. .. parcel of land lying in counties of Fauquier and Prince William .. bounded on **Richard Tidwill's Line** .. 275 a., being part of 576 acres granted to **John Madden** by a Proprietor's grant .. 6 April 1730. *Signed*: **Leonard Helm.** *Wit*: **John Catlett, Robert Catlett, Isaack Coppage.** *Rec*: 25 June 1761.

Release between **Leonard Helm** and **Moses Copedge** .. Ł85 .. bounded .. corner of **Richard Tidwell's** land .. by Goose Run .. 275 a. .. to him, his heirs, assigns, etc. except the "pretended claim of Brent Town patent only Accepted." *Rec*: 25 June 1761.

Pages 245-248. 25 June 1761. B & S. Between **James Arnold** and **Sarah**, his wife, and **John Fargurson** .. Ł15 .. 71 acres .. joining the lands of **Catsby Cock, Nathaniel Dod**, and **Joseph Jones** .. same purchased by Arnold of **John Pownal** .. rec. in Clerks Office, Prince William Co. *Signed*: **James Arnold, Sarah (x) Arnold.** *Wit*: **Thos. Garner, Rich'd Covington, Rich'd Mynatt.** *Rec*: 25 June 1761, with receipt for paynent.

Pages 248-251: 16 May 1761. Between **William Reading** and **Mary**, his wife, and **Phillip Huffman** .. Ł10 .. tract whereon Huffman now lives .. bounded cor. to **John Morehead** thence with Morehead's line .. cor. to said Morehead and the land of **Tilman Wever** dec'd .. line of **Joseph Martin** .. 104 a., more or less .. *Signed*: **Wm. (X) Reading, Mary (X) Reading.** *Wit*: **Wm. Walker, Jac'b. Wever, Thos. Marshall.** *Rec*: 25 June 1761.

Pages 251-253. 24 June 1761. Lease. Between **George Johnson,** of Co. of Fairfax and **John Doonis,** of Fauquier .. plantation whereon the said John Doonis now dwells .. 200 a. .. for his natural life .. annual rent of one pepper corn on 25 Dec., if demanded .. Doonis to pay all quit rents and taxes .. *Signed*: **George Johnston.** *Wit*: **Cuthb't. Bullett, Wm. Ellzey, Francis Dade.** *Rec*: 25 June 1761.

Pages 253-259. 23 July 1760. Lease & release. Between **Alexander Beach,** Planter and **William Eaves** .. 100 a. .. known by the name of the long point .. part of a larger tract whereon Beach now lives .. bounded by Middle Branch being a branch of Deep Run .. Beginning at **Bryant Breedings** line .. up Deep Run joining the land of **John Buttler** to **Joseph Blackwell's** line .. *Signed*: **Alexander (B) Beach.** *Wit*: **Rodham Tullos, Jos'h Williams, Moses Coppedge.** *Rec*: 23 July 1761.

Pages 259-265. 22 August 1761. Lease & release. Between **Catesby Cocke,** of Parish of Dittingen, Prince William Co., Gent. and **William Stuart,** of Parish of St. Paul, Stafford Co., Clerk .. plantation containing 1555 acres .. same granted unto **John Blackley** from the Proprietor .. 9 Sept 1731 and by said Blackley sold to **Ralph Falkner** of Parish of Hanover, King George Co., Gent. .. 24 & 25 Aug 1733 and by Falkner sold to Catesby Cocke, 9 & 10 Aug 1737 .. bounded .. where the Great Branch runs into the Broad Run of Occoquan .. corner tree of the land of Mr. **George Rust** .. near the land of **John Fishback** .. near the land of Mr. **John Warner** .. down Broad Run .. *Signed*: **Catesby Cocke.** *Wit*: **Wm. Ellzey, Fran's. Dade, Wm. Carr, Wm. Grant.** *Rec*: 27 August 1761.

Pages 265-268. 26 August 1761. B & S. Between **James Willson** and **Judith,** his wife, of Prince William Co. and **Rodham Tillos,** of Fauquier Co. .. Ł15 .. 100 a. .. remaining part of a tract of land taken up by **William Gleek** by deed from the Proprietors .. 22 June 1725 .. 124 a. out of the first grant of 224 and some poles was sold unto **Joseph Allen** by William Gleek and the remaining 100 acres and some poles was left by the said Gleek to his wife who intermarried with one **Abraham Crandon** and by them sold to **John Wilcox** and by him to James Wilson. *Signed*: **James (X) Wilson, Judith (X) Wilson.** *Wit*: **Jos'h. Blackwell, Han. Lee, Wm. Walker.** *Rec*: 27 August 1761.

Pages 268-275. 26 & 27 March 1761. Lease & release. Between **William Ellzey,** Gent. and **Alice,** his wife, of Dittingen Parish, Prince William Co., and **Daniel Bradford,** planter of Hamilton Parish .. 309 a. .. lying on a branch of the Marsh Run called Marrs Run .. east side .. Chappel Branch .. line of the land surveyed for Mr. **John Coppedge** .. same granted to **William Macbee** from the Prop. Office .. and by sundry conveyances hath since become the estate of the said William Ellzey .. *Signed*: **Wm. Ellzey, Alice Ellzey.** *Wit*: **Jas. Mercer, Wm. Eustace, Wm. Grant, H. Brooke.** *Rec*: 27 August 1761. Dedimus, dated 1 July 1761, issued to **Henry Lee, Jno. Baylis, George Butt, Allan Macrae & William Tebbs,** Gent., to examine

Alice Ellzey to see if she willingly signed the above, wh returned 26 August 1761.

Pages 275-278. 27 August 1761. B & S. Between **George Williams** and **Alice**, his wife, of Hamilton Parish, and **Benjamin Butler** .. L 54.14s.6 1/2 d. .. 70 acres .. Beginning north side of the Hedgman River .. cor. to **Hancock Lee** and **Mr. Hedgman and Chambers** .. Chambers line .. *Signed*: **George Williams, Alice (X) Williams.** *Wit*: **Jas. Fletcher, Jas. Freeman.** *Rec*: 27 August 1761.

Pages 278-280: 27 March 1761. B & S. Between **James Morgan** and **Elizabeth**, his wife, and **Thomas Withers** .. L15.. 30 acres .. part of a tract of 425 acres .. *Signed*: **Jas. Morgan, Elizabeth Morgan.** *Wit*: **Peter Routt, John Hopper, Vinson (X) Garner.** *Rec*: 27 August 1761.

Pages 280-287. 16 & 17 September 1761. Lease & release. Between **Augustine Washington, Edward Randsdell & William Bernard**, of Westmoreland Co., Gent., surviving Trustees of **Robert Vaulx**, late of Parish of Washington, W'land Co., Gent., dec'd. and **Thomas Chilton**, Cople Parish, Gent. .. same Vaulx purchased of **Laurence Debutts**, late of Province of Maryland, Clerk, dec'd .. 11 & 12 June 1745 .. 1,475 a. .. Vaulx made his will 5 Aug 1754: Imprimis: I give unto my friend **John Elliot**, 400 a. of land in Prince William Co. during his natural life and after his decease to his two sons and their heirs forever: which 400 a. of land here intended to bo devised is part of a larger Tract in the aforesaid county, the residue of the said Tract of land together with another lying and being in the Prov. of Md. I devise to **John Bushrod**, Augustine Washington, Edward Ransdell & William Bernard .. in trust to be sold for the payment of my debts, But my will is that if **Mr. St. Clair** who formerly lived with my Mother should be inclinable to purchase the tract of land in Md. .. that my aforesaid Trustees convey it to him in fee simple upon his paying .. L100 .. John Bushrod one of the Trustees is since dec'd .. for L274.5s. current money to **Thomas Chilton**, now in his actual possession .. the remainder of the lands in Fauquier .. after the 400 a. .. devised to John Elliott is deducted .. *Signed*: **Augustine Washington, Edward Ransdell, William Bernard.** *Wit*: **Fox. Sturman, Eliza'th Ransdell, Thos. Chilton, Jr., Edwd. Ransdell, Jr.** Receipt to Thos. Chilton from August Washington, dtd. 16 Sept 1761, same witnesses as above. *Rec*: 24 September 1761, prov. by o. of **Foxhall Sturman, Thos. Chilton, Jun'r. and Edward Ransdell, Jr.**

Pages 287-291: 28 & 29 August 1761. Lease & release. Between **James Bland** of the province of North Carolina and County of Hanover and **Robert Scott** of Prince William, Mercht .. L33 current money of Virginia .. 357 a. .. in Fauquier formerly Prince William .. part of a tract .. granted to **William Johnston** by deed from the Prop. Office .. 1 Nov 1742 .. Beginning .. corner to **William Asberry** .. to **Youngs** cor. .. side of a Glade cor. of **John Toward** .. ridge in the line of **Owin Grinning** .. *Signed*: **James Bland.** *Wit*: **Thos. Machen, Dan'l. Grant, Alex'r. Scott, William Scott.** *Rec*: 24 September 1761. Dower released by **Mary Bland**, wife of James.

Pages 291-292. Bond of **John Bell** to the King as tax collector. *Securities*: **John Ashby, Nimrod Ashby, James Bell** and **Jeremiah Darnal**. *Rec*: 26 November 1761.

Pages 292-293. Same as above. *Securities*: **John Churchill, Jeremiah Darnall, William Pickett** and **Peter Kamper**. *Rec*: 26 November 1761.

Page 293. Same as above. *Securities*: **John Ashby, Nimrod Ashby** and **James Bell**. *Rec*: 26 November 1761.

Pages 293-295. 24 September 1761. Lease and release. Between **Peter Taylor** and **William Robertson Taylor** .. 50 a. .. where **Richard Pickrill** formerly lived .. being part or parcel of land that **Miles Ward** had taken up & pattened by **Charles Taylor** .. adjoining the lands of Doctor **Alexander Bell** now in the possession of **William Morgan** of Middlesex Co. & the land of **John Hudnall** of Northumberland Co., now in the possession of Joseph Hudnall and **John Basye** being near Miles Mt. & on the branches of Cedar Run .. Beginning cor. to John Hudnall .. with Morgan's line .. rent of one peppercorn at Feast of St. Michael the Arch Angel only if same be lawfully demanded .. *Signed*: **P e t e r** **Taylor**. *Wit*: **Jos'h. Hudnall, Jr., John Stone, Jun'r., Samuel Porter**. *Rec*: 26 November 1761. *Release*: **Peter Taylor** to **William Robertson** (not **W. R. Taylor**) .. and the said Peter Taylor his heirs, exors .. the said mentioned granted. Premises with the Appurtenances unto the said **William Robartson** his heirs and assigns shall & will warrant & forever Defend by these Presents & the said **Peter Newport** for himself, his heirs .. doth Covenant with the said William Robertson .. In Witness whereof the said Peter Newport have Interchangeably set his hand and affixed his Seal .. *Signed*: **Peter Taylor**. *Wit*: **Jos. Hudnall, Jun'r., John Stone, Samuel Porter**. Receipt from Taylor to Robertson for ₤18. *Rec*: 26 November 1761, ack. by **Peter Taylor**.

Pages 298-300. 26 November 1761. B & S. Between **Peter Kamper** and **Elizabeth**, his wife, and **Henry Kamper** .. ₤40 .. tract in his actual possession .. on waters of Carters Run .. Beginning .. cor. to the land of **Michael Meldrum** .. cor. to **Benjamin King** .. drain making down Piney Mt. .. east side of Rosser's Run .. large white oak marked I W H W cor. to **Buckner** .. 187 acres .. being a tract taken up by the said Peter .. 1746. *Signed*: **Peter Kamper, Eliz'th (X) Kamper**. *Rec*: 26 November 1761.

Pages 300-302. 26 November 1761. B & S. Between **J o h n   B e l l** and **Frances**, his wife, and **James Bashaw** .. ₤45 .. Beginning .. cor. to **Waugh Darnall** .. with the line that divides the said land hereby conveyed from another part of the same tract sold by Mr. **Thomas Bell** to **William Norriss** .. 570 acres .. *Signed*: **John Bell**. *Wit*: **James Pendleton, Jr., James Bell, William Hunton**. *Rec*: 25 March 1762.

Pages 302-304. 25 March 1762. B & S. Between **David Welsh, Joshua Welsh, John Welsh, William Welsh, John Barbey** and **James Slaugh-**

ter, are held and firmly bound unto **John Withers** of Stafford Co., Planter .. Ł723 .. whereas **Thomas Welsh** late of Prince William Co. Planter, dec'd, was seized of a tract in Prince William now Fauquier .. 764 a. .. had contracted with **Thomas Withers**, bro. of John Withers, to whom it hath been sinco conveyed by David Welsh, the oldest son and heir at law of Thomas Welsh .. Thomas Welsh by his will dated 13 April 1752, did devise his land as follows: Item I give unto my six sons the land I now live upon till my son **Benjamin Welsh** comes to the age of 20 and then the whole tract to be sold and the money equally divided amongst all my sons as is then alive .. said will is duly recorded in Prince William Co. and whereas the aforesaid David, Joshua, John and William Welsh .. the four eldest sons (his two youngest sons **Daniel** and Benjamin who enlisted in the Virginia Regiment being absent) did expose to public sale .. the remaining part of said tract .. 664 acres .. John Withers was the highest bidder at Ł 361.10s. but it was doubted whether or not Benjamin Welsh was 20 years old aud whether 664 acres was the exact acerage of the tract .. John Withers demanded a good title, the above give security that they will do so, and also refund any balance if the survey proves the tract to be less than 664 acres. *Signed*: **David Welsh, Joshua Welsh, John Welsh, William Welsh, John Barbee, James Slaughter**. *Wit*: **Joseph Blackwell, Andrew Edwards**. *Rec*: 26 March 1762.

Pages 304–305. 30 & 31 October 1761. Lease & release. Between **Joseph Hackney & Sarah**, his wife, and **William Duty** and **Caty**, his wife, of Prov. of North Carolina and **John Duncan** .. Ł60 .. adjoining the lands formerly Colonel **Page** (now **Churchhill's**) **Nicholas Russells & William Russells** .. 100 a. +/– .. is the land given by Captain Russell to his son **Martin Russell** dec'd. whose daughter, the said Caty Duty is .. *Signed*: **Joseph (H) Hackney, William (P) Duty. Caty (X) Duty** signed release. *Wit*: **Thomas McClanaham, Samuel Porter, Joseph Duncan, Joseph (I) Duncan, William Walker, Jacob Wever, Samuel Walker**. (**Thomas Parker**, wit. on receipt). *Rec*: 25 March 1762.

Pages 309–310. 10 February 1762. Deed of Gift. **William Powell** of Prince William, Parish of Dittengen, to **Leven Powell**, for natural love and affection for which I have and do bear unto my son .. tract in Fauquier and Loudon taken up and pattented by William Powell and surveyed by **Thomas Davis** .. 22 Oct 1741 .. 557 acres. *Signed*: **William Powell**. *Wit*: **William Seale, Robert Peyton, Samson Demovel**. *Rec*: 25 February 1762, prov. by o. of **Robert Peyton**. 25 March 1762, prov. by o. of **William Seale and Sampson Demovel**.

Pages 310–313. 1762. Lease & release. Between **Simon Miller** and **David Robertson** .. 5s. .. 125 acres .. where David Robertson now lives .. being part of a greater tract of land taken up and surveyed by a grant .. by the said Simon Miller .. to Goose Creek thence down the said Creek .. *Signed*: **Simon Miller**. *Rec*: 25 March 1762.

Pages 313–316. 26 & 27 May 1761. Lease & release. Between **Joseph Delany** and **William Demsie**, of Culpeper Co. .. all that tract ..

200 a. in Fauquier Co. .. head of branch cor. to **Ludwell** now **Hedgmans** .. dividing line between **Charles** and Joseph Delany .. 3 pines in Old Line. *Signed*: **Joseph Delany, Jun'r.** *Wit*: **William Delany, Charles Delany, Morace (X) Jacobs.** *Rec*: 27 May 1762, ack. by grantor.

Pages 316-319. 27 & 28 May 1762. Lease & release. Between **Henry Harding & Wilmoth**, his wife, of Frederick Co. and **John Nelson** .. 180 a. .. corner to land of **William Allan** .. fork of Elk Run .. oak on north side of Elk Run that divides the said Hardings land & **John Delashumate's** .. to line of **Nicholas George** .. same being part of 360 a. purchased by Henry Harding Father to sd. Henry Harding from **William Allen** to whom the same was granted by Patent .. 5 March 1718/19. *Signed*: **Henry (//) Harding, Wilmoth (M) Harding.** *Wit*: **James Pendleton, Jr.** *Rec*: 28 May 1762, ack. by grantor & wife.

Pages 320-323. 27 May 1762. Lease & release. Between **Henry Harding & Wilmoth**, his wife, of Frederick Co. and **Nicholas George** of Stafford Co. .. 180 a. .. to the dividing line between the said Harding & **John Delashumate** .. part of 360 a. purchased by Henry Harding Father of the said Henry Harding from **William Allen** .. *Signed*: **Henry (//) Harding, Wilmoth (W) Harding.** *Wit*: **James Pendleton.** *Rec*: 28 May 1762, ack. by grantor & wife.

Pages 323-328. 27 May 1762. Lease. **Joseph Hitt & Mary**, his wife, **Harman Kamper & Catherine**, his wife, and **Ann Elizabeth Weaver** to **William Hunton** .. 100 a. .. bounded by lands of **Armistead Churchhill**, Esq., **William Russell** and the lands of the said William Hunton which he purchased of **Thomas** and **Samuel Porter** and is the land which descended to the said Mary, Catherine, and Ann Elizabeth as sisters and coheiresses of **Tilman Weaver**, dec'd .. for one year .. *Signed*: all grantors. *Rec*: 28 May 1762, ack. by grantors.

Page 328. 29 May 1762. Bond of **John Bell, Elias Edmonds** and **Thomas McClanahame**, Gent. to **Thomas Harrison, William Blackwell, John Wright, William Grant** and **Jeremiah Darnall**, Gent., Justices of Fauquier Co. .. Ł1000 .. condition .. John Bell on 29 August 1760, did undertake to Build a Courthouse for the use of said County .. whereas the Court .. have thought proper to have an alteration in the Courthouse agreeable to an Order of Court .. said John Bell is willing to make said alteration .. for same consideration .. to be void by performance. *Signed*: **John Bell, Elias Edmonds, Thomas McClanaham.** *Rec*: 29 May 1762, ack. by above.

Page 328. 27 May 1762. Receipt from **Benjamin Robinson** to **John Rout** for Ł20. *Rec*: 27 May 1762, ack. by **Benjamin Robinson.**

Pages 329-330. 24 June 1762. B & S. Between **John Duncan** and **Elizabeth**, his wife, and **Samuel Porter** .. Ł100 .. 150 a. where Samuel Porter now lives .. near Turkey Run .. to **Churchhill's** line .. part of tract purchased by **John Holtzclaw**, dec'd. from **William Russell** and by Holtzclaw the above 150 a. was in his Last Will and Testament given to his daughter Elizabeth, now the wife of the said John Duncan. *Signed*: **John Duncan, Elizabeth Duncan.** *Rec*: 24 May 1762, ack. by grantors, with receipt.

Pages 330-331. 21 June 1762. Agreement. **John Twentyman** and **Sarah Twentyman** .. confirm unto **James Crap, Jun'r.** of Brunswick Parish, King George Co. .. tract in Fauquier .. 214 a. .. part of tract granted to **Edward Twentyman** by Patent .. 13 Oct 1726, whereon John Twentyman and Sarah, his wife, now lives .. Ł25 with interest from 21 June 1762 .. if the said Twentyman & wife do not Contest and pay him (Crap) the above said Ł25 with interest by 21 June 1763, it will be lawful for Crap to enter, hold, possess, and enjoy the said Tract .. *Signed*: **John (+) Twentyman, Sarah (z) Twentyman.** *Wit*: **William Dulany, William Stanton, Charles Dulany.** *Rec*: 25 May 1762, ack. by **John Twentyman.**

Pages 331-333. 9 June 1762. B & S. Between **James Ball, Gent.** of Lancaster Co. and **Elias Edmonds, Gent.** .. Ł225 .. 2,003 a. tract which was granted to James Ball, Father of aforesaid James Ball, by Deed .. 5 May 1732 .. *Signed*: **James Ball.** *Wit*: **James Craig, Howson Kenner, William Pickett, Wm. Davis, Joseph Duncan.** *Rec*: 25 June 1762, prov. by o. of wits.

Pages 333-339. 19 July 1762. Lease & release. Between **Gilson Foote, Gent.** .. and **Thomas Fitzhugh,** of Stafford Co. .. (Ł38.14s.) tract on north side of Cedar Run .. 36 a. .. in bounds of Mr. Thomas Fitzhugh's former purchase of the said Foote .. the said Land being part of Brenttown Patent and was devised to the said Gilson by his Father **George Foote** in his Will bearing date 31 May 1759. *Signed*: **Gilson Foote.** *Wit*: **Richard Foote, Jun'r., Benj'a Pope, William Foote.** *Rec*: 22 July 1762, ack. by Gilson Foote, Gent. *Release wit*: **Richard Foote, Jun'r., Benj'a. Pope** and **Leonard Helm.**

Pages 339-344. 7 July 1762. Lease & release. Between **Leonard Helm** of Prince William Co. and **Hugh Guttray** of Co. aforesaid .. 283 a. .. (Ł64) .. which said land was taken up by **Thomas Helm,** Father of the said Leonard Helm by Patent dated 25 Jan 1720 and by him devised to the said Leonard Helm in his last will and testament .. cor. to land of **John Catlett** thence up Dorrels Run .. Cor. to land of Leonard Helm. *Signed*: **Leonard Helm.** *Wit*: **W. Ellzey, John Moffett, Scarlet Madden, Dan'l. Kincheloe, Henry Peyton.** *Rec*: 22 July 1762.

Pages 344-350. 21 July 1762. Lease & release. Between **Linaugh Helm, Gent.** of Prince William Co. and **Hester,** his wife, and **Thomas Helm** .. 200 a. .. in Co. of Fauquier .. purchased by the said Linaugh Helm from **Parish Garner** as by a Deed of Bargain and Sale duly proved in the General Court and recorded among the records in the Secretary's Office .. dividing cor. between the said Garner and his brother **Charles Garner** .. according to Survey and plat made by **George Hume,** Surveyor .. 7 Dec 1757. *Signed*: **Lynaugh Helm, Hester Helm.** *Rec*: 22 July 1762, ack. by grantors.

21

Pages 350-353. 29 May 1762. B & S. Between Peter Taylor and Elizabeth, his wife, and Gerrard McCarty .. L30 .. 80 a. being the land whereon the said Peter Taylor lately lived .. cor. to the land of Hudnall also the beg. tree to the land sold by the said Taylor to William Roberts .. cor. to Hudnall and tract of land formerly belonging to Colo. Barber now belonging to William Thornton .. cor. to sd. Thornton and Colo. John Bell .. north side of Cedar Run .. cor. to the land formerly taken up by Doctor Bell .. *Signed*: Peter Taylor, Elizabeth (+) Taylor. *Wit*: Chas. Morehead, Thos. Wood, Thos. (O) Older. *Rec̀*: 23 July 1762, ack. by grantors.

Pages 353-354. 1762. Deed of Gift. Betweon Harman Fishback of Culpepor Co. and Elizabeth Taylor, wife to Joseph Taylor and daughter to the said Harman Fishback of Fauquier Co. .. natural love and affection .. parcel whereon the said Elizabeth now lives being part of the German Town .. 66 a. *Signed*: Harman (X) Fishback. *Wit*: Wm. Keirnes, Robert (RH) Hinson. *Rec*: 26 August 1762, ack. by grantor.

Pages 355-356. 26 August 1762. Release. Thomas Dodson release to Greenham Dodson of Amelia Co., Abraham Dodson, Joshua Dodson and Elisha Dodson of Fauquier Co. all claims on account of the Estate of Thomas Dodson, dec'd. which I the said Thomas Dodson do now declare that I have had .. from the Beginning of the World to the Day of the Date of these presents. *Signed*: Thomas Dodson. *Wit*: David Thomas, Gilbert Mason, Benj. (X) Morrice. *Rec*: 26 August 1762, ack. by Thomas Dodson.

Pages 356-362. 25-26 August 1762. Lease & release. Between William Colclough and Mary, his wife, .. Planter .. and Samuel Thornbury of Parish of St. Paul, Stafford Co., planter .. L250 .. 386 a. in Fauquier .. in line of Robert Carter, Esq. .. Cor. to lands of Robert Barber .. Spanish oak on a branch called the walnut branch .. *Signed*: William Colclough, Mary (X) Colclough. *Rec*: 26 August 1762, ack. by grantors.

Pages 362-363. 26 August 1762. Bond from William Colclough and Mary, his wife, to Samuel Thornbury in sum of L500. *Signed*: William Colclough. *Rec*: 26 August 1762, ack. by Wm. Colclough.

Pages 363-366. 25 August 1762. B & S. Between Daniel Hogan and Ann, his wife, and Mary Bashaw of Parish of Washington, Westmoreland Co. .. L18 .. 150 a. being part of a tract of 434 a. .. taken up by the said Daniel Hogan in the year 1742 .. cor. to land of Charles Hogan .. small branch of Cedar Run on the south side of a road .. *Signed*: Daniel (X) Hogan, Anne (X) Hogan. *Wit*: Thom. Marshall, Jas. Hathaway, Sennett Young. *Rec*: 26 August 1762, with receipt, ack. by grantors.

Pages 366-369. 24 July 1762. B & S. Between William Obannon the Younger and Mary, his wife, and Alexander Farrow of Loudoun Co. .. L25 .. 50 a. .. parcel lying on the Waggon Road that leads to Winchester it being part of a greater tract given the aforesaid William Obannon by his Grandfather, Mr. **Bryan Obannon**, dec'd., said Waggon Road at the head of Carters Run .. *Signed*: **William O'Bannon, Jun'r., Mary (X) O'Bannon.** *Wit*: **Sam'l Earle, Wm. (X) O'Bbannon, Sen'r., John O'Bannon.** *Rec*: 26 August 1762, ack. by grantors, with receipt wit. by above wits. and **Sarah (X) Obannon.**

Pages 369–375. 1762. Lease & release. Between **William Wright** and **Mary**, his wife, and **Thomas Edwards** .. L65 .. 125a. it being the said land whereon Wright now lives adjoining to the lands of **Simon Morgan** and **Jonas Williams** on the south side of the Pignut Ridge .. being part of a greater dividend taken up by **Waugh Darnall**, dec'd. by patent, dated 7 Feb. 1725. *Signed*: **William Wright, Mary (X) Wright.** *Wit*: **Isaac Judd, James Bashaw, Thomas Coleman.** *Rec*: 26 August 1762, ack. by grantors.

Pagos 375–377. 27 August 1762. B & S. Between **Thomas Hudnall** of St. Stephens Parish, Northumberland Co. and **Gerrard Edwards** of Hamilton Parish .. 219 acres .. which **William Hudnall** of Northumberland Co. made a Deed to the said Thomas, his son, for L26 to him in hand paid by the said Gerrard Edwards. *Signed*: **Thomas Hudnall.** *Wit*: **Martin Pickett, James Fletcher.** *Rec*: 27 August 1762, with receipt, ack. by grantor.

Pages 378–380. 23 September 1762. Lease. Between **John Sias** and **George Leach** .. 150 a. .. south end of the tract whereon the said John Sias lives and joining to the land of **Richard Healey** .. during the natural lives of George Leach and his wife, **Elizabeth** .. annual rent of 450 lbs. of lawful tobacco yearly or 900 lbs. and cask in 2 years if not paid yearly .. to pay all taxes, Quit rents on the same to the Chief Lord of the Fee. *Signed*: **John Siers, George (X) Leach.** *Wit*: **Richard Healey, James Siers, Ann Champe.** *Rec*: 23 September 1762, ack. by **John Sias.**

Pages 381–383. 23 September 1762. B & S. Between **William Redding & Mary**, his wife, and **John Ashby, Gent.** .. L18.5s. .. tract on the drains of Elk Lick Run .. cor. to the said John Ashby and **Martin Harding** .. cor. to **John Morehead** .. cor. to **Tilman Weaver** .. 73 acres. *Signed*: **William (X) Redding, Mary (/) Redding.** *Rec*: 23 September 1762, with receipt, ack. by grantors.

Pages 384–389. 20–21 August 1761. Lease & release. Between **James Bland** of Hannover Co., Province of North Carolina, Yeoman, and **William Asberry** of Prince William Co., planter .. 5 s. sterling .. tract in Fauquier on the head branch of the Broad Run of Occoquan .. cor. of **Major Ball** .. cor. to land of the late Rev. Mr. **Alexander Scott** .. cor. to sd. Scott .. 201 a. .. said part of which was purchased by the sd. Wm. Asberry of the said James Bland being 125 a. but by intersecting the lines of the said Scott 40 a. was taken away and to the 75 a. remaining in the possession of the sd. **William Asbury** was by the said Bland added 126 a. .. being part of a tract containing 598 a. .. formerly granted to **William Johnson** by deed dated 1 Nov. 1742.

Signed: **James Bland.** *Wit*: **John Basye, John Moffett, Thomas El-liott.** *Rec*: 25 March 1762, prov. by o. of wits.

Pages 389-393: 23 September 1762. Lease. Between **Thomas Lord Fairfax** and **Robert Bolt** .. tract in Manor of Leeds .. 200 acres .. during natural life of Robert Bolt, **Elizabeth**, his wife, and **John**, his son. *Signed*: **Fairfax.** *Rec*: 23 September 1762, ack. by **Lord Fairfax.**

Pages 393-397. 23 September 1762. Lease. Between **Thomas Lord Fairfax** and **Henry Holtzclaw** .. tract in Manor of Leeds .. 200 a. .. during his natural life and the lives of **Susanna**, his wife and **William**, his son .. yearly rent of 40s. sterling .. *Signed*: **F a i r f a x.** *Rec*: 23 Sept. 1762, ack. by **Lord Fairfax.**

Pages 397-401. 23 September 1762. Lease .. Between **Thomas Lord Fairfax** and **James Frazier** .. tract in Manor of Leeds .. cor. to lot surveyed for **Holtzclaw** .. 200 a. .. for his natural life and lives of **Mary**, his wife and **William**, his son .. *Signed*: **Fairfax.** *Rec*: 23 September 1762, ack. by **Lord Fairfax.**

Pages 401-405. 23 September 1762. Lease. Between **Thomas Lord Fairfax** and **Dixon Brown** .. tract in Manor of Leeds .. Beginning two pines on top of a large hill .. on east side of Thumb Run .. in the line of **John Hoppers** Lott .. 213 a. .. during his natural life and lives of **Mary**, his wife, and **Winiford Brown**, his daughter. *Signed*: **Fairfax.** *Rec*: 23 September 1762, ack. by **Lord Fairfax.**

Pages 405-409. 19 October 1761. Lease. Between **Charles Carter**, Esq., and **Zacharias Lewis** .. 200 a. .. Beginning at a red oak in the German Town line cor. to **John Page**, Esq., with his Line .. west side of old run in the sd. Page line .. Mr. **Charles Carter's** line .. during Lewis' natural life and that of his wife during her widowhood .. rent of 650 lbs. good sound merchantable top tobacco clear of ground leaves & trash .. with Cask .. due 25 Nov. 1763, plus quit rents & taxes. *Signed*: **Charles Carter, Zacharias Lewis.** *Wit*: **Charles Carter, Jr., Jno. Churchill, Arm'd. Churchill, Jr.** *Rec*: 28 October 1762, prov. by oath of **John** and **Armistead Churchill**, wits.

Pages 409-414. 4 & 5 October 1762. Lease & release. Between **Henry Foote** and **Margaret**, his wife, and **William Stuart**, Clerk, of Stafford Co. .. £90 .. 100 a. .. same devised to Henry Foote by will of **George Foote** his father .. steep bank of Cedar Run .. cor. to sd. Foote's tract and land of George Foote. *Signed*: **Henry Foote, Margaret Foote.** *Wit*: **Thomas Harrison, Gilson Foote, Richard Foote, Jr., Morias Hansbrough.** *Rec*: 24 March 1763, OR.

Pages 414-418. 24 Maroh 1763. Lease & release. Between **Catherine Holtzclaw** and **Zacharias Lewis** .. parcel in Parish of Hamilton .. 300 a. same granted unto the sd. Catherine Holtzclaw (by the name of **Catherine Thomas** of Stafford Co. she then being the widow and relict of ---- Thomas, dec'd. by patent .. dated 22 January

24

1727/8 .. *Signed*: **Catherine (X) Holtzclaw**. *Rec*: 24 March 1763, ack. by **Catherine Holtzclaw**.

Pages 418-422. 13 & 14 March 1763. Lease & release. Between **Jacob Thomas** and **Judith**, his wife, and **Zacharias Lewis** .. tract in Hamilton Parish bounded by lands of **Robert Burwell**, Esq., **Joseph Martin** and **John Morehead** and is the land granted to **Catherine Thomas** .. 22 Jan. 1727/8 .. *Signed*: **Jacob (X) Thomas, Judith (X) Thomas**. *Wit*: **Joseph Holtzclaw, Joseph Martin, Thomas Batheney**. *Rec*: 24 March 1763, prov. by wits., OR.

Pages 422-426. 24 & 25 March 1762. B & S. Between **Simon Miller** and **David Robertson** .. 125 a. .. £5 .. whereon the sd. **Robinson** now lives .. part of greater tract granted to Simon Miller by the Prop. .. Goose Creek .. (Both Robertson & Robinson used in deed; correct spelling thought to actually be Robinson.) *Signed*: **Simon Miller**. *Rec*: 24 March 1763, ack. by **Simon Miller**.

Pages 426-427. 2 December 1762. Bill of Sale. **William Bannister** to **James Drummond** .. personal estate, corn on plantation of **Richard Foote, Sr.**, on acct. of James Drummond being my security to **William Carr**, Merc't. at Dumfries. *Signed*: **William (+) Banister**. *Wit*: **William Walker**. *Rec*: 24 Maroh 1763, prov. by wit.

Pages 427-428. 24 December 1762. Deed of Gift. **George Wheatley**, by judgment of the County Court of Prince William, recovered of **Honour Williams**, mother of **Sarah**, my late wife in right of the sd. Sarah, 3 slaves **(Sampson, Pompey** and **Will)** and had 3 children by sd. Sarah: **Honour, Betty** and **George**, for whose use and benefit I intend the sd. slaves .. natural love and affection for daughter Betty .. Negro Pompey .. *Signed*: **George Wheatley**. *Wits*: **Thomas Withers, Paul Williams, John Morgan**. George Wheatley to keep sd. Pompey until his daughter, **Elizabeth** marries or comes of age. *Rec*: 24 March 1763, ack. by **George Wheatley**.

Pages 428-429. 24 December 1762. Deed of Gift. **George Wheatley** to daughter, **Honour Wheatley** .. Negro **Sampson**. George Wheatley to keep sd. Negro until Honour marries or comes to age.

Pages 429-430. Same to son, **George Wheatley, Jr.** .. the sd. Negro **Will** .. said George Wheatley, Jr. not to have or enjoy sd. Will until his marriage or his coming to age.

Pages 430-431. 25 September 1762. Deed of Gift. **Joseph Neavill** to **George Neavill** .. for natural love and affection to loving son .. tract whereon he now lives .. on the head of Cedar Run .. formerly pur. of **Thomas Walker** being part of a tract taken up by **John Hudnall** of Northumberland Co. *Signed*: **Joseph Neavill**. *Wit*: **Lazarus Taylor, Walter Moffett, Samuel Earle**. *Rec*: 24 March 1763, ack. by **Joseph Neavill**.

Pages 431–433. 26 November 1762. Bond. **James Scott, Clerk,** of Dittengen Parish, Prince William Co., **John Moncure,** Clerk of Overwharton Parish, Stafford Co., and **George Mason,** Gent., of Truro Parish, Fairfax Co. .. bound unto **James Scott, Jr.** of Hamilton Parish, Fauquier Co. in the sum of Ł2,000 sterling .. James Scott, Clerk and James Scott, Jr., his son and heir apparent have petitioned the General Assembly to dock the Intail of certain lands and settle other lands in Lieu thereof and annex certain slaves thereto as will enable the said James Scott, Clerk, to make an equitable provision for his younger children as to provide during his life a maintenance for the sd. James Scott, Jr. and his family .. if the petition is granted .. the sd. James Scott, Clerk, as well for and in consideration of the sd. James, Jr. having concurred .. as for the love, affection and esteem which the said James Scott, Clerk, hath for the said James, his son .. he agrees to make over to his son in Fee Simple the whole tract whereon he now lives .. 970 a. .. reserving only liberty for James Stewart to reside thereon during the life of the said James Scott, Clerk, without paying rent and also put him in immediate possession of that tract of land upon Carters Run except such part as shall be engaged to tenants, with slaves, .. *Signed*: **James Scott, John Moncure, George Mason.** *Wit*: **Archibald Henderson, John Riddill.** *Rec*: 24 March 1763, prov. by oath of **Arohibald Henderson.**

Pages 433–437. 13 & 14 October 1762. Lease & release. Between **William Wright** and **Mary,** his wife, and **David Williams** and **Betty,** his wife, and **John Waddle** .. Ł35 .. 60 acres .. on side of the Pignut Ridge .. **Simon Morgan's** line .. being part of a tract taken up by **Waugh Darnall,** dec'd. *Signed*: **William Wright, Mary (X) Wright, David Williams.** *Wit*: **Simon Morgan, Thomas Carter, William Norriss, Charles Morgan, Thomas Grubbs.** *Rec*: 25 March 1763, prov. by o. of **Simon Morgan, Norriss, Charles Morgan, Jr.,** wits.

Pages 437–441. 24 & 25 March 1763. Lease & release. Between **John Spilman** of Frederick Co. and **John Morgan** .. 100 a. .. same in Fauquier Co. on Licking Run in the German Town, the land which the sd. Spilman recovered by a decree of the County Court of Fauquier in Chancery of **Mary Gent,** his grandmother .. cor. to the land of **Thomas Marshall,** with his line to another cor. .. cor. to the land of **Peter Hitt.** *Signed*: **John (+) Spilman.** *Wit*: **William Ellzey, Martin Pickett, John Blackwell, William Pickett.** *Rec*: 25 March 1763, prov. by o. of wits.

Pages 442–446. 24–25 March 1763. Lease & release. Between **William Redding,** planter, and **Mary,** his wife, and **William Keirns** .. 347 a. .. part of a greater tract of the sd. William Redding .. cor. to Capt. **John Ashby's** in the line of **Mark Hardin.** *Signed*: **William (+) Redding.** *Rec*: 25 March 1763, ack. by **William Redding.**

Pages 446–451. 20–21 April 1763. Lease & release. Between **Richard Foote the Elder,** Gent. of St. Paul's Parish, Stafford Co. and **John Fitzhugh,** Gent. of Overwharton Parish, Stafford Co. .. 8 3/4 a. .. on north side of Cedar Run .. sd. Fitzhugh's line .. Spanish oak by

Cedar Run. *Signed*: **Richard Foote**. *Wit*: **Gilson Foote, Leonard Helm, William Foote, Richard Foote, Jr.** *Rec*: 28 April 1763, prov. by o. of **Gilson Foote, Helm, and William Foote**, wits.

Pages 451-454: 10 April 1763. **B & S**. Between **Francis Tennell**, Planter, and **Margaret**, his wife, and **Thomas Hord, Jr.**, Gent. of K. G. Co. .. Ŀ50 .. 157 a. .. part of 300 a. sold by **Howsen Kenner & Margaret**, his wife, to **Alexander Sinkler** and Francis Tennell .. 25 July 1743 and recorded in Prince William Co. .. stake in **J o h n s o n**'s line .. white oak on the Marsh run .. west side of sd. run cor. to the line that divides the above sd. land from the land of the sd. Francis Tennell .. cor. to Tennell's land & that of **Edward Wilburn**. *Signed*: **Francis Tennell, Margaret (+) Tennell**. *Wit*: **John Dunlops, Benj. Douglass**. *Rec*: 28 April 1763, ack. by Francis Tennell.

Pages 454-455. 19 February 1763. Deed of Gift. Between **Benjamin Taylor and Elizabeth**, his wife, and **Joseph Taylor**, their son .. for natural love and affection .. plantation whereon we now dwell .. 200 a. .. bounded by the lands of **William Morgan** and **Elias Edmonds** up to the divining line of the land given son **Richard Taylor** and the lands of **Edmund Basye**. Also one Negro woman **Hannah**, stock .. household furniture .. reserving a life interest for themselves .. after their death to pay the following legacies to his sisters: to **Winifred Bayse**, one bed & furniture; to **Hannah Bayse, Elizabeth Morgan** and **Mary Hudnall**, the sum of Ŀ10 each. *Signed*: **Benjamin Taylor, Elizabeth (X) Taylor, Joseph Taylor**. *Wit*: **John Gibbins, William Kitson, Elias Edmonds**. *Rec*: 28 April 1763, prov. by o. of wits.

Pages 456-459. 20 November 1762. Between **Richard Foote**, Gent. of Stafford Co. and **William Stuart**, Clerk, **George Foote, Gilson Foote, Richard Foote** and **William Foote**, four of the sons of George Foote, dec'd. .. Whereas heretofore many years ago **George Brent, Robert Bristow, Nicholas Hayward** and Richard Foote, grandfather of the first named Richard Foote, party to these presents, obtained a patent from the Prop. of the Northern Neck of Virginia for 30,000 acres .. known by the name of the Brent Town Tract .. and whereas at the death of the said Richard Foote the patentee an undivided fourth part of the said .. Land descended to his son Richard Foote, the Father of the first named Richard who having been seised of the said undivided 4th part in his Demesal as of fee simple made his last will and testament .. gave 800 a. of his Brent Town Land to two of his daughters in fee Tail and .. he gave the same by the said Will to his sons Richard (first party to these presents) George and **John Foote** and to their heirs forever equally to be divided .. the said John Foote died intestate without issue, the said Richard, party of 1st part, became intituled to the said John's land .. said Richard was therefore intituled to 2/3rds and George Foote the other devisee was intituled to one-third of an undivided 4th part of the whole Brent Town Land except 800 a. devised to their sisters ... in the years 1737 and 1738 by consent of the Props. of the Brent Town Land the said Land was divided into four Lots and it was the prop's. intention that every lot should contain an equal quantity of land to wit, 7,500 a. .. after the Lots were drawn the first named Richard supposing that the Lot which fell to the Footes contained the full compliment, he soon after allotted to his sisters 800 a. thereof and to his bro. George the Devissee 1/3rd part of 6700 a., to wit, the quantity of 2,233 1/3 a. believing that there remained to him the quantity of 4,466 2/3 acres, but after repeated Tryals it has been found that there remained to the sd. Richard no more than 3,017 a. and that he wanted about 1,450 a. of his compliment which 1,450 a. by the mistake of the surveyor at the division of the whole Tract had been chiefly thrown into the Lot held by Mr. Brent and whereas the said Richard commenced a suit in Chancery against the said Brent and others to have the said mistake rectified and hath expended considerable sums of mnoney in prosecuting the said suit in which however he was cast in the General Court and therefore if these things had been known before or at the time when the said allotment was made to the said George Foote the Devisee could only have claimed 1/3 part of 5,250 a. to wit 1,750 a. and consequently there is contained in his, the said Devisee's part the quantity of 483 a. or thereabouts more than a 1/3 part of the said 5,250 a. and whereas the said George Foote the Devisee by Deeds executed in his lifetime and by his will hath given the said 2,233 1/3 a. of land to his sons **Henry Foote,** who hath sold & conveyed the same to the said **William Stuart** and to **George Gilson,** Richard and William Foote .. and whereas Richard Foote, first party, had resolved to reclaim the said 483 a. and to prevent a suit he and the other parties (except William Stuart in whose stead Henry Foote acted, submitted the said difference to arbitration .. Richard Foote should accept Ł100 for his claim and he (Richard) should execute such release to the other parties .. Richard Foote to the other above mentioned parties .. 2,233 1/3 acres .. *Signed*: **Richard Foote.** *Wit*: **Absolem (+) Ramey, Benjamin Pope, James (+) Drummond.** *Rec*: 26 May 1763, proven by o. of wits.

Pages 459-461. 6 May 1763. B & S. Between **William Hammitt,** Planter, and **Catherine,** his wife, and **William Bronaugh,** Gent. of Stafford Co. .. Ł60 .. 270 a. .. same granted to Hammitt by deed from the Prop. .. 27 May 1748 .. cor. to Mr. **John Savage's** survey .. red oak by branch of Cannon's Run .. box oak near a branch of Dorrils Run .. line of **Taylor** .. stake by Brent Town Road side cor. to the land of Mr. John Savage, dec'd. *Signed*: **William Hammett, Catherine (C) Hammett.** *Wit*: **John Ralls, Alex'r. Jameson, Morias Hansbrough, John Brahan, James Peters.** *Rec*: 26 May 1763, ack. by **William Hammett.**

Pages 461-467. 7-8 February 1763. Lease & release. Between **John Mercer** of Marlborough, Stafford Co., Gent. and **Duff Green,** Gent. of Fauquier .. 405 a. .. on some of the small branches of Cedar Run, joining the lands of **Col. Carter, Col. Tarpley** and **Parson Scott** .. corner of **Peter Lehugh** now Parson Scott's Land .. line of Col. Carter alias **Col. Page** .. said Lehugh alias Scott's land .. same from Prop. to **John Blower** .. 13 Feb. 1728/9 and from Blower to **John Mercer** .. 15 May 1733. *Signed*: **John Mercer, Ann Mercer.** *Wit*: **J. Moncure, Travers Daniel, Dan'l. McCarty, Jas. Mercer, Alex'r. Cuninghame, Jas. Buchanan, William Bronaugh, Yelverton Peyton.** *Rec*: 26 May

1763, prov. by o. of wits. Certificate of examination of Ann Mercer returned by John Moncure and Travers Daniel, dated 9 Feb. 1763.

Pages 467–473. 21–22 December 1762. Lease & release. Between **Rice Duncan** and **Ann Hooe, Sarah Hooe** and **Susannah Hooe** of Stafford Co. .. daughters of **John Hooe** .. tract .. 189a. .. from Prop. to Duncan .. 17 Feb. 1743. *Signed*: **Rice (R) Duncan**. *Wit*: **Thomas McClanaham, William McClanaham, Francis (X) Self, William Marshall**. *Rec*: 26 May 1763, ack. by **Rice Duncan**.

Pages 473–479. 22–23 February 1763. Lease & release. Between **Henry Moffett** and **Hannah**, his wife, and **John Moffett** .. tract .. on Carters Run that was granted to **Walter Anderson** of K. G. Co. for 818 a. .. he devised one moiety to his son **Cyprain** and his daughter **Mary**, late wife of the said Henry .. Cyprain conveyed his right and property .. to **Thomas Turner** who conveyed the same to Henry Moffett .. the moiety devised to the said Mary by Walter Anderson's will to her & the heirs of her body lawfully begotten, the said John Moffett being that legal and lawful heir is possessed of the same .. Henry Moffett doth hereby relinquish all his right of dower .. Ł100 ..containing by est. 200 a. more or less, adjoining the lands of the **Rev. Mr. Scott**, the **Rt. Hon. Lord Fairfaxes** Manor of Leeds, the land of **William Fairfax**, dec'd. *Signed*: **Henry Moffett**. *Wit*: **Original Young, Wm. Neavill, John Blakemore, John Shumate**. *Rec*: 26 May 1763, prov. by o. of **William Neavill, Original Young, John Blakemore**, wits.

Pages 479–483. 26–27 April 1763. Lease & release. Between **Hugh Guttray**, Taylor, in Dumfries, Dittingen Parish, Prince William Co. and **John Gunyon**, Merch't. of same .. tract on Dorrells Run purch. by Hugh Guttray by deeds from **Leonard Helm** .. 286 acres .. *Signed*: **Hugh Guttray**. *Wit*: **Hubbard Prince, Nathaniel Wickliffe, Robt. P. Downman**. *Rec*: 26 May 1763, ack. by **Hugh Guttray**.

Pages 483–485. 26 May 1763. B & S. Between **Simon Miller** and **William Furr** of Loudoun Co. .. Ł10 .. being the said William Furr's proportionable part of the charges that accrued upon taking up a Tract of Land by the said Simon Miller .. 280 a. .. whereon the sd. Furr now dwells .. taken up by Simon Miller ., one part in Fauquier Co. and one part in Loudoun Co. .. in line of **Mr. Burgess**, dec'd. .. line of **Nichols** and **Triplett** .. down to Goose Creek. *Signed*: **Simon Miller**. *Rec*: 26 May 1763, ack. by **Simon Miller**.

Pages 485–489. 29–30 April 1763. Lease & release. Between **Catesby Cocke** of Prince William Co., Esq. and **David Williams** .. Ł15 .. 77 a. .. on one of the branches of the Elk Marsh joining the lands of **David Darnall, Maj. Thornton** and one Smith .. main fork of the Elk Marsh branch cor. to Maj. Thornton .. cor. to **George Wheatley** .. cor. to **John Smith**. *Signed*: **Catesby Cocke**. *Wit*: **Dan'l. Payne, Robert Mackie, William Ellzey, William Carr, John Gunyon**. *Rec*: 26 May 1763, prov. by o. of **Robert Mackie, Ellzey** and **Gunyon**, wits.

Pages 489–492. 5 November 1762. B & S. Between **Thomas Hudnall** of Northumberland Co. and **Joseph Morehead** .. ₤12.12 .. 123 a. .. cor. to Morehead, **Brooke** and Hudnall .. part of tract given Thomas Hudnall by his father **William Hudnall** by deed of gift dated August 1762 and rec. in Northumberland Co. *Signed*: **Thomas Hudnall**. *Wit*: **William Blackwell, Thos. Matthews, Geo. Crump, Samuel Blackwell**. *Rec*: 26 May 1763, ack. by **Thomas Hudnall**.

Pages 492–494. 5 November 1762. B & S. Between **Thomas Hudnall** of Northumberland Co. and **William Blackwell** .. ₤5 .. 50 a. adjoining the land lately sold to **Gerrard Edwards** called Sereans and Wm. Blackwell's part of the said 50 a. lying on Marsh Run and part on Brown's Run it being all the remainder of a tract given to Thomas Hudnall by his father **William Hudnall**. *Signed*: **Thomas Hudnall**. *Wit*: **Thomas Matthews, Samuel Blackwell, Wm. Blackwell, Jr.** *Rec*: 26 May 1763, ack. by **Thomas Hudnall**.

Pages 495–500. 3–4 November 1762. Lease & release. Between **Thomas Hudnall** of Northumberland Co. and **Humphrey Brooke** .. 2 tracts .. 105 a. on a branch by the road .. Brown's Run .. crossing the Church road .. near Hoppers line .. cor. to said Brooke and **Joseph Morehead** .. 75 a. Norman Ford Road .. cor. to another tract of said Brooke .. cor. between said Brooke & Joseph Morehead .. ₤18 .. *Signed*: **Thomas Hudnall**. *Wit*: **Wm. Blackwell, Joseph Morehead, Wm. Blackwell, Jr., Philip Pendleton**. *Rec*: 26 May 1763, ack. by **Thomas Hudnall**.

Pages 500–503. 5 November 1762. B & S. Between **Thomas Hudnall** of Northumberland Co. and **Thomas Matthews** .. ₤25 .. 253 a. .. lying on Brown's Run .. formerly a tract called Mr. Hudnall's .. taken up by **John Hudnall** father to the said **William Hudnall** .. same from Wm. Hudnall to his son Thomas Hudnall .. 1762. *Signed*: **Thomas Hudnall**. *Wit*: **William Blackwell, George Crump, Samuel Blackwell**. *Rec*: 27 May 1763, ack. by **Thomas Hudnall**.

Pages 503–504. 27 May 1763. Bill of Sale. **Matthew Fisher**, Planter, to **Samuel Pepper**, Planter .. 2 mares of a Bald Eagle color, both branded on the near shoulder N.C., one grey horse branded on the near shoulder M.C., cattled sheep, feather beds, pewter, iron pots and skillets, chests, all other personal and real estate and woman's side saddle .. ₤20. *Signed*: **Matthew (+) Fisher**. *Wit*: **John Moffett, Leonard Helm**. *Rec*: 27 May 1763, prov. by wits.

Pages 504–510. 22 November 1762. Lease & release. Between **David Robinson** and **George Lamkin** .. 3.5 .. 125 a. land whereon said Robinson now lives same from Prop. to **Simon Miller** .. Goose Creek. *Signed*: **David Robinson, Catron (X) Robinson**. *Wit*: **John Rust, Chattin Lamkin, Stanley Singleton**. *Rec*: 23 June 1763, prov. by wits.

Pages 510–511. 6 June 1763. Bill of Sale. **George Bell** to **Lazarus Taylor** .. beds, grey horse branded on the near buttock C, livestock all marked with an underkeel, personal property, in consideration of a debt due **Martin Pickett** for Ł32 .. *Signed*: **George (O) Bell.** *Wits*: **Jesse Alexander, William Neavill.** *Rec*: 23 June 1763, prov. by o. of Jesse Alexander and George Neavill.

Pages 511–517. 1–2 June 1763. Lease & release. Between **David Welch** and **Frances**, his wife, **John Welch** and **Elizabeth**, his wife, **William Welch** and **Alice**, his wife, **Joshua Welch, Daniel Welch** and **Benjamin Welch**, sons of and devisees of **Thomas Welch**, late of Prince William Co., dec'd. now the county of Fauquier and **John Withers** of Stafford Co., Planter .. 498 a. .. on the waters of Tin Pott and Great Run .. box oak in **Bronaugh's** Division line .. **Garners** line .. sold according to the will of Thomas Welch, dec'd. .. Ł270 .. *Signed*: **David Welch, Joshua Welch, John Welch, William Welch, Alice Welch, Benj'n. Welch.** *Wit*: **Joseph Hudnall, Paul Williams, William Withers.** *Rec*: 23 June 1763, ack. by grantors.

END OF DEED BOOK NO. 1

DEED BOOK NO. 2

1763 - 1767

Pages 1-7. 8-9 March 1763. Lease & Release. Between **John Grant** of K. G. Co. and **Daniel Grant** of Prince William Co. 158 1/2 a. ... 1/2 of tract containing 317 a. in Fauquier Co. ... same purchased by John Grant, dec'd., father of John & Daniel Grant, of **Howsen Kenner & Margaret**, his wife, part of larger tract granted to **George Eskridge** for 2,060 a. and by him bequeathed to Howsen Kenner and Margaret, his wife, dau. to George Eskridge ... lyes binding on the Marsh commonly called by the name of Jeffrys Marsh ... L5 and nat. love and affection for his brother. *Signed*: **John Grant**. *Wit*: **John Wright, William Bronaugh, William Grant, Winfield Wright, John Kyes**. *Rec*: 28 July 1763, prov. by o. of **William Grant, Winfield Wright** and **John Kyes**.

Pages 7-9. 28 July 1763. Exchange of land. Between **Richard Hampton** and **Charles Morehead** ... parties traded a small tract of land on Cedar Run ... part of the land they now live on ... confirms said exchange and establishes division line ... Mr. Thornton's line ... cor. by Baileys rolling road .. *Signed*: **Richard Hampton, Charles Morehead**. *Wit*: **Joseph Blackwell, Wm. Ransdell, Wharton Ransdell**. *Rec*: 28 July 1763, ack. by parties.

Pages 9-14. 22 September 1760. Power of Attorney. **Joseph Ashworth** of Little Lever near Bolton, Great Britain, Weaver, appoints son **John Ashworth** of or near York River in King Wm. Co. or New Kent Co., province of Virginia, linen weaver, true and lawful attorney to dispose of all lands in North America, late the estate of my mother **Alice Ashworth**, widow, dec'd. which come to me by will or descent .. *Signed*: **Joseph Ashworth**. *Wit*: **James Cock, John McCormick**. James Cock at LiverPoole, in the Co. of Lancaster, Mariner, made oath to above. Sworn to in Liverpoole before **Lawrence Spincer**, Mayor of Liverpoole. *Rec*: 28 July 1763, with cert. of execution, on motion of **John Ashworth**.

Pages 14-19. 27 July 1763. B & S. Between **John Ashworth** of Fauquier, late of Lancastershire, Great Britain and **William Barker** ... 197 a. ... Beginning at large oak marked TB standing at the foot of the Pignut Ridge ... cor. to **Waugh Darnall** ... cor. to **Macquire**, hence with **McGuire**'s line ... near a branch of Broad Run ... same granted

33

by Prop. to **William Bailey**, by him conveyed to **Jacob Holtzclaw** and by him conveyed to **Alice Ashworth** and by her devised to **Joseph Ashworth** ... Ł55 .. *Signed*: **John Ashworth**. *Rec*: 28 July 1763, ack. by **John Ashworth**.

Pages 19-27. 5-6 June 1763. Lease & Release. Between **Humphrey Brooke** and **Ann**, his wife, and **John Woodside** ... 271 a. ... on Brown's Run ... lower end of **Hopper**'s Old field ... pine marked I-F ... box oak by the Chappel Bridge ... Marr's line on the west side of the Chappell Run ... cor. to **Allen** and **Marr** ... to a white oak on the branch called the Rangers Tent ... cor. to **Capt. Grant** ... cor. to **John Brown** .. *Signed*: **H. Brooke, Ann Brooke**. *Wit*: **William Eustace, William Blackwell, Philip Pendleton**. *Rec*: 28 July 1763, ack. by **Humphrey Brooke**.

Pages 27-29. 28 July 1763. B & S. Between **Elias Edmonds** and **Simon Miller** ... Ł120 ... tract est. to be 1,002 a., half of a larger tract purchased by Elias Edmonds from **James Ball**, Gent. of Lan. Co. ... Beginning at lower end of said tract and beg. cor. of the said Edmond's patent ... east side of a glade of the north branch of the Piney Branch of the Broad Run of Occoquan ... cor. tree of **Parson Scott** in the head of a drain of the Horsepen Branch of the Piney Branch of the said Broad Run ... south branch of the sd. Piney Branch ... head of a drain of Goose Creek ... in a fork nigh to the head of a branch of Chattens Run ... on the west side the main branch of Cromwells Run ... *Signed*: **Elias Edmonds**. *Wit*: **William OBanon, John Fishback, William Kitson**. *Rec*: 28 July 1763, ack. by **Elias Edmonds**.

Pages 30-34. 25 November 1762. Mortgage. Between **George Lamkin** and **Sarah**, his wife, and **Daniel Jennifer** of Charles Co., Maryland, ... Ł706.4s ... tracts of land ... whereon said Lamkin lives, purchased of **Thomas Chattin** ... with 10 Negroes, **Harry, Titus, Timon, Bowman, Sibinah, Cook, Letty, Pleasant, Ruth, Young Letty** ... for <u>500</u> years ... however if said **Lamkin** shall pay the sum above with interest on or before the last day of April next ... this shall become void. *Signed*: **George Lamkin, Sarah Lamkin**. *Wit*: **William Ellzey, John Rust, William OBanon, Mary (+) OBanon, Stanley Singleton**. *Rec*: 29 July 1763, ack. by **George Lamkin**.

Pages 34-39. 28 July 1763. Lease. Between **Thomas Lord Fairfax** and **William Neavill** ... tract in Manor of Leeds ... 202 1/2 a. ... across the drains of Thumb Run ... during his natural life and lives of his wife **Winifred** and son **Yelverton Neavill** ... yearly rent of 40s.5d. ster. *Signed*: **Fairfax**. Rec: 29 July 1763, ack. by **Lord Fairfax**.

Pages 39-44. 28 July 1763. Lease. Between **Thomas Lord Fairfax** and **Gerrard Manifee** of Culpeper Co. ... 128 a. ... in Manor of Leeds ... in line of lott surveyed for **William Higgins** ... during his natural life and the lives of **William** and **Jonas Manifee**, his sons ... yearly rent of 25s.7d. *Signed*: **Fairfax**. Rec: 29 July 1763, ack. by **Lord Fairfax**.

Pages 45-50. 28 July 1763. Lease. Between **Thomas Lord Fairfax** and **James Jett** ... tract in Manor of Leeds ... 150 a. ... on Thumb Run cor. to Lott surveyed for **Neal Ju'r.** ... cor. to **Neavill's** lott ... cor. to **Gerrard's** Lott ... for Jett's natural life and the lives of **Elizabeth**, his wife, and **W i l l i a m**, his son, ... yearly rent of 30s. sterling. *Signed*: **Fairfax.** *Rec*: 29 July 1763, ack. by **Lord Fairfax.**

Pages 50-55. 28 July 1763. Lease. Between **Thomas Lord Fairfax** and **John Rogers** of Culp. Co. ... tract in Manor of Leeds ... 225 a. ... Beg. ... **Neal's** lott line ... cor. to **Jett's** Lott crossing Thumb Run ... **Norman's** Lott line ... line of **George's** lott ... cor. to **Neal Ju'r's.** Lott ... during his natural life and lives of **Henry Rogers** and **Stephen Rogers**, his sons ... yearly rent of 45s. ster. *Signed*: **Fairfax.** *Rec*: 29 July 1763, ack. by **Lord Fairfax.**

Pages 55-60. 28 July 1763. Lease. Between **Thomas Lord Fairfax** and **Clement Norman** ... tract in Manor of Leeds ... 200 a. ... corner of Lott surveyed for **William Higgins** ... saplin at foot of a little mountain ... during his natural life and the lives of **Jemimah Norman**, his wife and **Isaac Norman**, his son ... yearly rent of 40s. sterling. *Signed*: **Fairfax.** *Rec*: 29 July 1763, ack. by **Lord Fairfax.**

Pages 60-65. 28 July 1763. Lease. Between **Thomas Lord Fairfax** and **John Gerrard** ... tract in Manor of Leeds ... 145 a. ... cor. to **Mr. N e a v i l l** 's lott ... in the low grounds of Thumb Run ... for his natural life and lives of **Mary**, his wife and **Jacob**, his son ... yearly rent of 29s. sterling. *Signed*: **Fairfax.** *Rec*: 29 July 1763, ack. by **Lord Fairfax.**

Pages 65-66. 28 July 1763. Bond of **Armistead Churchill** for Ł 211.10s. to build a prison for the use of this county ... for the consideration of Ł105.15s. Obligation to be void if completed agreeable to order of the Court by November Court. *Inquiries*: **John Churchhill, Joseph Blackwell.** *Rec*: 29 July 1763

Pages 66-67. 30 March 1763. Bill of Sale. **William Corder** to **Martin Pickett** ... livestock ... for Ł24.5s.4d. in goods delivered to said Corder and son **William.** *Signed*: **William (W) Corder.** *Wit*: **William Pickett.** *Rec*: 30 July 1763, prov. by o. of wit.

Pages 67-69. 23 August 1763. Mortgage. **Daniel Horgain**, planter, to **James Horgain**, planter ... Ł16 ... cattle, horses, beds & furniture, personal property ... however, upon payment of above amount by 1 Sept. bill of sale to be void. *Signed*: **Daniel (X) Horgain.** *Wit*: **Gilson Foote, John Blackwell, Jeremiah Spiller.** *Rec*: 22 September 1763, ack. by **Daniel Hogain.**

Page 69. 30 October 1762. Bill of Sale. **Thomas Grubbs** to **Bennett Price** ... white horse ... to satisfy a debt of Ł10 to Messrs. **Andrew Cockran, Allan Dreghorn** and Co. *Signed*: **Thomas Grubbs.** *Wit*: **James McFerrand, William Wright.** *Rec*: 26 August 1763, prov. by

o. of **William Wright**.

Pages 69-70. 26 August 1762. Bill of Sale. **Henry Dickens to James Pendleton** on behalf of Messrs. **Andrew Cockran, Allan Dreghorn & Co.** ... Merch'ts, Glasgow ... Ł12 ... livestock ... personal property. *Signed*: **Henry Dickins**. *Wit*: **John Tomlin**. *Rec*: 26 August 1763, prov. by o. of **John Tomlin**.

Page 70. 13 September 1762. Bill of Sale. **Henry Dickens to James Pendleton**, horses ... to answer a debt to Messrs. **Andrew Cockran & Co.** of Ł12. *Signed*: **Henry Dickins**. *Wit*: **Bennett Price, George Rogers**. *Rec*: 26 August 1763, prov. by o. of **Bennett Price**.

Page 71. 28 March 1763. Bill of Sale. **Anthony Morgan to Bennett Price** ... slaves, livestock, personal estate ... Ł80, a debt due **Andrew Cockran, Esq. & Co.** *Signed*: **Anthony Morgan**. *Wit*: **Jesse Hamilton, William (X) Hamilton**.
Rec: 26 August 1763, prov. by o. of William Hamilton

Pages 71-75. 9-10 September 1763. Lease & Release. Between **Daniel Grant** and **Christian**, his wife, of Pr. Wm. Co. and **Allan Macrae** of the town of Dumfries ... Ł90 ... 162 1/2 a. ... 1/2 of a tract containing 325 a., part of tract granted to **George Eskridge** for 2,060 a., part given to Eskridge's son-in-law **Howsen Kenner** and wife **Margaret** and by them exchanged with **John Grant** of K. G. Co. for a larger tract in Fauquier ... present 325 a. devised by John Grant to his sons, **George & Daniel Grant** to be equally divided. *Signed*: **Daniel Grant, Christian Grant**. *Rec*: 22 September 1763, ack. by **Daniel Grant**.

Pages 76-78. 13 July 1763. B & S. Between **William Obannon** and **Mary**, his wife, and **Alexander Farrow** ... Ł150 tract of 256 a. ... on Broad Run ... north side of Broad Run ... cor. to tract formerly sold to said Farrow by the said Obannon ... line bet. tract and land of **John Obannon, Senior** ... part of the same tract left by **Bryan Obannon**, dec'd. to his grandson **Thomas Obannon** by will ... hence with Thomas Obannon's line ... a part of tract of Bryan Obannon left to his grandson, the said William Obannon. *Signed*: **William Obannon, Jun'r**. *Wit*: **James Kerr, John Obannon, Sr., Thomas Elliott, John Obannon, Jr.** *Rec*: 22 Sept. 1763, prov. by o. of **Kerr, John Obannon & Elliott**, wits.

Pages 79-82. 11-12 August 1763. Lease & Release. Between **Joseph Jones** of Spotsylvania Co. and **Mary**, his wife and **Francis Whiting** of W'land Co. ... Ł300 ... tract on Tin Pott Run ... 534 a. ... land that James Jones, dec'd. father to Joseph, purchased of **Nathaniel Hedgeman**. *Signed*: **Jos. Jones, Mary Jones**. *Wit*: **Matthew Whiting, H. Brooke, John Whiting**. *Rec*: 22 September 1763, prov. by o. of wits.

Pages 82-85. 29 June 1763. B & S. Between **Thomas Obannon** and **Samuel Rust** ... Ł70 ... 220 a. ... on South East side of Broad Run ...

part of two tracts formerly belonging to **Bryan Obannon**, dec'd. and by him devised to Thomas Obannon. *Signed*: **Thomas Obannon.** *Wit*: **Thom Marshall, Alex'r. Farrow, John Obannon, Sarah Obannon, John Rust.** *Rec*: 26 August 1763, prov. by o. of **Thomas Marshall** and **John Rust,** wits.

Pages 85–88. 5–6 November 1762. Lease & Release. Between **Thomas Hudnall** of N'land Co. and **John Barnes** ... 183 a. ... on the road cor. to **Humphrey Brooke** ... cor. to **Joseph Morehead.** *Signed*: **Thomas Hudnall.** *Rec*: 22 September 1763, ack. by **Thomas Hudnall.**

Pages 88–91. 15 September 1763. B & S. Between **Thomas Grining, John Courtney, William Courtney, George Henry, Joshua Wood & Charles Delaney** and **Joseph Blackwell** and **Richard Lewis** of Fauq. & K. G. Cos. ... L54 ... all the pine trees of a foot over at the stump now standing on the grantors' land about 938 a. ... the grantees may enter the premises to fell, cut, fetch & carry away the pine trees ... without any trouble ... the grantees may also erect mills they think proper to build or erect or a grist mill for grinding .. *Signed*: **Thomas (X) Grinning, John (X) Courtney, William (X) Courtney, George Henry, Joshua (X) Wood, Charles Dulany.** *Rec*: 27 October 1763, ack. by grantors.

Pages 91–93. 15 September 1763. B & S. Between **John Courtney** and **Joseph Blackwell** and **Richard Lewis** ... tract ... 2 a. ... 5s. ... on Rock Run being part of the tract said Courtney now lives on ... down several meanders of Rock Run, .. *Signed*: **John (X) Courtney.** *Wit*: **Joseph Sebastin, Henry Morless, Willian Dulaney, John Courtney.** *Rec*: 27 October 1763, ack. by grantor.

Pages 93–95. 27 July 1763. B & S. Between **William Dulaney** of Culp. Co. and **Joseph Blackwell** and **Richard Lewis** ... L15 ... 100 a. ... being part of a tract taken up by **Joseph Dulaney** and by him conveyed to **Charles Dulaney** by Deed of Gift and conveyed by Charles Dulaney to Wm. Dulaney ... southside Field's Road ... Crump's Path. *Signed*: **William Dulaney.** *Wit*: **George Henry, Jos. Williams, James Wheatley.** *Rec*: 27 October 1763, ack. by grantor.

Pages 95–96. 27 October 1763. B & S. Between **Joseph Williams** and **Elizabeth,** his wife, and **Joseph Blackwell** and **Richard Lewis** ... L10 ... 140 a. ... part of a tract taken up by **Joseph Delaney** and by him conveyed to **Charles Delaney** ... and by him conveyed to Joseph Williams. *Signed*: **Jos. Williams, Elizabeth (X) Williams.** *Wit*: **Rodham Tollos, Daniel Harrill, William Dulaney.** *Rec*: 27 October 1763, ack. by grantors.

Page 97. 24 November 1763. Bond of **William Grant** to collect and receive from Tithables their county levies. For: 60,176 lbs. tobacco. *Sec*: **Mamimillian Berryman.** *Rec*: 24 November 1763.

Pages 97–98. 24 November 1763. Bond of **William Grant** to collect and receive county levies. For: 1,000. *Sec*: **William Blackwell.** *Rec*:

37

24 November 1763.

Page 98. 27 October 1763. Bill of Sale. **William Welch** to **Thomas Hopper** of Culp. Co. ... Ł15 due Hopper ... crop of tobacco and corn, stock and personal estate. *Signed*: **William Welch**. *Wit*: **Joshua Welch**. *Rec*: 25 November 1763, prov. by o. of wit.

Pages 98-101. 25 November 1763. Lease & Release. Between **John Conyers** and **Alice**, his wife, and **William McClanahame** ... Ł50 ... 184 a. ... on east side of Carter's Run ... below Pickets Mill ... dividing line between John Conyers and **Samuel Conyers**. *Signed*: **John Conyers, Alice (X) Conyers**. *Wit*: **Thomas McClanahame, Samuel Conyers, William (X) Pritchett**. *Rec*: 25 November 1763, prov. by o. of wits.

Pages 102-103. 12 March 1764. B & S. Between **John Arnold, Jr.** and **Lutishea**, his wife, and **William Settle** ... Ł16 ... 50 a. whereon sd. Arnold now lives, being land given John Arnold by **John Arnold, Sr.**, his father ... deed recorded in Pr. Wm. Co. ... surveyed by **Thomas Marshall**, Surveyor of Fauq. Co. ... cor. to William Settle ... cor. to one other parcel ... given by the sd. John Arnold to his son **Moses**. *Signed*: **John Arnold, Lutishea (X) Arnold**. *Wit*: **Bushrode Doggett, Benjamin Settle, Fras. Bronaugh, John (X) Edwards**, the within delivered by turf & twig. *Rec*: 22 March 1764, prov. by o. of **Doggett, Bronaugh** and **Edwards**.

Pages 103-104. 22 March 1764. Deed of Gift. Between **John Morehead** and John Morehead, son of sd. Morehead ... for nat. love and affection ... 124 a. now in his possession. *Signed*: **John Morehead**. *Wit*: **Jos. Blackwell, Thos. McClanaham, Edward Humston**. *Rec*: 22 March 1764, ack. by **John Morehead**.

Pages 104-108. 22-23 March 1764. Lease & Release. Between **Elias Edmonds**, Gent. and **Betty**, his wife, and **Thomas Harrison**, Gent. ... Ł100 ... 400 a. ... cor. marked JB cor. to the land surveyed for **John Blowers** and by him sold to **John Mercer**, Esq. ... crossing Chattins Run ... in line of **Edmonds'** 220 a. lott ... crossing the main road & **Dixon**'s Quarter Road ... oak in Blower's alias **Mercer**'s line. *Signed*: **Elias Edmonds, Betty Edmonds**. *Wit*: **Jos. Blackwell, Han. Lee, Simon Miller**. *Rec*: 22 March 1764, ack. by grantors.

Pages 108-109. 31 October 1763. Bond. **Joseph Blackwell** and **Richard Lewis** bound to each other in sum of Ł10,000 ... they have purchased from parties (see above deeds) pine timber also property ... all on or near Rock Run ... where they intend to erect mills for sawing of the timber ... each relinquishes all right and title of Survivorship to above mentioned premises ... deeds to be executed to spell out their agreements. *Signed*: **Jos. Blackwell, Rich'd. Lewis**. *Wit*: **Jas. Ball, Nicholas Currell**. *Rec*: 23 March 1764.

Pages 109-110. 23 March 1764. Power of Attorney. **John Wright** of K.G. Co. planter, appoints trusty friend **John Wright, Jr.** of Fauquier,

Gent. ... full power of attorney. *Signed*: **John Wright**. *Wit*: **W. Edmonds, George Grant**. *Rec*: 23 March 1764, prov. by o. of **William Edmonds** and **George Grant**.

Pages 110-111. 24 October 1763. Bill of Sale. **George Coulson** to **James Siers** ... stock and personal estate for Ł18.10s. ... sum due **James Siers**. *Signed*: **George (X) Colson**. *Wit*: **Thomas Hogan, Joshua Ginnins**. *Rec*: 23 February 1764, ack. by **George Coulson**.

Page 111. 26 April 1764. Bond. Bond of **William Pickett, Jr.** to build a Prison for the Co. of Fauq. ... to be finished 26 July next ... to be paid Ł51.17s.6d. to be paid in July 1765. For: Ł500. *Sec*: **Thomas Marshall**. *Signed*: **Wm. Pickett, Jr., Thom. Marshall**. *Rec*: 26 April 1764, ack. by **Pickett** and **Marshall**.

Pages 112-115. 25-26 April 1764. Lease & Release. Between **George Wheatley & Dinah**, his wife, and **John Knox**, of K. G. Co., Merchant ... Ł150 ... 345 a. ... on the Wild Cat Run ... cor. to **John Duncan** ... part of the land patented by **George Wheatley**, dec'd., father to the Grantor in 159a. of which land **Mary**, the wife of **William Sturdie** has her Life ...

Pages 115-118. 25 April 1764. Lease & Release. Between **John Wright, Jr.**, Planter, and **Ann**, his wife, and **John Wright**, Gent. ... Ł 80 ... 116 a. ... part of a greater tract .. *Signed*: **John Wright, Ann Wright**. *Wit*: **George Wheatley, Gerrard Banks, Jr., Alexander Bradford**. *Rec*: 26 April 1764, ack. by grantors.

Pages 119-120. 26 April 1764. B & S. Between **Charles Morgan** and **Elizabeth**, his wife, and **Bushrod Doggett** ... Ł136.8s. ... 341 a. ... on the North Branch of Great Run ... cor. tree to **Charles Morgan, Sr.** and **Thomas Acresayers** and running along the said Ayres line (sic) ... line of **George Williams** ... Morgans antient Tract. *Signed*: **Chas. Morgan, Jr., Elizabeth Morgan**. *Rec*: 26 April 1764, ack. by grantors.

Pages 120-121. 27 October 1763. Bond of **John Johnson** and **Jeffrey Johnson**, his son, to convey to **Thos. Hord** a parcel of land cont. 100 a. ... at the Jefferys Marsh adj. a tract belonging to the sd. **Hord**. For: Ł500. *Signed*: **John (G) Johnson, Jeffery (L) Johnson**. *Wit*: **Wm. Pickett, Thos. Porter, William Withers**. *Rec*: 26 April 1764, ack. by **John** and **Jeffry Johnson**.

Pages 121-124. 15-16 February 1764. Lease & Release. Between **Peter Rout**, of Overwharton Par., Staf. Co., Planter, and **Martha**, his wife, and **James Withers** ... 50 a. ... upon the Rappahannock River opposite to Slaughters Mill ... Beg. at the mouth of a branch where he, the sd. **Peter Routt** formerly set his house. *Signed*: **Peter Routt**. *Wit*: **John Bell, Augustine Jennings**. *Rec*: 24 May 1764, ack. by **Routt**.

Pages 124-127. 23-24 May 1764. Lease & Release. Between **Henry Kemper** and **Lettis (Lettice)**, his wife, and **Jeremiah Darnall** ... 40 a.

on Licking Run ... part of a tract taken up by **John Fishback, John Huffman & Jacob Holtzclaw** by Patent ... 21 Aug. 1724 and conveyed from the above Persons to **John Kemper**, father to the sd. **Henry Kemper** ... to Licking Run ... **Mounjoys** line ... *Signed*: **H e n r y Kemper, Lettis (X) Kemper**. *Rec*: 24 May 1764, ack. by grantors.

Pages 127–128. 24 May 1764. Bill of Sale. **Waugh Darnall** to **George Wheatley** ... Ł12 ... personal estate, livestock, etc. *Signed*: **Waugh Darnall**. *Wit*: **Wm. Sturdy, James Wheatley**. *Rec*: 24 May 1764, prov. by o. of **William Sturdy**.

Pages 128–129. 9 April 1764. Lease. Between Col. **Richard Henry Lee** of W'land Co. and **Humphrey Arnold** ... for yearly rent of Ł5 to be paid by Humphrey Arnold, **Anne**, his wife, and **Samuel**, his son, during their nat. lives ... 100 a. ... **William Barton's** Tenement ... white oak near Tmrkey Run ... *Signed*: **Richard Henry Lee**. *Wit*: **James Craig, T. Bullett, John Oriss, Jos. Blackwell**. *Rec*: 24 May 1764, prov. by o. of **Craig, Blackwell and Oriss**. Ex'd. & del. to **T. Marshall**.

Pages 129–131. 9 April 1764. Lease. Between Col. **R. H. Lee** of W'land Co. and **Minor Winn** of Pr. Wm. Co. ... for yearly rent of Ł 11.8s. ... 228 a. to sd. **Winn, John Winn**, his son & **Dorothy**, the wife of John, and Minor Winn, the son of John Winn, for their nat. lives ... south side of the Great road leading to Ashby's Gap along an old Road binding on Captain **William Edmonds** ... Capt. Wm. Edmonds' cor. at Towsers Branch ... up sd. branch ... *Signed*: **Richard Henry Lee**. *Wit*: (same as above). *Rec*: 24 May 1764, prov. by o. wits. as above.

Pages 131–133. 9 April 1764. Lease. Between Col. **R. H. Lee** of W'land Co. and **William Jones** ... for yearly rent of Ł10.10s. ... 247 a. ... to sd. Jones, his wife, **Mary** and son, **William** and **James Jones** ... for their nat. lives ... line tree of **Thomas Grubbs** Tenement ... *Signed*: **Richard Henry Lee**. *Wit*: (same as above). *Rec*: 24 May 1764, prov. by o. of wits. as above.

Pages 133–134. 9 April 1764. Lease. Between Col. **R. H. Lee** of W'land Co. and **James Armstrong** ... 76 a. ... for yearly rent of 50s. ... cor. tree of **Willian Jones** tenement and **Thomas Grubbs** ... cor. to **William Barton**. *Signed*: **Richard Henry Lee**. *Wit*: (same as above). *Rec*: 24 May 1764, prov. by o. of **Craig, Blackwell & Oriss**.

Pages 134–136. 9 April 1764. Lease. Between Col. **R. H. Lee** of W'land Co. and **George Jeffries**, planter ... 123 a. ... for yearly rent of Ł6.5s. for his nat. life and lives of **Sarah**, his wife, and **Alexander**, his son ... **Humphrey Arnold's** Tenement ... cor. tree to **William Jones's** Lott ... *Signed*: **Richard Henry Lee**. *Wits*: **James Craig, T. Bullett, John Oriss, Jos. Blackwell**. *Rec*: 24 May 1764, prov. by o. of **Craig, Oriss, Blackwell**.

Pages 136–137. 9 April 1764. Lease. Between Col. **R. H. Lee** ... and **Thomas Grubbs** ... 100 a. ... for yearly rent of Ł5 for his nat. life and lives of **Sarah**, his wife, and **Darius Grubbs**, his son ... Beg. at

Turkey Run ... lines of **William Burton** and **Humphrey Arnold** ... cor. of tenement of **George Jeffries**. *Signed*: **Richard Henry Lee**. *Wits*: (same as above - **Thomas Bullett**). *Rec*: 24 May 1764, prov. by o. of wits. above. Ex'd. & del. to **T. Marshall**.

Pages 138-139. 9 April 1764. Lease. Between Col. **R. H. Lee** of W'land Co. and **Richard Lewis** of K. G. Co. ... 1 a. ... for yearly rent of Ł2.10s. to sd. Lewis, his wife, and **John Lewis**, his son, for their nat. lives ... cor. of **Minor Winn's** lott. *Signed*: **Richard Henry Lee**. *Wit*: (same as above). *Rec*: 24 May 1764, prov. by o. of wits. as above.

Pages 139-141. 9 April 1764. Lease. Between Col. **R. H. Lee** of W'land Co. and **William Burton** ... 200 a. ... for yearly rent of Ł10 ... for his nat. life and lives of **Rachael Burton**, his wife and **Samuel Burton**, his son ... near Turkey Run plantation .. *Signed*: **Richard Henry Lee**. *Wit*: (same as above). *Rec*: 24 May 1764, prov. by o. of above wits.

Pages 141-142. 9 April 1764. Lease. Between Col. **R. H. Lee** ... and **John Headley** ... 110 a. for yearly rent of Ł5 ... to sd. Headley, **Rebecca**, his wife, and **James Headley**, his son, for their nat. lives ... on road ... to post of the prison bounds ... out of which **John Winn** has 10 a. for Pasturage ... *Signed*: **Richard Henry Lee, John Headley**. *Wit*: **James Craig, T. Bullett, John Oriss, Jos. Blackwell**. *Rec*: 24 May 1764, prov. by o. of wits, except **Thomas Bullett**.

Pages 142-144. 9 April 1764. Lease. Between Col. **R. H. Lee** of W'land Co. and **Minor Winn**, of Pr. Wm. Co. ... 5 a. for yearly rent of ---- for nat. lives of sd. Winn, **John Winn**, his son, **Dorothy**, wife of John Winn & Minor Winn, son of John ... to post of prison bounds ... *Signed*: **Richard Henry Lee**. *Wit*: as above. *Rec*: 24 May 1764, prov. by o. wits as above.

Page 144. 24 May 1764. Deed of Gift. **Joseph Delaney** to son **Joseph Delaney** ... for nat. love and affection ... two Negroes named **Tom** and **Luce**. *Signed*: **Josep Delaney**. *Wit*: **George Threlkeld, George Rankins**. *Rec*: 24 May 1764, prov. by o. of wits.

Pages 144-145. 24 May 1764. Deed of Gift. **Joseph Delaney** to **Andrew Barbee** ... for nat. love and affection ... Negroe woman named **Sarah** ... *Signed*: **Joseph Delaney**. *Wit*: **George Threlkeld, George Rankins**. *Rec*: 24 May 1764, prov. by o. of wits.

Pages 145-146. 24 May 1764. Between **John Debity** and **Alexander Woodrow** & **John Neilson**, of K. G. Co., Merchants ... for Ł36.10s.5 1/2d. ... personal estate. *Signed*: **John Debity**. *Wit*: **James Withers, Edward Humston**. *Rec*: 24 May 1764, prov. by o. of above wits.

Pages 146-147. 5 April 1764. Bill of Sale. **Gaton Settle**, planter, to **Alexander Cuningham** of Falmouth, K. G. Co., merch't in behalf of Messrs. **Andrew Cockran, Allan Dreghorn & Co.** of the City of

Glassgow in Kingdom of Great Britain, Merchants ... for sum of Ł
116.10s. ... personal estate. *Signed*: **Gaton (+) Settle**. *Wit*: **William
Petty, James Robinson, Thomas Crawford, Hugh Hamilton**. *Rec*: 24
May 1764, ack. by **Gaton Settle**.

Pages 147-150. 23-24 May 1764. Lease & Release. Bet. **Parish
Garner** and **Margaret**, his wife, and **Thomas Helm** ... tract adj.
Thomas Withers and **Vincent Garner** and the land sold by the sd.
Garner to **Lynaugh Helm**, Gent. ... 39 a. ... for Ł16.10s. *Signed*:
Parish (X) Garner, Margaret (W) Garner. *Rec*: 24 May 1764, ack.
by **Parish Garner**.

Pages 150-153. 10-11 June 1764. Lease & release. Between **D a v i d
Williams** and **Elizabeth**, his wife, and **John Knox**, of K. G. Co., mer-
chant ... 77 a. ... on a branch of Elk Marsh joining to the lands of
David Darnall now in possession of one **Waugh, Major Thornton** and
one **Smith** ... main fork of the Elk Marsh branch cor. to Major Thornton
... cor. to **George Wheatley** ... cor. to **John Smith** ... for Ł20. *Signed*:
David Williams, Elizabeth (N) Williams. *Wit*: **John Dunlop, John
Shumate, Geo. Wheatley, William Sturdy, Waugh Darnall**. *Rec*: 28
June 1764, prov. by o. of **George Wheatley** and **Willian Sturdy**.

Pages 153-157. 23-24 June 1764. Lease & Release. Between **Moses
Copage & Jane**, his wife, of Par. of Brumfield, Culp. Co. and **Lynaugh
Helm**, Dittengen Par., Pr. Wm. Co., Gent. ... tract in counties of Pr.
Wm. and Fauq. bounded on **Richard Tidwell's** line ... 275 a. ... being
part of 576 a. granted to **John Madden** 6 Apr. 1730 ... cor. Richard
Tidwell's land ... by Goose Run ... Ł85. *Signed*: **Moses Coppedge,
Jane Coppedge**. *Rec*: 28 June 1764, ack. by **Moses Copage**.

Pages 157-159. 28 June 1764. B & S. Between **Jeffery Johnson**,
Planter, and **Sarah**, his wife, and **Thomas Hord**, Brunswick Par., K.
G. Co., Gent. ... Ł50 ... 100 a. ... part of 232 a. granted 20 July 1712
to **Jeffery Johnson**, grandfather to the above mentioned ... given to
John Johnson, son to Jeffery Johnson by his will dated 25 June 1725
... John Johnson by deed of gift to his son the sd. Jeffery Johnson ...
on the upper or north Little Marsh ... **Mr. Berriman's** plantation ...
Signed: **Jefery Johnson, Sarah (X) Johnson**. *Wit*: **Jos. Blackwell,
Richard Lewis, William Blackwell**. *Rec*: 28 June 1764, ack. by **Jef-
fery Johnson**.

Pages 159-160. 1 May 17. Deed of Gift. **John Johnson** to son **Jeffery**
... for nat. love and affection ... 100 a. ... *Signed*: **John (X) Johnson**.
Wit: **Thos. Porter, Wm. Underwood, Benjamin (X) Sebastin, Sam'l.
(X) H a d d o x**. *Rec*: 24 May 1764, prov. by o. of **P o r t e r** and
Underwood; 28 June 1764, prov. by o. of **Samuel Haddox**.

Page 161. 4 June 1764. Deed of Gift. **Joseph Dulaney** to **John Smith**
... for nat. love and affection ... one Negroe girl named **Grace** ...
Signed: **Joseph Dulaney**. *Wit*: **Wm Sturdy, George Threlkeld**. *Rec*:
28 June 1764, prov. by o. of wits.

Page 161. 26 June 1764. Deed of Gift. **Joseph Dulaney** ... for love and affection ... for son **William Dulaney** & his children, **Joseph & Anna Dulaney** of St. Marks Par., Culp. Co. ... to Wm. Dulaney one Negroe man named **J a c k** ... to his son Joseph one negroe woman named **Dinah** and his dau. Anna ... one negroe woman named **Hannah**. *Signed*: **Joseph Dulaney**. *Wit*: **W. Grant, James Duff**. *Rec*: 28 June 1764, prov. by o. of **William Grant** and **James Duff**.

Page 162. 13 February 1764. Power of Attorney. **James Edmondson** of Essex County appoints **Alex'r. Farrow** ... true and lawful attorney ... to act in Loudoun County. *Signed*: **Jas. Edmondson**. *Wit*: **Thomas Elliott, Wm. Farrow, Ann (ann) Farrow**. *Rec*: 28 June 1764, prov. by o. of **Elliott** and **Farrow**, wits.

Pages 163-164. 25 June 1764. B & S. Between **William Elliott** of Pr. Wm. Co. and **Thomas Chilton** of W'land Co., Gent. ... Ł100 half whereof is for the use of **Robert Elliott** his brother, an Infant under the age of 21 years ... tract ... 400 a. ... which was devised by the last will and testament of **Robert Vaulx**, late of W'land Co., Gent. dec'd to **John Elliott**, dec'd. during his nat. life, then to his two sons, the sd. William and Robert. *Signed*: **William Elliott**. *Wit*: **Charles Chilton**. *Receipt wit. by*: **Wm. Ransdell, Thos. Edwards**. *Rec*: 28 June 1764, ack. by **William Elliott**.

Pages 164-165. 25 June 1764. Bond of **William Elliott** and **John Linton** of Pr. Wm. Co. to **Thomas Chilton** of W'land Co. For: Ł500. When **Robert Elliott** arrives to age of 21 years he will make good his conveyance of the land conveyed above. *Signed*: **William Elliott, John Linton**. *Wit*: **Nathan Skipweth White, Thomas Chilton, Jr., Charles Chilton**. *Rec*: 28 June 1764, prov. by o. of **Thomas Chilton, Jr.** and **Charles Chilton**.

Pages 165-166. 11 February 1764. Bill of Sale. **Charles Dulaney** to **Martin Pickett** ... Ł55 ... two Negroes one a Wench named Nan, the other a fellow named **Jack** ... horse .. *Signed*: **Charles Dulaney**. *Wit*: **J. Blackwell, William Blackwell, Jr.** *Rec*: 28 June 1764, ack. by **Charles Dulaney**.

Pages 166-169. 28 July 1764. B & S. Between **William Thornton** and **Elizabeth**, his wife, of Hanover Par., K. G. Co. and **Charles Morehead** ... Ł48.10s. ... 148 a. ... on the branches of Cedar Run ... cor. to the land whereon the sd. Charles Morehead now lives ... cor. to Hudnall ... south side of the Main Road ... *Signed*: **William Thornton, Elizabeth Thornton**. *Wit*: **John Triplett, Will'm. Robinson, John Triplett, Thomas Jett** and **William Robinson** appointed to take the ack. of the above from **Elizabeth Thornton**. *Rec*: 26 July 1764, ack. by **William Thornton**.

Pages 169-170. 26 July 1764. Bond of **William Pickett, Jr.**, to build a Prison for Fauq. Co. agreeable to the Annexed Plan ... For: 65,000 lbs. tobacco. *Sec*: **Yelverton Peyton** and **John Ashby**. *Rec*: 20 July 1764, ack. by above.

Page 170. 28 Nov. 1763. Bill of Sale. **Alexander Parker** unto **Martin Pickett** ... Ł22 ... personal estate, stock, tobacco due from Parish ... *Signed*: **Alex'r. Parker**. *Wit*: **William McPherson**. *Rec*: 26 July 1764, ack. by **Alexander Parker**.

Pages 170-171. 15 April 1764. Bill of Sale. **Thomas Elliott** unto **Martin Pickett** ... Ł40 ... stock, personal property. *Signed*: **Thos. Parker**. *Wit*: **Jos. Smith, J. Blackwell**. *Rec*: 27 July 1764, ack. by **Thomas Elliott**.

Pages 171-176. 22-23 August 1764. Lease & Release. Between **Thomas Mitchell** and **Susannah**, his wife, of St. Mark's Par., Culp. Co. and **Thomas Garner** ... 100 a. cor. to **John Garner** ... Welch's line ... north side of Tinpott on line bet. John and Thomas Garner ... Ł 60 ... *Signed*: **Thomas Mitchell, Susannah (+) Mitchell**. *Wit*: **William Sturdy, Thomas Helm**. *Rec*: 23 August 1764, ack. by **Thomas Mitchell**.

Pages 176-181. 7-8 August 1764. Lease & Release. Between **David Welch** and **Frances**, his wife, **John Welch** and **Elizabeth**, his wife, **William Welch** and **Alice**, his wife, **Joshua Welch, Daniel Welch, Benjamin Welch**, sons and devisees of **Thomas Welch**, late of Pr. Wm. Co., dec'd and **John Withers** of Staf. Co., Planter ... 498 a. ... Ł 270 ... upon the waters of Tinpott and Great Run ... **Bronaugh's** Division Line ... **Garner's** line ... sold to John Withers as highest bidder ... *Signed*: **Daniel Walsh**. *Wit*: **Thomas Withers, Wm. Withers, James Pilsher, James Withers**. *Rec*: 23 August 1764, prov. by o. of **James** and **Wm. Withers** and **James Pilcher**, wits.

Pages 181-182. 12 October 1763. Lease. Between **Margaret Ralls** of Staf. Co. relict and widow of **John Ralls** ... and **John Ryley** of sd. Co., Taylor, ... 200 a. during the nat. life of sd. Margaret Ralls ... on east side of Rappahannock River which was left to me by my Father's last will and Testament ... for 800 lbs. of good merchantable tobacco. *Signed*: **Margaret Ralls, John (+) Ryley**. *Wit*: **Jno. Mauzy, Nath'l. Williams, Benj'n Williams**. *Rec*: 23 August 1764, prov. by o. of **Nathaniel** and **Benj'n. Williams**, wits. (Note: Margaret Ralls, widow of John Ralls, was the dau. of **George Williams** (d. 1750) of Staf. Co. See: G. H. S. King, *The Register of Overwharton Parish*, p. 98.)

Pages 182-185. 6 August 1764. Quiet Deed. Between **Daniel Grant** and **George Grant** of Pr. Wm. Co. and Fauq. and **Howson Kenner** ... all rights, etc. that they can any way have in ... 541 a. ... on branches of Town Run which was formerly ack. to Kenner by John Grant, dec'd., of K. G. Co. by deed dated 27 March 1758, joining lands of **M i c h a e l Dermont, Simon Cummings, Brereton Jones**, and land Kenner now lives on ... same **John Blackman** obtained by patent in 1724 from the prop., who sold to **William Grant**, late of K. G. Co., who died intestate ... fell to John Grant, dec'd. his son and heir at law ... cor. to parcel of land sold by **William Hackney** to the sd. Blackman ... crossing the middle run of Town Run ... Michael Dermont's line ... *Signed*:

Daniel Grant, George Grant. *Wit*: John Combs, Jr., Rich'd Mynatt, Thomas Reno ... quiet possession ... delivered by turf and twig ... *Rec*: 23 August 1764, prov. by o. of wits.

Pages 185-187. 10 August 1764. Bill of Sale. **Maximilian Berryman**, planter, to **Alexander Cunninghame** of Falmouth, K. G. Co., Merchant ... in behalf of **Andrew Cockran, William Cunninghame & Co.** of Glassgow, Kingdom of Great Britain, Merchants ... Ł439.6s.9d. ... 14 slaves. *Signed*: **Max'm. Berryman**. *Wit*: James Robison, John Neilson, William Henderson. *Rec*: 24 August 1764, ack. by M. Berryman.

Pages 187-190. 23 August 1764. Lease & Release. Between **W a u g h Darnall** and **Mary**, his wife, of the government of N. C. in Granvil County ... and **Morgan Darnall** ... two parcels ... in all ... 150 a. ... Ł 20 ... in **George Wheatley's** line ... Morgan Darnall's line ... **James Williams'** line ... **Squire Bushes** line ... **Hedgeman's** line ... 100 a. ... 50 acres on Marsh Run ... bounded by lines of George Wheatley, **John Smith & Jonas Williams**. *Signed*: **Morgan Darnall**. *Wit*: Geo. Wheatley, Wm. Sturdy. *Rec*: 24 August 1764, ack. by grantor.

Pages 191-193. 1764. Lease. Between **William Stuart** of Staf. Co., Clerk, and **Robert Matthews** of Pr. Wm. Co. Planter ... 300 a. part of greater tract belonging to sd. Stuart ... south run of Broad Run ... along **William Duff's** line ... cor. of **Dodson's** Tenement ... on South Run ... for nat. lives of sd. Robert Matthews, **Dudly Matthews** and **Chidester M a t t h e w s** ... yearly rent of 1,000 lbs. good tobacco with casks. *Signed*: William Stuart. *Wit*: Dan'l. Payne, Wm. Carr, John Riddell, Wm. Foote, T. Bullitt. *Rec*: 28 June 1764, prov. by o. of Daniel Payne, John Riddell, wits.

Page 193. 27 September 1764. Bill of Sale. **Maximilian Haynie** of Pr. Wm. Co. ... Ł50 ... to **Simon Boley** ... Negro slave named William. *Signed*: **Maximilian Haynie**. *Wit*: John Bell. *Rec*: 27 September 1764, ack, by **Maximilian Haynie**.

Pages 193-195. 26 September 1764. B & S. Between **Isaac Coppedge**, and **Elizabeth**, his wife, and **William Coppedge** ... Ł100 ... 800 a. ... which they hold in right of Dower of the sd. Elizabeth's former dec'd. husband **John Coppedge** ... bet. Dorrell's Run & Town Run. *Signed*: Isaac Coppedge, Elizabeth (=) Coppedge. *Wit*: Rodham Tullos, Joseph Taylor, John Whitledge. *Rec*: 27 September 1764, ack. by grantors.

Pages 195-197. 27 September 1764. Deed of Gift. Between **William Obanion**, planter, and **Elizabeth**, his wife and **Joseph Duncan, Jr.** ... for nat. love and affection for **Joseph Duncan** ... 50 a. ... part of greater tract whereon sd. Obanion now lives ... trees on the side of Broad Run. *Signed*: William (X) Obannon, Elizabeth (X) Obannon. *Wit*: Edward Humston, Thos. ____, Thomas Obannon. *Rec*: 27 September 1764, ack. by **William Obannion, Sr.**

Page 198. 7 June 1764. Bill of Sale. **William Roach** to **Bennett Price** ... on acc't. of Messrs. **Andrew Cockran, Allen Dreghorn & Co.** ... Negro slaves .. *Signed*: **William Roach.** *Wit*: **Bennett Price, Benj'a Robinson, Elizabeth (X) Roach.** *Rec*: 28 September 1764, prov. by o. of **B. Price,** wit.

Pages 198-199. 28 August 1764. Bill of Sale. **Thomas Grubbs** to **Bennett Price,** on acc't of Messrs. **Andrew Cookran, Allen Dreghorn & Co.** ... stock, personal est. *Signed*: **Thomas Grubb.** *Wit*: **Bennett Price, John Lee, Martin Pickett.** *Rec*: 28 September 1764, prov. by o. of **B. Price,** wit.

Pages 199-202. 6 February 1764. B & S. Between **Daniel Hogain** and **Ann,** his wife, and **William Triplett,** of W'land Co., Par. of Washington, Gent. ... Ł35 ... 280 a. ... cor. to **Mr. Savage** and **William Hogain** ... lines of **Ralph Hughs** ... line of **Col. Carter** ... cor. to **Mr. Debutts** ... containing 434 a. *Signed*: **Daniel (X) Hogains, Ann (A) Hogains.** *Wit*: **Absalom (A) Ramey, Betty (X) Legg, James (X) Young, Sarah (X) Ramey.** *Receipt further wit. by*: **Gideon (X) Wood.** *Rec*: 22 March 1764, prov. by o. of **Betty Legg, James Young.** 28 September 1764, by o. of **Sarah Ramey.**

Pages 202-204. 25 October 1764. B & S. Between **Martin Settle & Mary,** his wife, and **Anne Jordine** of Culp. Co. and **Peter Kamper** ... part of that tract ... bet. Carters Great Run and Barrows Run ... 196 a. ... granted by Prop. to **Thomas Jordine,** father of Mary Settle and Anne Jordine ... 24 Nov. 1740 ... 487 a. ... cor. to **Harmon Button** ... line of **Nathaniel Rector** ... Ł18. *Signed*: **Martin (X) Settle, Mary (X) Settle, Ann (X) Jordine.** *Wit*: **W. Grant, Wm. Ransdell.** *Rec*: 26 October 1764, ack. by grantors.

Pages 204-205. 25 October 1764. B & S. Between **Anne Jordine** of Culp. Co. and **Harman Kemper** ... part of that tract bet. Carters, Great Run and Barrows Run ... (as above) ... Kempers line ... **George Williams'** line ... 52 a. *Signed*: **Ann (X) Jordine.** *Wit*: **W. Grant, Wm. Ransdell.** *Rec*: 26 October 1764, ack. by grantor.

Pages 205-206. 25 October 1764. B & S. Between **Anne Jordine** of Culp. Co. and **Harmon Button** ... 41 a. ... (desc. as above) ... Ł5. *Signed*: **Ann (X) Jordine.** *Wit*: **W. Grant, Wm. Ransdell.** *Rec*: 26 October 1764, ack. by **Ann Jordine.**

Pages 207-208. 25 October 1764. B & S. Between **Robert Duncan & wife Anne,** of Culp. Co. and **William Johnson** of K. G. Co. ... Ł25 ... 100 a. ... cor. to **Lott Hackley, Morris Jacobs** ... white oak on Rock Run, up same to New Road ... it being the reversion of a large tract of land. *Signed*: **Robert (R) Duncan, Sr., Robert (X) Duncan, Jr.** *Wit*: **James Arnold, Samuel Walker, Rodham Tullos.** *Rec*: 26 October 1764, ack. by **Robert Duncan, Sr.** and **Robert Duncan, Jr.**

Pages 208-212. 2-3 February 1764. Lease & Release. Bet. **Bertrand Ewell** of Pr. Wm. Co., Gent., and **John Gunyon,** of sd. Co., merchant

... four tracts, viz: one in Pr. Wm. Co. on both sides Quantico Run, granted to Ewell & William Riddle, cont. 400 a.; another in sd. co. on branches of Chapawamsick pur. by sd. Ewell of Mr. John Graham: 500 a.; tract of sd. co. on the br. of Occoquon pur. by Ewell of Col. John Tarpley, 500 a., except 100 a. heretofore sold to Rich'd. Rexay; tract in Fauq. Co. on both sides of Goose Creek, pur. by Ewell from Col. James Ball, containing 500 a. together with one Negro boy named Charles ... £400 ... Signed: Bertrand Ewell. Wit: W. Ellzey, Thomas Chapman, George Tebbs. Rec: 28 Sept. 1764, prov. by o. of Tebbs & Ellzey; 25 October 1764, by o. of Chapman.

Pages 212-216. 9-10 October 1764. Lease & Release. Between Timothy Stamps & Catharine, his wife, and Humphrey Brooke ... where Stamps now lives ... 160 a. ... £130 ... cor. to Joseph Dodson. Signed: Timothy Stamps, Catharine (C) Stamps. Wit: Yelv'n. Peyton, Duff Green, Wm. Hunton, Richard Drummond. Rec: 26 October 1764, prov. by o. of Yelverton Peyton, Green, and Richard Drummond, wits.

Pages 217-218. 15 September 1763. B & S. Between Thomas Grinan (also Grining) and Joseph Blackwell and Richard Lewis ... 1 a. ... 5s. ... part of tract sd. Grining now lives on ... Rock Run ... Signed: Thomas (X) Grining. Wit: Joseph Sebastin, Henry Morless, John Courtney, W. Blackwell, John Kirk, Zeph'a Philips. Rec: 22 November 1764, prov. by o. of William Blackwell, John Kirk, Zephaniah Philips, wits.

Page 219. 15 November 1764. Deed of Gift. William Douglass & Sarah, his wife, to the said William Douglass (sic) ... for nat. affection & fatherly love which we have for our well beloved son Benjamin Douglass of Pr. Wm. Co. ... to sd. Benj. ... Negroe man called Hanly. Signed: W. Douglass, Sarah Douglass. Wit: Mary Berryman, John Tenniel, Robert Berryman. Rec: 22 November 1764, prov. by o. of Robert Berryman and John Tenniel.

Pages 219-220. 10 October 1764. Bill of Sale. Thomas Matthew to William Blackwell ... personal property, stock, crops ... Signed: T'os. Matthews. Wit: Alex'r. Snelling, Rich'd. Mynatt. Rec: 22 November 1764, ack. by Thomas Matthews.

Pages 220-221. 22 November 1764. Bond of William Grant to collect from the Tithables the County levies. For: 89,000 lbs. tobacco. Sec: Jeremiah Darnall. Rec: 22 November 1764, ack. by Grant and Darnall.

Page 221. 22 November 1764. Bond of William Grant, to collect taxes. For: £1,000. Sec: William Blackwell, Joseph Blackwell. Rec: 22 November 1764.

Pages 221-223. 20 July 1764. Mortgage. Thomas Watts, planter, to Alexander Cuninghame of Falmouth, K. G. Co., merchant, for and in behalf of Messrs. Andrew Cockran, Allan Dreghorn & Co. of Glasgow ... £198.12s.5d. ... Negro slaves ... to be repaid 1 June 1766, with interest. *Signed*: **Thomas Watts.** *Wit*: **James Robison, Hugh Hamilton, Thomas Crawford.** *Rec*: 28 February 1765.

Pages 223-224. 25 July 1764. Mortgage. **Edward Dickenson, Senr.,** planter, to **Alexander Cuninghame** of Falmouth ... for £38 ... one Negro slave ... to be repaid by 1 June 1765, with interest. *Signed*: **Edward Dickenson.** *Wit*: **Thomas Crawford, Hugh Hamilton, John Neilson.** *Rec*: 28 February 1765, prov. by o. of **Neilson.**

Pages 224-226. 23 February 1765. Mortgage. Bet. **William Douglas** and **Sarah,** his wife, and **Gavin Lawson** of K. G. Co. ... £89.16s.6d. ... Negroes ... *Signed*: **Wm. Douglass, Sarah Douglass.** *Wit*: **John Dunlop, Henry Bramlet, Chas. Morgan, Jr., James Armstrong.** *Rec*: 28 February 1765, prov. by o. of **Dunlop & Morgan.**

Pages 226-228. 10 October 1764. Lease. Between Col. **R. H. Lee** of W'land Co. and **Alexander Cuninghame** of K. G. Co. ... 6 a. ... for his nat. life and the lives of **Bennett Price** and **Stewart Black** ... beg. near the south west cor. of the sd. Cuninghame's Storehouse ... large gum just below the spring ... yearly rent of £4 ... *Signed*: **R i c h a r d Henry Lee.** *Wit*: **Joseph Blackwell, Martin Pickett, John Winn.** *Rec*: 1 March 1765, prov. by o. of wits.

Pages 228-229. 12 March 1765. Bill of Sale. **John Matthews,** planter, to **Alexander Cuninghame** of Falmouth ... for £51 ... slaves, personal property, stock. *Signed*: **John Mathews.** *Wit*: **Jas. Buchanan, Robert Findlay, John Neilson.** *Rec*: 22 March 1765, ack. by **John Mathews.**

Pages 229-230, 25 March 1765. Bill of Sale. **J o h n W i n n,** planter, to **Minor Winn, Sr.** ... for £850 ... slave, personal estate, livestock. *Signed*: **John Winn.** *Wit*: **Alex'r. Cuninghame, Bennet Price, James Robison.** *Rec*: 22 March 1765, ack. by **John Winn.**

Pages 230-233. 10 October 1764. Lease. Between Col. **R. H. Lee** ... and **M i n o r W i n n** of Pr. Wm. Co. ... 228 a. ... for his nat. life and lives of **Margaret Winn,** his wife, **John Winn,** his son and **Minor Winn,** the son of John and **Dorothy Winn** ... south side of Great Road leading to Ashby's Gap ... old road binding on Capt. **W i l l i a m Edmonds'** ... Capt. Edmonds cor. at Towsers Branch ... yearly rent of £11.8s. *Signed*: **Richard Henry Lee.** *Wit*: **Jos. Blackwell, Bennett Price, Stewart Black.** *Rec*: 22 March 1765, prov. by o. of wits.

Pages 233-235. 10 October 1764. Lease. Between Col. **R. H. Lee** of W'land Co. and **Minor Winn** of Pr. Wm. Co. ... 5 a. ... for his life and lives of **Margaret,** his wife, **John Winn** and Minor Winn, son of John and **Dorothy Winn** ... to a post of the prison bounds ... *Signed*: **Richard Henry Lee.** *Wit*: **Jos. Blackwell, Martin Pickett, Bennett Price.** *Rec*: 22 March 1765, prov. by o. of wits.

Pages 235-239. 26 October 1764. B & S. Between **David Darnall,** planter, and **Gavin Lawson,** of K. G. Co., merchant ... £74.17s.6d. ... 152

a. ... same tract devised by will of **Thomas Carter**, dated 24 April 1728, in Tail to his son **Peter Carter**, and by him sold in fee simple, 19 Oct. 1738 to sd. David Darnall ... sd. deed is rec. in the Secretaries Office of the sd. Colony of Virginia. *Signed*: **David Darnall**. *Wit*: **Cuth't. Bullitt, W. Grant, Henry Mauzy**. *Rec*: 26 October 1764, prov. by o. of **Cuthbert Bullitt**; 25 March 1765, prov. by o. of **William Grant** and **Henry Mauzy**. "... possession delivered to **Lawson** by the delivery of a Turf & Twig ..."

Pages 239-240. 9 February 1764. B & S. Between **Morgan Darnall, Sr.**, planter, and **Gavin Lawson** of K. G. Co., Merchant ... Ł168.19s.7d. ... five Negroes ... cattle, household furniture. *Signed*: **Morgan (MD) Darnall**. *Wit*: **William Knox, Alex'r. Knox, John Dunlop, Adam Steuart**. *Rec*: 25 March 1765, prov. by o. of **William Knox, Dunlop**.

Pages 240-242. 24 October 1764. Mortgage. Between **Hugh Snelling** and **Alexander Wodrow & John Neilson**, of Falmouth, merchants ... Ł 56.4d. & 69 lbs. tobacco ... slaves ... sd. sum to be repaid by 1 Oct. 1766 with int. *Signed*: **Hugh Snelling**. *Wit*: **Adam Stewart, James Blain**. *Rec*: 25 March 1765, prov. by o. of wits.

Pages 242-243. 20 August 1764. Mortgage. Between **John Allen** and **Alex. Wodrow & John Neilson**, merchants of Falmouth ... Ł122.1a.1d. ... slaves ... sd. sum to be repaid by 22 Aug. 1765 ... with lawful interest. *Signed*: **John Allen**. *Wit*: **Adam Stewart, James Blain**. *Rec*: 25 March 1765, prov. by o. of wits.

Pages 244-248. 8-9 August 1764. Lease and Release. Between **Richard Haily & Honor**, his wife, and **William Carr** of Pr. Wm. Co. ... Ł60 ... 500 a. ... near the Pignut Ridge ... adj. the lands of **H e n r y Peyton, Jr., John Fishback, John Sias** and **William Stuart**, Clerk ... 100 a. was purchased by **Haily** of **Charles Barton** and the 400 a. taken up by him by deed from Prop. office. *Signed*: **Richard Healy, Honor (D) Healy**. *Wit*: **Cuth't. Bullitt, Thomas Chapman, James Nelson, Benjamin (ᴡ) Willoughby, James Markham**. *Rec*: 25 March 1765, ack. by **Richard Healy**.

Pages 248-249. 9 August 1764. Bill of Sale. **Richard Haily** to **Wi l l i a m C a r r** of Pr. Wm. Co. ... for Ł50 ... stock, household furniture. *Signed*: **Richard Healy**. *Wit*: (same as above). *Rec*: 25 March 1765, ack. by **Richard Healey**.

Pages 249-250. 9 August 1764. Bill of Sale. **John Roberson** to Martin **Pickett** for Ł37.15s.1d. in goods already advanced ... cattle, horse, household furniture. *Signed*: **John (Ɫ) Roberson**. *Wit*: **John Lee, Jr., John Blackwell**. *Rec*: 26 March 1765, prov. by o. of **John Blackwell (John Robertson)**.

Pages 250-253. 27 March 1765. B & S. Between **John Ballendine & Mary**, his wife, of Fairfax Co. and **Archibald Allan** ... Ł15 ... tract ... orig. granted to one **Lawrence Debutts** with a greater tract ... by the

Main Road ... 30 a. *Signed*: **John Ballendine.** *Wit*: **Cuth't. Bullitt, Js. Scott, Jr., James Craig.**

Pages 253-258. 8-9 April 1765. Lease & Release. Between **John Ballendine** of Fx. Co. and **Wharton Ransdell** ... Ł84.1s.4d. ... tract ... 194 a. ... in counties of Fauq. and Pr. Wm. ... cor. to sd. Ransdell ... cor. to **Mr. Scott** ... cor. to **Archibald Allan's** 30 a. tract ... Debutts line ... Mill run. *Signed*: **John Ballendine.** *Wit*: **Js. Scott, Jr., Wm. Ransdell, Gustavus Scott, John Chilton, John Bell.** *Rec*: 22 April 1765, prov. by o. of **William Randsdell, John Chilton** and **John Bell,** wits. Release states: "Being in Fauq. (formerly Pr. Wm.), being part of a patent granted to the Rev'd. **Lawrence Debutts** of the province of Maryland for 2,864 a. ... 18 Oct. 1727 ... cor. to Capt. Ransdell's land ... which sd. tract descended to **Sam'l. Debutts** Brother & Heir at Law to the sd. Lawrence Debutts, who died seized thereof and by his last will and Testament among other devisees devised the same to **Barnaby Egan** & the sd. Barn'a Egan by Indenture ... 1764 ... & duly rec. in the Gen'l Court conveyed the same to **John Ballendine** ..."

Pages 259-261. 22 April 1765. B & S. Between **Thomas Toms** and **Elizabeth,** his wife, and **Michael Marr** ... Ł8 ... 75 a. as surveyed by **George Hume** ... *Signed*: **Thomas (X) Toms.** *Wit*: **George Threlkeld, Joseph Sebastin, Alex. Woodside.** *Rec*: 22 April 1765, ack. by grantors.

Pages 261-264. 22 April 1765. B & S. Between **Joseph Sebastin** and **Elizabeth,** his wife, and **Michael Marr** ... Ł3 ... 50 a. as surveyed by **George Hume.** *Signed*: **Joseph Sebastin, Elizabeth Sebastin.** *Wit*: **Alander Woodside, George Threlkeld.** *Rec*: 22 April 1765, ack. by grantors.

Pages 264-271. 21-22 April 1765. Lease & Release. Between **John Allen,** Planter, and **Mary,** his wife, and **James Hunter** of K. G. Co., Merch't. ... 200 a. same devised to Allen by his father John Allen, late of the Co. of Pr. Wm. dec'd. who had a grant from the Prop. 19 Dec. 1731 ... on west side of Marsh Run ... 796 a. ... *Signed*: **John Allen, Mary Allen.** *Wit*: **W. Grant, Bushrode Doggett.** *Rec*: 22 April 1765. ack. by **John Allen.** Release states: "...and sd. John Allen, dec'd purchased from **John Frogg** of Pr. Wm. Co. ... 50 a., adj. to his said tract of 796 a. ... and by his will dated 3 Nov. 1759 devised to son John all his land in the Marsh neck above the Indian spring savanna in which the 50 acres from John Frogg is included ... Ł130 ...

Pages 271-274. 23 April 1765. B & S. Between **Bushrode Doggett** and **Nancy,** his wife, and **William Morgan** ... Ł16.8s. ... 41 a. ... same Doggett purchased of **Charles Morgan, Jr.,** on north branch of Great Run of Rappahannock ... cor. tree to **Charles Morgan, Sr.** and **Thomas Ayres.** *Signed*: **Bushrode Doggett, Nanney (X) Doggett.** *Wit*: **Thomas Bronaugh, Henry Mauzy, Francis Bronaugh.** *Rec*: 22 April 1765, ack. by **Busrode Doggett** and **Nancy,** his wife.

Pages 274-280. 27-28 August 1764. Lease & Release. Between **John Gunyon**, of Pr. Wm. Co., Merchant and **Robert Scott** of Pr. Wm. Co. ... 2 tracts ... one in Pr. Wm. Co. on branches of Chappawamksic, purchased by sd. Gunyon of **Bertrand Ewell** who purch. from **John Graham** ... 500 a. ... one other tract from Ewell to Gunyon in Fauq. on both sides of Goose Creek ... 500 a. ... Ł122 ... *Signed*: **John Gunyon**. *Wit*: **W. Ellzsy, William Scott, John Tyler.** On 3 Sept. 1764 **Robert Scott** signed over the lease & release to **John Knox.** *Wit*: **H. Brooke, Jas. Buchanan, Gavin Lawson, William Scott.** *Rec*: 22 April 1765, prov. by o. of **William Ellzey, William Scott, John Tyler,** wits.

Pages 280-290. 7-8 March 1765. Lease & Release. Between **James Campbell** of Charles Co., Maryland, Merchant and **Judith**, his wife, and **Judson Coolidge**, of Pr. Georges Co., Maryland, Gent. ... Ł300 sterling, money of Great Britain ... tract in Fauq. ... granted by the Prop. to **John Clark** of Salem, Essex Co., Mass. Bay in New England ... 15 Nov. 174- ... John Clark conveyed to sd. **James Campbell** ... marked oak ꟼF and ꟼCK ... on the east side a main branch of Goose Creek called Hunger Run cor. to the land of **John Fishback & Jacob Holtzclaw** ... up said Run along Fishback's line ... white oak in a fork nigh the head of the sd. Run ... cor. to Major **James Ball** ... ridge between two small branches of Crummys Run ... the land of **Doctor Thornton** ... 1,748 a. *Signed*: **Jas. Campbell, Judith Campbell.** *Wit*: **Duff Green, W. Ellzey, H. Brooke, Henry Peyton, Jr.** *Rec*: 23 April 1765, prov. by o. of **Green, Brooke and Ellzey,** wits.

Pages 290-292. 27 May 1765. B & S. Between **William Kerns, Sr.** and **John Sinclair** ... Ł10 ... tract whereon sd. Kerns now lives ... 13 a. *Signed*: **Wm. Keirnes.** *Wit*: **John Wright, James Wright, William Grant.** *Rec*: 27 May 1765, ack. by **William Keirnes.**

Pages 292-298. 30-31 October 1764. Lease & Release. Between **John Grant**, of Brunswick Par., K. G. Co., Planter and **George Grant** ... 162 a. ... part of a greater tract purchased by **John Grant, Sr.** father to **John Grant, Jr.** ... Beg. at G. which is the entrance of the Marsh ... cor. to Seaton standing in a branch of the Marsh run ... Ł60. *Signed*: **John Grant.** *Wit*: **John Wright, Wm. Bronaugh, Winfield Wright, John French, Axton Whitecotton.** *Rec*: 22 April 1765, prov. by o. of **John Wright, William Bronaugh;** 27 May 1765, prov. by o. of **Axton Whitecotton.**

Pages 298-301. 13 May 1765. Lease. Between the Rev. **William Stuart** of Par. of St. Paul, Staf. Co. and **Benjamin Robinson**, Planter ... tract ... on South Run of the Broad Run of Occoquan in Fauq. Co. ... 196 a. ... cor. to tenement of **William Roach** ... tenements of sd. Roach, **Robert Matthews** to Mr. **Joseph Minter's** cor. in the line of Mr. **Duff Green** ... for his nat. life and lives of **Sarah Robinson**, his wife, **George** and **Dickson Robinson**, his sons ... 1,050 lbs tobacco and cask per year ... at the most convenient warehouse on the Potomac River ... not to work more than 3 slaves on the sd. tenement. *Signed*: **William Stuart, Benj'a. Robinson.** *Wit*: **Yel'n Peyton, Jno. Mat-**

thews, John Ramy, Jno. (X) Ryley. *Rec*: 27 May 1765, prov. by o. of Yelverton Peyton, John Matthews, John Ryley.

Pages 301-307. 16 October 1764. Lease & Release. Between H e n r y Hitt & Alice, his wife, and Harmon Hitt ... 200 a. ... on Goose Creek being part of a greater tract ... formerly belonging to Thomas Chattin of Lancaster Co., dec'd ... cor. to Mr. George Johnston ... over Crommels Run ... joining to the land of Tilman Weaver on a hill ... joining to the land of Timothy Thornton ... Ł47. *Signed*: Henry (O) Hitt. *Wit*: Martin Pickett, Samuel Porter, Jesse Alexander, William Blackwell, Jr., John Smither. *Rec*: 27 May 1765, prov. by o. of Pickett, Alexander and Porter.

Pages 307-309. 24 June 1765. B & S. Between William Keirns and John Rector ... Ł20.12s.6d. ... part of a greater tract belonging to William Keirns ... 165 a. *Signed*: Wm. Keirns. *Wit*: James Wright, John Sincler, James Arnold. *Rec*: 24 June 1765, ack. by William Keirns.

Pages 310-312. 4 March 1765. B & S. Between Thomas Hudnall of St. Stephen's Par., W'land Co. and Daniel Newlin (or Newlan) 150 a. ... tract given to sd. Thomas Hudnall by his father William Hudnall of N'land Co., by deed of gift rec. in N'land Co. Court and adj. the lands of Col. Charles Carter ... on Summer duck run ... Ł15 ... *Signed*: Thos. Hudnall. *Wit*: W. Blackwell, William Kesterson, John Barber. *Rec*: 22 April 1765, prov. by o. of William Blackwell and John Barber; 24 June 1765, by o. of Wm. Kesterson.

Pages 312-314. 20 June 1765. Bond. Between John Churchill, Gent. and Nathaniel Harrison and William Fitzhugh, Jr. of Staf. Co. and William Churchill of Middlesex Co., Gentlemen ... at the request of John Churchill the parties of the 2nd part became securities for him in 2 bonds one payable to Armistead Lightfoot, Esq. of York Town in penalty of Ł157.9s.3d., payable with interest, the other payable to Mr. Gabriel Jones of Augusta Co. in penalty of Ł1200 ... payable with int. ... tract he bought of John Robinson and Lewis Burwell, Esq'rs. and the Exors. of Armistead Churchill, Esq., dec'd ... 1,367 a. ... 37 Negroes ... cattle. *Signed*: John Churchill. *Wit*: James Newman, William Thomson, Francis Young. *Rec*: 26 June 1765, ack. by John Churchill.

Pages 315-316. 9 October 1764. Mortgage. Between Edward Wilborn and Alexander Wodrow & John Neilson, of Falmouth, Merchants ... Ł 56.17s.2d. ... tract ... 135 1/2 a. ... Bounded on the West by Col. Gavin Corbin's tract, on the South by Capt. Housing Kinner's tract on the north and west by the Marsh Run ... same bought of Winkfield W r i g h t in or about the year 1759 ... to be void by payment of above plus interest by 1 Oct. 1765 ... *Signed*: Edward (u) Wilborn. *Wit*: Adam Steuart, James Blain, William Love. *Rec*: 25 March 1765, prov. by o. of Adam Stewart, James Blain; 25 June 1765, prov. by o. of William Love.

Pages 316-318. 20 June 1765. B & S. Between **Gerrard McCartie &
Sary Ann**, his wife, and **William Thornton**, Gent. of K. G. Co. ... Ł60
... 80 a. ... same formerly belonging to **Peter Taylor** ... cor. to land of
Hudnall ... land sold by **Peter Taylor** to **William Robinson** ... cor. to
land formerly belonging to **Col. Barber** now belonging to **William
Thornton** ... cor. to Thornton and **Col. John Bell** ... north side of
Cedar Run cor. to the land formerly taken up by Doctor Bell. *Signed*:
Gerrard McCartie, Sarah Ann McCartie. *Rec*: 20 June 1765, ack. by
grantors.

Pages 319-320. 13 March 1765. Mortgage. **Jefery Johnson, Jr.** to
Jefry Johnson, Sr. ... one Negroe man named **Ned** ... for Ł40 ... to be
void if Johnson, Jr. pays above amount to Johnson, Sr. by 10 Dec.
1765 ... Negro girl naned **G r a c e** to be substituted if Ned should die ..
Signed: **Jefery** (-/-/-) **Johnson.** *Wit*: **Thos. Porter, William Miller.**
Rec: 22 July 1765, prov. by o. of **Thomas Porter** and **William Miller.**

Pages 320-325. 17 April 1765. Lease & Release. Bet. **William Underwood** and **Richard Taylor** of Wecocomoco Par., N'land Co. ... 90
1/2 a. ... cor. trees to **Thomas Colson** ... line of trees belonging to
William Fairfax, Esq. near a place called Smiths Lick ... oaks on the
Rappahannock Ridge ... heap of stones on side of the Rappahannock
Mt. head of a Valley in **Thomas Colson** Line ... *Signed*: **Wm. Underwood.** *Wit*: **Thos. Porter, Alex'r. Bradford, Wm. Edmonds, James
Bell, Chas. Morgan, Jr.** *Rec*: 22 July 1765, ack. by **William Underwood.**

Pages 325-329. 22 July 1765. Trust. Between **Benjamin Tyler**, of
Pr. Wm. Co. and **M a r y**, his wife, late Mary Foote, widow & relict of
George Foote, late of Fauq. Co. dec'd., and **Cuthbert Bullitt**, of Pr.
Wm. Co., Gent. ... sd. Mary, before her marriage to Tyler, was
possessed of the dwelling plantation of her late husband George Foote,
by his last will & testament, during her nat. life for her own support
and the education of her children which she had by the sd. George and
280 a. of land in Fauq.; also slaves, stock, plantation and household
utensils ... on 12 April 1764 ... before the intended marriage between
Mary Foote and Benj. Tyler entered in a marriage contract, rec. in Pr.
Wm. Co. ... **Benjamin Tyler** gives up all rights he might have in Mary
Foote's estate ... and she relinquishes any rights she might have in
sd. Benjamin's estate ... to **Gilson Foote** the 280 a., slaves, utencils,
etc. ... in trust to Cuthbert Bullitt for the use of Mary during her
natural life ... *Signed*: **Benj. Tyler, Mary Tyler.** *Rec*: 22 July 1765,
ack. by **Benjamin Tyler**, and **Mary**, his wife.

Pages 329-331. 20 July 1765. B & S. Between **Harmon Fishback** and
Jeremiah Darnall & Catharine, his wife ... Ł10 ... part of a greater
tract ... w. side of the licking run ... with meanders of sd. run ... 40 a.
Signed: **Harmon** (X) **Fishback.** *Rec*: 22 July 1765, ack. by **Harmon
Fishback.**

Pages 331-333. 20 July 1765. B & S. Between **Jeremiah Darnall &
Catherine**, his wife, and **Harmon Fishback** ... Ł10 ... being part of a

tract belonging to sd. Darnall ... in line of **John Sinclor** ... 50 a. *Signed*: **Jeremiah Darnall, Catherine (A) Darnall**. *Rec*: 22 July 1765, ack. by **Jeremiah Darnall**.

Pages 333-338. 30-31 July 1764. Lease & Release. Between **John Willoughby**, planter, and **William Carr** of Pr. Wm. Co. ... 130 a. ... on a branch called Fornication Branch making in to the Broad Run of Occoquan ... where sd. Willoughby now lived ... which he purchased from **Mathew Moss & Sarah**, his wife, who Purchased the same from **John Glascock** ... Ł25. *Signed*: **John (E) Willoughby**. *Wit*: **Dan'l. Payne, W. Ellzey, Thomas Chapman, James Nelson**. *Rec*: 23 July 1765, ack. by **John Willoughby**.

Pages 338-343. 8 July 1765. B & S. Between **John Marcer** of Marlborough, Staff. Co., Gent. and **Anne**, his wife, and **Thomas Harrison**, Gent. ... Ł300 ... 1,000 a. ... same granted to sd. Mercer by the Props. of the Northern Neck ... 21 March 1730 on both side of the branches of Goose Creek near the Coblers Mountains ... on ridge between Carters Run and Goose Creek ... towards the middle of the Coblers Mountains. *Signed*: **J. Mercer, Anne Mercer**. *Wit*: **Thomson Mason, Clem't. Brooke, C. Rogers, Alex. Cuninghame, Hancock Lee, Dekar Thompson, Jas. Buchanan, John Glassell, Jr., Cuth. Bullitt**. Commission to examine Anne Mercer: **Thompson Mason, Peter Daniel, Traverse Daniel**, Gent. *Rec*: 20 August 1765, prov. by o. of **Dekar Thompson, James Buchanan & Cuthbert Bullitt**, wits.

Pages 343-345. 3 June 1765. Commission. To **Larkin Chew, Fielding Lewis** and **Wm. Smith**, Gent. to examine whether or not **Mary Jones**, wife of **Joseph Jones**, entered into a deed of her free will to convey tract to **Francis Whiting**, Gent. ... 500 a. **Field Lewis** and **William Smith** returned cert. that they had examined Mary Jones privily and she had signed freely. *Ret*: 26 August 1765, OR.

Pages 345-346. 23 July 1765. Marriage Contract. Bet. **Henry Mauzey** and **Elizabeth Morgan** ... a marriage soon to take place bet. the parties ... she grants to sd. Mauzey as soon as the marriage takes place, all her title to the lands of her dec'd. husband, **James Morgan**. Mauzey agrees to maintain two of the said Morgan's children until they arrive to full age and after the Payment of all debts of sd. James Morgan, the est. which remains to be used only by her & the six children of the said Morgan and to be equally divided between them and the sd. Elizabeth Morgan ... and she shall claim no part of sd. Henry Mauzey's estate. *Signed*: **Henry Mauzy, Elizabeth (X) Morgan**. *Wit*: **James Craig, Eli's. Edmonds, Fra's. Bronaugh, David Welch, William Jones**. *Rec*: 26 August 1765, prov. by o. of **Craig, Elias Edmonds**, and **David Welch**. Note: **Elizabeth Taylor**, dau. of **Benjamin & Elizabeth (_____) Taylor**, m. 1, **James Morgan**; m. 2, **Henry Mauzy**. The Taylors lived about 3 miles north of Warrenton, near Bethel – Taylor's Church in that area, was named for him. (*William & Mary Quarterly*, Vol. 6 (2), 1926, p. 331.)

Pages 347-352. 26 August 1765. B & S. Between **Joseph Japhrass** and **Margaret Japhrass**, his now wife and **Henry Smith** of Staff. Co. ... Ł 34 ... tract on branches of Middle Run ... 336 a., same granted to Mr. Henry Smith 2 Jan. 1751 ... cor. to tract granted to **John Blackman** ... cor. to tract granted to **Thos. Jones** ... branch of Middle Run in **Michael Dermons** line ... Rocky Run 16 links from Cimon Cunnings Cor. in sd. run ... to tract granted to Mr. **James Markham**, dec'd ... **Richard Youngs** Land ... Youngs land by **Robert Jones's** Line ... red oak being the place where sd. Thos. Jones's line crosses said Robert Jones's line .. *Signed*: **Joseph (Ɖ) Japhrass, Margaret (X) Japhrass.** *Rec*: 26 August 1765, ack. by **Joseph Japhrass.**

Pages 353-359. 25-26 August 1765. Lease & Release. Between **Thomas Marshall**, Gent. & **Mary**, his wife, and **John Ariss**, Gent. ... 250 a. ... north side of Licking Run ... where the German Road crosses the red branch ... by **Jane Smith's** fence ... cor. to **John Morgan's** land ... line tree to **M r . N e l s o n's** ... land purchased by Marshall of **Frederick Fishback, Timothy Redding & John Huffman,** by their several deeds, rec. in Pr. Wm. Co. ... Ł250 ... *Signed*: **Thom Marshall, Mary Marshall.** *Rec*: 26 August 1765, ack. by **Thomas Marshall,** Gent.

Pages 359-360. 11 March 1765. Bill of Sale. **David Darnall** to **Martin Pickett & Co.** ... slave, household, furniture, cattle, etc. ... Ł15 in goods already rec'd. *Signed*: **David Darnall.** *Wit*: **Francis Attwell, Mary (S) Corder.** *Rec*: 27 August 1765, prov. by o. of **Francis Attwell.**

Pages 360-361. 22 May 1765. Bill of Sale. **Betty Snelling** and **John Snelling** to **Martin Pickett** ... for Ł12.10s. ... negroe & horse. *Signed*: **Betty (X) Snelling, John Snelling.** *Wit*: **Arther Harriss, Wm. Blackwell.** *Rec*: 27 August 1765, prov. by o. of **William Blackwell.**

Pages 361-367. 23 September 1765. Lease & Release. Between **Richard Taylor** and **Judith**, his wife, and **Thomas Smith** ... 218 a. ... cor. to **Thomas Colsen** ... line of marked trees belonging to **William Fairfax**, Esq. near a place called Smiths Lick ... Rappahannock Ridge ... straight course to **Brian Fairfax** line on the head of Cedar Run ... Ł 35. *Signed*: **Richard Taylor, Judith (X) Taylor.** *Rec*: 23 September 1765, ack. by grantors.

Pages 367-368. 4 February 1765. Bill of Sale. **Josias Brausum** to **Original Young** ... household furniture, ducks, drakes, crop of tobacco in hands of **Jeremiah Darnall** ... for Ł64.15s.10d. *Signed*: **Josias (O) Bransum.** *Wit*: **Richard Luttrell, John Rousau.** *Rec*: 23 September 1765, prov. by o. of wits.

Pages 368-369. 23 September 1765. Deed of Gift. **Joseph Dodson**, wheelright, for consideration of the love, good will, and affection which I have and do bear towards my loving Brethren & sisters of the Baptist Church and their successors in this place and with a desire to promote the Glory of God have ... granted ... unto **William Stamps,**

Deacon in the said Church and his successors forever ... parcel of land ... on Barkers Branch ... part whereon I now live ... on which the new Meeting House is already partly Built containing one acre. *Signed*: **Joseph Dodson.** *Wit*: **John Creell, Thomas Dodson, Jr., James Shackelford.** *Rec*: 23 September 1765, ack. by **Joseph Dodson.**

Pages 370-373. 23 September 1765. B & S. **William Stamps and Ann,** his wife, and **James Shackelford** of Hamilton Par., Pr. Wm. Co. ... L 100 ... 631 a. joining to the land of **Docktor Parker** on the Walnut Branch of Cedar Run ... granted by Prop. to **Thomas Stamps,** dec'd. and by him by will to said William Stamps. *Signed*: **William Stamps, Anne Stamps.** *Wit*: **Geo. Lamkin, Jos. Smith, Thomas Smith.** *Rec*: 23 September 1765, ack. by grantors.

Pages 373-376. 23 September 1765. Deed of Gift. Between **Joseph Hudnall** and **John Hudnall,** son of the said Joseph Hudnall ... for nat. love and affection ... plantation and land whereon he now lives ... 127 a. ... part of tract of 250 a. obtained by sd. Joseph from John Hudnall, dec'd. of the Co. of N'land, grandfather to the aforesaid John Hudnall ... cor. to land of Mr. Barber ... near the Hopp Yard Branch. *Signed*: **Jos. Hudnall.** *Wit*: **Charles Morehead, Elias Edmonds, John Hammett.** *Rec*: 23 September 1765, ack. by **Joseph Hudnall.**

Pages 376-381. 22-23 September 1765. Lease & Release. Between **Joseph Hudnall** and **Charles Morehead** ... L100 ... 114 a. ... cor. to **John Hudnall** ... road, dividing line bet. John Hudnall and Joseph Hudnall. *Signed*: **Jos. Hudnall.** *Wit*: **Eli's. Edmonds, Benjamin Crump, John Hudnall.** *Rec*: 23 September 1765, ack. by **Joseph Hudnall.**

Pages 381-386. 23 September 1765. B & S. Between **Isaac Eustace & Agatha,** his wife, of Staff. Co. and **Elias Edmonds** ... L25 cash and 10,000 lbs. of Lawful tobacco ... tract on Pignut Ridge ... 450 a. ... same granted to **Peter Byrum** of Staff. Co. by the Prop. ... 1 March 1730 ... by him conveyed to Capt. **John Lee** of Staff. Co. 18-19 May 1735 and from him to Capt. **William Eustace** of Lan. Co., father of Isaac ... who bequeathed the land to Isaac ... Beg. near the land of **John McGuire** ... east side of the Pignut Ridge ... *Signed*: **Isaac Eustace, Agatha Eustace.** *Wit*: **Jos. Blackwell, Martin Pickett.** *Rec*: 24 September 1765, ack. by grantors.

Pages 386-389. 12 September 1765. Release of Bond. Between **Thomas Machen** of Pr. Wm. Co. and **William Pickett** ... whereas by a bond of sd. Pickett's given to **Thomas Chilton,** formerly of Pr. Wm. Co. ... to ack. a parcel of land in Culp. Co. ... bond is now delivered to said Pickett and Thomas Machen with power of atty. from Thomas Chilton, 24 Nov. 1763, rec. in Pr. Wm. Co. empowering him to settle the affairs of sd. Chilton ... the sd. Pickett never made a conveyance to Chilton ... relinquishes the right and title of said Chilton ... to Pickett in the land mentioned in the Bond. *Signed*: **Thos. Machen.** *Wit*: **James Winn, William Blackwell, Rich'd Winn, Martin Picket.** *Rec*: 24 September 1765, prov. by o. of **Blackwell, Richard Winn** and **Martin Pickett.**

Page 389. 4 March 1765. Bill of Sale. **Sampson Demovel** to **Bennett Price**, on account of Messrs. **And'w Cockrane, William Cuninghame & Co.** ... Negro Man named **William** ... in consideration of a debt due ... *Signed*: **Samson Demovel.** *Wit*: **Bennett Price, Wm. Powell.** *Rec*: 24 September 1765, prov. by o. of **Bennett Price.**

Pages 390-393. 25-26 October 1765. Lease & Release. Between **George Neavil, Jr.** and **Rachel**, his wife, and **Joseph Smith** ... Ł60 ... 260 a. ... whereon sd. Neavil now lives ... one half of 412 a. taken up by **John Hudnall** of N'land Co. ... said 1/2 pur. by **Thomas Walker** thence sold to **Joseph Neavil** and to George Neavil, Jr. by Deed of Gift ... Beg. at tree marked I W. WFX 1739, cor. to **William Fairfax, Esq.** and Johnson ... north side of Carters Run ... line of **Jeffry Johnson**, son of **John Johnson.** *Signed*: **George Neavil, Rachel Neavil.** *Wit*: **Geo. Lamkin, Joseph Smith, Wm. Smith, John Conderre, John Smith, Benj. (X) Sebastian, Peter Taylor.** *Rec*: 26 May 1766, prov. by o. of **George Lamkin, Joseph Smith, Benjamin Sebastian**, wits.

Pages 394-395. 20 December 1765. B & S. Between **John Duncan & Wilkey**, his wife, and **Augustine Jennings** ... Ł100 ... tract whereon son of sd. **John Duncan** now lives ... dividing line between **Peter Hedgman, Jr.** and **Nathaniel Hedgman** ... 200 a. *Signed*: **John (X) Duncan, Wilkey (E) Duncan.** *Wit*: **Wm. Sturdy, Paul Williams, Jonas Williams, Augustine Jennings.** *Rec*: 26 May 1766, ack. by grantors.

Pages 395-396. 23 October 1765. Mortgage. **John Darnal** to **Francis Tennell** ... for Ł47 ... security unto **Gavin Lawson** of Falmouth, K.G. Co., merchant ... 150 a. whereon I now live ... bounded by lands of **Gowen Corbin**, dec'd., **Morgan Darnall & Wm. Smith** ... cattle, household furniture ... articles to revert to sd. Darnall upon repayment of above debt. *Signed*: **John Darnall.** *Wit*: **Wm. Pinchard, Edward Willbourn.** *Rec*: 26 May 1766, ack. by John Darnall.

Pages 396-397. 26 May 1766. Deed of Gift. **John Darnall** to loving son, **William Darnall** ... all est. real and personal ... *Signed*: **John Darnall, Thos. Garner, Jr.** *Wit*: **John Duncan.** *Rec*: 26 May 1766, ack. by **John Darnall.**

Pages 397-399. 28 September 1765. B & S. Between **William Churchhill, John Churchhill** and **Armistead Churchhill, Gent.**, exors of last will and testament of Armistead Churchhill, Esq., dec'd. and **Josiah Holtzclaw** ... Ł59.15s. ... 185 a. ... part of tract known as Pageland ... known as Lott No. 13 as surveyed by **Thomas Marshall, Gent.** ... cor. of Lott 12 ... *Signed*: **Will., John, A. Churchill.** *Wit*: **H. Brooke, Wm. Ellzey, John Ariss, Sam. Porter.** *Rec*: 26 May 1766, prov. by o. of **Humphrey Brooke, William Ellzey** and **Samuel Porter.**

Pages 399-401. 28 September 1765. B & S. Between (above Churchhills) and **Francis Whiting** of Fx. Co. ... Ł65.2s. ... 210 a. ... known as Pageland ... described in platt surveyed by **Thomas Mar-**

s h a l l , Gent. and known by the Lott No. 21 ... cor. to Lott No. 17 ...
Signed: **William, John, Armistead Churchhill.** *Wit*: **Humphrey
Brooke, Wm. Ellzey, John Ariss, Sam. Porter, Josiah Holtzclaw.**
Rec: 26 May 1766, prov. by o. of Ellzey, Porter and Holtzclaw.

Pages 401-405. 27-28 September 1765. Lease & Release. Between
(above Churchhills) and **Henry Fitzhugh** of Staff. Co., Gent. ... Ł
324.10s. ... two certain lotts of land ... part of Pageland ... surveyed
by **Thomas Marshall**, Gent. ... nos. 28 and 29, the 1st. cont. 349 a.,
... cor. to Lott No. 27 ... line of Mr. **John Churchhill** ... the last cont.
250 a. ... cor. to Lott No. 28 in line of lot No. 27 ... *Signed*: as above.
Wit: as above. *Rec*: 26 May 1766, prov. by o. of above wits.

Pages 405-409. 27-28 September 1766. Lease & Release. Between
William, John and **Armistead Churchhill**, exors. of last will and tes-
tament of **Armistead Churchhill**, Esq., dec'd. and **Thomas Porter** ...
Ł75 ... 250 a. ... cor. to Lotts Nos. 13 & 14 ... cor. to lotts 19 & 20 ...
Signed: **William, John, Armistead Churchhill.** *Wits*: **William Ellzey,
William Hunton, Sam'l. Porter, Josiah Holtzclaw.** *Rec*: 26 May
1766, prov. by o. of wits.

Pages 409-412. 27-28 September 1766. Lease & Release. Between
(above named Churchhills) and **Samuel Porter** ... part of Pageland ...
Lot No. 18 ... surveyed by **Thomas Marshall**, Gent. ... outside line of
the Patent ... 262 a. ... Ł81.4s. *Signed*: as above. *Wits*: as above.
Rec: 26 May 1766, prov. by o. of wits.

Pages 413-416. 12 October 1765. Lease. Between **Thomas Ludwell
Lee**, Esq. & **Molley**, his wife, of Staff. Co., Col. **R. H. Lee** & **Anne**,
his wife, of W'land Co. and **John Keith** of Fx. Co. ... lease ... for his
nat. life and lives of his brother, **Alexander** and **Isham Keith** ... 350 a.
lying on Goose Creek ... branch where **William Marshall's** northmost
line crosses the same ... cor. to **Thomas Marshall's** Lott ... side of a
mountain ... side of the Blue Ridge, cor. to **Benjamin Woods** Lott ...
yearly rent of Ł5. *Signed*: **Thomas Lud. Lee, Molly Lee, Richard
Henry Lee, Anne Lee, John Keith.** *Wit*: **Thos. Marshall, Wm. Marshall, William Hill.** Commission to **Peter Daniel, Samuel Selden,
Gowrey Waugh**, Gent. to examine the said Molly and Anne Lee,
privily, as to their signatures. Returned 15 Oct. 1765 from Staff. Co.
Rec: 26 May 1766, prov. by o. of wits.

Pages 416-420. 12 October 1765. Lease. Between (above named Lees)
and **Benjamin Wood** ... lease ... for his nat. life and lives of Sarah,
his wife, and **Lewis Wood**, his son ... 130 a. ... Beg. at a branch of
Goose Creek where **William Marshalls** line crosses same ... side of
the Blue Ridge ... yearly rent of 50s. *Signed*: **Benjamin (X) Wood,
Thos. Lud. Lee, Molly Lee, Richard Henry Lee, Anne Lee.** *Wits*:
Thom. Marshall, John Keith, William Marshall. *Rec*: 26 May 1766,
prov. by o. of wits.

Pages 420-424. 12 October 1765. Lease. Between (above named Lees)
and **William Marshall** ... lease ... for his nat. life and lives of **Mary**

Ann, his wife and **Lewis Marshall**, his son ... 150 a. ... lying on Goose Creek ... southside of Goose Creek ... red oak known cor. to **Thomas Marshall's Lott** ... yearly rent of 50s. *Signed*: **Thos. Lud. Lee, Molly Lee, Richard Henry Lee, Anne Lee, Wm. Marshall.** *Wit*: **Thom Marshall, William Hill, John Keith.** *Rec*: 26 May 1766, prov. by o. of wits.

Pages 424–429. 12 October 1765. Lease. Between (above named Lees) and **Thomas Marshall** ... tenement ... whereon sd. Marshall now lives ... small branch of Goose Creek ... spur of the Naked Mountain cor. to one other lott ... 330 a. ... to sd. Marshall during his nat. life and the lives of **Mary Marshall**, his wife, and **John Marshall**, his son ... yearly rent of Ł5. *Signed*: **Thos. Ludwell Lee, Molly Lee, Richard Henry Lee, Anne Lee, Thom. Marshall.** *Wit*: **Wm. Marshall, J. Keith, William Hill.** *Rec*: 26 May 1766, prov. by o. of wits.

Pages 429–433. 12 October 1765. Lease. Between (above named Lees) and **William Hill** ... lease ... during his nat. life and lives of **George Holmes, Anne**, his wife and **John**, his son ... 150 a. ... north side of Goose Creek then up sd. Creek ... mouth of small branch cor. to **Thos. Marshall** ... yearly rent of 50s. *Signed*: **Thos. Lud. Lee, Molly Lee, Richard Henry Lee, Anne Lee, William Hill.** *Wit*: **Thom. Marshall, Wm. Marshall, J. Keith.** *Rec*: 26 May 1766, prov. by o. of wits.

Pages 433–436. 12 October 1765. Lease. Between (above named Lees) and **William Hill**, during the nat. life of **Thomas Masters** & the nat. life of **Anne**, his wife and **Mary**, his daughter ... 150 a. ... cor. to one other lot to sd. Hill ... 50s. yearly. *Signed*: **Thos. Lud. Lee, Molly Lee, Richard Henry Lee, Anne Lee, William Hill.** *Wit*: **Thom Marshall, Wm. Marshall, J. Keith.** *Rec*: 26 May 1766, prov. by o. of wits.

Pages 436–441. 12 October 1765. Lease. Between (above named Lees) and **William Hill** ... during his nat. life and nat. lives of **Katherine**, his wife and **John** his son ... yearly rent of 50s. *Signed*: **Thos. Lud. Lee, Molly Lee, Richard Henry Lee, Anne Lee, William Hill.** *Wits*: **Thom Marshall, Wm. Marshall, J. Keith.** *Rec*: 26 May 1766, prov. by o. of wits.

Pages 441–448. 25–26 May 1766. Lease & Release. Between **Thomas Dodson, Sr.** & **Elizabeth**, his wife, and **Thomas Dodson, Jr.** & **Mary**, his wife, and **William Hunton** ... 400 a. ... white oak in **Debutts** line on the low grounds of the south run of the Broad Run of Occoquan ... thence across the road that leads to Chapmans Mill ... red oak on the side of the mountain ... Barkers Branch in the hollow of the mountains ... cor. to **Joseph** and **George Dodson** ... cor. to **Humphrey Brooke** ... in or near the **Reverend Mr. Stuart's** line ... lines of the sd. Stuart and **Duff Green** dec'd ... Ł224. *Signed*: **Thomas Dodson, Sen'r., Thomas Dodson, Jun'r., Elizabeth Dodson, Mary Dodson.** *Rec*: 26 May 1766, ack. by grantors.

Pages 448-455. 25-26 May 1766. Lease & Release. Between **John Stamps** & **Leanna**, his wife, and **Thomas Dodson, Sr.**, and **Elizabeth**, his wife, and **Parnak George** ... 149 a. ... on the Mine Branch cor. to **Humphrey Brooke** ... oak in **Henry Taylor's** line ... **Mr. Stuart's** Line ... cor. to **Brookes** and John Stamps ... same devised to sd. John Stamps by will of his father, **Thomas Stamps**, dec'd. ... where John Stamps now lives ... Ł90. *Signed*: **John Stamps, Leanna (X) Stamps, Thomas Dodson, Sr., Elizabeth Dodson.** *Rec*: 26 May 1766, ack. by grantors.

Pages 455-457. 26 May 1766. Bond of **William Blackwell**, as Sheriff of Fauq. Co. For: Ł500. *Sec*: **Joseph Blackwell, Cuthbert Bullitt.** *Signed*: **W. Blackwell, Jos. Blackwell, Cut't. Bullitt.** *Rec*: 26 May 1766, ack. by **Wm. Blackwell, Joseph Blackwell, Cuthbert Bullitt.**

Pages 458-459. 26 May 1766. Bond of **William Blackwell**, as Sheriff of Fauq. Co. For: Ł1,000. Same as above.

Pages 459-460. 26 May 1766. Bond of **William Blackwell**, as Sheriff of Fauq. Co. For: Ł1,000. *Sec*: **Wm. Grant and Cuthbert Bullitt.** *Signed*: **W. Blackwell, W. Grant, Cuth't. Bullitt.** *Rec*: 26 May 1766.

Pages 460-461. 26 May 1766. Bond of **William Blackwell**, as Tax Collector of Fauq. Co. For: 58,162 lbs. of tobacco. *Sec*: **Wm. Grant, Cuthbert Bullitt.** *Signed*: **W. Blackwell, W. Grant, Cuth't. Bullitt.** *Rec*: 26 May 1766.

Pages 461-467. 22-23 June 1766. Lease & Release. Between **William Hunton** and **Judith**, his wife, and **Richard Chichester**, of Lan. Co., Gent. ... whereon Wm. Hunton lately lived ... 328 a. ... 128 a. purch. of **Thomas Porter** and **Sarah**, his wife ... 25 & 26 March 1761 and 100 a. purch. of **Samuel Porter** and **Eve**, his wife ... 26 March 1761 and 100 a. purch. of **Joseph Hitt** and **Mary**, his wife, **Harman Kamper & Catherine**, his wife and **Ann Elizabeth Weaver** ... 27-28 May 1762 ... Ł310. *Signed*: **Wm. Hunton, Judith Hunton.** *Rec*: 23 June 1766, ack. by grantors.

Pages 467-473. 22-23 June 1766. Lease & Release. Between **G e o r g e Dodson** and **Anna**, his wife and **Robert Sanders** of Culp. Co. ... 100 a. ... cor. to tract of **Joseph Dodson** ... with **Debutts'** upper line ... near **Carters** line ... east side of mountain ... cor. of tract which formerly belonged to **Thomas Dodson** ... Barkers branch ... land given to sd. George Dodson by his father, Thomas Dodson, by deed ... 8 May 1761 ... Ł50. *Signed*: **George Dodson.** *Rec*: 23 June 1766, ack. by **George Dodson.**

Pages 473-477. 1 June 1765. B & S. Between **Joseph Duncan** and **Caty**, his wife, and **Martin Pickett** ... Ł15 ... 70 a. on Broad Run ... same conveyed by **William OBanion** to Joseph Duncan out of a larger tract whereon the sd. OBanion now lives ... ash on side of Broad Run ... *Signed*: **Joseph Duncan, Caty Duncan.** *Wit*: **Chattin Lamkin, Francis**

Attwell, William Blackwell, Joseph Williams. Rec: 25 June 1765, prov. by o. of Francis Attwell and William Blackwell, Jr.

Pages 477-484. 27-28 October 1765. Lease & Release. Between William Churchill, John Churchill, & Armistead Churchill, Gent., Exors. of Armistead Churchill, Esq., dec'd., and Martin Pickett ... 2 lotts adjacent to each other, part of a larger tract commonly called Pageland ... surveyed by Thomas Marshall, Gent. ... Lot No. 15: 195 a. ... cor. to Lot No. 9 ... Lot No. 16: cor. to lot No. 15 ... 203 a. ... Ł 139.6s. Signed: Will Churchhill, John Churchill, A. Churchill. Wit: W. Ellzey, Thos. Porter, Wm. Hunton, Sam'l Porter. Rec: 23 June 1766, prov. by o. of Thomas Porter, Samuel Porter and William Hunton, wits.

Pages 485-493. 21-22 June 1766. Lease & Release. Between Benjamin Morris & Elizabeth, his wife, and Robert Matthis, of Cameron Par., Loud. Co. ... 127 a. ... south side of South Run of Broad Run of Occoquan ... by patent granted to the Rev. Lawrence Debutts of Maryland ... 19 Oct. 1727 ... bounded by land of Col. Charles Carter, the Rev'd Mr. Stuart, William Duff ... same from Debutts to Thomas Dodson and by sundry conveyances to Benjamin Morris ... Ł50. Signed: Benjamin (X) Morris, Elizabeth (X) Morris. Wit: G. Bennett, James Winn, John Tomlin, Benjamin Ballard, Arch'd. Allan. Rec: 23 June 1766, ack, by grantors.

Pages 493-496. 28 October 1765. Lease. Between Col. R. H. Lee of W'land Co. and Joseph Williams ... 50 a. for his nat. life and nat. lives of Elizabeth Williams and Frances Williams ... cor. of Headley ... Ł2 yearly rent. Signed: Richard Henry Lee, Joseph Williams. Wit: Jos. Blackwell, Martin Picket, James Winn, John Winn. Rec: 24 June 1766, prov. by o. of Joseph Blackwell, Martin Picket, James Winn, wits.

Pages 496-500. 3 June 1766. B & S. Between Alexander Farrow and Anna, his wife, and John Obannon, Sr. ... Ł200 ... 256 a. ... on Broad Run and its drains ... cor. to the land sold by Thomas Obannon to Rust ... the other or lessor tract ... by the Waggon Road at the Head of Carters Run ... 50 a. ... above tracts are parts of a tract granted to Bryan Obannon dec'd. by the Prop. of the No. Neck and who bequeathed the two tracts to William Obannon, the Younger, who conveyed them to Alexander Farrow. Signed: Alex'r. Farrow, Anne (X) Farrow. Wits: Simon Miller, George Bennett, John Obannon, Jr., William Obannon, James Nelson, Samuel Rust. Memorandum wit: John Rust, Samuel Rust, Robert Bolt. Rec: 24 June 1766, prov. by o. of John and Samuel Rust, Robert Bolt, wits.

Pages 501-502. 21 June 1766. Commission. Joseph Blackwell, Jeremiah Darnall and Gilson Foote, Gent. commissioned to examine Rachel Neavil, wife of George Neavil, Jr., who entered into a deed to Joseph Smith, 26 October 1765. Signed: H. Brooke. Ret. & Rec: 23 June 1766, by Jeremiah Darnall and Gilson Foote.

Pages 502-504. 16 January 1766. B & S. Between **Peter Kamper** & **Elizabeth**, his wife, and **William Jennings** ... Ł5.10s. ... 31 1/2 a. ... part of tract formerly belonging to **Thomas Jourdan**, dec'd. ... dividing line between **Augustine Jennings** and Peter Kamper. *Signed*: **Peter Kamper, Elizabeth (X) Kamper**. *Wit*: **William Settle, Benj'a. Snelling, John Obannon**. *Rec*: 29 July 1766, ack. by grantors.

Pages 504-508. 16 July 1766. B & S. Between **Henry Smith, Jr.**, of Staff. Co. and **John Cummings**, Planter ... Ł4 ... 40 a. ... part of 336 a. granted by Prop. to Mr. **Henry Smith, Sr.** ... 2 Jan. 1751 ... cor. to **Simon Cummings** ... Rocky Run ... cor. to **Markham's** land ... *Signed*: **H. Smith**. *Wit*: **John Edge, George Byram, Rich'd. Mynatt**. *Rec*: 29 July 1766, ack. by **Henry Smith, Jr.**

Page 508. 2 May 1766. Assignment. **John Blowers** to **William Barker** ... all rights, etc. in above mentioned (sic) Land & Promises for one horse, Saddle & Bridle and one Great Coat. *Signed*: **John Blowers**. *Wit*: **Wm. Norris, James Walker, Elias Edmonds**. *Rec*: 29 July 1766, prov. by o. of **William Norris** and **Elias Edmonds**.

Pages 508-510. 1 October 1765. B & S. Between **Henry Morless** and **Sarah**, his wife, and **William Millard** & **Elizabeth**, his wife, **John Kite** & **Charity**, his wife, **Lewis Prichet** & **Mary**, his wife, aforesd. daughters of **John Lattimore**, dec'd. and **John Robertson** ... Ł10 to each ... two negro slaves named **Joe** and **Solomon**, property of sd. John Lattimore, dec'd. *Signed*: **Henry Morless, Sarah Morless, William (W) Millard, Elizabeth (X) Millard, Lewis Prichett, Mary (X) Prichett, John Kight, Charity Kight**. *Wit*: **John Peters, John Roussau, Sinet Young, Robert (R) Ashby, Wm. Ashby**. *Rec*: 27 May 1765, prov. by o. of grantors and o. of wits. Rousseau and Peters. 29 July 1766, OR.

Pages 510-518. 20-21 August 1766. Lease & Release. Between **Humphrey Brooke**, Gent. and **Ann**, his wife, and **Allan Macrae** of Pr. Wm. Co. ... following tracts: 115 a. remainder of Tract of 386 a. granted to **John Frogg** from the Prop., 13 March 1742, 171 a. whereof sd. Brooke sold to **John Woodside**, 5-6 June 1763; 167 a. granted by Prop. to **John Morehead**, 10 Sept. 1742; 25 a. purch. by John Frogg of sd. Morehead, 28-29 April 1746; 105 a. and 75 a. both purch. by Brooke of **Thomas Hudnall**, 3-4 Nov. 1762; 30 a. purch. by Brooke of **John Hopper** & **Ann**, his wife, 27-28 May 1761 ... tracts lie contiguous and adj. to one another ... Ł230 ... 512 a. *Signed*: **H. Brooke, Ann Brooke**. *Rec*: 25 August 1766, ack. by **Humphrey Brooke** and a commission annexed taking ack. of said **Ann Brooke**.

Pages 518-522. 24-25 August 1766. Lease & Release. Between **James Bashaw** and **Frances Bashaw**, his wife, and **John James** ... Ł15 ... 300 a. ... cor. of **William Norris** ... cor. to **Waugh Darnall**. *Signed*: **James Bashaw, Frances Bashaw**. *Wit*: **John Chilton, Ben Bradford, John Bell**. *Rec*: 25 August 1766. ack. by grantors.

Pages 522-530. 2-3 August 1765. Lease & Release. Between **John Balendine** of Fx. Co. and **Mary**, his wife, and **Wharton Ransdell** ...

194 a. ... cor. to sd. Ransdell ... cor. to **Mr. Scott** ... saplin in Debutts and Allen's line ... cor. to **Archibald Allen**, his 30 a. tract ... part of 2,864 a. granted to the Rev. **Laurance Debutts** of Maryland ... 18 Oct. 1727, from sd. Debutts to his brother and heir at law **Samuel Debutts**, by him devised to **Barnaby Egan** and by him by indenture rec. in the General Court of the Colony conveyed the same to John Balendine ... Ł84.1s.4d. *Signed*: **John Balendine.** *Wit*: **Matthew Whiting, Fran. Whiting, H. Brooke.** *Rec*: 23 September 1765 and 25 August 1766, prov. by o. wits. Commission to examine **Mary Balendine** from Fx. Co. signed by **Chas. Broadwater** and **Edwd. Blackburn.**

Pages 530-532. 25 August 1766. B & S. Between **William Smith** and **James Duff** ... Ł100 ... being part of a tract belonging to **John Smith** ... 156 a. *Signed*: **William Smith, John (+) Smith.** *Wit*: **Wm. McClanahan, Augustine Smith, Andrew Barbey.** *Rec*: 25 August 1766, ack. by **William Smith.**

Pages 532-534. 1 April 1766. Power of Attorney. **Alexander Farrow** appoints his trusty friend **George Bennitt**, true and lawfull attorney ... to collect debts due from Messrs. **Humphrey Brooke, Jos. Blackwell** and **A. Churchill, Jr.** ... from Capt. **Elias Edmonds** ... **Minor Winn, Sen'r.** *Signed*: **Alex'r. Farrow.** *Wit*: **Thom Marshall, Harmon Hitt, William Seaton, John (Ł) Rector.** *Rec*: 26 August 1766, prov. by o. of **Thomas Marshall.**

Pages 534-537. 26 August 1766. B & S. Between **John Hopper & Ann**, his wife, and **Allan Macrae** of Pr. Wm. Co. ... 200 a. given to sd. Hopper by Deed of Gift from his father, John Hopper, rec. in Pr. Wm. Co. about 24 years past ... adj. the lands of **Allen Macrae, Garrard Edwards** and **John Woodsides** ... Ł35. *Signed*: **John Hopper, Ann (A) Hopper.** *Wit*: **W. Blackwell, Rich'd. Covington, John Blackwell.** *Rec*: 26 August 1766, ack. by **John Hopper.**

Pages 537-538. 25 August 1766. Bond of **John Smith** to agree to the division of land made by **John Mare** bet. him and his brother **William.** For: Ł200. *Sec*: **James Duff.** *Signed*: **John (X) Smith.** *Wit*: **James Wright, John Obannon, John Wright.** *Rec*: 26 August 1766, prov. by o. of **James Wright.**

Pages 538-542. 21-22 September 1766. Lease & Release. Between **John Combs the Elder** and **Seth**, his wife, of Staff. Co. and **John Combs the Younger** for nat. love and affection for sd. **John Combs** their son ... tract ... whereon he now is ... **Michael Luttrell's** line ... **John Peters** line ... 265 a. *Signed*: **John Combs, Seth Combs.** *Wit*: **Thomas Mountjoy, George Crosby, Rich'd. Mynatt.** *Rec*: 22 September 1766, ack. by grantors.

Pages 542-544. 20 September 1766. B & S. Between **Charles Duncan** and **David Partlow** of Caroline Co. ... Ł100 ... plantation whereon I now live ... on the Summerduck Run ... 242 a. ... cor. to G e o r g e **Henry** ... **James Furnel's** line ... to Summerduck Run ... *Signed*: **Charles (X) Duncan.** *Wit*: **Jno. Hume, John Williams, Eliz'h. (X)**

Hume. Receipt wit. by **W. Blackwell.** *Rec*: 22 September 1766, ack. by **Charles Duncan.**

Pages 544-546. 22 September 1766. B & S. Between **John Rector** and **Rebecka**, his wife, and **Nathaniel Rector** ... Ŀ9.5s. ... in the line of the land of **John Kamper** ... thence along the mountain ... 115 a. *Signed*: **John (X) Rector, Rebecka (X) Rector.** *Wit*: **Thom Marshall, Edwin Fielding, Joseph Taylor.** *Rec*: 22 September 1766, ack. by grantors.

Pages 546-552. 22 September 1766. Lease & Release. Between **John Snelling**, Planter, and **Elizabeth**, his wife, and **Benjamin Snelling**, Planter ... 116 a. ... part of larger tract of 232 a. purch. by **Aquila Snelling** (father of the sd. **John & Benjamin**) of old **Joseph King**, who had the land by grant from the Prop. 30 July 1715 ... horsepen run and cor. to **Wm. Russell** ... Ŀ10. *Signed*: **John Snelling, Elizabeth (X) Snelling.** *Wit*: **Jno. Robinson, G. Lumkin, Rich'd Mynatt.** *Rec*: 22 September 1766, ack. by grantors.

Pages 552-556. 27 October 1766. B & S. Between **Joseph Morehead & Betty** (also **Elizabeth**), his wife, of Hallifax Co. and **Edward West** of K. G. Co. ... Ŀ60 ... 150 a. ... parcel given him by his father **John Morehead** by Deed of Gift ... 26 Nov. 1753 ... part of 200 a. tract purch. by John Morehead of **Henry Cafly** ... 28 June 1726 ... 2 a. of the 150 a. was sold by John Morehead to **John Frog** ... Beg. at oak on the Great Marsh Road Side ... cor. to 123 a. lot Purch. by Joseph Morehead of **Thomas Hudnall,** 5 Nov. 1760 ... part of greater tract given Thomas Hudnall by his father **William Hudnall** ... cor. of Morehead, Brooke & Hudnall. *Signed*: **Joseph Morehead, Betty Morehead.** *Wit*: **Jos. Blackwell, Chas. Morehead, Lettice Chilton.** *Rec*: 27 October 1766, ack. by **Joseph Morehead** and **Elizabeth**, his wife.

Pages 556-558. 14 September 1766. B & S. Between **George Crump** and **John Blackwell** ... 200 a. being tract bought by **John Crump,** father of George Crump of **Thomas Garner,** then of Pr. Wm. Co, which fell to George Crump as heir at law to his brother **Joseph Crump** ... Ŀ100. *Signed*: **Geo. Crump.** *Rec*: 27 October 1766, ack. by grantor.

Pages 558-559. 17 September 1766. Bill of Sale. **Joseph Douglas** of Fauq. Co., bricklayer, for Ŀ10 ... paid by **John Cummings,** Planter ... one Negro girl named **Hannah,** now in possession of Mr. **Gavin Lawson,** merchant at Falmouth by virtue of a Mortgage from **Wm. Douglas & Sarah,** his wife. *Signed*: **Joseph Douglas.** *Wit*: **Simon Cummings, James Armstrong, Richard Mynatt.** *Rec*: 27 October 1766, prov. by o. of **Simon Cummings and James Armstrong.**

Pages 559-560. 4 May 1766. Mortgage. **Joseph Settle** for better security of **Benj. Settle** for being my sec. for being Exor. to my father's estate ... 130 a. whereon I now live ... cattle, household furniture, Ŀ15 in hands of **George Settle,** Ŀ18 in hands of **George Whitley** and **John Frog,** part of money levied by an execution against **John Finey.** *Signed*: **Joseph Settle.** *Wit*: **Wm. Settle, Bushrod Dogget,**

George Settle. *Rec*: 27 October 1766, prov. by o. of **Doggett** and **William Settle.**

Pages 560-565. 27-28 October 1766. Lease & Release. Between **John Blackmore & Ann,** his wife, and **Thomas Lord Fairfax** ... parcel on some of the head Branches of the North River of Rappahannock ... at the foot of a mountain called Balls Mount on the east side thereof ... trees marked IB ... Hicory on the side of the Sugar Loaf Mt. ... 871 a. ... which sd. tract was granted by Thomas Lord Fairfax to **James Ball** of Lan. Co., Gent., 6 May 1732 ... £350. *Signed*: **John Blackmore.** *Rec*: 28 October 1766, ack. by grantor.

Pages 565-566. 3 May 1766. B & S. Between **Jeffery Johnson** and **Frances Moore** ... £50 ... One Negroe Woman Slave named Sue ... *Signed*: **Jeffery (I) Johnson.** *Wit*: **William Blackwell, Jr., John Rousaw, Harmon Hitt.** *Rec*: 28 October 1766, prov. by o. of **Blackwell** and **Rousau.**

Pages 567-570. 27-28 October 1766. Lease & Release. Between **David Darnal & Mary,** his wife, and **Reuben Bramlett** ... 152 a. ... part of larger tract of 304 a. ... devised by **Thom's Carter** to his son **Peter Carter** ... one-half sold by Peter Carter, 19 Oct. 1738, next to river, to sd. **David Darnal,** rec. in Secretary's Office of Colony of Virginia ... £ 80. *Signed*: **David Darnall.** *Wit*: **Peter Newport, Henry Mauzey, Edward Ball.** *Rec*: 28 October 1766, prov. by o. of wits.

Pages 570-572. 22 November 1766. B & S. Between **William Redding, Jr.** and **John Ariss** ... £25 ... 50 a. part of tract known by the name of the German Town ... Beg. in Mr. **William Nelson's** line ... where the old German Road crosses there a Branch ... where the said Nelson's line crosses the line of **John Rust** ... saplin standing on the old German Road. *Signed*: **William (M) Redding, Jr.** *Wit*: **H. Brooke, E. Edmonds, A. Churchhill.** *Rec*: 24 November 1766, ack. by grantor.

Pages 572-575. 12 November 1766. B & S. Between **John Ariss** and **Elizabeth,** his wife, and the Hon. **William Nelson,** Esq. of York Co. ... £220 ... 369 a. ... 319 a. being part purch. by John Ariss of **Thomas Marshall & Mary,** his wife, 25-26 Aug. 1765 ... north side of Licking Run ... stump on a small red nole where the German Road crosses the Red Branch ... hicory by **John Smith's** fence ... cor. to **John Morgan's** land ... live tree to **Mr. Wilson's** land ... 50 a. lately conveyed to Ariss by **William Redding, Jr.** *Signed*: **Jno. Ariss, Elizabeth Ariss.** *Rec*: 24 November 1766, ack. by grantors.

Pages 575-578. 12 October 1766. Lease. Between **Charles Carter,** Esq. and **Zacharias Lewis** ... 200 a. ... Beg. Oak in the German Town line cor. to **John Page,** Esq. ... to said Lewis and Mary his wife during her widowhood ... during his nat. life ... yearly rent of 650 lbs. good, sound, merchantable Top Tobacco, clear of ground leaves and Trash ... together with Cask ... to be delivered to some convenient Wharehouse on the Rappahannock River. *Signed*: **Chas. Carter,**

Zacharias Lewis. *Wit*: John Churchhill, Tho. Slaughter, John Campbell. *Rec*: 24 November 1766, prov. by o. of wits.

Pages 578-579. 24 November 1766. Deed of Gift. Between Thomas Conway & Elizabeth, his wife, and Thomas Conway their son ... for nat. love and affection ... one Negroe Boy named Benjamin. *Signed*: Thomas Conway, Elizabeth Conway. *Wit*: Mary Doniphan, John Mauzey, Henry Conway. *Rec*: 24 November 1766, ack. by Thomas Conway.

Pages 579-580. 24 November 1766. Deed of Gift. Between Thomas Conway & Elizabeth, his wife, and William Conway, their son ... nat. love & affection ... 200 a. part of tract containing 307 a. given to the sd. Elizabeth by Mary Waugh her mother ... being part of 607 a. by patent from Prop. 14 March 1718 and the 307 a. being the upper part of the 607 a., which being divided from the lower part, rec. in sd. County ... on Elk Run joining the lands of Mr. Waggoner, Mr. Gibson and Mr. Thomas Bullitt ... for the nat. life of sd. Elizabeth Conway and after her death to be peaceably held by William Conway. *Signed*: Thomas Conway, Elizabeth Conway. *Wit*: Mary Doniphan, John Mauzey, Henry Conway. *Rec*: 24 November 1766, ack. by Thomas Conway.

Pages 580-584. 2-3 June 1766. Lease & Release. Between Thomas Dodson and Humphrey Brooke ... 150 a. ... Dodson's Spring Branch ... oak on the Mine Branch cor. to James Bailey and the land lately owned by John Stamps ... Mr. Stuart's line ... line of William Hunton and Joseph Dodson ... Ł20. *Signed*: Thomas Dodson, Sr. *Wit*: Thomas Dodson, Jr., William Stamps, Abraham Dodson, Wm. Hunton. *Rec*: 27 Oct. 1766, prov. by o. of Thomas Dodson, Jr. and William Stamps; 24 Nov. 1766, prov. by o. of Hunton.

Page 584. 24 November 1766. Bond of William Blackwell to collect the taxes to be laid and paid to the Treasurer of this Colony ... For: Ł 1,000. *Sec*: Joseph Blackwell. *Signed*: W. Blackwell, Jos. Blackwell. *Rec*: 24 Nov. 1766, ack. by William & Joseph Blackwell.

Pages 584-585. 24 November 1766. Bond of William Blackwell to receive from tithables the county levies. For: 28,000 lbs. tobacco. *Sec*: Joseph Blackwell. *Signed*: W. Blackwell, Jos. Blackwell. *Rec*: 24 Nov. 1766, prov. by o. of William & Joseph Blackwell.

Pages 585-588. 5-6 September 1766. Lease & Release. Between John McGuire of Craven Co., North Carolina, and Richard Jackman ... tract on the Head of the South Run of Broad Run of Occoquan on the south side of the Pignutt Ridge ... Beg. percill of land lately surveyed for Mr. Samuel Skinker ... small hill between Ceddar Run and aforesd. run ... 282 a. ... Ł100 ... tract granted by Prop. to John McGuire, dec'd. 26 Jan. 1726, and left it by will to his sons John and James McGuire and Jas. dying without heirs - John being the sole surviving heir of John McGuire, dec'd. *Signed*: John McGuire. *Wit*: Jeremiah (X) Sousbery, George Mills, Jas. Lindsey, John Justise. *Rec*: 24 Nov. 1766, prov. by o. of **Jeremiah Sousbery, George Mills, James Lindsey.**

Pages 588-589. 29 October 1766. Deed of Gift. **John Mauzey, Sr.** ... for good will and affection towards my granddaughter **Esther Mauzey,** the dau. of **Henry Mauzey** ... one Negroe girl named **Basha.** *Signed*: **John Mauzy.** *Wit*: **Peter (X) Murphey, John Mauzy, Jr.,** son of **Peter Mauzy, Thomas Conway.** *Rec*: 24 Nov. 1766, ack. by **John Mauzy.**

Page 589. 11 October 1766. B & S. **Francis Bronaugh** to **John Blackwell** ... one Negroe boy named **Robin** ... Ł25. *Signed*: **Fran's. Bronaugh.** *Wit*: **Wm. Martin, John Nelson, Jr.** Receipt wit. by **John Peters, John Nelson, Jr., Wm. Martin.** *Rec*: 25 Nov. 1766, prov. by o. of **William Martin** and **John Nelson.**

Pages 589-590. 22 December 1766. Deed of Gift. Bet. **Michael Luttrell** and **James Luttrell,** his brother ... nat. love and affection ... half my new patten of land ... adjoining the sd. **James Luttrell** ... southside of Town Run ... strate line to **Combses** line ... along Combses line to **Mawzey's** line ... 54 a. *Signed*: **Michael Luttrell.** *Wit*: **Wm. Harison, Richard Larance, Charles Waller.** *Rec*: 22 Dec. 1766, ack. by **Michael Luttrell.**

Pages 590-592. 19 December 1766. B & S. Between **John Luttrell,** planter, and **James Luttrell,** planter ... Ł25 ... 70 a. whereon sd. **John** now lives ... part of larger tract belonging to **Richard Luttrell,** dec'd. ... west side of Town Run ... **Richard Luttrell's** rolling road ... to a branch called Cabin Branch ... down said branch to Town Run. *Signed*: **John Luttrell.** *Wit*: **Richard Larrance, Wm. Harrison, Charles Waller.** *Rec*: 22 Dec. 1766, ack. by **John Luttrell.**

Pages 592-596. 25 September 1766. B & S. Between **Burges Smith** of Lan. Co., Gent. & **Alice,** his wife, and **James Strother,** Planter ... Ł40 ... 218 a. ... part of tract containing 13,000 & od acres ... sd. tract **Charles Burgess,** Gent. rec'd a patent from the Prop. ... on Goose Creek ... the 218 a. is comprehended in Lott No. 36 as appears on a plott rec. in the Clerks Office of Fauq. Co. done by **Thomas Marshall,** Gent., Surveyor of sd. Co. ... cor. to Lotts 33, 34 and sd. Lott 36 ... to the road. *Signed*: **Burgess Smith, Alice Smith.** *Wit*: **Jos. Blackwell, John Chilton, Lettice Chilton.** *Rec*: 23 Feb. 1767, with commission to examine **Alice Smith,** prov. by o. of wits.

Pages 596-599. 25 September 1766. B & S. Between **Burges Smit,** Gent., ... and **Alice,** his wife, and **John Rector** ... Ł50 ... 234 a. ... part of tract granted to **Charles Burgess,** Gent., dec'd ... (as above) ... Lott No. 34 ... cor. to Lotts No. 31, 32, 33, & 34. *Signed*: **Burges Smith, Alice Smith.** *Wit*: (same as above). *Rec*: 23 Feb. 1767, prov. by o. of wits. (as above).

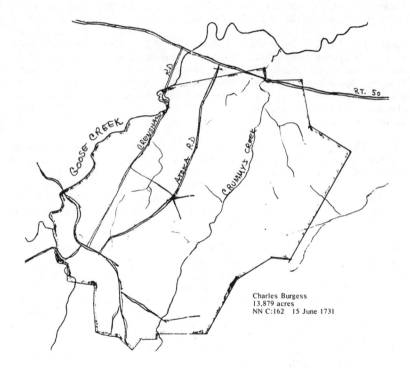

GOOSE CREEK

CRENSHAW RD.

ATOKA RD.

CROMMYS CREEK

RT. 50

Charles Burgess
13,879 acres
NN C:162   15 June 1731

Pages 599-602. 25 September 1766. B & S. Between **Burges Smith** and **Alice**, his wife, of Christ Church Par., Lan. Co., and **Charles Chinn**, planter, ... L60 ... 399 a. ... part of **Charles Burgess**, Gent., dec'd. grant of 13,000 odd acres ... Lotts Nos. 1 & 2 ... cor. for No. 1 and No. 2 ... cor. to Lotts 1, 2, 3, 4. *Signed*: (as above). *Wit*: (as above). *Rec*: 23 Febr. 1767, prov. by o. of wits (as above).

Pages 602-605. 25 September 1766. B & S. Between **Burges Smith**, Gent. and **Alice**, his wife, and **Rubin Ellit** of Pr. Wm. Co. ... L111 ... 295 a. ... part of **Charles Burgess**, dec'd., grant of 13,000 odd a. ... Lot No. 35 ... *Signed*: (as above). *Wit*: (as above). *Rec*: 23 Febr. 1767, prov. by o. of wits (as above).

Pages 605-609. 26-27 December 1766. Lease & Release. Between **John Nevile** (also **Neavile**) and **William Carr** of Pr. Wm. Co. ... two tracts of land ... one of which was purch. of **William Hackney** and rec. in Pr. Wm. Co., 20 Oct. 1766, the other granted by Prop., 5 Jan. 1745, lying on branches of Cedar Run ... survey made by Mr. **James Ginn** ... cor. tree to **Col. Carter** and a tract formerly surveyed for Mr. **William Hackney** ... cor. tree to **Thomas Barber** and **Thomas Garman** ... hill side on the west side the Walnut Branch ... 53 a. ... L100. *Signed*: **John Nevill**. *Wit*: **James Young, Edw'd. Dickinson, Patt (X) Muskett, John Dickinson**. *Rec*: 23 March 1767, ack. by **John Neavil**.

Pages 609-611. 29 September 1766. B & S. Between **Joseph Dodson** and **Ann**, his wife, and **Jacob Hays** ... L40 ... 150 a. ... adj. land of Mr. **Humphrey Brooke** & Mr. **William Hunton** ... high hill ... Mr. Wm. Hunton's line ... land formerly owned by **Thomas Dodson, Sr.** ... given by him to Joseph Dodson by deed of gift. *Signed*: **Joseph Dodson, Ann (X) Dodson**. *Wit*: **John Creel, Lazarus Dodson, Benjamin Edward, Rosannah Creel, Obed Cornwell, William Davis, Thomas Dodson, Sr., Abraham Dodson, Robert Sanders, John Benett, Edmund Hays**. *Rec*: 23 March 1767, ack. by **Joseph Dodson**.

Pages 611-613. 1 March 1767. B & S. **Martin Pickett** and **Ann**, his wife, and **William Gibson** ... L28 ... tract on Broad Run ... 82 a. ... tract to Pickett from **Jos. Duncan** out of larger tract whereon **William Obannon** now lives ... side of Broad Run. *Signed*: **Martin Pickett, Anne Pickett**. *Rec*: 23 March 1767, ack. by grantor.

Pages 613-615. 23 March 1767. B & S. Between **Samuel Porter** and **Eve**, his wife, and **Charles** and **James Taylor** ... L40 ... cor. of Ball's and **Tilman Weaver** ... a hiccory on the side of a Hill cor. of Mr. **Burgess** Goose Creek Tract ... 150 a. *Signed*: **Sam'l. Porter, Eve Porter**. *Rec*: 23 March 1767, ack. by grantor.

Pages 615-616. 24 March 1767. Bill of Sale. **Gaton Settle**, Planter, to **Alexander Cuningham** of Falmouth, merchant, for L70 ... all goods and chattels ... *Signed*: **Gaton (X) Settle**. *Wit*: **Francis Payne, Bennett Price**. *Rec*: 24 March 1767, ack. by **Gayton Settle**.

Pages 616–619. 1 November 1766. Lease. Between **Thomas Lord Fairfax** and **Edward Larrance** ... parcel in Manor of Leeds ... a Lot formerly leased to **Thomas George** who has since forfeited said lot ... 200 a. ... yearly rent of 40s. sterling ... *Signed*: **Fairfax**. *Wit*: **Joseph Barbey, Matthew Neale, John Priest**. *Rec*: 27 April 1767, prov. by o. of wits.

Pages 619–622. 1 November 1766. Between **Thomas Lord Fairfax** and **Samuel Luttrell** ... 150 a. in Manor of Leeds ... red oak in **Mr. Neils** lott ... yearly rent of 30s. sterling. *Signed*: **Fairfax**. *Wit*: **Joseph Barbey, Matthew Neiles, John Priest**. *Rec*: 27 April 1767, prov. by o. of wits.

Pages 622–625. 1 November 1766. Lease. Between **Thomas Lord Fairfax** and **William Norman** ... 140 a. in Manor of Leeds ... cor. to **Blackemores** lott ... Spanish oak in Burgesses line ... cor. to **Jno.** Smith's lott ... for Norman's nat. life and lives of **Lettice**, his wife, and **John Norman**, his son ... yearly rent of 28s. ster. *Signed*: **Fairfax**. *Wit*: **Matthew Neale, Edward Lawrence, Joseph Barbey**. *Rec*: 27 April 1767, prov. by o. of wits.

Pages 625–628. 1 November 1766. Lease. Between **Thomas Lord Fairfax** and **John Priest** of Pr. Wm. Co. ... 200 a. in Manor of Leeds ... oak by little Thumb Run cor. to **J e t t s** lott ... for his nat. life and lives of **Elizabeth**, his wife and **Mason Priest**, his son ... yearly rent of 40s. sterling. *Signed*: **Fairfax**. *Wit*: **Joseph Barbey, Matthew Neale, Edward Larrance**. *Rec*: 27 April 1767, proved by o. of wits.

Pages 628–631. No date. Lease. Between **Thomas Lord Fairfax** and **Andrew Barbey** ... 126 a. in Manour of Leeds ... oak in **Georges** lott line ... for his nat. life and lives of **J a n e**, his wife, and Andrew Barbey, his son ... yearly rent of 25s.2d. sterling. *Signed*: **Fairfax**. *Wit*: **John Priest, Edward Larrance, Matthew Neale**. *Ret*: 27 April 1767, prov. by o. of wits.

Pages 631–634. 23 October 1766. Lease. Between **Thomas Lord Fairfax** and **Archibald Allen** ... lot formerly leased to **Morgan Darnall, Jr.** and by him forfeited and absconded to another government ... in Manour of Leeds ... 200 a. ... cor. to **Charles Jones's Lott** ... for sd. Allen's nat. life and lives of **William and Moses Allen**, his sons ... yearly rent of 40s. *Signed*: **Fairfax**. *Wit*: **John Priest, Joseph Barbey, Edward Larrance**. *Rec*: 27 April 1766, prov. by o. of wits.

Pages 635–637. 17 December 1766. B & S. Between **Joseph Sebastian** of Christ Par., Lan. Co. and **Thomas Skinker** ... Ł30 ... 130 a. ... on the main county road ... same land being part of a larger tract taken up by **Howsen Kenner** and by him conveyed to **William Wood** and by him to his son Joshua 130 a. ... the balance, upper part, containing 135 a., by deed to Joseph Sebastian ... divided from the land of **Joshua Wood** by a stream known by the name of the great branch of Rock Run ... *Signed*: **Joseph Sebastin**. *Wit*: **James Crap, David Partlow, Joseph(Ł)**

Williams, William (X) Elkins, George (Ⱶ) Williams. *Rec*: 27 April 1767, prov. by o. of **J. Crap, Elkins,** and **Partlow,** wits.

Page 637. 8 April 1767. Bond of **William Blackwell** to receive from Tithables their public levies. For: 224,424 lbs. tobacco. *Sec*: **Joseph Blackwell.** *Signed*: **W. Blackwell, Jos. Blackwell.** *Rec*: 27 April 1767, ack. by makers.

Pages 637-639. 25 May 1767. B & S. Between **Joseph Blackwell & Lucy,** his wife, and **Richard Lewis** of K. G. Co. ... Ⱡ350 ... 100 a. ... near Summerduck Run ... which sd. land was purch. of **William Delaney** by the sd. Joseph Blackwell and Richard Lewis ... 1764 ... also another tract ... 140 a. purch. by them of **Joseph Williams** and adj. the aforesd. 100 a. ... also 2 a. purch. of **John Courtney** whereon the sd. Blackwell and Lewis hath built a saw mill and made other improvements lying on Rock Run ... also 1 a. on the opposite side from the sd. mill purch. of **Thomas Grinning** ... also pine trees of a foot over at the stump that is upon the land of **William Courtney, Joshua Wood, George Henry,** Thomas Grinning ... also all the pine and all timber on the land of **Charles Delany** ... to Richard Lewis all of Joseph Blackwell's right & title in sd. granted lands, timbers and appurtenances ... *Signed*: **Jos. Blackwell, Lucy Blackwell.** *Wit*: **Martin Pickett, Bennitt Price, W. Edmonds.** *Rec*: 25 May 1767, ack. by grantors.

Pages 639-641. 25 May 1766. B & S. Between **Thomas Furr & Elizabeth,** his wife, and **Symon Miller,** Planters ... and **George Lamkin** ... Ⱡ30 ... in hand paid Thomas Furr by George Lamkin ... 150 a. ... Beg. at cor. dividing Thomas Furr and George Lamkin ... cor. on side of Chattins Run ... down the meanders of sd. Run running into Goose Creek thence down the meanders of Goose Creek ... cor. to Furr and Lamkin ... also all claim of **Simon Miller** in said line. *Signed*: **Simon Miller, Thos. (T) Furr.** *Wit*: **John (Ⱶ) Siarss, John Obannon, John Morehead, Richard Larrance.** *Rec*: 25 May 1767, ack. by grantors.

Pages 641-643. 23 May 1767. B & S. Between **William Red(d)ing** and **John Rector** ... Ⱡ15 ... tract ... cor. of **John Holtzclaw's** land and land of **Mr. Burrell** ... to **Phillip Hufman's** cor. ... cor. of **Kearnes** land ... cor. of **Russ's** ... 170 a. ... part of larger tract granted to Redding 24 Febr. 1761. *Signed*: **William (+) Reading.** *Rec*: 26 May 1767, ack. by **William Reding.**

Pages 643-646. 24 November 1766. B & S. Between **Thomas Garner & Elinson,** his wife, and **Susannah Hewitt** of K. G. Co. ... 150 a. ... which Thomas Garner inherits as heir at law of his father, **John Garner** who obtained a Patent for the land ... Beg. at a bridge in the Road that leads from Falmouth to Great Run ... lines of **Parish Garner** ... oak by another bridge in the line of Parish Garner ... line of **Thomas Welch's** dec'd. ... cor. to Mr. **Thomas Mitchell** ... to Tin Pot Run ... in lines of Messrs. **John** and **Thomas Garner, Jr.** ... Ⱡ90 ... *Signed*: **Thos. Garner, Elinson Garner.** *Wit*: **W. Blackwell, John Blackwell,**

Joseph Seavell. *Rec*: 26 May 1767, prov. by o. of **William & John Blackwell** and **Joseph Seavell.**

Pages 646-649. 23 February 1766. B & S. Between **Thomas Renoe & Jane**, his wife, of Detingen Par., Pr. Wm. Co. and **Thomas Garner** (son of the sd. Jane) ... 150 a. ... which the sd. Jane, wife of Thomas Renoe, chose for her Dowry of all the land of **John Garner**, dec'd. (late husband of sd. Jane) ... L22. *Signed*: **Thos. Reno, Jane** (X) **Reno.** *Wit*: **John Blackwell, Original Young, James Winn, John Nelson, Jos. Hudnall, John Wright, James Baley.** *Rec*: 28 April 1767, prov. by o. of **John Nelson, Jr.** and **Original Young**; 29 April, by o. of **Joseph Hudnall, John Wright** and **James Baily**, but before the execution thereof she declared she would not execute the same unless the consideration money was paid or secured to be paid to her and at a Court continued on 27 May 1767 the same was OR.

Pages 649-653. 30-31 March 1767. Lease & Release. Between **William Durham**, of Bute Co., North Carolina and **Caleb Smith**, of Pr. Wm. Co. ... 75 a. ... being part of a greater tract patented by **William Hackney** ... conveyed by him to **John Calfee** and by him sold to **William Colcouth** and by him conveyed to Durham ... rec. in Pr. Wm. Co. ... cor. to Wm. Colcough ... **Carters** line ... cor. of **James Green** ... L20. *Signed*: **William Durham.** *Wit*: **Fortunatus Legg, George Reeve, John Reeve, James Wyat.** *Rec*: 25 May 1767, prov. by o. of **George & John Reeves**; 22 June, by o. of **James Wyat.**

Pages 653-655. 22 June 1767. B & S. Between **John Forguson & Martha**, his wife, and **Peter Pearce** ... L15 ... 70 a. ... joining the lands of **Catesby Cocke, Nathaniel Dodd, & Hedgemans**, land which the sd. Fauguson purch. of **James Arnold**. *Signed*: **John Forgueson, Martha** (X) **Forgueson.** *Wit*: **James Arnold, Stephen Threlkeld, James Wheatly.** *Rec*: 22 June 1767, ack. by **John Forguson & Martha**, his wife.

Pages 655-657. 6 December 1766. B & S. Between **John Darnall & Jean**, his wife, and **William Darnall**, there son and **John Duncan, Jr.** son of **John Duncan** ... L60 ... part of greater tract ... near the main road in **Corbin's** line ... Ratliss Run ... horsepenn run ... mouth of Smiths Spring Branch ... 125 a. *Signed*: **John Darnall, Jean** (X) **Darnall, William Darnall.** *Wit*: **Paul Williams, James** (X) **Duncan, James Wright, Morgan** (X) **Darnall, John** (X) **Duncan.** *Rec*: 22 June 1767, prov. by o. of **Wright, Morgan, Darnall, John Duncan.**

Pages 657-658. 22 June 1767. Deed of Gift. **John Duncan** ... for nat. love & affection ... to granddaughters **Elizabeth McCormick** (dau. of **William Morgan** and wife of **John McCormick**) ... Negroe woman Jude ... gr.dau. **Phebe Morgan** (dau. of Wm. Morgan) ... one negroe woman named **Carner** ... gr.dau. **Alice Morgan** (dau. of **William**) negroe woman named **Jay** ... gr.dau. **Rosannah Morgan** (dau. of **William**) ... one negroe woman named **Luce** ... *Signed*: *John* (I) **Duncan.** *Wit*: **Thom Marshall, Wm. Settle, Henry Mauzy. William**

72

Morgan then relinquished all his claim against the estate of **John Duncan**. *Rec*: 22 June 1767, ack. by **John Duncan**.

Pages 658-661. 22 June 1767. B & S. Between **John Rector & Catherine**, his wife, and **Hugh Morrison** ... £30 ... part of larger tract taken up 15 June 1731 ... cor. to Strother ... 115 a. *Signed*: **John** (R) **Rector, Catherine** (C) **Rector**. *Wit*: **Jos. Blackwell, W. Kincheloe, Henry Rector**. *Rec*: 22 June 1767, ack. by grantors.

Pages 661-666. 20 July 1767. B & S. Between **William, John & Armistead Churchhill**, Exors. of Armistead Churchhill, dec'd. of Middlesex Co., **Edmond Pendleton**, Gent., of Caroline Co., Admr. of **John Robinson**, late of K. G. Co., Esq. dec'd. and **Warner Lewis** of Glou. Co., Gent., of one part and **Richard Chichester**, Gent. of the other part ... Armistead Churchhill, dec'd, did mortgage to Warner Lewis and John Robinson ... sd. Churchhill's lands ... were sold to the highest bidder and Richard Chichester purch. 1,192 a. out of the tract ... to make a clear title the sd. Pendleton and Warner join in conveying the tract to Chichester ... for £455.1s. ... part of larger tract purch. of sd. Warner Lewis by sd. **Armistead Churchhill the Elder** and by him mortgaged to sd. Lewis first and then to sd. John Robinson, dec'd. ... Bounded ... north side of Cedar Run ... John Churchhill's line ... south side of Cedar Run and down the meanders thereof ... *Signed*: **Warner Lewis, Will. Churchhill, John Churchhill, A. Churchhill**. *Wit*: **Benj'a. Churchhill, Churchhill Jones, William Jones**. *Rec*: 27 July 1767, ack. by o. of wits.

Pages 666-669. 1 June 1767. B & S. Between **William Waugh**, of K. G. Co. and **Peter Pearce** ... £47 ... 150 a. ... same from **Joseph Duncan & Lydia**, his wife, to Wm. Waugh, father of the grantor ... who obtained by will from his father ... will rec. in Pr. Wm. Co. *Signed*: **William Waugh**. *Wit*: **Gavin Lawson, John Dunlop, Alex'r. Wodrow, John Sincler, Debar Thompson, Alex'r. Cunninghame**. *Rec*: 27 July 1767, prov. by o. of **Debar Johnson** (sic) 22 June 1767, prov. by o. of **A. Cunninghame & John Sincler**.

Pages 669-676. 2-3 June 1767. Lease & Release. Between **Burgess Smith & Alice**, his wife, of Lan. Co. and **William Peake** ... 187 a. ... line bet. sd. Burgess Smith and **Burgess Ball** ... cor. to Lot No. 27 & 32 ... cor. to lots No. 28, 31 & 32 ... cor. to lots Nos. 25, 26, & 28 ... part of larger grant to Mr. **Charles Burgess**, dated 15 June 1731 ... £ 46.15s. *Signed*: **Burgess Smith, Alice Smith**. *Wit*: **Jos. Blackwell, John** (X) **Rector, Will'm. Fitzgarrel, Wm. Kincheloe**. *Rec*: 27 July 1767, prov. by o. of wits.

Pages 676-682. 2-3 June 1767. Lease & Release. Between **Burgess Smith & Alice**, his wife ... and **William Kincheloe** ... 400 a. ... part of **Charles Burgess** grant ... 15 June 1731 ... line bet. Burgess Smith and **Burgess Ball** ... cor. of lotts 18 & 19 ... cor. of lotts 26 & 27 ... cor. of lotts 25, 26, 27 & 28 ... £90 ... *Signed*: **Burges Smith, Alice Smith**. *Wit*: **Jos. Blackwell, John** (X) **Rector, Will'm.** (X) **Fitzgarril, Wil-**

liam Peake. *Rec*: 27 July 1767, prov. by o. of **Joseph Blackwell, John Rector** and **William Peake.**

Pages 682-690. 2-3 June 1767. Lease & Release. Between **Burges Smith & Alice,** his wife ... and **Daniel Flowree** ... 955 a. ... beg. ... oak by Crummies Run ... o. in the head of a Branch of Chattins Run ... cor. to **George Lamkin** ... cor. to **George Johnston,** Gent., dec'd. ... cor. to **Harmon Hitt** ... cor. to **Stanley Singleton** ... **Strother's** line ... Ł114.12s. *Signed*: **Burges Smith, Alice Smith.** *Wit*: **Jos. Blackwell, Martin Pickett, Tilman Weaver, William Peake, John Boley.** *Rec*: 27 July 1767, prov. by o. of **Joseph Blackwell, Martin Pickett,** and **William Peake.**

Pages 690-696. 24-25 July 1767. Lease & Release. Between **Ge o. Barry & Mary,** his wife, and **Edward Feagan** of Pr. Wm. Co. ... 150 a. ... on the waters of Broad Run and near the mountain called & known by the name of Old Mother Leather Coat ... Beg. at black oak by Fornication Branch & near the Thoroughfare Road ... binding on Glascock's lines ... Ł75 ... *Signed*: **George Berry, Mary Berry.** *Rec*: 27 July 1767, ack. by grantors.

Pages 696-698. 25 July 1767. Agreement. **John Adams** of Charles Co., Md. and **Zephaniah Turner** of the same ... purchased as joint tenants of **James Ewell** of Lan. Co. ... 1,000 a. ... and have received lease & release for same and obtained his security for one other plot adjoing the aforesd. containing 1,000 a. and to be confirmed to them when James Ewell, son of **Solomon** or **Eve Ewell** shall arrive at full age ... both parties agree to divided the land equally, whether they survive each other or not. *Signed*: **John Adams, Zeph. Turner.** *Wit*: **Robert Scott, William Cave, John Gunyon.** *Rec*: 27 July 1767.

Page 698. 26 May 1767. Deed of Gift. Between **John Peters,** Planter ... for nat. love & affection for his brother and in compliance with a request of his father, **James Peters,** dec'd ... one Negroe boy named **George,** about 13 years old ... *Signed*: **John Peters.** *Wit*: **H. Smith, Betty Mauzy, Elizabeth (X) Phillips.** *Rec*: 27 July 1767, ack. by **John Peters.**

Pages 699-702. 4 August 1767. B & S. Between **Benjamin Drummond** of Pr. Wm. Co., Planter and **John Mercer, George Mercer** and **James Mercer,** Esqrs. ... 221 a. Drummond has by deed from Prop. ... 26 April 1742 ... within the bounds of 2 larger tracts granted to John Mercer, Esq. by two deeds ... 9 & 11 June 1737 ... sd. John Mercer and **Anne,** his wife, by lease & re]ease to George and James Mercer ... 2-3 April 1759 ... one half of the two tracts ... the bounds established in a suit in the General Court styled John Mercer, Esq. plt. ag. **John Leachman,** Deft. ... the Mercers are willing to reimburse Benj. Drummond for his expenses in obtaining the grant, clearing the 221 a. ... Ł 21.8s. ... cor. to land surveyed for **Burr Barton.** *Signed*: **Benjamin (B) Drummond.** *Rec*: 24 August 1767, ack. by **Benjamin Drummond.**

END OF DEED BOOK N0. 2

DEED BOOK NO. 3

1767 - 1770

Pages 1-6. 25 May 1767. Lease & Release. Between **Wm. Churchhill & Elizabeth**, his wife, of Middlesex Co. and **Samuel Thornsberry** of Staff. Co. ... Ł20 ... 200 a. ... same granted by Patent 5 Jan. 1741 to **John Higgins**, containing 110 a. ... cor. to **Benj. Newton** ... line of **Col. Carter's** ... cor. to tract of 900 a. surveyed by Mr. **John Warner** for **Lord Fairfax** ... small branch of Walnut Branch ... another tract granted by Patent ... 5 Aug. 1747 to **James Genn** ... cor. to John Higgins tract in the late **Secretary Carter's** line ... cor. marked LF cor. to Lord Fairfax ... to Falmouth Road ... to Quantico Road ... cor. to Higgins and Benj. Newton ... large oak on Walnut Branch marked WM C B T T T D cor. to sd. Newton, **Thomas Stamps**, and **Timothy Dorgain**. *Signed*: **Will. Churchhill, Elizabeth Churchhill**. *Wit*: **John Catlett, George Catlett, William (X) Thornberry**. *Rec*: 28 September 1767, prov. by o. of wits.

Pages 7-9. 15 September 1767. B & S. Between **John Pope Williams, James Williams** and **Charles Williams** of Staff. Co. and **Henry Mauzy** ... Ł130 ... 1/3 of larger tract devised by **George Williams**, father of grantors ... 250 a. ... beg. ... cor. to **Ralls's** land ... branch side near Rappahannock River ... cor. to sd. Ralls & **Arnold** near a Cliff of Rocks ... down the meanders of said river ... *Signed*: **John Pope Williams, Jesse Williams, Charles Williams**. *Wit*: Jos. Hudnall, Wm. Settle, Bushrod Doggett, John Mauzy, Wm. Withers, Jr. *Rec*: 28 September 1767, prov. by o. of wits.

Pages 9-13. 13 March 1767. B & S. Between **Burgess Smith & Alice**, his wife, of Lan. Co. and **John Rector** ... Ł40 ... 200 a. ... part of larger tract taken up by Mr. **Chas. Burgess**, dec'd. ... lott No. 33 on survey in Fauq. Co. Clerk's Office ... cor. to lott No. 32 and on the dividing line bet. Burges Smith and **Burges Ball** ... cor. to lott No. 36 and **Chattins** cor. ... corner to lotts Nos. 34, 32, 31. *Signed*: Burges Smith, Alice Smith. *Wit*: **Gregory Glascock, Elijah Glascock, Joseph (X) Robinson**. *Rec*: 28 Sept. 1767, with proof of Alice Smith's signature cert. by **Jas. Ball, John Chinn** of Lan. Co., ack. by **Burges Smith**.

Pages 13-17. 21 March 1767. B & S. Between **Burges Smith & Alice**, his wife ... and **Roger Towls** ... Ł54 ... 180 a. ... near Goose Creek and part of **Charles Burges**, grant ... cor. to lotts No. 21, 16 and 15 ... cor. to lotts No. 20, 23, 24 ... *Signed*: **Burges Smith, Alice Smith**.

Wit: **James Murrey, Robt (X) Munday, Wm. (X) Pearice.** *Rec*: 28 September 1767, ack. by **Burgess Smith.**

Pages 18–22. 4 June 1767. B & S. Between **Burges Smith & Alice,** his wife ... and **John Rector** ... Ł50 ... 198 a. ... near Goose Creek part of larger tract of Mr. **Charles Burgess,** dec'd., by deed 15 June 1767 ... being lotts 29 & 30 ... cor. to lot No. 35 ... cor. to lot No. 24 ... cor. to lots 22, 25, 28 ... *Signed*: **Burges Smith, Alice Smith.** *Wit*: **James Pendleton, James Slaughter, John Blackwell, James Woodburn, Peter Grant, Hancock Lee, Rich'd Lewis.** *Rec*: 28 September 1767, ack. by **Burgess Smith.**

Pages 22–27. 3 June 1767. B & S. Between **Burges Smith & Alice,** his wife ... and **Wm. Fitzgarrald** ... Ł68 ... 305 a. ... near Goose Creek ... part of grant to Mr. **Chas. Burgess,** dec'd ... lotts No. 23 & 24 ... lot No. 23 bounded: cor. to lots no. 21, 22, & 24; lot No. 24; cor. to lotts No. 21, 25 ... lots No. 25, 28 & 29 ... cor. to lotts No. 21, 22, 23 ... *Signed*: **Burges Smith, Alice Smith.** *Wit*: **William Peake, John Boley, John (X) Rector.** *Rec*: 28 September 1767, ack. by **Burgess Smith.**

Page 27. 10 July 1767. Bill of Sale. **Alexander Parker** to **William Parker** ... Ł35.18s.6d. ... livestock, crops. *Signed*: **Alex. Parker.** *Wit*: **Martin Pickett, James Hathaway.** *Rec*: 28 September 1767, ack. by **Alexander Parker.**

Pages 28–31. 26 August 1767. B & S. Between **John Morgan** and **Elizabeth,** his wife, and **Peter Pearce** ... Ł30 ... part of a greater tract ... cor. to **Sturd** ... **Foote's** cor. ... course of **Morgan Darnall's** Pattern ... cor. in **Sturde's** line ... 136 a. ... *Signed*: **John Morgan, Elizabeth (X) Morgan.** *Wit*: **Rich'd Bryan, Henry Utterback, John (X) Utterback.** *Rec*: 28 September 1767, ack. by grantors.

Pages 31–36. 27–28 September 1767. Lease & Release. Between **William Robinson & Frances Ann,** his wife, and **John James,** Bricklayer ... 50 a. ... Ł30 ... cor. to **John Hudnall** ... **Morgan's** line ... and is the land the sd. **Wm. Robinson** purch. of **Peter Taylor** ... *Signed*: **Wm. Robertson, Frances Ann Robertson.** *Wit*: **Wm. Brent, James (X) Williams, Henry Martin.** *Ret*: 28 September 1767, ack. by **William Robertson & wife.**

Pages 36–39. 8 October 1767. B & S. Between **Burges Smith,** Gent. & **Alice,** his wife, and **John Rector,** Planter ... Ł25.4s. ... 168 a. ... near Goose Creek, part of Mr. **Burgess's** grant and grandfather of the sd. **Burges Smith** ... lot No. 28 ... cor. of lots No. 25, 6, 7 ... cor. of lots 27, 31, & 2 ... cor. to lots 20, 30, 31 ... cor. to lots 24, 29, 25 ... *Signed*: **Burges Smith, Alice Smith.** *Wit*: **Richard Chichester, Jos. Blackwell, J. Moffett, John Blackwell, Jas. Scott, Jr.** *Rec*: 26 October 1767, prov. by o. of wits.

Pages 39–42. 8 October 1767. B & S. Between **Burges Smith,** Gent. & **Alice,** his wife, and **James Ball,** Gent. of Lan. Co. ... Ł275 ... tract ... Beg. ... cor. bet. the lots No. 1, 4 & 5 ... cor. bet. lotts No. 8, 9, 12 &

13 ... in line of the Patent and cor. of lots No. 7, 14 ... cor. of lotts No. 15, 22 ... cor. to lotts No. 15, 16, 21 & 22 ... cor. of the lotts 21, 22, 23, 24 ... cor. of lotts No. 20, 21, 24, 25 ... cor. of lotts No. 24, 25, 28, 29 ... cor. of Iotts No. 25, 26, 27 & 28 ... cor. of lotts No. 17, 18, 19, 20 ... line that divides this land from the land of **Burges Ball** & cor. of the lotts 18 & 19 ... cor. of the lotts No. 3 & 4 ... cor. of the lotts 1, 2, 3 & 4 ... Including lotts No. 3, 4, 9, 10, 11, 12, 13, 14, 15, 16, 17, 18, 20, 21, & 25 ... 2, 746 acres. *Signed*: **Burges Smith, Alice Smith.** *Wit*: **Richard Chichester, Jos. Blackwell, J. Moffett, John Blackwell, Jas. Scott, Jr.** *Rec*: 26 October 1767, prov. by o. of wits.

Pages 42-49. 1-2 May 1767. Lease & Release. Between **B u r g e s Smith, Gent.** & **Alice**, his wife, of Lan. Co. and **William Pearl** of Loud. Co. ... Ł240 ... part of **Charles Burgess'** grant near Goose Creek ... Beg. for Lotts No. 5, 6, 7 & 8 ... cor. of the Grand Pattent ... cor. of lotts 8, 9, 12, 13 ... cor. 1, 4, 5 ... 720 a. ... and for the lotts 31 & 32 ... Beg. ... cor. of the lotts 31, 34, 35 ... **Burges Ball's** line ... cor. of lotts no. 28, 29, 30, 31 ... 393 a. ... in all 1,113 a. *Signed*: **Burges Smith, Alice Smith.** *Wit*: **Jas. Ball, Oswald Newby, Robt. Mctire, Lazarus (X) Webbs, Jos. Blackwell, W. Kincheloe, John (X) Rector, Will'm. (X) Fitzgarrell.** *Rec*: 26 October 1767, prov. by o. of **Joseph Blackwell, John Rector,** and **William Fitzgarrell**, wits.

Pages 49-52. 26 October 1767. B & S. Between **Reuben Ellett** of Pr. Wm. Co. & **Ruth**, his wife, and **William Smith** ... Ł40 ... 147 a. ... being of tract containing 295 a. which being a Lott sd. Ellett purch. of **Burges Smith, Gent.** ... Lot No. 35 ... cor. to **Strawder** ... to a Road ... to the old line of **Fairfax's.** *Signed*: **Reuben (X) Ellet, Ruth (X) Ellet.** *Wit*: **John Mauzy, John Baley, John Obannon.** *Rec*: 26 October 1767, ack. by grantors.

Pages 52-56. 22 October 1767. Lease. Between **Samuel Luttrill** and **Samuel Wood** ... part of **Richard Luttrill**, dec'd., tract ... by Town Run ... **Mauzy's** line, **William Wright's** line, **Malica Cumming's** and the Cabben Branch ... 70 a. ... for his nat. life and lives of his wife, **Sarah Wood** ... yearly rent of 530 lbs. of Crop Tobacco. *Signed*: **Samuel Luttrell.** *Rec*: 26 October 1767, ack. by **Samuel Luttrell.**

Pages 56-61. 23-24 October 1767. Lease & Release. Between **John Bell, Gent.** & **Frances**, his wife, and **Joseph Neavil, Sr.**, planter ... point on line of **Walter Anderson** ... line of the Hon. **George Wm. Fairfax, Esq.** ... 187 a. ... being on Carters Run ... *Signed*: **John Bell, Frankey Bell.** *Rec*: 16 October 1767, ack. by grantors.

Pages 61-67. 26-27 October 1767. Lease & Release. Between **John Bell, Gent.** and **John Waddle** (also **Waddell**) ... Ł18 ... 375 a. cor. to **John Blowers** ... hiccory in **Darnall's** line ... cor. bet. **Samuel Skinker** and **John Mcguire** ... part of larger grant to Doct. **Alexander Bell.** *Signed*: **John Bell.** *Rec*: 28 October 1767, ack. by **John Bell.**

Pages 67-69. 26 October 1767. B & S. Between **Thomas Bell** & **Elizabeth**, his wife, of Orange Co., Par. of St. Thomas ... and **James**

Bell ... £280 ... tract devised to Thomas Bell by his father **John Bell,** dec'd, being part of a larger tract granted to sd. John Bell ... lies at the lower end of the sd. larger tract bounded by lands of **Richard Henry Lee, John Hitt, Richard Grubbs** and **Wharton Ransdell** and to be divided by a line bet. Thomas and John Bell ... approx. 600 a. ... *Signed*: **Thos. Bell, Eliza. (E) Bell.** *Rec*: 26 October 1767, ack. by grantors.

Pages 69-70. 30 July 1767. Bill of Sale. **John Conyers** to **Martin Pickett** ... £45 ... household furniture and cattle ... *Signed*: **John Conyers.** *Wit*: **Joseph Williams.** *Rec*: 28 October 1767, prov. by o. of wit.

Pages 70-71. 26 October 1767. Bond of **Thomas Marshall,** for sheriff of Fauquier County. *Sec*: **Jeremiah Darnall, James Scott, Jr., William Pickett,** Gent. For: £1000. *Rec*: 26 October 1767, ack. by **Marshall** and Securities.

Pages 71-72. 26 October 1767. Bond of **Thomas Marshall,** appointed Sheriff, 20 October, for performance of duties. *Sec*: **Jeremiah Darnall, James Scott, Jr., William Pickett,** Gent. *Rec*: 26 October 1767, ack. by **Marshall** and securities.

Pages 73-83. 24-25 July 1767. Lease & Release. Between **J a m e s Ewell** of Lan. Co., Gent. & **Mary,** his wife, and **John Adams** and **Zephaniah Turner** of Charles Co., Maryland, Gent. ... tract ... 1,000 a. being part of larger tract containing 7,800 a. ... 5,000 a. of sd. tract was by **James Ball,** late of Lan. Co., dec'd. by his last will, dated 15 July 1754, devised to his dau. **Sinah** and his four grandsons, **Jesse Ball,** son of his dau. **Frances, James Ewell,** son of **Eve Ewell** and **John Seldon** to be equally divided among them ... division by **Bertrand Ewell,** surveyor of Pr. Wm. Co. ... 21 Nov. 1759, made in presence of **John Bell, George Neavill** and **Wharton Ransdell,** Gent., Commr's appointed by Pr. Wm. Court for that purpose ... by lott assigned to said James Ewell and marked by No. 4 on the plat ... main road that leads by **Robert Ashby's** house to that part of the Blue Ridge commonly called Ashbys Gap and known for a cor. tree of Col. **Landon Carter's** land and the end of the 11th line of the aforesaid mountain tract of the aforesd. James Ball ... 1,000 a. ... £250. *Signed*: **James Ewell, Mary Ewell.** *Wit*: **Robert Scott, Dan'l. Payne, William Carr, John Gunnyon, Thomas Chapman, John Riddell.** *Rec*: 27 July 1767, prov. by o. of **Wm. Carr** and **John Gunnyon.** *Wits*: 23 Nov. 1767 by **John Riddell** and **Thomas Chapman.** Certificate of examination of **Mary Ewell.**

Pages 83-88. 20-21 November 1767. Lease & Release. Between **Thomas Stone & Mary,** his wife, and **Thomas James** ... 184 a. ... on the drains of Carters Run, being part of the lands purch. by the sd. Stone of **John Dagg** ... £70. *Signed*: **Thos. (X) Stone, Mary (X) Stone.** *Wit*: **Wm. McClanaham, W. Blackwell.** *Rec*: 23 November 1767, ack. by grantors.

Pages 89-92. 25 July 1767. Bond. **James Ewell** of Lan. Co. and **Jesse Ewell** of Pr. Wm. Co., Gent. and **James Craik** of Charles Co., Maryland, Surgeon, bound to **John Adams** and **Zephaniah Turner** of Charles Co., sd. for the sum of Ł1,500 ... Adams and Turner agreed to purch. Lot No. 5 in division of **James Ball's** estate from **James Ewell, Jr.**, a minor ... they agreed to pay Ł250 for 1,000 a. ... the above James Ewell to cause James Ewell, son of **Eve**, after his 21st birthday to execute deed ... this bond will be invalid thereafter ... *Signed*: **James Ewell, Jesse Ewell, James Craik.** *Wit*: **Robert Scott, Dan'l. Payne, William Carr, John Gunnyon, Thomas Chapman, John Riddell.** *Rec*: 27 July 1767 and 23 November 1767, prov. by o. of wits.

Pages 92-98. 24-25 February 1768. Lease & Release. Between **George Lamkin** and **Sarah**, his wife, of Pr. Wm. Co. and **Daniel Jenifer** of Charles Co., Maryland, Esq. ... Ł100 ... tracts ... 17 a. on which the sd. Lamkins Mill stands ... together with the Mill & 275 a. between Chattin Run & Goose Creek contiguous to the sd. mill 125 a. of which **Lamkin** purch. from **David Robinson** and the remainder from **Thomas Furr** ... the 275 a. was from **Simon Miller** to Lamkin ... "the Robinson & Furr was paid for" ... *Signed*: **G. Lamkin, Sarah Lamkin.** *Wit*: **Margaret Lamkin, Wm. (X) Wilson, Mary (X) Reeves, Wm. (X) Hayne, Chattin Lamkin.** *Rec*: 25 April 1768, ack. by **George Lamkin**.

Pages 98-100. October 1767. B & S. Between **Gavin Lawson** of K. G. Co., Merchant and **Reubin Bramlett**, planter ... Ł80 ... 152 a. ... same mortgaged to Gavin Lawson by **David Darnall** ... and divided from the lands of one **Thomas Carter** by a dividing line as mentioned in Carter's last will and testament ... *Signed*: **Gavin Lawson**. *Rec*: 25 April 1768, ack. by **Lawson**.

Pages 100-103. 21 October 1767. Lease. Betwesn Col. **R. H. Lee** of W'land Co. and **Martin Pickett** ... 108 a. for nat. life of sd. Pickett and lives of **Anne**, his wife and **George Steptoe Blackwell** ... Cattail Branch on road side ... edge of Col. Lee's old field ... yearly rent of Ł 5.8s. *Signed*: **Richard Henry Lee, Martin Pickett.** *Wit*: **James Craig, Jos. Blackwell, Francis Atwell.** *Rec*: 25 April 1768, prov. by o. of wits.

Pages 103-106. 19 January 1768. Cert. of Acknowledgement. From Fauq. Co. Court to **Richard Mitchell, Thomas Bertrand Griffin** and **John Chinn**, Gent. to rec. the ack. of **Alice Smith** to a conveyance to **John Rector** for 168 a. Also to obtain Alice Smith's ack. to deed to **James Ball** for 2,746 acres.

Pages 107-111. 24 August 1767. Lease. Between **Thomas Lord Fairfax** and **William Morgan** ... tract in Manor of Leeds ... 200 a. ... for his nat. life and lives of **Charles Morgan** and **John Morgan** his 2 sons ... yearly rent of 40s. sterling ... *Signed*: **Fairfax**. *Wit*: **H. Brooke, Martin Pickett, Jas. Scott.** *Rec*: 24 May 1768, prov. by o. of wits.

Pages 111-115. 24 August 1767. Lease. Between **Thomas Lord Fairfax** and **Henry Jones** ... tract in Manor of Leeds ... 200 a. ... for his nat. life and lives of **Lermah Jones**, his wife, and **Joseph Jones**, his son ... yearly rent of 40s. sterling ... *Signed*: **Fairfax**. *Wit*: **H. Brooke, Jas. Scott, Martin Pickett**. *Rec*: 24 May 1768, prov. by o. of wits.

Pages 115–118. 1 October 1767. Lease. Between **Thomas Lord Fairfax** and **John Allis** ... tract in Manor of Leeds ... 100 a. ... by a road in the line of **John Hoppers** Lott ... for his nat. life and lives of **Anne**, his wife, and **John Allis, Jr.**, his son ... Yearly rent of 20s. sterling ... *Signed*: **Fairfax**. *Wit*: **Jas. Scott, H. Brooke, Martin Pickett**. *Rec*: 24 May 1768, prov. by o. of wits.

Pages 119–122. 24 August 1767. Lease. Between **Thomas Lord Fairfax** and **Richard Crawley** of Culp. Co. ... tract in Manour of Leeds ... 200 a. ... north side of the Hedgman River ... down the river ... cor. to **Edward Douglas'** lot ... for his nat. life and lives of **Effirella**, his wife, and **M e n o h**, his son ... yearly rent of 40s. sterling ... *Signed*: **Fairfax**. *Wit*: **Jas. Scott, H. Brooke, Martin Pickett**. *Rec*: 24 May 1768, prov. by o. of wits.

Pages 122–126. 24 August 1767. Lease. Between **Thomas Lord Fairfax** and **William Fletcher** ... tract in Manor of Leeds ... cor. to Lot No. 9 ... line of Lot No. 5 ... line of the Lot No. 2 ... cor. of the Laller Lot ... cor. to **Thomas Withers** and the Lot No. 1 ... cor. to Lot No. 1 & 8 ... in the line of No. 9 ... thence with the Laller line ... 200 a. ... for his nat. life and lives of **Elizabeth**, his wife, and **Spencer Fletcher**, his son ... yearly rent of 40s. sterling ... *Signed*: **Fairfax**. *Wit*: **Jas. Scott, H. Brooke, Martin Pickett**. *Rec*: 24 May 1768, prov. by o. of wits.

Pages 127–131. 24 August 1767. Lease. **Thomas Lord Fairfax** and **George Settell** ... tract in Manor of Leeds ... on the Catemount Branch ... 200 a. ... for his nat. life and lives of **Mary**, his wife, and **Thomas Settell**, his son ... yearly rent of 40s. sterling. *Signed*: **Fairfax**. *Wit*: (as above). *Rec*: 24 May 1768, prov. by o. of wits.

Pages 131–137. 23 March 1768. Articles of Agreement. Between **James Scott, Jr.**, and **James Scott**, Clerk, his father, of Pr. Wm. Co., both parties in 1762 agreed to the docking the Intail of sundry lands of the sd. James Scott, Clerk ... and settling other lands in lieu of the same ... (recites petition to Gen'l. Assembly) ... **Alex'r. Scott**, Clerk, dec'd. of Overwharton Par., brother of one and uncle of the other, died possessed of land in Staff., Fx., and Pr. Wm. Cos. (that part now called Fauq.) ... 2,823 a. in Fauq. on Carters Run ... James Scott, Clerk, to make over to James Scott, Jr. the tract of 970 a. ... and the Carters Run Tract ... (The Act was paused in Dec. 1762) but was not exactly what the Scotts meant ... therefore this Article of Agreement ... that James Scott, Jr., nor his heirs, will ever take advantage of any mistakes in the Act of Assembly ... that James Scott, Clerk, is to have his life in his plantation "Westwood" of 2,000 a. in Pr. Wm. Co. ... that James Scott, Clerk, to have a nat. life interest in the Carters Run tract ... that James, Jr. is to make over to his Mother, Mrs. **Sarah**

Scott, wife of James, Clerk, the plantation Westwood in Pr. Wm. Co. for her nat. life ... together with 300 a. annexed ... James, Clerk, to convey in fee simple to James, Jr. the tract of 970 a. whereon he now lives ... and the unseated part of the Carters Run tract, with all slaves on both places ... *Signed*: **James Scott, Jas. Scott, Jr.** *Wit*: **Geo. Graham, John McMillian, Cuth. McMillian, Gustavus Scott.** *Rec*: 24 May 1768, ack. by James Scott, Clerk, and James Scott, Jr.

Page 138. 27 March 1768. Release of Bond. Between **James Scott,** Clerk, and **James Scott, Jr.** ... sd. James Scott, Clerk has performed all the intents of the bond ... made Nov. 1762 ... *Signed*: **Jas. Scott, Jun'r.** *Wit*: **John Mcmillian, Cuth. Mcmillian, Gustavus Scott.** *Rec*: 24 May 1768, ack. by James Scott, Jr.

Pages 139-143. 29 Feb. - 1 March 1768. Leaae & Release. Between **John Duncan, Jr.** and **Dinah**, his wife, and **Thomas Pope** ... 125 a. ... cor. near the main road in **Corbin's** line ... crossing Ratlifs Run ... to the horsepen run ... to the mouth of Smiths Spring Branch ... same purch. by Duncan of **John Darnall** and **Jane**, his wife, and **William Darnall** ... 6 Dec. 1766 ... L60. *Signed*: **John Duncan, Dinah Duncan.** *Wit*: **James Arnold, Thomas (X) Bennett, Edward Newgent, Wm. Sturdy.** *Rec*: 24 May 1768, prov. by o. of Arnold, Bennett and Newgent.

Pages 143-148. 26 March 1768. B & S. Between **James Scott,** Clerk & **Sarah**, his wife, of Pr. Wm. Co. and **James Scott, Jr.** ... son and heir apparent of the sd. James Scott, Clerk ... according to agreement ... 970 a. ... originally granted to a certain **Peter Lehugh** and by him conveyed to **Alexander Scott,** late of Staff. Co., dec'd., Clerk, who devised the same to James Scott, Clerk, In Tail ... cor. to **Mann Page** in the north fork of Cedar Tun ... in a large poison'd field in view of the Mountains ... reserving unto **James Stewart,** his heirs, etc. ... use of the house and Plantation whereon he now lives to be held by him or them under James Scott, Jr., free from the paiment of rent during the life of the sd. James Scott, Clerk. *Signed*: **James Scott, Sarah Scott.** *Wit*: **Geo. Graham, John Mcmillian, Cuth. McMillian, Gustavus Scott.** *Rec*: 24 May 1768, ack. by grantors

Pages 148-151. 23 October 1767. Lease. Between **R. H. Lee** and **Martin Pickett** ... tenement whereon the sd. Picketts storehouse now stands containing 1/2 a. ... during his nat. life and lives of **Anne**, his wife, and **Lucy Pickett**, his daughter ... in line of **John Winn's** lot ... to **Minor Winn's** line ... also another parcel whereon Pickett's dwelling house stands, containing 3 acres including the sd. dwelling house, the garden, outhouses &c ... yearly rent of L3.2s. ... *Signed*: **Richard Henry Lee, Martin Pickett.** *Wit*: **Bennett Price, James Winn, Jos. Blackwell, Jos. Williams.** *Rec*: 25 April 1768, prov. by o. of Joseph Blackwell, Joseph Williams, wits. 24 May 1768, prov. by o. of James Winn.

Pages 151-153. 22 February 1768. B & S. Between **Jacob Hays** & **Katharine**, his wife and **Abraham Dodson** and **William Stamps**, who were apptd. trustees for the Baptist Church ... L1 ... tract ... 1 a. ... part of tract whereon Hays lived and the land the new Meeting House is built upon ... *Signed*: **Jacob Hays, Katey (X) Hays.** *Wit*: **John Hathaway, Robert Sanders.** *Rec*: 24 May 1768, ack. by grantors.

Pages 153-154. 24 May 1768. Apprentice Bond. Bet. **Elijah Nash** and **Robert Sanders,** Carpenter and House Joiner ... **Elijah Nash,** with consent of his gdn. **James Nash** and approval of the Court ... voluntarily ... apprectices to the sd. Sanders to learn his art, Trade or Mistery ... until he arrives to the age of 21 years. *Signed*: **Elijah Nash, Robert Sanders.** *Rec*: 24 May 1768, ack. by parties.

Pages 155-159. 25-26 March 1768. Lease & Release. Between **George Rogers & Elizabeth,** his wife, **William Flourence, Jr.** of Pr. Wm. Co. & Dittingen Par. ... tract on Branches of Broad Run of Occoquan ... granted 18 Nov. 1740 to **George Rogers** ... survey made by **James Thomas, the Younger** ... west side of a Branch falling into the branch called Fornicating Branch, called the Glady Branchand Cor. to the land surveyed for **Valentine Barton** and **John Sias** ... cor. to land surveyed for **Thomas Barton** ... side of Fornicating Branch opposite to land of **Bradly Garner** ... 227 a. ... L50 ... *Signed*: **George Rogers, Betty (B) Rogers.** *Wit*: **John (I) Seirs, Henry Herryford, John Chilton.** *Rec*: 24 May 1768, ack. by **George Rogers.**

Pages 160-166. 27-28 October 1767. Lease & Release. Between **James Ball,** Gent. of Lan. Co. & **Lettice,** his wife, and **Henry Lee,** of Pr. Wm. Co., Gent. ... tract lately purch. by Ball of **Burges Smith,** Gent. ... Cor. hiccory in the line that divides this land from the land of **Burges Ball** ... outward line of the Patent ... including Lots No. 3. 4, 9. ten, 11, 12, 13, 14, 15, 16, 17, 18, 20, 21, & 25 ... 2,746 acres ... L 500 ... *Signed*: **Jas. Ball, Lettice Ball.** *Wit*: **George Glascock, Robt. Downman, Rawleigh Downman, Jr., Alex'r. Bennehan, William (X) Bonis, Thomas Elliott, Ann Blackwell, William Ball, James Blackwell, Rawleigh Chinn, Jesse Ewell.** *Rec*: 24 May 1768, prov. by o. of **Ann Blackwell, William Ball, James Blackwell.**

Pages 166-167. 28 October 1767. Bond. **James Ball** to **Henry Lee** for L1.000 ... to keep the covenants, etc. in the above indenture ... *Signed*: **Jas. Ball.** *Wit*: (all above wits.) *Rec*: 24 May 1768, pro. by o. of **Ann & James Blackwell, William Ball,** wits.

Pages 167-169. 23 June 1768. B & S. Between **Thomas Harrison,** Gent. and **William Harrison** ... L150 ... 520 a. as laid off by **John Moffett** ... part of land Harrison purch. of **John Mercer** lying on the branches of Goose Creek near the Coblers Mountains ... saplin by the road side leading to **Robert Ashby's** ... *Signed*: **Thos. Harrison.** *Wit*: **Betty Quarles, Anne Gillison, Frances Harrison, Elizabeth Bullitt.** *Rec*: 27 June 1768, ack. by **Thomas Harrison.**

Pages 169-175. 14-15 April 1767. Lease & Release. Between **John Barker & Mary,** his wife of Dittingen Par., Pr. Wm. Co. and **James Grinstead** of sd. co. .... 125 a. ... part of greater tract granted to

Joseph Chambers and sold by him to John Dagg, late of Pr. Wm. Co. and by sd. Dagg given to his dau. the sd. M a r y B a r k e r by his last will and testament ... Thomas Stone's tenement ... £18.5s. *Signed*: John Barker, Mary (X) Barker. *Wit*: Wm. Grant, Ben. Bradford, Sam'l. Jackson. *Rec*: 27 July 1767, prov. by o. of William Grant and Samuel Jackson; 27 June 1768, by o. of Benjamin Bradford.

Pages 175-180. 1 September 1767. Lease. Between Thomas Lord Fairfax and John Crimm, Sr. ... tract in Manor of Leeds ... cor. to J o h n R o b i n s o n's lot ... 200 a. during his nat. life and lives of Catherine, his wife, and Jacob Crim, his son ... yearly rent of 40s. sterling. *Signed*: Fairfax. *Wit*: Jas. Scott, H. Brooke, Martin Pickett. *Rec*: 28 June 1768.

Pages 180-183. 1 September 1767. Lease. Between Thomas Lord Fairfax and John Crim, Jr. ... tract in Manor of Leeds ... to the line of his father's lott ... 100 a. ... during his nat. life and lives of P e t e r Crimm and Mary Crimm ... yearly rent of 20s. sterling. *Signed*: Fairfax. *Wit*: Jas. Scott, H. Brooke, Mart'n Pickett. *Rec*: 28 June 1768, prov. by o. of wits.

Pages 183-186. 1 September 1767. Lease. Between Thomas Lord Fairfax and John Crimm, Jr. ... tract in Manor of Leeds ... on west side of Thumb Run cor. to John Crimm, Sr.'s lott ... 100 a. ... for his nat. life and lives of Peter Crimm, his brother and Mary Crim ... yearly rent of 20 s. sterling. *Signed*: Fairfax. *Wit*: Jas. Scott, H. Brooke, Martin Pickett. *Rec*: 28 June 1768, prov. by o. of wits.

Pages 186-188. 14 April 1768. B & S. Between John Henry, Planter & Mary, his wife and John Henry, cousin to sd. John ... £9.10s. ... 80 a. ... part of tract George Henry, father to John Henry bought of Jasper Billings in 1742 ... on Summer duck run ... *Signed*: John (X) Henry, Mary (X) Henry. *Wit*: Wm. Blackwell, Thos. Matthews, Joseph Odor. *Rec*: 27 June 1768, ack. by grantors.

Page 188. 23 April 1767. Receipt. From Thomas Chinn, gdn. of orphans of Chichester Chinn, late of Pr. Wm. Co. to Mr. T h o m a s T h o r n t o n, former gdn., for £4.10s.10d. for the estate of the orphans. *Signed*: Thos. Chinn. *Wit*: Jno. Matthews. *Rec*: 28 June 1768, prov. by o. of John Matthews.

Pages 188-194. 25-27 February 1768. Lease & Release. Bet. J e f f r y Johnson, Jr. and Rachael, his wife, of Cameron Par., Loud. Co. and Peter Cornwell ... tract lying bet. the Pignut ridge and the Rappahannock Mountains ... cor. to Moses Johnson ... oak in Col. Fairfax's line ... 130 a. ... £100 ... *Signed*: Jeffry (J/J/J) Johnson, Rachel Johnson. *Wit*: Simon Triplett, Jas. Lane, William Read. *Rec*: 29 June 1768, ack. by Jeffry Johnson, with Commission to Loud. Court to examine Rachel Johnson.

Pages 194-197. 16 June 1768. Lease. Bet. Francis Hackley and Joseph Odor ... 186 a. ... for his nat. life and the lives of Joseph and

Thomas Odor ... for yearly rent of £4 ... *Signed*: Fran's. Hackley. *Wit*: John Morgan, Thomas Conway, Alex'r. Woodside. *Rec*: 25 July 1768, prov. by o. of wits. *Desc*: ... cor. to Capt. Lott Hackley. This is the first deed to have a plat recorded in the deed book.

Pages 197-199. 29 April 1768. Deed of Gift. Bet. George Hopper of Amherst Co. and Joseph Hopper and Thomas Hopper ... for nat. love and affection for his brothers ... tract whereon their father Blagro Hopper, dec'd. did live ... 377 a. ... except 130 a. which said George hath reserved for himself ... 80 a. taken from the old Patent and 50 a. from the new Patent ... whereon Thomas Matthews now lives and has a right to the sd. 50 a. for and during his life and his wife's ... boundary of 80 a. ... cor. on west side of Jeffrys Branch ... br. of Deep Run ... 50 a. bounded as follows: ... cor. of old patent and Joseph Blackwell ... to be equally divided bet. them. *Signed*: George Hopper. *Wit*: Jos. Blackwell, John Chilton, Thomas Matthews. *Rec*: 25 July 1768, prov. by o. of wits.

Pages 199-202. 29 April 1768. B & S. Bet. George Hopper, Joseph Hopper and Thomas Hopper and Joseph Blackwell ... £50 ... tract of 80 a. ... which was granted to Blagro Hopper by Patent containing 246 a. in 1715. *Signed*: George, Joseph, Thomas Hopper. *Wit*: Thomas Smith, Thos. Matthews, John Smith. *Rec*: 25 July 1768, prov. by o. of wits.

Pages 202-204. 19 July 1768. B & S. Bet. James Scott & Elizabeth, his wife, and William Stamps ... £100 ... 200 a. ... part of tract whereon Scott now lives ... cor. bet. the lott and the lott surveyed for James Stewart ... west side of the Mill Run ... oak on the Church Path ... oak on Cedar Run a cor. of Capt. Scott and William Ransdell. *Signed*: Jas. Scott. *Wit*: John Chilton, Sarah (X) Davis, W. Ellzey. *Rec*: 25 July 1768, ack. by James Scott, Jr.

Page 204. 19 July 1768. Bond. James Scott, Jr. and William Ellzey bond to William Stamps for £500 ... to fulfill the articles in the above deed. *Signed*: Jas. Scott, Jr., William Ellzey. *Wit*: John Shumate, Chas. Morgan, Joseph Holtzclaw. *Rec*: 25 July 1768, ack. by Scott and Ellzey.

Pages 205-211. 27-28 June 1768. Lease & Release. Bet. Joseph Combs and Elizabeth, his wife, of Loud. Co. and Original Young ... part of tract given by Joseph Combs, Sr. to his son Joseph Combs, Jr. (of 1st part) by deed of lease & release rec. in Pr. Wm. Co., 22 Nov. 1756 ... oak on hillside in the dividing line bet. John and Joseph Combs ... cor. to Mr. John Combs ... cor. to Combs and Coppage ... saplin on East side of Brenton Road ... 100 a. ... £40 ... *Signed*: Joseph Combs, Elizabeth Combs. *Wit*: John Lee, Jr., Joseph Barbey, Rich'd. Luttrell, Sinit Young, John Peters, Charles Waller. *Rec*: 25 July 1768, prov. by o. of Lee, Barbey, and Sinnet Young, wits.

Pages 212-213. 26 July 1768. B & S. Bet. Benjamin Settle & Katharine, his wife, and George Settle ... £30 ... tract formerly belonging to **Joseph Settle** and by mortgage to sd. Benjamin Settle ... 132 a. ... north branch of Rappahannock River cor. to **Ralls** ... in **William Settle's** lines ... *Signed*: **Benjamin Settle, Katharine (X) Settle.** *Rec*: 26 July 1768, ack. by grantors.

Pages 214-217. 1 August 1768. Lease. Between **Thomas Lord Fairfax** and **David Darnall** ... tract in Manor of Leeds ... pine in Darnall's own line ... **Mr. Blackwell's** line ... 100 a. ... for his natural life and lives of **Mary**, his wife and **Reubin Bramlett** ... yearly rent of 20s. *Signed:* **Fairfax.** *Wit*: **Jas. Scott, Wm. Ransdell, William Ball, J. Moffett.** *Rec*: 22 Aug. 1768, prov. by oaths of witnesses.

Pages 218-221. 1 July 1768. Lease. Between **Thomas Lord Fairfax** and **Thomas Hickerson** ... tract in Manor of Leeds ... 200 a. ... for his natural life and lives of **Mary**, his wife, and **John Hickerson**, his son ... 40s. sterling, yearly rent. *Signed*: **Fairfax.** *Wit*: as above. *Rec*: 22 August 1768, prov. by oaths of wits.

Pages 222-225. 1 August 1768. Lease. Between **Thomas Lord Fairfax** and **William Grimsley** ... parcel of land in Manor of Leeds ... oak on the Hedgman River corner to **William Day's** lott ... down river ... 100 a. ... during his natural life and lives of **Joannah**, his wife and **Nimrod Grimsley**, his son ... yearly rent of 20s. *Signed*: **Fairfax.** *Wits*: as above. *Rec*: 22 August 1768, prov. by oaths of wits.

Pages 226-230. 1 August 1768. Lease. Between **Thomas Lord Fairfax** and **Daniel Rector** ... tract in Manor of Leeds ... cor. to **Woodyard's** Lott ... to **Scott's** line ... oak marked TF in **Flynn's** lott line ... 175 a. ... for his natural life and lives of **Anne**, his wife and **Conway Rector**, his son ... yearly rent of 35s. *Signed*: **Fairfax.** *Wit*: **Jas. Scott, Wm. Ransdell, William Ball, J. Moffett.** *Rec*: 22 Aug. 1768, prov. by oaths of wits.

Pages 230-234. 1 August 1768. Lease. Between **Thomas Lord Fairfax** and **John Marshall** ... tract in Manor of Leeds ... oak by a branch of Buck Run ... 146 a. ... for his natural life and the lives of **M a r y**, his wife and **Thomas Marshall**, his son ... yearly rent of 29s.2 1/2d. *Signed*: **Fairfax.** *Wit*: as above. *Rec*: 22 Aug. 1768, prov. by oaths of wits.

Pages 234-238. 5 August 1768. Lease. Between **Thomas Lord Fairfax** and **William Day** ... tract in Manor of Leeds ... oak on bank of Hedgman River ... 200 a. ... for his natural life and the lives of **J a n e**, his wife and **John Day**, his son ... 40s. sterling, yearly rent. *Signed*: **Fairfax.** *Wit*: as above. *Rec*: 22 August 1768, prov. by oaths of wits.

Pages 238-242. 1 August 1768. Lease. Between **Thomas Lord Fairfax** and **William Felkins** ... tract in Manor of Leeds ... oak on a hillside near South Run ... 150 a. ... during his natural life and lives of **Sarah**, his wife and **John Felkins**, his son ... yearly rent of 30 shillings, sterling. *Signed*: **Fairfax.** *Wit*: **Jas. Scott, Wm. Ransdell, William Ball, J. Moffett.** *Rec*: 22 Aug. 1768, proved by oaths of witnesses.

Pages 242–246. 1 August 1768. Lease. Between **Thomas Lord Fairfax** and **David Barton** ... tract in Manor of Leeds ... oak in the **Rev'd Mr. Scott's** line, cor. to **Daniel Rector's** lott ... binding on Scott's line and **Woodyard's** line ... 225 a. ... during his natural life and lives of Benjamin Barton and John Barton, his sons ... yearly rent of 45s. *Signed:* Fairfax. *Wit:* as above. *Rec:* 22 Aug. 1768, prov. by o. of wits.

Pages 246–250. 1 August 1768. Lease. Between **Thomas Lord Fairfax** and **Lewis Woodyard** ... tract in Manor of Leeds ... crossing Beaver Dam Branch ... 200 a. ... for his. natural life and lives of **N e s s y**, his wife and **James Woodyard** his brother ... yearly rent of 40s. *Signed:* Fairfax. *Wit:* as above. *Rec:* 22 Aug. 1768, prov. by o. wits.

Pages 250–253. 1 August 1768. Lease. Between **Thomas Lord Fairfax** and **Benjamin Piper** ... tract in Manor of Leeds ... cor. to **John Robinson's** Lott ... 200 a. ... during his natural life and lives of **Winniford**, his wife and **Thomas Bryan Ashby** ... yearly rent of 40s. sterling ... *Signed:* Fairfax. *Wit:* **Jas. Scott, Wm. Ransdell, William Ball, J. Moffett.** *Rec:* 22 Aug. 1768, prov. by oaths of wits.

Pages 254–257. 1 August 1768. Lease. Between **Thomas Lord Fairfax** and **Jacob Utterback** ... tract in Manor of Leeds ... 100 a. ... for his natural life and lives of **Elizabeth**, his wife and **Martin Utterback**, his son ... yearly rent of 20 shillings, sterling. *Signed:* **Fairfax**. *Wit:* as above. *Rec:* 22 Aug. 1768, prov. by oaths of wits.

Pages 257–261. 1 August 1768. Lease. Between **Thomas Lord Fairfax** and **William Dulin** ... parcel in Manor of Leeds ... oaks below the forks of Carter's Run ... Piney Ridge ... 200 a. ... for his nat. life and lives of **Clemance**, his wife and **John Dulin**, his son ... yearly rent of 40 s. *Signed:* **Fairfax**. *Wit:* as above. *Rec:* 22 Aug. 1768, prov. by o. of wits.

Pages 261–265. 24 August 1767. Lease. Between **Thomas Lord Fairfax** and **Simon Heflin** ... parcel of land in Manor of Leeds ... small ridge near drain of Thumb Run ... 200 a. for his nat. life and nat. lives of **Alice Heflin** and **Augustus Heflin**, his son ... yearly rent of 40 s. sterling. *Signed:* **Fairfax**. *Wit:* **James Scott, H. Brooke, Martin Pickett.** *Rec:* 22 Aug. 1768, prov. by o. of wits.

Pages 265–269. 1 September 1767. Lease. Between **Thomas Lord Fairfax** and **John Payne** ... tract in Manor of Leeds ... pines on the west side of the Cobler Ridge ... 100 a. ... for his nat. life and lives of **William** and **Augustine Payne**, his sons ... yearly rent of 20 s. sterling. *Signed:* **Fairfax**. *Wit:* **James Scott, H. Brooke, Martin Pickett.** *Rec:* 22 Aug. 1768, prov. by o. of wits.

Pages 269–273. 14 August 1768. Lease. Between **Thomas Lord Fairfax** and **Elizabeth Marshall** ... tract in Manor of Leeds ... oak in **Barbay's (Barbee)** Lott line ... 150 a. ... for her nat. life and lives of

Sarah Lavel and William Lavel ... yearly rent of 30s. sterling. *Signed*: **Fairfax**. *Wit*: as above. *Rec*: 22 Aug. 1768, prov. by o. of wits.

Pages 273-277. 22 August 1768. Lease & Release. Bet. **Joseph Thomas & Catey**, his wife and **Joseph Holtzclaw** ... 163 a. ... part of a larger tract taken up by **Henry Martin** and **Mary Martin** ... 1729 ... cor. to dividing line between sd. Thomas and Henry Martin ... ₤30 ... *Signed*: **Joseph Thomas, Caty (X) Thomas**. *Rec*: 22 Aug. 1768, acknowledged by grantors.

Pages 277-280. 22 August 1768. B & S. Between **George Henry & Lydia**, his wife and **Richard Lewis** ... ₤9 ... 13 a. part of tract where Henry liveth lying on Rock Land being the southside of Rock Run. *Signed*: **George Henry, Lydey (X) Henry**. *Wit*: **Hugh Brent, Thomas James, James Garner**. *Rec*: 22 Aug. 1768, ack. by grantors.

Pages 280-283. 22 August 1768. B & S. Between **Edward Ball & Elizabeth**, his wife and **Richard Covington** ... 358 a. ... cor. of **Henry Chalpee** ... oak in **Rodham Tulloss'** line ... stump in **Brown's** old field ... cor. of **Col. Carter** ... oak on the Marsh Road ... being reversion of two tracts of land Edward Ball, father of grantor, bought of **Owen Grinnan** and fell to **Edward Ball, Jr.** by the death of his brother, **John Ball's** son, the sd. Edward being heir at law to the said lands ... ₤ 42.10s. ... *Signed*: **Edward Ball, Elizabeth (X) Ball**. *Wit*: **W. Blackwell, John Hopper**. *Rec*: 22 Aug. 1768, ack. by grantors.

Pages 284-286. 12 May 1768. Division. Between **John Adams**, late of Charles Co., Md., now of Fauq. Co., Va. and **Zephenia Turner** of Chas. Co., Md. ... the parties in July 1767, for ₤200, paid to **James Ewell**, obtained a joint Bond from James Ewell, **Dr. James Craik**, and **Jesse Ewell** ... for the conveyance of tract of land of 1,000 a. as soon as James Ewell son of **Eve Ewell** became 21 yrs. of age ... also pur. another lot of 1,000 a. adjoining the former purchase ... this deed is for the purpose of dividing the 1st tract bet. Adams and Turner ... tree on Crooked Run to be marked EA.ZT ... the northern most to belong to John Adams and the southern most half to Z. Turner ... Also, for a div. of the 2nd Tract ... the northern part to Z. Turner and the southern part to John Adams. *Signed*: **John Adams, Zeph. Turner**. *Wit*: **Robert (R) Ashby, John Williams, Hez'h Turner, John Ashby, George Adams, John Thomas Chunn**. *Rec*: 23 Aug. 1768, prov. by o. of **Robert Ashby, Hezekiah Turner**, and **John Ashby**, wits.

Pages 287-288. 13 May 1768. B & S. Between **Zepheniah Turner** of Chas. Co., Md. and **Hezekiah Turner** ... ₤125 ... half of a lott of 1,000 a. from **James Ewell** of Lancaster Co. to sd. Z. Turner and **John Adams** ... 518 a. *Signed*: **Zeph. Turner**. *Wit*: **Robert (R) Ashby, John Adams, John Thomas Chunn, George Adams**. *Rec*: 23 Aug. 1768, prov. by o. of **John Adams, Robert Ashby** and **John Ashby**, wits.

Pages 289-293. 26 July 1768. Deed of Trust. Between **Peter Grant, Gent.** and **Thomas Marshall** and **James Scott, Gent.** ... whereas John

Grant, dec'd. father of sd. Peter, devised to his wife, **Margaret Grant,** the use of a certain tenement on the lower side of Browns Run ... together with Negroes ... during her nat. life ... and after her death one-half of sd. slaves to Peter Grant ... also 1/5th of all household goods and stock to Peter ... and sd. Peter borrowed, with int.. £170 from **Gabriel Jones, Gent.,** for which Marshall and Scott are securities ... sd. Scott also loaned to Peter Grant £85.4s.9d. ... to Marshall & Scott to secure them, as securities on debt to Jones and Scott's debt ... personal property ... real estate ... *Signed*: **P. Grant.** *Wit*: **Wm. Pickett, Thos. Keith, Martin Pickett.** *Rec*: 23 Aug. 1768, prov. by o. of wits.

Pages 293–294. No date. Plat of land whereon Mr. **Samuel Fox** (on Tin Pot Run) lives ... divided into three equal parts, by **Thomas Marshall,** Surveyor of Fauq. Co. Chainmen: **James Arnold, Augustine Jennings, Richard Green, John Lee, Samuel Blackwell.** Report of **Jos. Blackwell, Jeremiah Darnall, Daniel Bradford,** apptd. to assign the wife of **Paul Williams** her Dower ... the Williams's refused to chose one, so the Court gave them Lot No. 1 as their equal third ... 211 a. 2 R. 15 Po. of total of 634 a. 3 R. 15 Po. *Rec*: 23 Aug. 1768, OR

Pages 294–295. 26 July 1768. B & S. Between **Joseph Settle** of Oraine Co., North Carolina, & **Mary,** his wife, and **Benjamin Settle** ... £30 ... tract whereon Joseph Settle formerly lived ... mortgaged, 4 May 1766, to Benj. Settle 130 a. ... devised to sd. Joseph by will of **Isaac Settle,** dec'd. *Signed*: **Joseph Settle, Mary (X) Settle.** *Rec*: 26 July 1768, ack. by grantors.

Pages 295–300. 10 February 1768. B & S. Between **Jesse Ewell** of Pr. Wm. Co. & **Charlotte,** his wife and **James Ewell** of Lan. Co. & **Mary,** his wife and **Robert Scott** of Pr. Wm. Co. ... **Charles Ewell,** dec'd, of Pr. Wm. Co., on 31 Dec. 1741 was granted 2,000 a. situated on branches of Goose Creek in that part of Pr. Wm. Co. now called Fauq. ... surveyed by **John Warner** ... now vested in Jesse & James Ewell in fee simple ... Pr. Wm. Co. Court decreed, 5 June 1766, that they convey to **Thomas Thornton,** late of Pr. Wm. Co., one moiety of the land. T. Thornton requested that the Ewells convey the same to Robert Scott ... sd. Scott has purch. the other moiety for £160 ... entire tract of 2,000 acres ... *Signed*: **Jesse Ewell, Charlotte Ewell, James Ewell, Mary Ewell.** *Wit*: **W. Ellzey, William Carr, John Riddell, Thomas Chapman, William Dobbie.** *Rec*: 25 Apr. 1768 & 26 Sept. 1768, with commission & return of cert. of exam. of **Mary Ewell,** prov. by o. of wits. and ack. by certificate.

Pages 300–304. 7-8 March 1768. Lease & Release. Between **R o b e r t S c o t t** of Pr. Wm. Co. and John Knox of Staff. Co., late Agent and Factor for Messrs. Bogles & Co. ... 2,000 a. ... tract taken up by **Charles Ewell,** dec'd, of Pr. Wm. Co., Gent. by Pattent, 31 Dec. 1741 ... £122 ... *Signed*: **Robert Scott.** *Wit*: **W. Ellzey, Evan Williams, Hugh Brent, Cuth. Bullitt, Foushe Tebbs.** *Rec*: 26 Sept. 1768, ack. by Robert Scott.

Pages 305-306. 8 March 1768. Release of Mortgage. **John Knox** of Staff. Co., whereas **John Gunnyon**, of Pr. Wm. Co. on 27-28 Aug. 1764 conveyed to **Robert Scott** ... by way of mortgage, securing the payment of Ł122 ... two tracts ... on the branches of Chappawamsic ... Pr. Wm. Co. ... purch. by Gunnyon of **Bertrand Ewell** who purch. the same of **John Graham** ... 500 a. ... and one other purch. by Gunnyon of B. Ewell in Fauq. Co. on both sides of Goose Creek ... 500 a. Robert Scott for securing like sum to John Knox, factor ... made over the above mortgage to sd. Knox ... having received other security releases the deeds to the above mentioned lands ... *Signed*: **John Knox**. *Wit*: **W. Ellzey, Evan Williams, Hugh Brent, Cuth. Bullitt, Foushee Tebbs**. *Rec*: 26 Sept. 1768, ack. by Knox.

Pages 306-307. 12 March 1768. B & S. **Robert Scott** to **Jesse Ewell**, all his right to mortgaged lands on Chappawamsic and Goose Creek, cited above ... *Signed*: **Robert Scott**. *Wit*: **John Gunnyon, William Carr, Thomas Chapman, Dan'l. Payne, Rob. Brent, Cumberland Willson, James Muschett**. *Rec*: 26 Sept. 1768, ack. by **Robert Scott**.

Pages 307-312. 24 May 1768. Lease & Release. Between **John Bell** of N'land Co., Gent. & **Frankey**, his wife, and **William Ball** ... 600 a. ... tract left to John Bell by his father, the Rev'd. John Bell ... on north side of Cedar Run ... line dividing this tract from Capt. **Elias Edmonds** ... cor. to Capt. **William Edmonds'** land ... oak in line of Col. **Richard Henry Lee** ... land of Capt. **James Bell** ... Ł1,000 .. *Signed*: **John Bell, Frankey Bell**. *Wit*: **John Hathaway, Francis Atwell, Randolph Spicer, John Wright**. *Rec*: 26 Sept. 1768, prov. by o. of Spicer, Atwell & Wright.

Pages 312-313. 24 May 1768. Bond. **John Bell** of N'land Co., bound to **William Ball** for Ł2,000 ... to keep the covenants, etc. in the above deed. *Signed*: **John Bell**. *Wit*: as above. *Rec*: 26 Sept. 1768, prov. by o. of witnesses.

Pages 313-314. 17 July 1767. Bill of Sale. **Thomas Chinn** ... Ł150 ... paid by **Bennitt Price** and **William Scott** of Pr. Wm. Co. ... slaves, personal estate, livestock ... *Signed*: **Thos. Chinn**. *Wit*: **Willm. Grayson, Robert Scott**. *Rec*: 23 Nov. 1767, prov. by o. of **Robert Scott**.

Pages 314-316. 24 October 1768. B & S. Between **Morias Hansbrough** of Staff. Co., Overwharton Par., Mill Wright, and **J a n e**, his wife, and **John Innas**, Planter, of same Co. and Par. ... Ł20 ... 105 a. ... on Branches of Aquia called Cannons Run ... *Signed*: **M o r r i a s Hansbrough, Jane Hansbrough**. *Rec*: 24 October 1768, ack. by grantors.

Pages 316-318. 17 September 1768. B & S. Between **Charles Waller** (son of Charles Waller) and **Cuthbert Bullitt** of Pr. Wm. Co. ... Ł95 ... tract purch. by Waller's father of **Thomas Hooper** ... on Town Run and Elk Run ... 200 a. + ... to sd. Charles devised by will to his son ...

Signed: **Charles (X) Waller.** *Wit*: **Original Young, John Peters, Jesse Norman, Hugh Norman.** *Rec*: 24 Oct. 1768, acknowledged by grantor.

Pages 318-320. 24 October 1768. B & S. Between **Charles Waller & Jesse Norman** ... in a marriage contract bet. **Charles Waller** and **Hester Norman**, 16 Sept. 1768, Waller agreed to settle on Hester and such issue of sd. marriage five slaves ... sd. marriage took place 28 Sept. 1768, according to the Church of England ceremonies ... therefore ... to Jesse Norman for Ł200 the said slaves ... for the payment of Waller's debts ... then to Hester for her life ... or to Charles for his natural life, if he is the longest liver ... after his death to the children of this marriage ... *Signed*: **Charles (X) Waller.** *Rec*: 24 October 1768, ack. by **Charles Waller.**

Pages 320-324. 21-22 October 1768. Lease & Release. Between **William Kincheloe & Molly**, his wife and **John Kincheloe** ... 183 1/2 a. ... oak in dividing line between **Burgess Smith** and **Burgess Ball** ... a large rock marked **K** ... part of 400 a. sold to William Kincheloe by Burgess Smith, 3 June 1767, part of larger tract granted to **Charles Burgess** by grant, 15 June 1731 ... Ł55.1s. ... *Signed*: **William Kinchiloe, Molly Kinchiloe.** *Wit*: **Jos. Hudnall, Ge. Bennitt, John Fishback.** *Rec*: 24 Oct. 1768, ack. by grantors.

Pages 324-329. 3 October 1768. Lease & Release. Between **John Mercer**, Gent. of Staff. Co. & **Ann**, his wife and **Carr Bailey**, Planter ... 343 a. ... oak in Poisoned Field near the line of Godfrey Ridge ... east side of a small branch of Cedar Run in the line of **Debutts** ... Ł 150 ... *Signed*: **J. Mercer, Anne Mercer.** *Wit*: **Jacob Minter, John Baley, James (Ł) Baley, Mungo Roy Mercer, Yelvn. Peyton.** *Rec*: 24 Oct. 1768, prov. by o. of **John & James Baley, Jacob Minter**, wits.

Pages 329-332. 10 September 1768. B & S. Between **John Lee** of Overwharton Par., Staf. Co. and Richard **Henry Lee** of Cople Par., W'land Co. ... Ł400 ... 4,000 a. ... issuing out of the north branch of Rappahannock River ... Great Run ... falling into sd. River above the second fork thereof and upon the heads of several branches issuing out of the main SW branch of Ocquaquan River ... Cedar Run, Turkey Run and Licking Run and near the foots of the Broken Hills or small mts. in the County of Richmond formerly but now Fauquier ... cor. of a tract taken up by Col. **Rice Hooe** ... opposite to Naked Mt. ... sd. land was granted to the Hon. **Thomas Lee**, Esq., late President of Virginia ... 28 Nov. 1718 ... by Thomas Lee devised In Tail to **R. H. Lee** and sold by R. H. Lee to John Lee ... 10 June last ... *Signed*: **Jno. Lee.** *Wit*: **Thom. Chilton, Charles Chilton, Benjamin Weaver, Alex'r. Balmain, William Aylett Booth, W. Blackwell, Willm. Blackwell, Jr., Joseph Blackwell, Han. Lee.** *Rec*: 24 Oct. 1768, prov. by o. of **William Blackwell, William Blackwell, Jr., Hancock Lee**, wits.

Page 332. 2 August 1768. Bill of Sale. **John Jett**, for Ł27 to **John Morehead** ... Negro girl named Sarah. *Signed*: **John Jett.** *Wit*: **Wil-**

liam Primm, Samuel Morehead, William Morehead. *Rec*: 24 Oct. 1768, ack. by John Jett.

Page 332. 8 August 1768. Assignment. John Morehead, Senr., after my death and my wife's do give the within named girl and her increase to my loving son Samuel Morehead ... *Signed*: John Morehead. *Wit*: John Jett, William Primm, William Morehead. *Rec*: 24 Oct. 1768, prov. by o. of Wm. Prim and John Jett, wits.

Pages 333–334. 24 October 1768. B & S. Between John Rector & Catherine, his wife, and Joseph Robinson ... Ł12 ... part of larger tract taken up 15 June 1731 ... cor. to Perils land ... 45 a. ... *Signed*: John Rector. *Wit*: Charles Chinn, John Hurmont, Jacob Rector. *Rec*: 24 Oct. 1768, ack. by grantor.

Pages 334–335. 26 September 1768 (?). B & S. Between George Settle & Mary, his wife and Thomas, his son, and Thomas Pope ... parcel rented by sd. Settle of Thomas Lord Fairfax ... in Manor of Leeds. *Signed*: George Settle, Mary Settle, Thos. Settle. *Wit*: Jas. Scott, Cuth. M'millian, Cuth't Harrison. *Rec*: 24 Oct. 1768, prov. by o. of wits. Thomas Lord Fairfax's cert. of consent to above transfer, 12 Aug. 1768. *Signed*: Fairfax. *Wit*: J. Moffett, Jas. Scott, Jr., William Ball.

Pages 336–338. 24 October 1768. B & S. Between William Courtney & Mary, his wife, and Richard Lewis of K. G. Co. ... Ł3.15s. ... 37 a. ... part of tract sd. Courtney now lives on ... on Rock Run ... cor. to 2 a. sold Lewis and Jos. Blackwell by John Courtney ... cor. to grant surveyed by John Chilton ... to the mill dam at the Western of the dwelling house ... along the dam to the Tumbling dam ... *Signed*: William (X) Courty. *Wit*: Jos. Blackwell, John Chilton, John (X) Henry. *Rec*: 24 Oct. 1768, ack. by grantor.

Pages 338–341. 23–24 October 1768. Lease & Release. Bet. William Pearle, of Cameron Par., Loud. Co. and John French ... part of larger tract from Burges Smith to Pearl ... cor. to Lot. No. 6 ... cor. to Lots No. 7, 8 ... cor. to Lots no. 4, 8, 9 ... cor. to lot No. 1, 4 ... 180 a. ... Ł40. *Signed*: William (P) Pearle, Martha (X) Pearle. *Wit*: Thom. Marshall, John Allan, Thomas Glascock. *Rec*: 24 October 1768, ack. by grantors.

Pages 341–343. October 1768. Division. Joseph and Thomas Hopper's division of deed of gift from George Hopper. *Wit*: Jos. Blackwell, Thomas (X) Matthews. *Signed*: Jos. (X) Hopper, Thos. (X) Hopper. *Rec*: 24 Oct. 1768, prov. by o. of wits.

Pages 343–345. 24 October 1768. B & S. Between William Stamps & Ann, his wife, and James Scott ... 200 a. ... west side of Mill Run ... oak on the Church path ... oak on Cedar Run a cor. to Capt. James Scott and William Ransdell. *Signed*: William Stamps, Anne Stamps. *Rec*: 25 Oct. 1768, ack. by grantors.

Pages 345-346. 25 October 1768. Lease. Between **James Scott**, Gent. and **William Stamps**, weaver, ... 200 a. ... tract whereon sd. Scott lives ... in the forks of Cedar Run and Mill Run ... bet. lott surveyed for **James Stuart** ... yearly rent of 600 lbs. of good legal and merchantable tobacco and cask to contain same ... for his natural life and lives of **Ann**, his wife and **John Stamps**, his son ... *Signed*: **Jas. Scott**. *Rec*: 25 October 1768, ack. by Scott.

Pages 346-347. 25 October 1768. Bond. **Elizabeth Etherington** bound to **John Etherington** in full sum of L500 ... the sd. Elizabeth gives up to the sd. John and the other children and representatives of John Etherington, her late husband dec'd. any right she has to land, slaves or personal estate of her sd. husband ... *Signed*: **Elizabeth** (E) **Etherington**. *Wit*: **Wm. Grant, Thos. Keith, Elis Edmonds**. *Rec*: 25 Oct. 1768, ack. by Elizabeth Etherington.

Pages 347-348. 25 October 1768. Bond. **John Etherington** to **Elizabeth Etherington** ... L500 ... John gives up any claim to slaves & personal estate possessed by sd. Elizabeth before her marriage to John Etherington, dec'd. father of said John, and obliges the other children to give up any claim ... except one negro man named **Tom** which she claims for her natural life, bought from the estate of **Bryant Obannon**, dec'd and one white horse belonging to est. of John Etherington, dec'd. *Signed*: **John Etherington**. *Wit*: **Wm. Grant, Thos. Keith, Eli's Edmonds**. *Rec*: 25 Oct. 1768, ack. by **John Etherington**.

Pages 348-349. 3 September 1768. Comm'r. to examine **Ann Dodson**. Commission to **Theophilus Lucy, John Wimbish,** and **John Donaldson**, Gent., of Pittsylvania Co., to examine Ann Dodson for her ack. to deed from **George Dodson**, her husband, to **Robert Sanders**. *Ret*: 25 October 1768, OR.

Pages 349-352. 27 September 1768. Lease. Bet. **James Scott**, Gent. and **William Stamps** ... 200 a. for his natural life and lives of **Anne**, his wife and **John Stamps**, his son ... yearly rent of 600 lbs. of tobacco ... *Signed*: **Jas. Scott**. *Wit*: **Archibald Allan, Will. Pickett**. *Rec*: 28 Nov. 1768, ack. by James Scott.

Pages 353-358. 23 August 1768. Lease. Between **Richard Henry Lee** and **Randolph Spiser** ... 196 a. ... for his nat. life ... oak on a branch of Great Run at ye ford on Pickett's Road ... hiccory in **Kittson's** line ... yearly rent of L10.10s.2d. *Signed*: **Richard Henry Lee, Randolph Spicer**. *Wit*: **Jos. Blackwell, Bennitt Price, James Winn, Martin Pickett, John Hathaway**. *Rec*: 28 Nov. 1768, prov. by o. of Hathaway, Winn, and Pickett, wits.

Page 358. 25 October 1768. Bond. **William Wheatley** bound unto **John Wheatly** for L100 ... condition: William to convey 287 a. to John ... being in Culp. Co. ... when done, this bond is void. *Signed*: **William Wheatly**. *Wit*: **John Morehead, Charles (X) Smith**. *Rec*: 28 March 1769, ack. by William Wheatly.

Page 359. 28 March 1769. Bond. **Thomas Marshall**, to collect and receive, from all the Tithables, taxes. For: 30,000 lbs. of tobacco. *Sec*: **Thomas Keith**. *Signed*: **Thomas Marshall, Thomas Keith**. *Rec*: 28 March 1769, ack. by Marshall and Keith.

Pages 360-365. 22 April 1769. Lease & Release. Bet. **Robert Elliston** of K. G. Co. & **Eleanor**, his wife, and **Richard Lewis** of Staf. Co. ... Ł 40 paid by **John Knox** ... tract granted to sd. Elliston, 22 Dec. 1740 ... on easternmost side of Rocky Run, cor. to land of **Giles Travers** and land of **John Courtney** ... **Col. Carter's** line ... cor. to William **Brooks** ... Cool Spring Branch ... 484 a. *Signed*: **Robt. Elliston, Eleanor (X) Elliston**. *Wit*: **James Crap, Thomas James, Jacob Elliston, Joseph (Ł) Williams**. *Rec*: 24 Apr. 1769, prov. by o. of **Thomas James, Joseph Williams, Jacob Elliston**.

Pages 365-367. 24 April 1769. B & S. Between **Thomas Eaves, Jr.** of Pr. Wm. Co. and **Alexander Woodside** ... Ł10 ... 100 a. ... by Aquia road and cor. to the land of Capt. **Augustine Washington** ... to a large stone called Peggs Stone ... *Signed*: **Thomas (X) Eaves**. *Wit*: **W. Blackwell**. *Rec*: 24 April 1769, ack. by grantor.

Pages 367-370. 25 January 1769. B & S. Between **Thomas Hopper & Anne Hopper**, his mother and **Joseph Blackwell** ... Ł40 ... 127 a. ... on the branches of Deep Run ... being part of a tract taken up by patent by **Blagro Hopper**, father of sd Thomas ... cor. to **Joseph Hopper** ... one lot of 85 1/2 a. and another of 40 1/2 a. ... cor. to **Thomas Matthews**. *Signed*: **Thomas Hopper, Anne (o) Hopper**. *Wit*: **W. Blackwell, Charles Chinn, Thomas Matthews, Elizabeth (X) Hopper**. *Rec*: 24 Apr. 1769, pro. by o. of Blackwell, Matthews, and Hopper.

Pages 370-373. 20 January 1769. B & S. Between **James Allan** and **James Hunter**, Gent., surviving exors. of the last will & testament of **John Allan**, late of the Town of Fredericksburg ... merchant ... dec'd ... and **George Yates** and **William Rogers**, acting exors of the last will & testament of **William Conner**, late of Caroline Co., dec'd. ... John Allan was possessed of 119 a. in Pr. Wm. Co. purch. of **Charles Baker** ... near the line of **Joseph Wright** ... cor. to the land of **Thomas Jackman** in the line of **Dr. Bell** ... Watry Mountain ... Allan's will dated 14 March 1750 ... apptd. **William Waller, Archbald McPherson, William Hunter, James Hunter**, James Allan and **Archibald Ingram**, Exors ... who agreed to sell the property to William Conner in his lifetime for Ł24, but before the conveyance could be made, Conner died and by his will apptd. George Yates and William Rogers, Exors. (with others who refused to serve) and the sd. Waller, McPherson, Wm. Hunter and Arch'd Ingram are also since dead ... by decree of the General Court, 11 Oct. 1765, order that the surviving exors. should convey the land to Conner's exors ... *Signed*: **James Allan, James Hunter**. *Wit*: **And. Buchanan, William Allason, James Robinson, Wm. Newton**. *Rec*: 24 April 1769, prov. by o. of **William Newton** and **James Robison** (signed both **Robinson & Robison**).

93

Pages 373–377. 9 February 1769. B & S. Between **Joseph Combs** of Pr. **Wm. Co. & Elizabeth,** his wife, and **Catharine Stark and Jeremiah Stark** ... Ł45 ... 100 a. ... Beg. white oak standing on the side of Brentown Road and in line of **William Coppage** and cor. to the purch. of **Original Young** of the sd. Combs ... saplins on Dorrills Run ... *Signed*: **Joseph Combs, Eliz'a Combs.** *Wit*: **Cuth't Bullitt, Cuth. Harrison, John McMillian, William Carr, Cumberland Willson, Thomas Chapman.** *Rec*: 24 April 1769, with commission to Court of Pr. Wm. to examine **Elizabeth Combs,** prov. by o. of Bullitt, Harrison and Chapman, wits.

Page 378. 24 April 1769. Bill of Sale. **Ephraim Hubbard** for Ł45 ... paid by **John Turner** in behalf of Messrs. **Andrew Cochrane, William Cunninghame & Co.,** Merch'ts. in Glasgow ... Slaves ... a Linnen Handk'r which I now deliver in the name of the whole. *Signed*: **E p h - raim Hubbard.** *Wit*: **Wm. Grant, A. Churchhill.** *Rec*: 24 April 1769, ack. by Hubbard.

Pages 378–382. 5 December 1768. B & S. Between **Thomas Matthews** and **Elizabeth,** his wife, and **James Robison** of Town of Falmouth in Co. of K. G., merchant, Factor and Atty. for **Andrew Cochrane, Wm. Cunninghame, John Murdock, Peter Murdock, Robert Boyle, Alexander Cunninghame, & John Stuart** of City of Glasgow, merchants & partners ... Ł50.12s.6d. ... tract on the branches of Brown Run granted to **John Hudnall** ... 15 Feb. 1725 ... cor. to land of **Henry Chalfee** and parcel surveyed for **Owen Grinnan** ... 253 a. *Signed*: **Thomas Matthews, Elizabeth (o) Matthews.** *Wit*: **Wm. Blackwell, John Barber, William (X) Kesterson.** Memorandum added stating that Matthews is indebted to Cochrane & Co. in the amount of Ł 50.12s.6d. but if the sd. James Robison cannot sell the property for that amount, Matthews shall bind himself to pay the balance. *Rec*: 24 April 1769, ack. by grantors.

Page 383. 13 April 1769. Bill of Sale. **Thomas Maddux, Jr.** farmer, to **John Moffett,** Gent. ... Ł20 ... household furniture, livestock ... *Signed*: **Thomas Maddux, Jr.** *Wit*: **James Neaville, Thomas Smith.** *Rec*: 27 May 1769, prov. by o. of wits.

Pages 384–388. 2 October 1765. Lease. Between **Richard Henry Lee** and **John Hathaway** ... 140 a. ... for his natural life and the lives of **Sarah Hathaway** and **John Hathaway,** his son ... cor. tree of the main tract on Turkey Run ... with a line of **Humphrey Arnold** ... cor. tree of **George Jeffries** ... line of **William Jones** ... yearly rent of Ł5 ... *Signed*: **Richard Henry Lee, John Hathaway.** *Wit*: **Jos. Blackwell, Joseph Blackwell, Randolph Spiser.** *Rec*: 23 May 1769, prov. by o. of wits.

Pages 388–391. 4 November 1768. B & S. Between **Richard Hackley & Elizabeth,** his wife, of Culp. Co. and **Thomas Grinham** ... Ł20 ... 186 a. on Summer duck Run ... part of larger tract taken up by **James Hackley** and by him bequeathed to his son **Joseph Hackley** the aforesd. 186 a. ... sd. Joseph dying without a will, it fell to his heir at law viz. to the sd. Richard, his son ... cor. to **John Eade** ... small branch in **Col. Carter's** line. *Signed*: **Richard Hackly, Elizabeth Hackly.** *Wit*: **David Partlow, James Hackly, William Delany, W. Child, Ambros (X) Arnold, Morris (X) Jacobs.** Receipt wit. by **William (X) Courtney** and signed **Richard Hackley.** *Rec*: 26 June 1769, prov. by o. of **Partlow, James Hackley, Ambrose Arnold, Jacobs,** wits.

Pages 391-392. 24 October 1768. Bond. **Richard Hackley** to **Thomas Grinham** for Ł50 ... in case **Elizabeth** should claim one-third of the above conveyed property. *Rec*: 26 July 1769, prov. by o. of **Francis Hackley** a wit.

Pages 392-395. 25 November 1768. B & S. Bet. **John Crump & Elizabeth,** his wife, **Thomas Harrison** and **Cuthbert Harrison** of Dittingen Par. ... Thomas Harrison of Fauq. Co. and Cuthbert Harrison of Pr. Wm. Co. ... and **Lynaugh Helm** of Pr. Wm. Co. ... confirm to Helm a part of a tract of land he had of Major **William Eustace,** also another tract the sd. Crump had given him by his father, John Crump, the whole containing 752 a. ... **Martin Hardin's** line ... cor. to Turner ... cor. of **Snellings** ... to the Marsh Road ... Ł229.4s. *Signed*: **John Crump, Betty Crump, Thos. Harrison, Cuth't. Harrison.** *Wit*: **W. Blackwell, William Blackwell, Jr., John Kerr, William Pope, Richard Lee, Elizabeth Bullitt.** Receipt signed by John and Betty Crump. *Rec*: 26 June 1769, prov. by o. of **William Blackwell, Wm. Blackwell, Jr., & John Kerr,** wits.

Pages 395-398. 22 June 1769. B & S. Between **Daniel Newlan** and **William Smith** ... 150 a. ... sd. Newland purch. tract of **Thomas Hudnall** of N'land Co. and joining the lands of **Edward West, John Barnes, Michael Marr, Charles Carter, Esq.** and **Robert Embry** it lying on Summer duck Run ... Ł25 ... *Signed*: **Daniel Newlan.** *Wit*: **W. Blackwell, James Blackwell.** *Rec*: 26 June 1769, ack. by grantor.

Pages 398-401. 17 June 1769. B & S. Between **Daniel Newlan** and **Stephen Pritchard** ... Ł75 ... 190 a., lying on Town Run, same Newland purch. of **John Lewis** for 147 a., part of tract granted to **William Hackney,** 11 March 1722 for 247 a. ... sd. 147 a. contained in survey made by Mr. **John Moffett** for Newland together with 43 a. more which was surplus, the said was re-issued by Lord Fairfax 17 Jan. 1764, rec. in N.N. Book J, folio 104 ... in Mr. **Mauzey's** line ... with **Fowk's** line ... **Righly's** line ... *Signed*: **Dan'l. Newlan.** *Wit*: **Original Young, William Blackwell, John Combs, Jr., Thomas Raily, Rodham Tullos.** *Rec*: 26 June 1769, ack. by **Daniel Newlan.**

Pages 401-405. 29 April 1769. B & S. Between **William Churchhill, John Churchhill** and **Armistead Churchhill,** Exors. of Col. Armistead Churchhill and **William Brent** ... Ł38.6s. ... 300 a., more or less ... part of Col. A. Churchhill's Page Land Tract ... oak opposite to the sd. Armistead Churchhill's dwelling house ... line of Mr. Carter ... oak near Licking Run ... *Signed*: **Will Churchhill, John Churchhill, A. Churchhill.** *Wit*: **Churchhill Jones, William Jones, Benj'a.**

Churchhill, Francis Ross, Philip (P) Allensworth. *Rec*: 22 June 1769, prov. by o. of C. Jones, W. Jones, Allensworth, wits.

Pages 405-407. 28 August 1769. B & S. Between **Jacob Hayes** and **Caty**, his wife, and **Humphrey Brooke** ... Ł80 ... 150 a. ... Bounded by lands of **William Hunton, Charles Carter, Robert Sanders, James Baily** and **Humphrey Brooke** ... same purch. by Hayes of **Joseph Dodson**, to whom it was given by his father, **Thomas Dodson**. *Signed*: **Jacob Hayes, Caty (X) Hayes.** *Rec*: 28 Aug. 1769, ack. by grantors.

Pages 407-413. 17 March 1769. Lease. Between **George Washington**, Esq. of Fx. Co. and **John Dyer**, farmer ... 227 a. ... partly in Loud. Co. and partly in Fauq. Co. ... Lott No. 13 ... part of a tract of land granted to **George Carter**, Esq., dec'd. for 3312 a. in Ashby's Bent of the Blue Ridge ... cor. to the Patent (above Fitzhugh's Quarter) ... swampy ground on the Panther Skin Run ... during his nat. life and the lives of his 2 sons: **William** and **Abraham Dyer** ... yearly rent of Ł10 ... *Signed*: **G. Washington, John Dyer.** *Wit*: **Robert Ashby, Jas. Wood, John Glascock, Jr., William Wood, Jr.** *Rec*: 28 Aug. 1769, prov. by o. of wits.

Pages 413-419. 17 March 1769. Lease. Between **George Washington**, Esq. of Fx. Co. and **George Russell**, farmer, ... 106 a. ... Lot No. 8, partly in Loud. & Fauq. Cos. ... cor. to Lot No. 7 ... branch which leads into the Panther Skin run ... for his nat. life and the lives of **Ann**, his wife and **Elizabeth**, their dau. ... yearly rent of Ł4. *Signed*: **G. Washington, George (X) Russell.** *Wit*: **Robert Ashby, Jas. Wood, William Wood, Jr., John Glascock, Jr.** *Rec*: 28 Aug. 1769, prov. by oath of wits.

Pages 419-424. 17 March 1769. Lease. Between **G. Washington**, Esq. of Fx. Co. and **James Wood**, farmer ... 100 a. ... Lott No. 6 ... line to where **Thomas Middleton** corners ... for his life and the lives of **Mary**, his wife and **Henry Machen Wood**, his son ... yearly rent of Ł 5. *Signed*: **G. Washington, James Wood.** *Wit*: **Robert Ashby, William Wood, Jr., John Glascock, Jr., Thomas Loyd.** *Rec*: 28 Aug. 1769, prov. by o. of Ashby, Wood and Glascock.

Pages 424-430. 17 March 1769. Lease. Between **G. Washington** ... and **Deel Clyman** of F'k. Co., Md. ... 160 a. ... Lot No. 19 ... oak in a hollow leading from the Lost Mountain ... cor. to Lott No. 18 ... branch from Lost Mt. to the Panther Skin Run thence up the same to Lot No. 10 ... to Lot No. 9 ... for his nat. life and the lives of **Mary**, his wife and **Philip Clyman**, his son ... yearly rent of Ł5 ... *Signed*: **G. Washington, Deel Clyman.** *Wit*: **Robert Ashby, William Wood, Jr., John Glascock, Jr., Thomas Loyd.** *Rec*: 28 Aug. 1769, prov. by o. of wits.

Pages 430-436. 17 March 1769. Lease. Between **George Washington**, Esq. of Fx. Co. and **Israel Morris**, Farmer, ... 100 a. ... Lot No. 3 ... cor. to Lot No. 2 ... to **James Wood's** line ... for his nat. life the lives of **Lettice**, his wife and **John**, his son ... yearly rent of Ł5. *Signed*: **G.**

Washington, Israel Morris. *Wit*: Robert Ashby, James Wood, William Wood, Jr., John Glascock, Jr. *Rec*: 28 Aug. 1769, prov. by o. of wits.

Pages 436-441. 17 March 1769. Lease. Between G. Washington ... and Thomas Loyd, farmer ... 100 a. ... Lot No. 17 ... cor. to Lot No. 16 ... for his nat. life and the lives of Ann, his wife and Sarah Shears, dau. to Thomas and Sarah Shears ... yearly rent of Ł5. *Signed*: G. Washington, Thomas Loyd. *Wit*: Robert Ashby, John Glascock, Jr., William Wood, Jr. *Rec*: 28 Aug. 1769, prov. by oaths of wits.

Pages 441-447. 17 March 1769. Lease. Between G. Washington ... and Robert Thompson, farmer ... 150 a. ... partly in Fauq. and partly in Loud. Cos. Lot No. 10 ... cor. to Lot No. 8 ... for his nat. life and lives of Daniel McPherson, son of Rich'd. McPherson and Alice Gibson, dau. of Joseph Gibson ... yearly rent of Ł7. *Signed*: G. Washington, Robert (e) Thompson. *Wit*: Robert Ashby, James Wood, William Wood, Jr., John Glascock, Jr. *Rec*: 28 Aug. 1769, prov. by oath of wits.

Pages 447-454. 17 March 1769. Lease. Between G. Washington ... and William Donaldson, farmer ... 100 a. ... Lot No. 15 ... cor. of original Patent and cor. to Lott No. 14 ... to a point bet. the Panther Skin and Cabbin Branch ... for his nat. life and the lives of Mary, his wife and Andrew, his son ... yearly rent of Ł4 ... *Signed*: G. Washington, Wm. Donaldson. *Wit*: Robert Ashby, William Wood, Jr., John Glascock, Jr., Thomas Loyd. *Rec*: 28 Aug. 1769, prov. by oaths of wits.

Pages 454-460. 17 March 1769. Lease. Between G. Washington ... and William Wood of Loud. Co., farmer ... 220 a. ... partly in Loud. & partly in Fauq. Cos. ... Lotts Nos. 11 & 12 ... oak by the Rattlesnake Den, cor. to the Patent and to Lot No. 10 ... to the Pantherskin Run ... small br. which heads up at the end of the Lost Mt. ... for his nat. life and John Wood, his brother and William Young, son to John & Margaret Young ... yearly rent of Ł9. *Signed*: G. Washington, William Wood, Junior. *Wit*: Robert Ashby, Thomas Loyd, John Glascock, Jr., B. Ashby. *Rec*: 28 Aug. 1769, prov. by o. of Robert Ashby, Loyd, Glascock.

Pages 460-465. 17 March 1769. Lease. Between G. Washington ... and John Glasscock, farmer ... 100 a. ... Lot No. 16 ... oak in line of original Patent ... poplar standing in the fork of the Panther Skin run and Cabbin Branch ... cor. to Lot No. 15 ... during his nat. life and the lives of Elizabeth, his wife and Hezekiah, his son ... annual rent of Ł 5. *Signed*: G. Washington, John Glascock, Jr. *Wit*: Robert Ashby, William Wood, Jr., Thomas Loyd. *Rec*: 28 Aug. 1769, prov. by o. of wits.

Pages 465-470. 1-2 July 1769. Lease & Release. Bet. Henry Lee & Lucy, his wife, of Pr. Wm. Co. and Edward Turner ... 180 a. ... Lot No. 21 ... part of tract patented by Charles Burgess, grandfather of Burgess Smith, heir at law to sd. Charles, who sold the same to

James Ball, who sold to Lee ... L45 ... *Signed*: Henry Lee, Lucy Lee. *Wit*: Original Young, Thomas Chapman, John Riddell, John Neilson, Dan'l Payne, Cumberland Wilson. *Rec*: 28 Aug. 1769, prov. by o. of Young, Payne & Wilson, wits.

Pages 470-471. 19 July 1769. Bill of Sale. John Back of Culp. Co. to Joseph Blackwell ... L22.19s.6d. ... horse, etc. at my mill on Rappahannock River. *Signed*: John Back. *Wit*: Samuel Blackwell. *Rec*: 28 Aug. 1769, prov. by o. of Anne Steptoe Lawson and Samuel Blackwell.

Pages 471-472. 13 June 1769. Mortgage. Francis Bronaugh, Planter to James Robison of Falmouth for L241.16s. ... slaves ... Bronaugh to pay to Robison as factor for Cochrane & Cunningham, merchants ... 10 Sept. 1769, with interest ... then this bill of sale shall be null and void. *Signed*: Fra's Bronaugh. *Wit*: James Woodburn, Reginald Graham, William Cunninghame. *Rec*: 28 Aug. 1769, ack. by Bronaugh.

Pages 472-475. 20 June 1769. Lease. Between Thomas Lord Fairfax and Samuel Harris ... tract in Manor of Leeds ... on SW side of Buck run ... cor. to Lots 2, 3, 4 ... 300 a. ... for his nat. life and lives of Martha, his wife and George Harris, his son ... yearly rent of L3 sterling ... *Signed*: Fairfax. *Wit*: Jas. Scott, Jr., William Ransdall, William Ball, J. Moffett. *Rec*: 29 Aug. 1769. prov. by o. of James Scott and Ransdall, wits.

Pages 476-477. 1 Sept. 1769. Bond. William Eustace, who is appointed Sheriff of Fauq. Co. ... 28 Aug. 1769 ... For: L1000. *Sec*: Thomas Marshall and Martin Pickett. *Signed*: Wm. Eustace, Thom Marshall, Martin Pickett. *Rec*: 1 Sept. 1769, ack. by parties. Also another bond for L500 for same.

Pages 477-480. 24-25 Sept. 1769. Lease & Release. Bet. Benjamin Cundiff of Bedford Co. and James Baily ... tract bounded by lands of sd. James Baily, Parnack George, Sarah Dodson & Humphrey Brooke ... 100 a. ... L45. *Signed*: Benjamin Cundiff. *Rec*: 25 Sept. 1769, ack. by grantor.

Pages 480-482. 25 Sept. 1769. B & S. Between Thomas Pope and Ann, his wife and Francis Suddoth of Overwharton Par., Staff. Co. ... L70 ... part of greater tract taken up by Morgan Darnall and by him devised to his son, John Darnall, conveyed by sd. John & Jane his wife and William, his son and heir, to John Duncan, Jr. and by Duncan to Thomas Pope ... near main road in C o r b i n's line ... crossing Ratcliff's Run ... 125 a. *Signed*: Thos. Pope, Ann (X) Pope. *Wit*: Josh'a. Lampton, John Johnson, John Jeffris. *Rec*: 25 Sept. 1769, ack. by grantors.

Page 483. 28 August 1769. Deed of Gift. Between John Woodside, Sr. and John Woodside, Jr., son to sd. Woodside ... for nat. love & affection ... 250 a. 1/3 of the whole plantation now in possession of sd.

Woodside, Sr. *Signed*: **John (X) Woodside, Sen.** *Wit*: **Thom. shall, Wm. Blackwell, Original Young.** *Rec*: 31 Aug. 1769, prₒ.. o. of Marshall & Blackwell.

Pages 484–485. 19 August 1769. Lease. Between **Thomas James** and **Joseph Williams** ... for his nat. life and lives of **Mary**, his wife and Joseph Williams, his son, the younger ... 100 a. ... on Deep Run ... tract James now lives on ... mouth of a branch, lower cor. to a tract of land purch. of **Simon Sallard** ... yearly rent of 600 lbs. tobacco. *Signed*: **Thomas James, Joseph (Ɫ) Williams.** *Wit*: **J. Markham, Jas. Scott, Jr., Thom Marshall.** *Rec*: 28 Aug. 1769, prov. by o. of Marshall & Scott.

Pages 485–490. 17 March 1769. Lease. Between **George Washington,** Esq. of Fx. Co. and **Francis Ballenger** ... 120 a. ... Lott No. 5 ... cor. to Lot No. 4 and in line of Lot No. 3 ... on the side of Lost Mountain ... cor. to Mr. **James Wood** ... for his nat. life and lives of **Edward Ballenger,** his son and **Frances Ballenger,** his dau. ... yearly rent of Ɫ4. *Signed*: **G. Washington, Francis (F) Ballenger.** *Wit*: **James Wood, Jos. Berry, Ezekel (X) Jenkens.** *Rec*: 28 Aug. 1769, prov. by o. of **James Wood.** 25 Sept. 1769, prov. by o. of **Joseph Berry** and **Thomas Hathaway** (sic) witnesses.

Pages 490–495. 17 March 1769. Lease. Between **G. Washington** ... and **James Ballenger** of Fred'k Co., farmer ... 120 a. ... Lot No. 4 ... oak on the west side of Lost Mt. cor. to Lot No. 2 ... cor. to Lott No. 3 ... for his nat. life and lives of **Dorcas,** his wife and **John Ballenger,** his son ... yearly rent of Ɫ4 ... *Signed*: **G. Washington, James Ballenger.** *Wit*: **James Wood, Joseph Berry, Ezeken (X) Jenkins, Thomas Hathaway.** *Rec*: 28 Aug. 1769, prov. by o. of **James Wood.** 25 Sept. 1769, prov. by o. of **Joseph Berry and Thomas Hathaway.**

Pages 495–498. 17 April 1769. Lease. Between **Richard Henry Lee** of W'land Co., Esq. and **Joseph Hudnall, Jr.** ... 111 1/4 a. ... cor. of **Peter Grant's** ... saplin on edge of **Harmon Hitt's** old field ... oak in **Martin Pickett's** line ... during his nat. life and lives of **Mary**, his wife and his son, **R i c h a r d** ... yearly rent of Ɫ6.14s. 2d. *Signed*: **Richard Henry Lee, Jos. Hudnall, Jr.** *Wit*: **Jos. Blackwell, John Smith, Sam'l Blackwell, Original Young, Wm. Blackwell, Jr.** *Rec*: 25 Sept. 1769, prov. by o. of **Joseph & Samuel Blackwell** and **John Smith,** wits.

Pages 498–501. 17 April 1769. Lease. Between **R. H. Lee** ... and **Peter Grant** ... 203 1/4 a. ... cor. of **Martin Pickett** and runs across the Cattail Run ... with **W i n n**'s old line ... up Towzers Branch ... for his nat. life and lives of **Susannah,** his wife and **William Grant** ... yearly rent of Ɫ12.3s.7d. *Signed*: **Richard Henry Lee.** *Wit*: **Jos. Blackwell, John Smith, Sam'l. Blackwell.** *Rec*: 25 Sept. 1769, prov. by o. of wits.

Pages 501–504. 17 April 1769. Lease. Between **R. H. Lee** ... and **William Kittson** ... 86 1/2 a. ... oak in Pickett's line, cor. to **John Smith**

... cor. of **Martin Pickett** and **John Headly** ... cor. to Headly and **Robertson** ... during his nat. life and lives of **Jean**, his wife and **James Burch Kitson** ... yearly rent of ₤?.4s.1d. *Signed*: **R. H. Lee, William Kittson**. *Wit*: **Jos. Blackwell, John Smith, Sam'l Blackwell, Wm. Grant, Wm. Eustace**. *Rec*: 25 Sept. 1769, prov. by o. of Blackwells and Smith.

Pages 504-507. 17 April 1769. Lease. Between **R. H. Lee** ... and **Joseph Bragg** ... 227 a. ... cor. of **Kamper's** lease of Lee on the low grounds of Great Run ... with Price to Great Run ... for his nat. life and lives of his dau. **Elizabeth** and his son, **Isaac** ... yearly rent of ₤ 7.2s.9d. *Signed*: **R. H. Lee, Joseph Bragg**. *Wit*: **Jos. Blackwell, John Smith, Sam'l Blackwell, George (+) Green**. *Rec*: 25 Sept. 1769, prov. by o. of **Blackwells & Smith**.

Pages 510-512. 18 October 1769. B & S. Between **Joshua Tulloss** and **Susannah**, his mother and **Rodham Tullos** ... ₤18 ... 100 a. ... joining the land of **Howson Kenner, Thomas Raley & John Allan**. *Signed*: **Joshua Tullos, Susannah (S) Tullos**. *Wit*: **W. Blackwell**. *Rec*: 23 Oct. 1769, ack. by grantors.

Pages 512-513. 23 October 1769. B & S. Between **Henry Boatman** and **Margaret**, his wife and **John Ball** ... ₤45 ... 100 a. ... oak on east side of a branch of Licking Run ... cor. to **Hooe**'s land. *Signed*: **Henry Boatman, Margaret (X) Boatman**. *Wit*: **H. Brooke, Ch. Simms, W. Underwood**. *Rec*: 23 Oct. 1769, ack. by grantors.

Pages 514-517. 14-15 July 1769. Lease & Release. Bet. **Daniel McCarty** and Sinah, his wife of Fx. Co. and **Richard Chichester** ... 1,000 a. ... allotted to said **Sinah McCarty** as part of a tract of land containing 7,000 a. whereof her father, Col. **James Ball**, died seized upon a survey and div. made 21 Nov. 1759 by **Bertrand Ewell**, Surveyor of Pr. Wm. Co. bet. **Jesse Ball**, Sinah McCarty, **John Selden**, James Ewell and James Ewell, in purs. of an order of Pr. Wm. Co. Court, 29 Nov. 1757 ... ₤200. *Signed*: **Daniel McCarty, Sinah McCarty**. *Wit*: **Jos. Blackwell, Charles Chilton, Stephen Chilton**. *Rec*: 23 Oct. 1769, ack. by grantors.

Pages 517-521. 20-21 Oct. 1769. Lease & Release. Bet. **Richard Chichester & Sarah**, his wife and **Daniel McCarty** of Fx. Co. ... 1,000 a. ... same conveyed to Chichester by Daniel McCarty and wife ... ₤ 200 ... *Signed*: **Richard Chichester, Sarah Chichester**. *Wit*: **Jos. Blackwell, Charles Childton, Stephen Chilton**. *Rec*: 23 Oct. 1769, ack. by grantors.

Page 521. 2 March 1769. Bill of Sale. **Vall. Barton** to **John Waddell** for sum of ₤9.17s. ... household furniture, cropy in **Thomas Legg's** hands ... livestock. *Signed*: **Vall. (B) Barton**. *Wit*: **Peter Carter, Norris Carter**. *Rec*: 23 Oct. 1769, prov. by o. of **Norris Carter**, wit.

Pages 521-522. 27 September 1769. Bill of Sale. **Valentine Barton** to **John Waddell** ... for ₤18.9s.11d. ... furniture ... crops. *Signed*: **Valen-**

tine (B) Barton. *Wit*: **Henry Peyton, Peter Carter.** *Rec*: 23 Oct. 1769, ack. by **Valentine Barton.**

Pages 522–523. 26 February 1770. Bond of Apprentice. Bet. **Henry Bradford** and **John Cooke,** Taylor ... Henry Bradford by consent of his mother, **Mary Nash,** and the approbation of the County Court ... apprentices himself to Cooke, Taylor, to learn his art trade or mistery ... until he arrives at the age of 21. *Signed*: **Henry Bradford, John Cooke.** *Wit*: **William Stamps, Ch. Simms.** *Rec*: 26 Feb. 1770, ack. by **Henry Bradford.**

Pages 523–525. 16 October 1769. B & S. Between **Morgan Darnall** and **John Darnall,** his son, and **Thomas Obannon** ... L35 ... part of tract formerly belonging to **Waugh Darnall** ... 77 a. *Signed*: **John Darnall, Morgan (M) Darnall.** *Wit*: **Joshua Shumate, Augustine Jennings, Jr., James Wright, Augustine Jennings.** *Rec*: 26 Feb. 1770, prov. by o. of **James Wright, Augustine Jennings, Jr. & Sr.**

Pages 525–531. 20–21 December 1769. Lease & Release. Bet. **Richard Grubbs & Susannah,** his wife of Pr. Wm. Co. and **James Stuart** ... 80 a. ... same taken up by Richard Grubbs, 13 July 1727 ... poplar in line of **William Russell** ... hickory in **Barber's** line ... one other tract, patented by Grubb, 26 Feb. 1727/8 ... 107 a. contiguous to the above 80 a. ... oak corner of Russell & Hitt ... cor. to **Bell & Hitt** ... L50 ... *Signed*: **Richard Grubbs, Susannah (X) Grubbs.** *Wit*: **John Chilton, Charles Chilton, Thos. Damkins, Allan Stewart, Richard (X) Grubbs.** *Rec*: 26 Mar. 1770, ack. by grantors.

Pages 531–534. 21–22 December 1769. Lease & Release. Bet. **John Duncan & Elizabeth,** his wife and **Richard Chichester** ... whereon sd. Duncan lately lived ... oak on side of a ridge (where the lands of **William Russell** and the said Richard Chichester corners) ... Main Road ... to **Page** line ... 100 a. ... which was purch. by sd. Duncan of **Joseph Hackney & Sarah,** his wife and **William Duty & Caty,** his wife, 30–31 Oct. 1761 ... L75. *Signed*: **John Duncan, Elizabeth (X) Duncan.** *Wit*: **William Russell, Sr., William Russell, Jr., Jesse Russell, Mary McCarty, Sinah McCarty, James Hathaway.** *Rec*: 26 Mar. 1770, ack. by grantors.

Pages 535–536. 26 March 1770. Bill of Sale. **George Boswell,** Planter, to **James Robison,** of Falmouth, for L200, merchant in behalf of Messrs. **Andrew Cochrane, Wm. Cunninghame & Co.** of Glasgow ... 18 Negroe slaves ... if L200 is paid by 10 Sept. 1770 ... this present Bill of Sale shall become & be utterly void and of no effect. *Signed*: **George Boswell.** *Wit*: **Bennitt Brown, James Woodburn, Maxwell Flynd.** *Rec*: 26 Mar. 1770, ack. by **G. Boswell.**

Pages 536–539. 24 March 1770. Lease. Between **Pearson Chapman** of Charles Co., Md. and **Samuel Grigsby** ... tract on south side of north run of Broad Run of Occoquan ... part of tract granted by Prop., 10 June 1731, for 757 a. to **John Toward** of Staff. Co. ... the sd. demised premises containing 378 1/2 a. the moiety of sd. tract ... during his nat. life and lives of **Aaron Grigsby** his son and **Susannah Grigsby**, his dau. ... yearly rent of Ł10 ... if Aaron Grigsby survives Samuel, he is to pay Ł12.10s. same for Susannah Grigsby, if she survives ... *Signed*: **Pearson Chapman, by J. Moffett,** his Atty. *Rec*: 26 Mar. 1770, ack. by parties.

Pages 539–541. 24 March 1770. Lease. Between **Pearson Chapman** ... and **Samuel Grigsby** ... tract on north side of north run of Broad Run of Occoquan ... 378 1/2 a. being the plantation and adjacent lands thereto whereon the sd. Grigsby now dwelleth ... part of tract to **John Toward** ... by patent, 10 June 1731 ... for his nat. life and lives of **Anne**, his wife and **Talliaferro Grigsby,** his son ... yearly rent of Ł12.10s. (recites terms for changing or adding children). *Signed*: **Pearson Chapman, by J. Moffett,** his atty. *Rec*: 26 Mar. 1770, ack. by **John Moffett & Samuel Grigsby.**

Pages 541–544. 23 December 1769. Lease. Between **Richard Henry Lee** and **Randolph Spicer** ... (Randall Spicer) ... 196 a. ... for his nat. life and lives of **Randolph Spiser,** son to **William Spicer & Levina Bronnen** ... west side of Jones's spring branch ... oak in Kitson's line ... ford on Picketts Road ... yearly rent of Ł10.10s.2d. *Signed*: **Randolph Spiser, Richard Henry Lee.** *Wit*: **Jos. Blackwell, Bennett Price, James Winn.** *Rec*: 26 Mar. 1770, prov. by o. of wits.

Page 545. 27 March 1770. Bond of Apprentice. Between **Spencer Morgan** and **Thomas Hathaway,** Sadler, ... sd. Morgan with consent of his mother, **Elizabeth Mauzey** and the County Court ... apprentices himself to Hathaway ... until he reaches the age of 21 ... *Signed*: **Spencer Morgan, Thos. Hathaway.** *Rec*: 27 Mar. 1770, ack. by parties.

END OF DEED BOOK NO. 3

DEED BOOK NO. 4

1770 - 1772

Page 1. 23 April 1770. Bond of Apprentice. Between **William Strother** and **Robert Sanders**, Carpenter and house joiner .. Strother with approbation of County Court, voluntarily apprentices himself to Sanders .. until he arrives to the age of 21 years. *Signed*: **William Strother, Robert Sanders**. *Rec*: 23 Apr. 1770, ack. by parties.

Pages 2-5. 4 September 1769. Lease. Between **Simon Miller** and **John Davis** .. part of that tract known by the name of Ball's Horsepen Tract .. stake by Siers Road .. 150 a. .. during his nat. life and lives of **Eli Davis** and **Joel Ankram Davis** his sons .. yearly rent of 530 lbs good tobacco and the quit-rents. *Signed*: **Simon Miller, John** (X) **Davis**. *Wit*: **Henry Peyton, James Foley, Joshua Yeates**. *Rec*: 25 Sept. 1769, prov. by o. of Peyton & Yates, wits. 23 Apr. 1770, by o. of Foley, wit.

Pages 5-9. 21 April 1770. B & S. Between **Robert Elliott & Elizabeth**, his wife, of Pr. Wm. Co. and **William Chilton** of W'land Co. .. Ł50 .. 200 a. .. in **Joseph Minter's** line .. is a moiety of 400 a. given by **Robert Vaulx**, Gent. dec'd to **William** and Robert Elliott. *Signed*: **Robert Elliott, Elizabeth Elliott**. *Wit*: **Edward Ransdall, William Stewart, John Crittenden, Charles Chilton, John Chilton**. *Rec*: 23 Apr. 1770, prov. by o. of **Ransdell, Stewart** and **C. Chilton**, wits.

Pages 9-11. 12 October 1769. Lease. Between **James Murray** and **Peter Hodo** of Loud. Co. .. whereon Murray now lives lying on a branch of Elk Run near Brent town .. 188 a. .. for 15 years .. yearly rent of Ł7.10s. *Signed*: **James Murry, Peter Hodo**. *Wit*: **William Vaughan, Joseph Stricklan, Abigail Stricklan, Jane Conway**. *Rec*: 26 Mar. 1770, prov. by o. of **Vaughan & J. Strickland**. 23 Apr. 1770, by o. of **Jane Conway**.

Pages 12-15. 23 April 1770. B & S. Between **Thomas Ayres & Milly**, h. w. and **John Edwards** .. Ł38.10s .. 100 a. of which the sd. Ayres formerly made a deed of gift to the sd. Edwards and since has made over 70 a. more to Edwards .. 170 acres. *Signed*: **Thomas Ayres, Milly Ayres**. *Rec*: 23 Apr. 1770, ack. by grantors. Plat included - near land formerly belonging to **Charles Morgan** .. cor. to **Wm. Settle** .. cor. to sd. Settle, **Augustine Jennings & George Williams** .. in line of **Wm. Williams** .. binding with lands of **Wm.**

Withers, Henry Mauzey & James Withers .. 478 a. Plat of John Edwards' gift and purchase .. Surveyed by Chas. Morgan, 30 Jan. 1770.

Pages 16-18. 20 October 1769. B & S. Between **John Crump & Betty**, h. w. and **Lynaugh Helm** of Pr. Wm. Co. .. £15 .. beg. in the road at Cattail Run in the line of the sd. Helm .. to **Humston**'s line .. to the land of **Martin Hardin** .. 70 a. *Signed*: **John Crump, Betty Crump**. *Wit*: **Wm. Blackwell, Jr., Sam'l Blackwell, W. Blackwell, Francis Hume, Susannah (X) Tullos**. *Rec*: 23 Oct. 1769, prov. by o. of **Wm. Blackwell, Sr.** and **F. Hume**. 23 Apr. 1770, by o. of **Wm. Blackwell, Jr.**

Pages 18-19. 23 April 1770. Bond. **William Eustace**, as collector of levies. For: 100,000 lbs. tobacco. *Sec*: **Martin Pickett**. *Signed*: **W. Eustace, Martin Pickett**. *Rec*: 23 Apr. 1770, ack. by parties.

Page 19: 23 April 1770. Bond. **William Eustace** as collector of all public levies from the Tithables .. For: 19,928 lbs. tob. *Sec*: **Martin Pickett**. *Signed*: **Wm. Eustace, Martin Pickett**. *Rec*: 23 Apr. 1770, ack. by parties.

Pages 20-23. 14 January 1770. B & S. Between **Daniel Feagin & Violety**, h. w. of Loud. Co. and **John Wood** .. £49 .. on north side of Town Run .. 3 poles from **George Crosby**'s 2 cors. .. oak on side of Town Run .. 2 cor. hiccories of Brent Town .. hence with Brent town line .. 130 a. *Signed*: **Daniel Feagins, Violety Feagins**. *Wits*: **John (X) Tullos, James (X) Wood, Peter Wood, John (X) Johnson**. *Rec*: 28 May 1770, prov. by o. of **James & John Wood, John Johnson**, wits.

Pages 23-25. 10 December 1769. Bill of Sale. **William Waite** to the Hon. **John Tayloe** of R'mond Co., Esq. for £500 .. household goods, slaves, livestock .. *Signed*: **William Waite**. *Wit*: **Francis Nash, Thos. Lawson, Thos. Beale, William Griffin**. Rec. with Memorandum by **Thos. Lawson**, agent of **John Tayloe**, to the effect that the slaves were sold at public auction to satisby an execution of Mr. **William Hicks**, merchant, in White Haven agst. Mr. **Wm. Waite** .. 28 May 1770. *Rec*: 28 May 1770, ack. by **William Waite**.

Pages 25-26. 29 March 1770. Deed of Gift. Bet. **Christian Young** and **Original Young** .. nat. love & affection for her son, Original Young .. parcel of land (being part of greater tract) to include house where O. Young now lives .. south side of Negro Run in and near a line of **John Combs** .. oaks standing near a cowhouse .. to the line of **Joseph Combs**'s land .. which the sd. Young purchased .. *Signed*: **Christian (X) Young**. *Wit*: **Thos. Harrison, John Combs, Smith Hansbrough**. *Rec*: 28 May 1770, ack. by **Christian Young**.

Pages 27-32. 23 April 1770. B & S. Between **Thomas Middleton & Anne**, h. w. and **James Wood** .. £43 .. where Wood now lives near Ashby's Gap being part of a tract of 630 a. purch. by Middleton of the Hon. **Robert Burwell, George Washington** and **Fielding Lewis**, Esq'rs.

Trustees apptd. by Act of Assembly to sell certain lands whereof **George Carter**, dec'd, died possessed of .. 1768 .. cor. to Col. George Washington's land .. oak by the Main road and near the Gap Branch .. cor. to the sd. Middleton and the land of **John Young** .. 215 a. *Signed*: **Thomas (X) Middleton, Anne (X) Middleton**. *Wit*: **J. Moffett, Thom Marshall, Daniel Floweree, Daniel Brown, James Nellson**. *Rec*: 28 May 1770, prov. by o. of Moffett, Brown and Nellson, wits.

Pages 32-37. 23 April 1770. B & S. Between **Thomas Middleton & Anne**, h. w. and **John Young** .. Ł40 .. near Ashby's Gap .. part of George Carter dec'd, tract (as above).. poplar on east side of the Blue Ridge & cor. to Carter's orig. survey .. cor. of sd. Middleton and **James Wood** .. 200 a. .. *Signed*: **Thomas (X) Middleton, Anne (X) Middleton**. *Wit*: (as above). *Rec*: 28 May 1770, prov. by o. of **John Moffett, Daniel Brown, James Nellson**, wits.

Pages 37-39. 25 June 1770. Lease. Between **Daniel Bradford** and **John Burdett** .. tract .. in **Waugh Darnall's** line .. 154 a. .. during the life of John Burdett, **Mary Burdett & Frederick Burdett** yearly rent of 530 lbs. tobacco. *Signed*: **Daniel Bradford, John (X) Burdett**. *Wit*: **John Blackwell, Joseph Blackwell, Joseph Smith**. *Rec*: 25 June 1770, ack. by parties.

Pages 39-45. 24-25 May 1769. Between **Martin Pickett & Ann**, h. w. and **George Boswell** .. 2 certain lotts adjacent to each other .. being land purch. of the Exors. of **Armistead Churchill**, Esq., dec'd. .. part of larger tract called Page Land .. surveyed by **Thomas Marshall**, Gent. .. first plot if Lott No. I5 .. 195 a. .. cor. to Lott No. 9 .. The other is lot No. 16 .. cor. to lott no. 15 .. 203 a. .. Ł200. *Signed*: **Martin Pickett, Anne Pickett**. *Rec*: 26 June 1770, ack. by grantors.

Pages 45-48. 26 May 1770. B & S. Between **William Smith & Margaret**, h. w. and **Reubin Elliott** .. Ł40 147 a. part of tract of 295 a. which the sd. Reubin Elliott purch. of Mr. **Burgess Smith**, Gent. .. Lot No. 35 .. on Goose Creek .. cor. to **Strawder** .. to the old line of **Fairfax**. *Signed*: **Wiilliam (X) Smith, Margaret (X) Smith**. *Rec*: 23 July 1770, ack. by grantors.

Pages 48-50. 22 October 1770. Lease. Between **Pearson Chapman** of Charles Co., Md. and **George Kennard**, Planter .. elm in a branch in **Fairfax's** line and cor. to one of **Cornwell's** lotts .. oaks in the Waggon Road .. to **Johnson's** line .. 93 a. .. for 25 years .. yearly rent of 50s. *Signed*: **Pearson Chapman** by J. Moffett his atty., **George Kinnaird**. *Rec*: 22 Oct. 1770, ack. by **John Moffett** and **George Cenard**.

Pages 50-52. 24 September 1770. B & S. Between **Joseph Hitt & Mary**, h. w. and **John Duncan** .. Ł120 .. part of larger tract which Hitt purch. of **Nath'l. Hitt** (or Hilten) .. oak in Capt. **Wm. Russell's** line .. head of a branch of Turkey Run .. line of **Rich'd Grubbs** .. drain falling into the Parsons Branch .. large white oak in the view of the Mountains .. 214 a. *Signed*: **Joseph Hitt, Mary (X) Hitt**. *Wit*: **Thomas**

Marshall, Benjamin Garner, Elvin Porter. *Rec*: 22 Oct. 1770, ack. by grantors.

Pages 52-55. 25 August 1770. B & S. Between **Henry Moffett** and **Hannah**, h. w. of Leeds Parish, Fauq. Co. and **John Moffett** .. Ł1000 .. tract on Carters Run .. beech on east side of sd. run & cor. tree to **Parson Scott** .. oak on foot of Rappahannock Mountain .. 600 a. *Signed*: **Henry Moffett, Hannah** (H) **Moffett**. *Rec*: 22 Oct. 1770 ack. by grantors.

[Note: This is the first deed recorded to mention Leeds Parish, formed from Hamilton Parish in 1769.]

Pages 55-58. 10 March 1770. Lease. Between **William Ellzey**, of Pr. Wm. Co., Atty at Law, and **David Cael**, Planter .. 800 a. ... part of larger tract of 1700 a. which Ellzey purch. of Exors. of **Armistead Churchill**, Esq., dec'd .. to be divided by agreement bet. **Cail** and **Will'm Bryant** and **James Bryant**, being the upper part of the said 1700 a. .. during nat. lives of **Peter Cail, David Cail, Jr., Jacob Cail, John Cail** and **William Cail**, sons of **David Cail** .. yearly rent of Ł15 .. *Signed*: **W. Ellzey, David** (D) **Cail**. *Wit*: **Daniel Payne, Thomas Chapman, William Bryant, Evan Williams, Minor Winn, Original Young, John Churchill, James Bryan, Peter Cail**. *Rec*: 22 Oct. 1770, prov. by o. of **John Churchill, Peter Cail & James Bryantt**, wits.

Pages 58-60. 10 March 1770. Lease. Between **William Ellzey** of Pr. Wm., Atty at Law and **William Bryant** and **James Bryant** .. 900 a. .. part of 1700 a. (as above) .. being lower part of tract .. during nat. lives of sd. William Bryant, James Bryant, **John Bryant, Rachel Bryant**, dau. of sd. Wm. Bryant, and **William Ellzey, Jr.**, son of William Ellzey .. Ł15 yearly rent .. *Signed*: **W. Ellzey, William & James Bryant**. *Wit*: **Daniel Payne, Thomas Chapman, David** (D) **Cail, James Young, Minor Winn, John Churchill, Peter Cail, Evan Williams, Original Young**. *Rec*: 22 October 1770, on o. of **John Churchill, David** and **Peter Cail**.

Pages 61-62. 25 August 1770. B & S. Between **William Blackwell & Elizabeth**, h. w. and **Joshua Tullos** .. Ł25 .. 100 a. ... adjoining lands of sd. Tullos, **Joseph Waugh** and Messre. Cockran & Co., part of tract sd. Blackwell bought of **George Rose**. *Signed*: **W. Blackwell, Eliz'h Blackwell**. *Rec*: 22 October 1770, ack. by grantors.

Pages 62-64. 18 September 1770. Deed of Gift. Bet. **William Blackwell & Elizabeth**, h. w. and **William Blackwell, Jr.**, son of the above .. tract of 733 A. .. part of tract sd. Blackwell pur. of **George Rose** .. Also one other tract .. 50 A. which sd. Blackwell bought of **Thomas Hudnall** of Northumberland Co. .. on Marrs Run, Brown Run & branch of Deep Run. *Signed*: **William Blackwell, Elizabeth Blackwell**. *Rec*: 22 October 1770, ack. by Grantors.

Pages 64-66. 27 August 1770. Lease. Between **Daniel Flowerree** of Leeds Par. and **William Hawkins** of same .. on waters of Goose Creek

.. part of **Charles Burgess** tract .. 102 A. .. for nat. life of sd. Hawkins and lives of **Elizabeth, h. w.** and **Thomas Hawkins,** his son .. for yearly rent of £4, except for first year, which is one Ear of Indian Corn .. *Signed:* **Daniel Flowerree, Will'm (S) Hawkins.** *Rec:* 22 October 1770, ack. by parties.

Pages 66-71. 22 October 1770. B & S. Bet. **John O'Bannon** and **Sarah, h. w.** of Leeds Par. and **James Nelson** .. £70 .. tract .. at the Pignut Ridge .. Beg. at a hic. by the Waggon Road cor. to **Chapman** and **Scott** .. 100 A. *Signed:* **John O'Bannon, Sarah (X) O'Bannon.** *Wit:* **J. Moffett, Jeremiah Darnall, Charles Chinn, William Nelson.** *Rec:* 23 October 1770, ack. by Grantors.

Pages 71-77. 3 October 1770. B & S. Bet. **Elias Edmonds** of Leeds Par., Gent. & **Betty, h. w.** and **William OBannon, Jr.** .. £130 .. in his actual possession .. part of tract granted to Capt. **James Ball,** late of Lan. Co. commonly called the horspen tract .. cor. to **John Blowers &** others .. cor. to Col. **Thos. Harrison's** 400 A. .. 400 A. .. with all houses (except **David Barton's** dwelling house). *Signed:* **Elias Edmonds, Betty Edmonds.** *Wit:* **W. Edmonds, J. Moffett, Wm. Ball, James Thomson.** *Rec:* 23 October 1770, ack. by Grantors.

Pages 77-79. 27 August 1770. Lease. Bet. **Pearson Chapman** of Charles Co., Md. and **James Nelson** of Leeds Par .. 150 A. .. on head waters of Carters Run .. gum in the Rev'd Mr. **Scott's** line of his Carters Run tract and by the sd. Run Road .. Scott's Line of a tract joining to **O'Bannon** and **Toward** .. for his nat. life and **Betty Nelson** his wife .. year rent of £5 ... *Signed:* **Pearson Chapman,** by **John Moffett,** his Atty., **James Nelson.** *Rec:* 23 October 1770, ack. by parties.

Pages 80-82. 27 February 1770. B & S. Bet. **James Syars & Alice, h. w.** and **William Pearle, Jr.** .. £50 .. 122 A. .. on drains of Little River being a tract of land patented by Syars .. cor. to land surveyed for **Barton** .. **Gibson's** cor. .. **Walker's** line .. **Holtzclaw's** line .. *Signed:* **James (E) Syars.** *Wit:* **John Field, Nathaniel Weadon, James Murry.** *Rec:* 23 July 1770, prov. by o. of **John Field & Nathaniel Weadon.** 23 Oct. 1770, prov. by o. of **James Murry.**

Pages 82-85. 22 May 1770. Deed of Gift. Bet. **Henry Peyton** of Pr. Wm. Co. and **Timothy Peyton** of same .. nat. love & affection for his son Timothy .. .. also £20 .. tract in Fauq. Co. on the branches of Little River part of tract granted to **Thomas Thornton** of Lan. Co. & by sd. Thornton devised to his dau., **Anne,** who married sd. Henry Peyton .. cor. to **William Faulin's** land .. to the line of **Agatha Chinn** .. hic. in **Burgesses** line .. cor. to **Faulin** .. 254 A. *Signed:* **Henry Peyton.** *Wit:* **Thomas Marshall.** *Rec:* 23 October 1770.

Pages 85-89. 30 April 1770. Lease. Bet. **Richard Henry Lee,** Esq. of W'land Co. and **Francis Attwell** .. tract in Hamilton Par. .. 200 A. .. cor. to **Randolph Spicer** .. oak in **Kitson's** line and cor. to Spicer .. oak in **Smith's** line .. cor. to **Bradford** .. for his nat. life and the lives of **Mary, h.w.** and of **William Churchill** the son of **Armistead Chur-**

chill .. yearly rent of £12 .. *Signed*: **Richard Henry Lee**. *Wit*: **William Blackwell, Randolph Spicer, George Boswell, Joseph Blackwell, Bennett Price, A. Churchill**. *Rec*: 23 Oct. 1770, prov. by o. of **Joseph Blackwell, William Blackwell** and **Armistead Churchill**.

Pages 89-95. 23-24 March 1769. Lease & release. Bet. **J a m e s Ginstead & Elizabeth**, h. w. of Dittingen Par., Pr. Wm. Co. and **William Duling** .. 125 A. .. £30 .. in Hamilton Par. .. part of larger tract granted to **Joseph Chambers** and conveyed by him to **John Dagg** and by sd. Dagg given to his dau., **Mary Barker** .. **Thomas Stone's** tenement ... *Signed*: **James Grinstead, Elizabeth (X) Grinstead**. *Wit*: **William Ellzey, William Carr, Thomas Chapman, Daniel Payne, John Whitledge, Original Young**. *Rec*: 25 June 1769, prov. by o. of **William Carr, Original Young**. 23 Oct. 1770, prov. by o. of **Thomas Chapman**.

Pages 95-96. 18 June 1770. Quiet Title. Between **Lewis Burwell**, Esq. of James City Co., of 1st part and **Edmund Pendleton** and **Peter Lyons**, Gent. surviving admors. of est. of **John Robinson**, Esq., dec'd. of 2nd part and **Richard Chichester** of 3rd pt. .. tract of land, which Burwell & Robinson had, .. 1192 A. part of a tract called Pageland .. and conveyed to the sd. Chichester by **Warner Lewis, William Churchill, John Churchill** and **Armistead Churchill**, Gent. .. 20 July 1767 .. of which Chichester is now possessed .. that Burwell and Robinson will have no further claim to the estate ... *Signed*: **Lewis Burwell, Edm'd Pendleton, Peter Lyons**. *Wit*: **Thomas Marshall, James Robinson, Henry Field, Jr., James Scott, Jr.** *Rec*: 23 July 1770, prov. by o. of Marshall and Scott. 26 Nov. 1770, proved by o. of **James Robinson**.

Page 97. 25 April 1770. Bill of Sale. **William Ball** to **Martin Pickett** and **Thomas Keith** .. £105 .. three Negroes ... *Signed*: **William Ball**. *Wit*: **William Blackwell**. *Rec*: 26 November 1770, prov. by o. of **Wm. Blackwell**.

Pages 97-98. 27 March 1770. Bill of Sale. **Charles Eskridge** to **James French** of Pr. Wm. Co., planter, for £70 .. two Negroe men slaves. *Signed*: **Chrles. Eskridge**. *Wit*: **Cuth. Bullitt, George Maddox, James Scott, Jr.** *Rec*: 26 Nov. 1770, ack. by **Charles Eskridge**.

Pages 98-103. 28-29 September 1770. Lease & release. Bet. **Francis Whiting** of Fairfax Co., Gent. and **Betty**, h. w. and **James Slaughter** of Culp. Co., Gent. .. tract on Tin Pott Run .. 534 A. .. land sd. Francis Whiting pur. of **Joseph Jones**, Gent. .. except 34 A. which is claimed by a certain **John Duncan** .. £300 .. *Signed*: **Francis Whiting, Betty Whiting**. *Wit*: **Alexander Parker, Jr., Parnack George, Humphrey Brooke**. *Rec*: 26 Nov. 1770, ack. by **Francis Whiting**.

Pages 103-104. 1770. B & S. Bet. **James Slaughter** of Culp. Co. and **John Duncan** .. £24 .. 40 A. .. part of land Slaughter pur. of **Whiting** joining the plantation whereon the sd. Duncan now lives .. *Signed*: **James Slaughter**. *Wit*: **Robert Lawson**. *Rec*: 26 Nov. 1770, ack. by Slaughter.

Pages 104–106. 28 March 1770. Bill of Sale. Bet. **Charles Eskridge & Elizabeth Salkield** of 1st part and **William Carr Lane, Martin Pickett** and **Cuthbert Bullett** .. Ł224.14s. .. slaves, livestock, household furniture .. *Signed*: **Charles Eskridge, Eliz'h (X) Salkield.** *Wit*: **John Turner, And'r Buckhanan, William Grant.** The slaves were taken in Exec. to satisfy **Henry Ellison,** Esq. of Fx. Co. agst. **Charles Eskridge,** and the Sheriff refused to sell them unless I (**William Templeman,** atty for Ellison) would oblidge myself to make good title .. **W. C. Lane, Martin Pickett** and **C. Bullett** have become security for Ł224.14s. .. bond to stand for their bonds .. in that case I am to deduct out of their Bonds so much of the Slaves Effects as the sd. Eskridge and Salkeld cannot make a sufficient title to .. if it sells for less than will pay the said Bonds. *Signed*: **William Templeman.** *Ret*: 26 Nov. 1770, ack. by **Charles Eskridge** and o. of **Andrew Buckhannon** as to **Elizabeth Salkild.**

Pages 106–108. 26 November 1770. B & S. Bet. **Jeremiah Darnall** and **John Blackwell,** Gent., Church wardens of Ham. Par. and **Martin Pickett** of Ham. Par. .. whereas by Act of Assembly the Par. of Hamilton in Fauq. and Pr. Wm. was divided it was ordered that the Glebe should be sold .. wardens advertised the same .. sold at public auction .. Martin Pickett was the highest bidder .. Ł200.5s. .. The Glebe of 240 A. .. northeast side of Licking Run .. cor. in **Carter's** Line .. *Signed*: **Jeremiah Darnall, John Blackwell.** *Rec*: 26 Nov. 1770, ack. by **Jeremiah Darnall & John Blackwell.**

Pages 108–110. 26 November 1770. B & S. Bet. **Martin Pickett** of Ham. Par. and **Jeremiah Darnall** .. Ł200.5s. .. 240 A. .. is the land commonly called the glebe land .. *Signed*: **Martin Pickett.** *Rec*: 26 Nov. 1770, ack. by **Martin Pickett.**

Pages 110–111. 26 November 1770. B & S. Bet. **James Slaughter** of Culp. Co. and **John Blackwell** .. Ł160 .. part of that Tract .. on the north side of Tinn Pott Run .. 200 A. adjoining the plantation whereon the sd. Blackwell now lives .. part of tract to Slaughter from **Francis Whiting** .. *Signed*: **James Slaughter.** *Rec*: 26 Nov. 1770, ack. by grantor.

Pages 111–113. 30 June 1770. Mortgage. Bet. **David Barton** and **Bryan Bruin** of F'rick Co. .. Ł124 .. tract of leased land in his Lordships Manor .. granted for lives of sd. David Barton and **Benjamin** and **John Barton,** his sons .. same on which David Barton's Mill stands .. if Barton pays Bruin the sum of Ł31 before 1 July 1771 and like sum by 1 July 1772 .. and same by 1 July '73 and 1 July 1774 .. this Indenture to be void .. *Signed*: **David Barton.** *Wit*: **Robert (R) Ashby, Alex. White, John Suthard.** *Rec*: 26 Nov. 1770, prov. by o. of wits.

Pages 114–119. 26 November 1770. Lease & release. Bet. **Alice Conyers,** the wife of **John Conyers,** dec'd., John Conyers and **William Conyers** and **Peggy,** h. w. and **Samuel Porter** .. hic. on the lower most side of the upper fork of Licking Run .. cor. to **Mr. Withers** .. dividing cor. bet. John Conyers, dec'd. and Samuel Conyers .. dividing cor. standing in the line of Col. **R i c e   H o o e** .. Cor. to Hoe's land and the land of Col. **Thomas Lee** .. 348 A. .. which sd. land was divided to sd. Alice Conyers wife of John Conyers, dec'd, John and William Conyers by their Grandfather **Denis Conyers**, dec'd .. Ł140 .. *Signed*: **Alice (L) Conyers, John (X) Conyers, William (X) Conyers, Peggy (X) Conyers**. *Rec*: 27 Nov. 1770, ack. by grantors.

Pages 119–123. 27 November 1770. B & S. Bet. **William Conyers** and **Peggy, h. w.** and **William Sutten** .. 298 A. .. cor. to land of **John D a g g** .. oak on the lower side the mouth of a branch falling in a br. of Carters Run cor. to sd. Dagg .. cor. to the land of Capt. **T h o m a s Carter** .. to Carters Run .. *Signed*: **William (X) Conyers, Peggy (X) Conyers**. *Rec*: 27 Nov. 1770, ack. by grantors.

Pages 123–127. 24–25 November 1770. Lease & release. Bet. **Martin Pickett** of Ham. Par. and **Ann, h. w.** and **George Boswell** .. two lotts of land adjacent to each other, sd. Pickett pur. of Exors. of **A r mistead Churchill**, dec'd., part of large tract commonly called Page Land .. surveyed by **Thomas Marshall, Gent.** Lott No. 15, 195 A .. Lott No. 16, 203 A. Ł200 *Signed*: **Martin Pickett, Anne Pickett**. *Rec*: 27 Nov. 1770, ack. by grantors.

Pages 127–128. 26 November 1770. Bill of Sale. **Charles Eskridge** to **Hector Ross** of Fx. Co. on behalf of **George Oswald, David Dalyell & Co.** of Great Britain .. Ł65 .. Negroes and horse ... *Signed*: **C h a s. Eskridge**. *Wit*: **Joseph Blackwell, Thomas Keith**. *Rec*: 28 Nov. 1770, ack. by **Charles Eskridge**.

Pages 128–130. 22 October 1770. B & S. Bet. **Daniel dela Shumate & Mary, h. w.** of Pr. Wm. Co. and **John dela Shumate** .. Ł30 .. 100 A. .. adj. the lands of **John Kerr, Nicholas George, John Neilson** and the above sd. John dela Shumate .. which said 100 A. was given to the sd. Daniel by his father, John dela Shumate .. taken up by **William Allen** then Staff. Co. and conveyed by sd. Allen to sd. Shumate, father of John dela Shumate. *Signed*: **Daniel (X) Dela Shumate, Mary (X) Dela Shumate**. *Wit*: **W. Blackwell**. *Rec*: 25 March 1771. ack. by grantors.

Pages 130–132. 23 June 1770. B & S. Between **William Eves**, of Pr. Wm. Co. and **William Kesterson** of Ham. Par. .. Ł8 .. 100 A. .. on branch of Deep Run .. bounded on a br. of Deep Run called Middle Branch & on lines of Mr. **Joseph Blackwell** .. *Signed*: **William Eves**. *Wit*: **Joseph Blackwell, Thomas Smith, John Smith**. *Rec*: 25 March 1771, prov. by o. of wits.

Pages 132–135. 25 September 1770. B & S. Bet. **James Ball, Gent.** of Lan. Co. and **John Adams**, Planter .. Ł400 .. residue of tract granted to Capt. James Ball (father of sd. James Ball) by deed from Proprietor, 1 July 1731 for 7,883 A. .. 690 A. or thereabouts of which was taken away by an elder grant to **Charles Burgess**, Gent. and 5,000 A. more thereof was devised by sd. Capt. James Ball unto his dau.

Sineh and four grandchildren, **Jesse Ball, John Selden, James Ewell**
and **James Ewell** .. remainder 2,193 A. was devised to Capt. Ball's
son, **James Ball** .. sd. 2,193 A. (+/-) to John Adams .. *Signed*: **James
Ball**. *Wit*: **Thomas Smith, Hez'h Turner, John Thos. Chunn, Thomas
Vowles, Joseph Blackwell**. *Rec*: 25 March 1771, proved by o. of **Thos.
Smith, J. T. Chunn** and **Joseph Blackwell**. Also recorded is a bond of
James Ball to **John Adams** to perform all the covenants and agree-
ments in above Indenture.

Pages 135-139. 8 October 1770. B & S. Bet. **Richard Henry Lee**,
Esq. of Cople Par., W'land Co. and **Anne**, h. w. and **William Edmonds**
of Leeds Par., Gent. .. Lee by lease & release .. 19, 20 June 1759, for
Ł230 .. 514 A. 2 R. 2 P. .. near Main road to Winchester .. stone
marked TL near Capt. **Elias Edmonds'** plantation .. part of larger tract
containing 4,200 A. devised by the Hon. **Thomas Lee** dec'd to sd. **R.
H. Lee** .. the 4,200 A. was entailed which R. H. had docked .. on 13
June 1768 he conveyed the same to **John Lee** of Staff. Co. Gent. and
on 10 Sept. 1768 sd. John Lee convyed the same to R. H. Lee in fee
simple .. to **William Edmonds** in Fee Simple .. *Signed*: **Richard
Henry Lee**. *Wit*: **Martin Pickett, John Likly, James Craig, Joseph
Blackwell, James Thomson, Martin Pickett**. *Rec*: 25 March 1771,
prov. by o. of **Blackwell, Thomson,** and **Pickett** and commission for
taking ack. and examination of **Ann Lee**.

Pages 139-141. 29 November 1770. B & S. Bet. **Waugh Darnall,
Morgan Darnall & Sarah**, h. w. of Ham. Par. and **Nathaniel Dodd** .. Ł
81.10s .. 163 A. .. cor. to **Jonas Williams** .. *Signed*: **Waugh Darnall,
Morgain (MD) Darnall, Sarah (X) Darnall**. *Wit*: **Paul Williams,
James Wright, William Shumate, Wm. Pinckard, Joseph Wheatley,
James Wheatley**. *Rec*: 25 March 1771, prov. by o. of **Wm. Pinkard,
James Wheatley** and **Jos. Wheatley**, wits.

Pages 141-142. 23 September 1770. Deed of Gift. **Robert Lovell** for
natural love and affection for my dau. **Elizabeth Lovell** .. one Negroe
girl .. *Signed*: **Robert Lovell**. *Wit*: **Thomas Marshall, John Ashby,
Robert Fristoe**. *Rec*: 25 March 1771, prov. by o. of **Marshall &
Ashby**.

Pages 142-146. 22-23 March 1771. Lease & release. Bet. **Burges(s)
Ball**, Gent. of Lan. Co. & **Mary**, h. w. and **James Young** and **John
Thornberry**, planter .. all his moeity of a tract .. upon Kettle Run &
for the greater part in Fauq. Co. .. Beg. where the Line of the whole
tract crosses **Burwell**'s road .. to **Brenton** line .. to a cor. of
Harrison's land .. edge of **Samuel Thornberry**'s old field .. oak near
James Young's fence .. on a track of the Walnut Branch .. bet. Lick
and Kettle run .. said moiety containing 2,074 A. (+/-) .. Ł710 ..
Signed: **Burges Ball**. *Rec*: 26 March 1771, ack. by **Burgess Ball**.
N.B. Some part of the above premises are incumbered with the Curte
Sy of Colo. **James Ball** in the same this Ind. witnesseth that no more
is intended to be conveyed thereby than the Reversion in such part so
Incumbered.

Pages 146-147. 26 March 1771. Bond of Apprentice. Bet. **John Davis** and **John Headley** .. sd. Davis of his own free will and with the approbation of the County Court .. binds himself to Headley .. aged 18 .. until he is 21 years old .. to be taught the trade of a Blacksmith ..Headley to give Davis 6 mos. schooling. *Signed*: **John** (X) **Davis**, **John** (X) **Headley**. *Rec*: 26 March 1771, ack. by parties.

Pages 147-151. 27 December 1770. B & S. Bet. **Burges Ball**, Gent. of Lan. Co. and **Mary**, h. w. and **John Rector**, planter .. Ł1940.12s. .. tract near Goose Creek, being part of a large tract formerly granted to **Charles Burgess**, Gent. late of Lan. Co. bounded on the dividing line made bet. the sd. **Burges Ball** and **Burges Smith**, the line run for **Thomas Chattin** is part of this Tract the Line run by **William West** now held by **John Anderson** and on the land of **Elias Edmonds**, formerly **Simon Miller**, containing by est. 4,874 A. .. in Par. of Leeds. *Signed*: **Burges Ball, Mary Ball**. *Wit*: **Henry Rector, James Selden, George Carter, Jesse Ball, John Squiers**. Commission to examine **Mary Ball** and take her ack. of above deed. *Rec*: 26 March 1771, ack. by **Burges Ball**.

Pages 151-152. 1771. B & S. Bet. **Thomas Jackman** and **Elias Edmonds** .. 4,000 lbs. tobacco .. tract .. 128 A. .. part of tract granted to sd. Jackman by Proprietor .. 1 Dec. 1742 .. Beg. at small hic. in **Charles Baker's** yard, now **James Nelson's** .. hic. on a mt. thence along mt. .. in a line of the land of **Joseph Wright** (now the sd. Edmonds) .. oak on side of Cedar Run .. cor. to sd. Wright and Col. Thos. Lee and the Rev. **John Bell** .. trees in line of Doctor **Alexander Bell** (now **Richard Taylor**) .. *Signed*: **Thomas Jackman**. *Wit*: **Wm. Ransdell, Jos. Taylor, Jno. Cooke**. *Rec*: 26 March 1771. ack. by Jackman.

Pages 152-154. 16 April 1771. B & S. Bet. **Landon & Charles Carter**, Exors. of the last will & testament of Charles Carter of K. George Co., Esq. dec'd .. and **James McCanahan** of Lunenberg Par., R'mond Co., planter .. Charles Carter dec'd was possessed of sundry tracts in fee tail .. one on Kettle Run in Fauq. Co. .. 190 A. .. he was indebted to sundry person in Great Britain and this Colony .. in order to discharge sd. debts .. Exors. applied to Gen'l. Assembly to dock the intail, which was done by Act .. Ł95 .. part of Kettle Run Tract .. corner to **Joseph Hedger** .. 190 A. .. *Signed*: **Landon Carter, Charles Carter**. *Rec*: 22 April 1771, prov. by o. of **William McClanaham, Henry Asbury, Peter Moore**, wits.

Pages 154-158. 22 April 1771. Lease & release. Bet. **Josiah Holtzclaw & Susanna**, h. w. and **Richard Chichester, John Hathaway, John Wright, Jr., James Brient** and **Peter Kamper, Jr.**, Trustees for the Presbyterian Society in the Par. of Hambleton .. 20s. .. tract .. 1 A. .. whereon there is to be built a house for the only use of Divine worship for the benefit of the said Society .. *Signed*: **Josiah Holtzclaw, Susanna** (X) **Holtzclaw**. *Rec*: 22 April 1771, ack. by grantors.

Pages 158-160. 22 April 1771. B & S. Bet. James Duff & Sarah, h. w. of Ham. Par. and John Ball of same .. L40 .. 100 A. .. on branch of Licking Run .. *Signed*: James Duff, Sarah (X) Duff. *Rec*: 22 April 1771, ack. by James Duff & Sarah.

Pages 160-162. 5 January 1771. B & S. Bet. Zacharias Lewis & Mary, h. w. and Alexander Morehead .. L100 .. cor. bet. sd. land and land of Joseph Martin .. standing in Carters line .. sm. br. of Licking Run, ano. of Carter's cors .. 277 A. *Signed*: Zacharias Lewis, Mary Lewis. *Wit*: Charity Brent, George Brent, Daniel Shumate. *Rec*: 22 April 1771, ack. by grantors.

Pages 163-165. 22 April 1771. B & S. Bet. William Grant & Judith, h. w. and John Thomas and Margret Thomas .. L150 .. tract .. on the br. of Broad Run .. cor. on the Bisket Mt. ..north East of the Piny Mt. .. stake on the Wolf Trap Br. .. 353 A. .. moiety of larger tract pur. by sd. Grant of John Madison of Augusta County .. *Signed*: William Grant. *Rec*: 22 April 1771, ack. by William Grant, Gent.

Pages 165-166. 23 April 1771. Bond. John Wright, Jr., for Surveyor of Fauq. Co., by Commission of the President and Masters of the College of William and Mary, 17 April 1771 .. For: L5,000. *Sec*: Cuthbert Bullitt, William Blackwell, Jr. *Signed*: John Wright, William Blackwell, Jr., Cuth. Bullitt. *Rec*: 23 April 1771, ack. by parties.

Pages 166-167. 27 April 1771. Release of Mort. Bet. Nathaniel Harrison, William Fitzhugh of Somerset, Staff. Co., William Churchill of Middlesex Co., Gent. and John Churchill, Gent. .. parties of 1st part, became securities of party of 2nd part .. 19 June 1765 .. in 2 bonds .. one payable to Armistead Lightfoot, Esq. for L786.14s. the other payable to Gabriel Jones, Gent. of Augusta Co. .. L600 .. to secure sd. securities .. mort. to them .. tract .. pur. of John Robinson and Lewis Burwell, Esqrs. .. 1,366 A. .. same released to John Churchill. *Signed*: Natha. Harrison, William Fitzhugh, Will. Churchill. *Wit*: A. Churchill, Joseph Hedger, George Nicholson, Jr. *Rec*: 27 May 1771, prov. by o. of Armistead Churchill and George Nicholson, Jr.

Pages 167-171. 6 May 1771. B & S. Indenture Quinquepartite .. Bet. William Churchill and Armistead Churchill, Gent., Exors of Armistead Churchill late of Middlesex Co., dec'd of 1st part, Lewis Burwell, Esq. of James City Co., 2nd pt., Edmond Pendleton of Caroline Co. and Peter Lyons of Hanover Co., Gent. .. sur. admrs. of John Robinson, of K. & Q. Co. dec'd of 3rd pt. .. Warner Lewis of Glou. Co., Esq. of 4th pt. and John Churchill, Gent. of Fauq. of the 5th part .. Armistead Churchill, dec'd on 17 June 1757 gave a mortgage whereby he B & S to sd. Robinson and Lewis Burwell all of that tract .. by the name of Pageland .. 10,600 A. (+/-) .. 73 slaves, 13 horses, 62 cattle, 90 hogs, 29 sheep .. Robinson and Burwell brought their Bill in Chan. in Fauq. Co. agst. Exors. of A. Churchill, Hannah Churchill, widow, John Robinson & Mary, h. w., John Gordon & Lucy, h. w., Hannah Churchill, Priscilla Spann, widow, Benj. Churchill, Judith

Churchill & Betty Churchill .. on 28 Feb. 1765 .. the Defts. Hannah and Wm. Churchill were apptd. gdns. of Judith & Betty Churchill, infants .. Pageland to be sold to pay certain mortgages .. for £655 .. pd. by John Churchill .. tract cont. 1,582 A. .. and as shown by platt made by **Thomas Marshall** as Lotts No. 42, 43, 44, 45, & 46 .. on Cedar Run .. cor. to **Col. Fitzhugh** .. running with the Carolina or Teisy [sic] Road ... *Signed*: **Will. Churchill, A. Churchill, Lewis Burwell, Pet'r. Lyons, Edm'd. Pendleton, Warner Lewis.** *Wit*: **Benjamin Churchill, George Nicholson, Jr., Joseph Hedger.** Receipt to **John Churchill**. *Rec*: 27 May 1771, prov. by o. of **Benjamin Churchill, Nicholson** and by affirmation of **Joseph Hedger**, wits.

Pages 171-174. 27-28 May 1771. Lease & release. Bet. **William Triplett & Mary, h. w.** and **Arthur Moreson & David Cheves** of K. Geo. Co. .. tract on Licking Run .. same pur. from **Daniel Hogains** .. 410 A. .. £60 .. *Signed*: **William Triplett.** *Wit*: **William Blackwell, A. Buchanan, Joseph Blackwell, Jr., Benj'a. Snelling.** *Rec*: 29 May 1771, prov. by o. of wits.

Pages 174-176. 26 May 1771. B & S. Bet. **John Churchhill**, Gent. & **Sarah, h. w.** and **Richard Chichester** .. £791 .. 791 A .. bank of Cedar Run .. in the line of Acre of Land granted to **George Neavil** .. part of Pageland .. John Churchill pur. of **John Robinson** and **Lewis Burwell**, Esqrs., Exor. of **Armistead Churchill**. *Signed*: **John Churchhill, Sarah Churchill.** *Wit*: **William Edmonds, William Ball, Martin Pickett, Jeremiah Darnall, Humphrey Brooke.** *Rec*: 24 June 1771, ack. by grantors.

Pages 176-178. 29 May 1771. B & S. Bet. **John Churchill**, Gent. & **Sarah, h. w.** and **Francis Whiting** of Fx. Co., Gent. .. £791 .. 820 1/2 A. .. bank of Cedar Run .. near Carolina or Ousy [sic] Road .. in line of an acre of Land granted to Capt. **George Neavil** by order of Fauq. Court ... *Signed*: **John Churchill, Sarah Churchhill.** *Wit*: **A. Churchill, Jeremiah Darnall, Richard Chichester, H. Brooke.** *Rec*: 24 June 1771, ack. by grantors.

Pages 178-180. 22 April 1771. B & S. Bet. **Peter Hitt, Jacob Wever, Peter Kemper** of Fauq. and **Harman Fishback** of Culp. Co. of one pt. and **Tilman Martin** .. £24 .. lot .. cont..100 A. whereon sd. Tilman Martin now lives .. binding on land of **Charles Carter** of Lan. Co. and **Jeremiah Darnall** .. being one of the lotts of land in the German Town formerly set apart for a German glebe .. *Signed*: **Peter (X) Hitt, Jacob Wever, Herman Fishback, Peter Kamper.** *Wit*: **Thomas Marshall, Tilman Wever, Joseph Martin, Josiah Holtzclaw.** *Rec*: 24 June 1771, prov. by o. of **Tilman Wever, Joseph Martin & Josiah Holtzclaw.**

Pages 180-184. 5 May 1771. Lease & release. Bet. **William Churchill, John Churchill** and **Armistead Churchill**, Exors. of Col. Armistead Churchill, dec'd, and **Andrew Buchanan** of Town of Falmouth, K. Geo. Co. tract .. part of Pageland .. in line of Crab tree, lot No. 24 opposite to dwelling house of sd. Armistead Churchill and marked for the

Cor. end Beg. of a part of the sd. large tract consisting of No. 1 & a small pt. of No. 8 conveyed by sd. Exors to **William Brent**, 29 April 1769 .. cor. to lots 3, 4, 7, & 8 .. cor. to lots No. 4, 5, 6, 7 and cor. to lots 6, 7, 10 .. cor. to Lot No. 7, 8, 9 & 10 .. line of Lot No. 26 and cor. to Lot No. 9 & 15, cor. of Lot No. 24 .. cor. of lots No. 7,9 & 8 .. Ł50 .. 620 A. inc. Lots 7, 9 & 8, except so much of last as conveyed to Wm. Brent. *Signed*: **Will., John** and **A. Churchill.** *Wit*: **Churchill Jones, Benjamin Churchill, George Nicholson, Jr., Joseph Hedger.** *Rec*: 29 May 1771, prov. by o. of **Benjamin Churchill, Nicholson** and by affirmation of **Hedger.** 24 June 1771, ack. by **John Churchill.**

Pages 184-187. 1 May 1771. Lease & release. Bet. Exors of **Armistead Churchill** (as above) and **Martin Pickett** .. part of Pageland .. Lot No. 14, containing 250 A. *Signed*: as above. *Wit*: as above. *Rec*: 27 May 1771, prov. as above, 24 June 1771 ack. by **John Churchill.**

Pages 188-189. 8 May 1771. B & S. Bet. **Andrew Buchanan** of Falmouth and **Armistead Churchill,** Gent. .. Lot 7, 8, 9, except so much of Lot 8 as was conveyed to **William Brent.** *Signed*: **Andrew Buchanan.** *Wit*: **Will'm Blackwell, John Blackwell, James Blackwell, Will'm (X) Jones.** *Rec*: 24 June 1771, ack. by grantor.

Pages 189-192. 6 May 1771. Ind. of Quinque-partite Bet. **W a r n e r Lewis,** Esq. of Glou. Co., 1st pt.; **Lewis Burwell** of James City Co., 2nd pt.; **Edmond Pendleton** of Car. Co. & **Peter Lyons,** Gent., sur. admrs. of est. of **John Robinson,** late of K. & Q. Co., Gent. and **John Churchill,** 4th pt.; and **Armistead Churchill,** 5th pt. .. Armistead Churchill late of Middlesex Co. died possessed of Pageland .. 10,600 A. .. so much to be sold to satisfy mortgage to Warner Lewis .. recites suit in Fauq. Co. of Robinson & Burwell vs. Churchill heirs .. slaves and stock were not sufficient to satisfy the debt .. the heirs proceeded to sell so much of Pageland to make up the difference .. to **Armistead Churchill, the Younger,** 1,262 A. of Pageland.. incl. Lots No. 24,25,26,27 .. Ł500.16s. .. *Signed*: **W a r n e r Lewis, Lewis Burwell, Edm'd Pendleton, Pet'r. Lyons, Will. Churchill, John Churchill.** *Wit*: **Benjamin Churchill, George Nicholson, Jr., Joseph Hedger.** *Rec*: 27 May 1771 (as above); 24 June 1771 (as above).

Pages 192-193. 28 May 1771. Comm. to obtain ack. To: **Joseph Blackwell, William Edmonds** and **Martin Pickett,** Gent., to examine **Mary Ball,** wife of **Burges Ball,** to obtain her ack. to conveyance to **James Young** and **John Thornberry.** *Signed*: **Joseph Blackwell, Martin Pickett.** *Rec*: 24 June 1771, Commission & cert. of Execution returned, O.R.

Pages 193-195. 26 April 1771. B & S. Bet. **John Barnes & Rebecca,** h. w. of Culp. Co. and **Thomas Sheppard** .. Ł50 .. [also **Shephard**] .. 183 A. .. adj. land of **Edward West, William Smith, Allen Macrae's** heirs and the land called Skinkers .. same to Barnes from Mr. **Thomas Hudnall** of N'land Co. .. *Signed*: **John Barnes, Rebecca (R) Barnes.** *Wit*: **William Blackwell, George (H) Wright, William Grant.** *Rec*: 24 June 1771, prov. by o. of wits.

Pages 195-196. 7 June 1771. B & S. Bet. **James Wood & Mary, h. w.** of Leeds Par .. and **Randle Morgan,** of same .. Ł200 .. where Morgain now lives .. near Ashbys Gap .. pt. of 630 A. lot .. cor. to Col. **George Washington's** land .. cor. to **Thomas Middleton** .. side of the Blue Ridge .. near the Gap Branch .. land of **John Young** .. Carter's old line .. 215 A. *Signed*: **James Wood, Mary Wood.** *Wit*: **John Connor, John (Ɖ) Young, John Wood, Margaret Young.** *Rec*: 24 June 1771, prov. by o. of **John** and **Margaret Young, John Wood,** wits.

Pages 197-198. 18 June 1771. B & S. Bet. **John Young & Margaret, h. w.** of Leeds Par and **Nathaniel Moss** of same .. Ł160 .. whereon Young now lives .. near Ashbys Gap .. part of 630 A. tract pur. of **Thomas Middleton** .. poplar on E. side of Blue Ridge and cor. to Carter's orig. survey .. cor. to Middleton and **James Wood** .. 200 A. *Signed*: **John (ƗY) Young, Margaret Young.** *Wit*: **John Ashby, Jr., John Barton, Robert Bolt, John Southard.** *Rec*: 24 June 1771, ack. by grantors.

Pages 198-200. 24 June 1771 B & S. Bet. **George Grant** of Ham. Par. and **James Gillison** of same .. Ł90 .. 171 1/2 A. .. 1/2 of tract cont. 343 A. formerly pur. by **John Grant,** father of sd. George, of **Howson Kenner,** devised to sd. George by sd. John in his will .. oak standing on the Marsh Run .. cor. to Seaton .. *Signed*: **G e o r g e   G r a n t.** *Wit*: **Joseph Blackwell, Benjamin Snelling, William Boswell.** *Rec*: 24 June 1771, ack. by **George Grant.**

Pages 200-203. 22 June 1771. Lease & release. Bet. **Edmund Basey & Winnifred, h. w.** and **Traverse Downman** of Pr. Wm. Co. .. tract on branches of Cedar Run, pur. by Basey of **James Taylor** .. cor. to Benjamin Taylor on Taylor's Spring Branch .. 125 A. .. Ł100 .. *Signed*: **Edmond Basye, Winnefred Basye.** *Wit*: **Joseph Taylor, Richard Taylor, Edwin Fielding.** *Rec*: 24 June 1771, ack. by grantors.

Page 203. 11 October 1770. Bill of Sale. **David Barton** of Leeds Par. to **John Morehead** .. Ł10 .. all household furniture .. *Signed*: **David Barton.** *Wit*: **John Moffett, Peter Lawrance.** *Rec*: 24 June 1771.

Pages 203-204. 15 June 1771. Deed of Gift. **Robert Monday** of Leeds Par .. for nat. love and affection for my loving son **John Monday** of same .. Negroes .. all residue of estate after debts are paid and such things as given to wife **Catherine** and other children in a will dated 15 June 1771. *Signed*: **Robert (X) Monday.** *Wit*: **William Pickett, Peter Obryants, William Owens.** *Rec*: 24 June 1771 prov. by o. of **William Pickett** and **William Owens.**

Pages 204-206. 5 May 1771. B & S. Bet. **William Churchill, John Churchill** and **Armistead Churchill,** Gent., devisees & exors. of Armistead Churchill, dec'd and **W i l l i a m   B r y a n** .. Ł105 .. part of Pageland .. oak on Licking Run cor. of Lot No. 3 .. cor. to Lot No. 4, 5, & 6 .. including Lots No. 2, 3, 4, 5 and a part of 6 .. 906 A. *Signed*: **Will. Churchill, John Churchill, Armistead Churchill.** *Wit*: **Chur-**

chill James, Benjamin Churchill, George Nicholson, Jr., Joseph Hedger. *Rec*: 29 May 1771, prov. by o. Church, Nicholson and affirmation of Hedger. 24 June 1777, ack. by **John Churchill.**

Pages 206-208. 31 May 1771. B & S. Bet. **William Brien [Bryan] & Elizabeth,** h. w. and **James Brien** and **William Lynne,** of the Township of Bernard, Somerset Co., N. Y. .. Ł500 .. part of Pageland .. including Lots No. 2, 3, 4, 5 and part of Lot No. 6 .. 906 A. .. same that William and **James Bryan** pur. of Exors of **Armistead Churchill,** dec'd. *Signed*: **Willaim Bryan, Elizabeth Bryan, James Bryan.** *Wit*: **John** and **Armistead Churchill, John Brian.** *Rec*: 24 June 1771, ack. by grantors.

Pages 208-211. 9 May 1771. Lease & release. Bet. **William Ball,** Gent. & **Sarah,** h. w. and **Martin Pickett** .. 600 A. .. same pur. by Ball of Col. **John Bell** .. stone on the north side of Cedar Run .. line that divides land from Capt. **Elias Edmonds** .. stone marked TL cor. to Capt. **Wm. Edmonds'** land .. line of Col. **Richard Henry Lee** .. dividing line bet Ball and Capt. **James Bell** .. low grounds of Cedar Run .. Ł700 .. *Signed*: **William Ball, Sarah Ball.** *Wit*: **William Blackwell, Thomas Keith, Samuel Boyd, Aylett Buckner.** *Rec*: 24 June 1771, ack. by grantors.

Pages 211-215. 29 May 1771. Lease & release. Bet. **Martin Pickett,** Gent. & **Ann,** his wife and **John Churchill,** Gent. .. 600 A. .. same Pickett pur. of **William Ball,** Gent. .. Ł730 .. *Signed*: **Martin Pickett, Anne Pickett.** *Wit*: **H. Brooke, Jeremiah Darnall, Richard Chichester, A. Churchill.** *Rec*: 24 June 1771, ack. by grantors.

Pages 215-216. 24 June 1771. B & S. Bet. **Wharton Ransdall,** Gent. and **Margaret,** h. w. and **John Churchill,** Gent. .. Ł100 .. parcel on both sides of Cedar Run for a mill seat .. 4 A. .. also 4 more acres which he overflowed by means of building a mill.. *Signed*: **Whart'n. Ransdell, Margarett Ransdell.** *Rec*: 24 June 1771, ack. by grantors.

Pages 217-219. 24-25 June 1771. Lease & release. Bet. **James Withers** and **Catharine,** h. w. and **Gavin Lawson,** merchant of K. Geo. Co. .. on n. side of Hedgman River opposite or nearly opposite to the lands of sd. Lawson on the other side .. pur. by sd. Withers of **P e t e r Rout,** late of Staff. Co. .. 50 A. .. Ł150. *Signed*: **James Withers, Catherine Withers.** *Rec*: 21 June 1771, ack. by grantors.

Pages 220-221. 25 April 1771. Trust. Bet. **Robert Monday** and **Charles Haney** .. whereas a marriage has been solemnized bet. sd. Monday and **Catherine** the dau. of sd. Haney .. in order to provide for his wife and 5 shillings paid by Haney .. slaves, furniture, stock, pewter .. to the proper use of Catherine and her heirs forever .. *Signed*: **Robert (X) Monday.** *Wit*: **Henry Berry, George Berry, Winifred Haynie.** *Rec*: 26 Aug. 1771. prov. by o. of **Joseph** and **Henry Berry.**

Pages 221-223. 26 August 1771. Deed of Gift. Bet. **William Coppage** and **John Coppage** .. brothers .. nat. love & affection .. 150 A. ..

on the west side of the White Oake Branch .. to the Main County Road
.. *Signed*: **William Coppedge**. *Wit*: **John Lee Wright, George Bennett**. *Rec*: 26 Aug. 1777, ack. by **William Coppedge**.

Pages 223-225. 10 May 1771. Lease. Bet. **Bryan Fairfax** of Fx.
Co., Gent. and **Joseph Jackson** .. on Little River or Hunger Run ..
Chinn's line .. 150 A. .. for his nat. life and lives of his wife, **Ann** and
his son **George Jackson** .. Ł4 yearly rent .. *Signed*: **Bryan Fairfax,
Joseph Jackson**. *Wit*: **Leven Powell, Thomas Chinn, Peyton Harrison, William Smith**. *Rec*: 24 June 1771, prov. by o. of Powell,
Chinn and on 26 Aug. 1771 by o. of Harrison.

Pages 225-228. 26 July 1771. B & S Bet. **William Grant & Judith**, h.
w. of Ham. Par. and **William Nalls** of Leeds Par., Blacksmith .. Ł105
.. tract on Broad Run and the Wolf Trap Branch .. on the Broad Run at
the Thoroughfare of the Biskett and Leathercoat Mountains .. cor. to
Nelms .. Wolf Trap Branch at the road that leads to **Neavils** .. oak
near the top of the Biskett Mt. thence along the top of the Mt. .. 354
A. .. *Signed*: **William Grant, Judith Grant**. *Wit*: **William Edmonds,
William Blackwell, John Combs**. *Rec*: 26 August 1771, ack. by **William Grant, Gent**.

Page 228. 25 December 1770. Survey & Divison. Survey made by order of County Court, for div. of the tract .. bet. Miss **Emelia Macrae**,
orph. of **Allan Macrae**, Gent., dec'd and **George Grant** .. in presence
of **William Blackwell, William Eustace & William Grant**, Gent. .. to
George Grant, 171 1/2 A. on Marsh Run .. to Miss Emelia Macrae a
like quantity .. surveyed by **Thomas Marshall** .. 13 & 14 December
1770. *Rec*: 27 August 1771.

Pages 228-231. 1 May 1771. Lease. Bet. **Daniel Payne** of Pr. Wm.
Co., Merchant, and **Edward Ball**, Planter .. tract whereon Ball now
dwells .. **Alexander Jeffries'** plantation .. adj. **Pickett's** land .. for
Ball's nat. life .. yearly rent of 1,000 lbs. tobacco in one cask .. Ball
not to sell lease before giving Payne an opportunity to buy on equal
terms .. *Signed*: **Daniel Payne, Edward Ball**. *Wit*: **William Ball,
John Smith, William (X) Haddox**. *Rec*: 26 August 1771, prov. by o. of
wits.

Pages 231-233. 27 August 1771. Lease. Bet. **Henry Peyton, Jr.** of
Leeds Par. and **James Gray** .. in a Bottom by the Rattle Snake Den up
sd. bottom to the top of the mt. and along the top of the sd. mt. to
Fishback's cor. .. to **Chapman's** cor .. North Run .. down North Run
and Broad Run .. 200 A. .. during his nat. life & life of **Elizabeth** h. w.
.. 530 lbs tobacco yearly rent or cash at the market price .. *Signed*:
Henry Peyton, James Gray. *Rec*: 27 August 1771, ack. by parties.

Pages 233-236. 25 May 1771. Lease. Bet. **Henry Peyton, Jr.** of
Leeds Par .. and **William Kidwell** of same .. on Et. side of Millers
Spring Branch .. to Broad Run .. for his nat. life and lives of **Mary**, h.
w. and **John Kidwell**, his son .. 530 lbs Tobacco yearly rent .. *Signed*:

Henry Peyton, William Kidwell. *Rec*: 27 August 1771, ack. by parties.

Pages 236-239. 23 August 1771. B & S. Bet. William Nalls & Sarah, h. w. of Leeds Par. and James Whaley of Loud. Co. .. Ł 130.10s. .. 261 A. .. part of larger tract granted by Proprietor to Capt. John Frogg .. 29 March 1744 for 1,837 A. .. oak near the top of Biskett Mt. by a ledge of rocks being cor. to the sd. Patent .. cor. to John Thomas .. to the pt. of an island in the Wolf Trap Br. .. cor. bet. the sd. Patent and Mr. Downing .. *Signed*: William Nalls, Sarah Nalls. *Wit*: The Court. *Rec*: 27 August 1771, ack. by grantors.

Pages 239-241. 26 August 1771. B & S. Bet. William Dulin, Jr. of Leeds Par & Elizabeth, h. w. and Thomas James of same .. Ł30 .. 125 A. .. Beg. of main tract (called Daggs) and Thomas Stone's former tenement .. part of larger tract granted to Joseph Chambers who conveyed it to John Dagg and became prop. of James Grinstead who conveyed to sd. William Dulin .. *Signed*: William Dulin, Elizabeth Dulin. *Wit*: John Moffett, Thos. Nelson, William Blackwell. *Ret*: 27 Aug. 1771, ack. by William Duling and Elizabeth, his wife.

Pages 241-243. 4 May 1771. B & S. Bet. James Stevenson & Betty, h. w. and Thomas Withers .. 1,000 lbs. Crop Tobacco .. tract in Ham. Par., part of larger tract granted by Prop. to William Kerns, Sr., 1 March 1754 and by him revised to sd. James Stevenson .. 10 A. .. cor. to Cox's land .. *Signed*: James (I) Stevenson, Betty (X) Stevenson. *Rec*: 28 Aug. 1771, ack. by grantors.

Pages 243-246. 2 February 1771. B & S. Bet. William Obannon, Sr. and Elizabeth, h. w. of Leeds Par .. and John Obannon, Jr. of same .. Ł100 .. tract at the Pignut Ridge .. oak on side of Ridge being corner to John Obanon, Sr. .. ash on side of Broad Run .. outline of Bryant Obanon's patent .. 232 A. *Signed*: William (X) Obannon, Elizabeth (꜉) Obanon. *Wit*: J. Moffett, Isham Keith, Wm. Phillips. *Rec*: 23 Sept. 1771, ack. by grantors.

Pages 246-247. 2 February 1771. Bill of Sale. William OBannon of Par. of Leeds to John OBannon, Jr. of same .. for Ł80 .. Slave, livestock and household furniture .. *Signed*: William (X) Obanon. *Wit*: J. Moffett, Isham Keith, Wm. Phillips. *Rec*: 23 Sept. 1771, ack. by William OBannon.

Pages 247-249. 14 September 1771. B & S. Bet. John Debutts of Md. and William Hunton .. Ł20 .. 100 A. .. on South Run of Broad Run of Occoquan .. Capt. Ransdell's line at the north end of the ridge .. Debutt's patent line .. oaks in Green's line .. oak near the top of Baldwin's Ridge .. *Signed*: John DeButts. *Wit*: Jas. Scott, Jr., John Duncan, Wharton Ransdell, Edwr' Fielding. William Hunton agrees to pay unto Ld. Fairfax all quit rents now due on the sd. lands which are part of a tract of 2,864 A. patented to the Rev. Laurance Debutts exclusive of a tract of 1,475 sold R o b e r t V a u x and one of 450 sold

Wharton Ransdell, part of sd. 2,864 A. *Rec:* 23 Sept. 1771, prov. by o. of **Scott, Ransdell** and **Edwin Fielding,** wits.

Pages 250-252. 14 September 1771. B & S. Bet. **John Debutts** of Ann Arundel Co., Md. and **Wharton Ransdell** .. Ł84.1s.4d. .. 194 A. .. cor. to sd. Ransdell .. cor. to **Mr. Scott** .. saplin in Debutts & Allans line .. cor. to **Archibald Allan** .. part of tract of 2,864 A. granted to the Rev. **Lawrence Debutts** of Md. .. 18 Oct. 1727, descended to **Samuel Debutts,** bro. and heir-at-law of the sd. Laurence .. from sd. Samuel to John Debutts .. *Signed:* **John DeButts.** *Wit:* **James Scott, Jr., Wm. Hunton, John Duncan, Thomas Maddux, Jr.** *Rec:* 23 Sept. 1771, prov. by o. of **Scott, Hunton** and **Maddux.**

Pages 253-255. 14 September 1771. B & S. Bet. **John Debutts** of Annapolis, Md. and **Wharton Ransdell** .. Ł20 .. all the residue of the Rev. **Laurence Debutts** grant .. 18 Oct. 1727 .. 150 A. in the possession of **John Chilton** and 30 A. in the possession of **Archibald Allan** only excepted. *Signed:* **John DeButts.** *Wit:* **Jas. Scott, Wm. Ransdell, Edwin Fielding, Elizabeth Scott.** *Rec:* 23 Sept. 1771, prov. by o. of **James Scott, William Ransdell & Edwin Fielding,** wits.

Pages 255-257. 14 September 1771. B & S. Bet. **John Debutts** of Ann Arundel Co., Md. and **James Scott** .. Ł13.6s. .. 66 A. .. stone on top of Baldwins Ridge by the roadside .. to **Chilton's** cor .. cor. to Capt. Scott .. part of Debutt's patent .. 18 October 1727 .. *Signed:* **John DeButts.** *Wit:* **Wharton Ransdell, Wm. Ransdell, Edwin Fielding.** *Rec:* 23 Sept. 1771, prov. by o. of wits.

Pages 258-260. 15 September 1771. B & S. Bet. **John Debutts** of Ann Arundel Co., Md. and **John Chilton** .. Ł30 .. 150 A. .. one the sides of Baldwins Ridge .. cor. to Chilton's pur. of **V a u l x** .. cor. of Blowers Patent now held by **Green** .. *Signed:* **John DeButts.** *Wit:* **George Neavil, John Sutton, William Thornberry.** *Rec:* 23 Sept. 1771, prov. by o. of wits.

Pages 260-264. 3-4 September 1771. Lease & release. Bet. **Thomas Neavil,** son & devisee of **John Neavil** of Fauq. Co., dec'd. and **William Carr** of Dumfries, Pr. Wm. Co., Gent. and **George Lowry** of Pr. Wm. Co. .. 2 tracts .. on branches of Cedar Run .. whereon sd. John Neavil lived and died which he pur. of **William Hackney** .. rec. in Pr. Wm. Co., 20 Oct. 1736 .. the other tract was granted to John Neavil, 5 Jan. 1745 .. survey made by **James Genn** .. adjacent to each other .. 240 A. .. conveyed by John Neavil in his lifetime to William Carr by way of Mortgage, since paid, and devised by John Neavil to his son, Thomas, will dated 24 April 1767 .. Ł146.8s. *Signed:* **Thomas Neavill, William Carr.** *Wit:* **Step'n Lee, William Bayles, William Parker, Thomas Matterson, W. Ellzey.** *Rec:* 23 Sept. 1771, prov. by o. of **William Ellzey, Parker** and **Matterson.**

Pages 265-269. 6-7 November 1769. Lease & release. Bet. **J o h n Syas** and **William Carr** of Pr. Wm. Co. .. on branch of North West Branch of the broad run of Occoquan called Fornicating Branch .. by

survey made by Mr. James Thomas the Younger .. cor. to land sur-
veyed for Valentine Barton .. 639 A. .. ₤75 .. Signed: John (Ɨ) Sias.
Wit: James Muschett, Thomas Chapman, Robt. Singleton, George
Newman Brown, John Riddell. Rec: 26 Mar. 1770, prov. by o. of
Brown and on 23 Sept. 1771 ack. by John Sias.

Pages 269-273. 1-2 January 1768. Lease & release. Bet. Henry
Peyton of Pr. Wm. Co. and Cuthbert Bullitt of same .. 1,710 A. on
Little River .. same granted to Allan Macrae Exors. for the security
of a debt due the sd. Macrae in his lifetime .. 254 A. which the said
Peyton is tenant by the curtesy of England & 293 A. in F'rick from the
Prop. to Henry Peyton .. ₤1,000. Signed: Henry Peyton. Wit: Hugh
Brent, George Brent, Wm. Brent, Francis Triplett, W. Ellzey. Rec:
24 Aug. 1768, prov. by o. of William Ellzey & Geo. Brent and on 23
Sept. 1771, prov. by o. of Hugh Brent.

Page 273. 28 October 1771. Bond. Armistead Churchill apptd.
Sheriff .. 18 October .. (no amount) .. Sec: John Churchill, William
Blackwell, Jr. Rec: 28 Oct. 1771, ack. by parties.

Page 274. 28 October 1771. Bond. Armistead Churchill for Sheriff ..
For: ₤1,000 .. Securities as above. Rec: 28 Oct. 1771, ack. by parties.

Pages 275-277. 28 October 1771. B & S. Bet. Archibald Allen &
Abigail, h. w. and Wharton Ransdell .. ₤52 .. tract .. on east side of
br. of the North Fork of Cedar Run .. line of marked trees of Rev.
Laurence Debutts and cor. tree to John Blowers .. Rev. Mr. James
Scott's line .. cor. to Thomas Barber and John Blowers .. 108 A.
Signed: Archibald Allan, Abigail Allan. Wit: Jas. Scott, Jr., Ran-
dolph Spicer, George Rogers. Rec: 28 Oct. 1771, prov. by o. of wits.

Pages 277-280. 23 September 1771. B & S. Bet. John Rector &
Catherine, h. w. of Leeds Par. and John Kincheloe .. ₤62.16s. .. 157
A. .. cor. to Isaac Cundiff .. in dividing line bet. Burges Ball and
Burges Smith, Gent. .. oak standing in Thomas Glascock's line ..
being part of a larger Tract of land formerly pur. by the Rector of
Burges Ball, Gent. .. 7 September 1771 .. Signed: John (ꞮR) Rector,
Catherine (CR) Rector. Wit: Thomas Marshall, Thomas Glascock,
John Squires. Rec: 28 Oct. 1771, ack. by grantors.

Pages 280-282. 10 October 1771. B & S. Bet. John Rector &
Catherine, h. w. of Leeds Par and Henry Rector, Jr. of same .. ₤
62.16s. .. 157 A. cor. to the Lotts of Charles Rector and John Rector
.. oak cor. standing in Isaac Cundiff's line .. part of tract (as above) ..
Signed: (as above). Wit: Thom. Marshall, Aaron Drummond, Daniel
Brown. Rec: 28 Oct. 1771, ack. by grantors.

Pages 282-285. 1 October 1771. B & S. Bet. John Rector &
Catherine, h. w. of Leeds Par and Charles Rector .. ₤62.16s. .. 157
A. .. Beg. .. oak cor. in Chattins line .. oak, cor. to Henry Rector ..
cor. to Jacob Rector, Jr. .. part of larger tract .. (as above) ...
Signed: (as above). Wit: (as above). Rec: (as above).

Pages 285-287. 28 October 1771. B & S. Bet. John Rector & Catherine, h. w. .. and George Glascock .. Ł102.16s. .. 257 A. .. part of larger tract (as above) .. Beg. at oak in John Anderson's line .. cor. to Jacob Rector & Thomas Glascock .. cor. to Clark .. *Signed*: John Rector, Catherine Rector. *Wit*: Thom. Marshall. *Rec*: 28 Oct. 1771, ack. by grantors.

Pages 288-290. 28 October 1771. B & S. Bet. John Rector & Catherine, h. w. and Richard McPherson .. Ł60 .. 150 A. .. part of larger tract (as above) .. oak in dividing line formerly run bet. Smith and Ball, being James Murry's .. cor. Thomas Priest .. cor. to Ephraim Furr .. cor to James Murry .. *Signed*: John Rector, Catherine Rector. *Wit*: Thom. Marshall. *Rec*: 28 October 1771, ack. by grantors.

Pages 290-292. 28 October 1771. B & S. Bet. John Rector & Catherine, h. w. and John Squires .. Ł74.16s. .. 187 A. .. oak in dividing line formerly run bet. Ball & Smith .. Thomas Glascock's corner .. *Signed*: John Rector, Catherine Rector. *Wit*: Thom. Marshall. *Rec*: 28 Oct. 1771, ack. by grantors.

Pages 292-294. 1771. B & S. Bet. John Rector & Catherine, h. w. and William Murry .. Ł62.16s. .. 157 A. .. dividing line bet. Ball & Smith .. cor. to John Kincheloe's Lott .. part of larger tract (as above) .. (Thomas Glascock and Agnes, h. w. mentioned as grantors in body of deed?) .. *Signed*: John Rector. *Wit*: Thom Marshall. *Rec*: 28 Oct. 1771, ack. by grantor.

Pages 294-296. 1 October 1771. B & S. Bet. John Rector & Catherine, h. w. of Par. of Leeds and Isaac Cundiff .. Ł62.16s. .. 157 A. .. oak in Henry Rector's line & cor. to Jacob Rector, standing on dividing line formerly run bet. Ball and Smith .. cor. to John Kincheloe .. cor. to Thomas Glascock .. being part of larger tract .. *Signed*: John (IR) Rector, Catherine (CR) Rector. *Wit*: Thom. Marshall, Aaron Drummond, Daniel Brown. *Rec*: 28 October 1771, ack. by grantors.

Pages 296-299. 1 October 1771. B & S. Bet. John Rector and Catherine, h. w. of Leeds Par. and Hezekiah Glascock .. Ł68.. 170 A. .. cor. to Henry Rector .. to Anderson's line .. part of larger tract (as above) .. *Signed*: (as above). *Wit*: (as above). *Rec*: 28 Oct. 1771, ack. by grantors.

Pages 299-301. 28 October 1771. B & S. Bet. John Rector & Catherine, h. w. and James Murry .. Ł127.4s. .. 318 A. .. saplins in dividing line formerly run, etc. .. Burgesses old line .. cor. to Richard McPherson .. *Signed*: John Rector, Catherine Rector. *Wit*: Thom. Marshall. *Rec*: 28 Oct. 1771, ack. by John Rector & wife.

Pages 301-304. 1 October 1771. B & S. Bet. John Rector, Sr. & Catherine, h. w. and John Rector, Jr. .. Ł62.16s. .. 157 A. .. cor. to Henry Rector and George Glascock .. part of larger tract, etc.

Signed: **John (℟) Rector, Catherine (CR) Rector.** *Wit*: **Thom. Marshall, Aaron Drummond, Daniel Brown.** *Rec*: 28 Oct. 1771, ack. by grantors.

Pages 304-306. 1 October 1771. B & S. Bet. **John Rector & Catherine**, h. w. and **Jacob Rector** .. Ł62.16s. .. 157 A. .. cor. to **George Glascock** and John Rector .. cor. to **John Rector, Jr.** and **Henry Rector's** lotts .. *Signed*: **John (℟) Rector, Catherine (CR) Rector.** *Wit*: Marshall, Drummond and Brown. *Rec*: 28 October 1771, ack. by grantors.

Pages 306-309. 1 October 1771. B & S. Bet. **John Rector & Catherine**, h. w. and **Henry Rector, Sr.** .. Ł60 .. 150 A. .. being part of tract pur. by Rector of **Burgess Ball** .. 1770 .. cor. to sd. John Rector .. cor. to **George Glascock** .. to **John Anderson's** line .. to **Chattins** line .. *Signed*: (as above). *Wit*: (as above). *Rec*: 28 Oct. 1771, ack. by grantors.

Pages 309-311. 1 October 1771. B & S. Bet. **Thomas Glascock & Agnes**, h. w. of Leeds Par. and **Margaret Hardwick** .. Ł74.16s. (mentions **John Rector** & wife as Grantors ?) .. 244 A. .. oak in **Kincheloe's** line .. cor. to Thomas Glascock .. cor. to **Jacob Rector** .. part of larger tract to Rector .. *Signed*: **Thomas Glascock, Agnes Glascock** *Wit*: **Thom. Marshall.** *Rec*: 28 Oct. 1771, ack. by Glascock & wife.

Pages 311-313. 30 April 1771. B & S. Bet. **William Walker** of Brunswick Co. and **William Barkley** of Loud. Co. and **William Picket Sandford** .. Ł131 .. 524 A. .. fork in br. of Hunger Run & cor. to **Jacob Holtzclaw** .. lower side of Hunger run .. same granted to William Walker father of sd. William .. 16 June 1741.. *Signed*: **William Walker.** *Wit*: **William Monday, Peter O'Bryant, John Monday.** *Rec*: 24 June 1771, prov. by o. of **Wm.** & **John Monday**; 29 Oct. 1771, prov. by o. of **Peter O'Briant.**

Pages 313-315. 29 October 1771. B & S. Bet. **James Bashaw & Frances**, h. w. and **Peter Bashaw** .. Ł30 .. tract adj. **Waugh Darnel** land sold to the sd. James Bashaw by **John Bell**, dec'd... with **John James's** .. cor. of sd. James .. 167 A. .. *Signed*: James Bashaw, Frances Bashaw. *Wit*: **Joseph Basye, Elizabeth Edwards.** *Rec*: 29 Oct. 1771, ack. by grantors.

Pages 316-318. 29 October 1771. B & S. Bet. **James Bashaw & Frances**, h. w. and **James Genn** .. Ł70 .. joining the land of **Simon Morgan** sold to the sd. Bashaw by **John Bell**, dec'd .. in Simon Morgan's line .. oak in **William Norris's** line .. oak cor. in **Peter Bashaw's** line .. 120 A. .. *Signed*: **James Bashaw, Frances Bashaw.** *Wit*: **Joseph Basye, Elizabeth Edwards.** *Rec*: 29 October 1771, ack. by grantors.

Pages 318-321. 23 May 1771. B & S. Bet. **Landon Carter** and **Charles Carter**, Exors. of Charles Carter, Esq., dec'd. and **Benjamin**

Morris .. 131 A. .. part of Tract called Kettle Run .. in Par. of Hambleton .. Ł65.10s. .. cor. on Kettle Run .. road that leads from Thornton's to Neavill's .. *Signed*: **Landon Carter, Char's. Carter**. *Wit*: **Landon Carter, Jr., Gawin Corbin, Jr., Catesby Woodford, Wm. F. Brazun**. *Rec*: 24 June 1771, prov. by o. of **L. Carter, Jr., C. Woodford**, ack. by **Landon & Charles Carter** .. 25 Nov. 1771, prov. by o. of **Gawin Corbin, Jr.** and **William F. Brazun**.

Pages 321–323. 23 May 1771. B & S. Bet. (same as above) and **George Reeves** .. recites Act of Assembly, 1769, which enabled the Grantors to sell the land to pay the debts of **Charles Carter**, dec'd .. 420 A. .. part of Kettle Run Tract .. Ł210 .. cor. to **H e a l e** .. cor. with **H o r n e r** .. hic. on Burwell's Road .. (marked RH GR) .. *Signed*: (as above). *Wit*: (as above). *Rec*: (as above).

Pages 324–326. 23 May 1771. B & S. Bet. .. (same as above) .. and **John Churchill** and **Armistead Churchill** .. 178 A. .. part of Kettle Run Tract .. Ł89 .. oak in **Morris'** line .. cor. to **George Steel** .. *Signed*: (as above). *Wit*: (as above). *Rec*: (as above).

Pages 326–329. 23 May 1771. B & S. Bet. (as above) .. and **William Warren** of Pr. Wm. Co. .. 460 A. .. Ł230 .. oak in a branch on SE side of the Carolina Road .. south branch of Broad Run in the Broad Run patent line .. *Signed*: (as above). *Wit*: (as above). *Rec*: (as above).

Pages 329–331. 23 May 1771. B & S. Bet. (as above) .. and **J o h n Tomlin** .. 141 A. .. Ł70 .. Cor. to **Morris** .. cor. to Morris and **Hedges** .. cor. to **Rogers** .. hic. in **Wm. Chilton's** line .. *Signed*: (as above). *Wit*: (as above). *Rec*: (as above).

Pages 331–334. 23 May 1771. B & S. Bet. (as above) .. and **George Rogers** .. 131 A. .. part of Kettle Run Tract .. Ł65.10s. .. with patent line and **Debutts'** line .. *Signed, wit, rec*: (as above).

Pages 334–336. 23 May 1771 .. B & S. Bet. (as above) .. and **Samuel Steele** .. 192 A. .. Kettle Run Tract .. Ł96 .. beg. with **Ambrose Barnard** in the road .. to **Hedgers** Cor. .. *Signed, wit, rec*: (as above).

Pages 336–339. 23 May 177I. B & S. Bet. (as above) and **John Shirley** .. 150 A. .. 175 .. cor. to **Ambrose Barnard** .. o. marked AB at end of Neavils old Meadow in one of the patent lines .. in **George Steele's** line .. *Signed, wit, rec*: (as above).

Pages 339–342. 23 May 1771. B & S. Bet. (as above) and **W a l k e r T a l i a f e r r o**, Esq. of Caroline Co. .. 1,120 A. .. part of tract of land called Broad Run in Hambleton Par .. Ł560 .. Beg. at mouth of south fork of Broad Run, thence up South Run .. cor. of patent and of Kettle Run patent .. cor. to **Charles Carter**, Esq. of Corotoman .. cor. to the Rev. Mr. **Isaac Campbell** .. *Signed, wit, rec*: (as above).

Pages 342–345. 23 May 1771. B & S. Bet. **Landon & Charles Carter**, Esq'rs., Exors. of **Charles Carter**, Esq., dec'd and **Ambrose**

Barnett [also spelled **Barnard**] .. Act of General Assembly 1769 empowering the Exors. to sell the lands of the dec'd for the payment of his debts .. 190 A. of Kettle Run Tract .. L95 .. *Signed*: **Landon Carter, Charles Carter.** *Wit*: **Landon Carter, Jr., Garwin Corbin, Jr., Wm. T. Brazier, Catesby Woodford.** *Ret*: 24 June 1771, prov. by o. of Carter & Woodford 25 Nov. 1771, prov. by o. of Corbin and Brazier.

Pages 345-347. 23 May 1771. B & S. Bet. (as above) and **W i l l i a m Watkins, Jr.** .. 119 1/2 A. .. L59.10s. .. Beg. at **Stephen Chilton's** cor. on the patent line .. cor. to **Shirley** .. *Signed, wit, rec*: (as above).

Pages 348-350. 23 May 1771. B & S. Bet. (as above) and **G e o r g e H e a l e** of Lanc. Co. .. 1,500 A. .. part of Kettle Run Tract .. L750 .. Beg. oak marked CC on the n.e. side of Kettle Run at Adams horse pen lick .. patent cor. & line .. oak on **Burwell's Road** .. Cattail bridge .. *Signed, wit, rec*: (as above).

Pages 351-353. 23 May 1771. B & S. Bet. (as above) and **C h a r l e s C h i l t o n** .. 126 1/2 A. .. part of Kettle Run Tract .. L65.3s. .. cor. to **R o g e r s** .. patent line .. to Debutts patent line cor. *Signed, wit, rec*: (as above).

Pages 354-356. 23 May 1771. B & S. Bet. (as above) and **S t e p h e n Chilton** of Westmoreland Co. .. 519 A. .. part of Kettle Run Tract .. L 259.10s. Beg. at **George Heale's** cor. on the Walnut Branch .. cor. to **Robert Horner** .. cor. to **James McClanaham** .. *Signed, wit, rec*: (as above).

Pages 357-359. 23 May 1771. B & S. Bet. (as above) and **Zachariah Lewis** .. 390 A. .. part of Kettle Run Tract .. L195 .. oak on **Burwell's** Road cor. of **Heale's** land near **Bullitts** and **John Thornberry's** cor. in the Patent line .. cor. to **Love** .. *Signed, wit, rec*: as above.

Pages 360-361. 25 November 1771. Mortgage. Bet. **Thomas Bullett** and **John McMillian** of Pr. Wm. Co. .. L500 .. 400 A. .. on Elk Run .. by Deed of Gift from **Benjamin Bullett**, father to said Thomas .. rec. in Pr. Wm. Co. .. Negroes .. cattle .. to be void on condition of payment with int. to sd. McMillian of L500 .. *Signed*: **Thomas Bullett.** *Rec*: 25 Nov. 1771, ack. by **Thomas Bullett.**

Pages 362-367. 25 November 1771. Lease & release. Bet. **G e o r g e Boswell** and **Judith,** h. w. and **Churchill Jones** of Middlesex Co., Gent. .. 305 A. .. L305 .. cor .. s. side of Turkey Run .. oak on east side of Main road .. same Boswell pur. of **Martin Pickett,** Gent. *Signed*: **George Boswell, Judith Boswell.** *Wit*: **Wm. Boswell, A. Churchhill, Benj'a. Churchhill.** *Rec*: 25 Nov. 1771, prov. by o. of wits.

Pages 367-370. October 1771. B & S. Bet. **John Rector & Catherine,** h. w. of Leeds Par .. **Thomas Glascock** of same .. L172.8s. .. 431 A. .. cor. to lott of Jacob Rector .. **John Kincheloe's** line near a cor. bet.

the sd. Kincheloe and **Isaac Cundiff** .. part of tract pur. by Rector of **Burgess Ball**, Gent. .. 7 Sept. 1770 .. *Signed*: **John (HR) Rector, Catherine (CR) Rector.** *Wit*: **Thomas Marshall, Aaron Drummond, Daniel Brown.** *Rec*: 25 Nov. 1771, ack. by **John Rector.**

Pages 370-374. 1 November 1770. Lease. Bet. **Thomas Lord Fairfax** and **Charles Waller** .. tract in Manor of Leeds .. cor. to **Garner Burgesses** Lott cor. to **Charles Pinchard** lott .. cor. to **James Jett** .. 250 A. .. for his nat. life and lives of **Easther Waller**, his wife and **John Waller** their son .. for yearly rent of 50s. sterling .. *Signed*: **Fairfax.** *Wit*: **Jas. Scott, Jr., John (X) Pepper, John Chilton.** *Rec*: 25 Nov. 1771. prov. by o. of wits.

Pages 375-378. 1 November 1771. Lease. Bet. **Thomas Lord Fairfax** and **Charles Taylor** .. parcel in Manor of Leeds .. cor. to **David Barton** .. oak in **Ball's** line .. 120 A. .. for his nat. life and lives of **Sarah**, h. w. and **Milly**, his dau. .. for yearly rent of 24s. sterling .. *Signed*: **Fairfax.** *Wit*: (as above). *Rec*: 25 Nov. 1771, ack. by wits.

Pages 378-381. 1 November 1771. Lease. Bet. **Thomas Lord Fairfax** and **Charles Morgan** .. parcel in Manor of Leeds .. in line of **Reuben Payne** .. line of **Wm. Morgan** .. road cor. to **Wm. Linagen** & **Wm. Walker** .. cor. to sd. Walker and **George Settle** .. 197 A. .. for his nat. life and lives of **Sukey**, h. w. & **Elizabeth**, his dau. .. yearly rent of 39s. sterling .. *Signed*: **Fairfax.** *Wit*: (as above). *Rec*: 25 Nov. 1771, ack. by wits.

Pages 381-383. 1 November 1771. Lease. Bet. **Thomas Lord Fairfax** and **Archibald Allan, Jr.**, parcel in Manor of Leeds .. oak on the end of the Poley Mt. .. 100 A. .. for his nat. life & lives of **Jemmima**, h. w. and **Martain Allan**, their son .. yearly rent of 20s. sterling .. *Signed, wit, rec*: (as above).

Pages 383-385. 1 November 1771. Lease. Bet. **Thos. Ld. Fx.** and **William Linager** .. parcel in Manor of Leeds .. **Morgan's** line .. 118 A. .. for his nat. life and lives of **Cauther**, h. w. and **Jesse**, his son .. yearly rent of 23s.7d. .. *Signed, wit, rec*: (as above).

Pages 386-388. 1 November 1771. Lease. Bet. **Thomas Lord Fairfax** and **John Allan** .. parcel in Manor of Leeds .. in line of **Chas. Jones** .. in line of **Archibald Allan, Sen'r** .. 104 A. .. for his nat. life and lives of **Elizabeth**, h. w. and **Nancy**, his dau. .. yearly rent of 20s.7d. *Signed, wit, rec*: (as above).

Pages 388-391: 1 November 1771. Lease. Bet. **Thos. Ld. Fx.** and **John Barton** .. in Manor of Leeds .. 100 A. .. during his nat. life and lives of **Rhoda**, h. w. and **Benjamin Barton**, their son .. yearly rent .. 20s. sterling. *Signed, wit, rec*: (as above).

Pages 391-394. 1 November 1771. Lease. Bet. **Thos. Ld. Fx.** and **David Sullivan** .. two parcels in Manor of Leeds .. cor. to **Guttriges** .. oak in **Dixon's** .. 125 A. .. also another lott 75 A. .. for his nat. life

126

and lives of **Mary**, h. w. and **Jonathan Sullivan**, their son .. yearly rent of 40s. sterling .. *Signed, wit, rec*: (as above).

Pages 394–397. 1 November 1771. Lease. Bet. **Thos. Ld. Fx.** and **John McCormick** .. in Manor of Leeds .. 200 A. .. for his nat. life and lives of **Elizabeth**, h. w. and **Margaret**, his dau. .. yearly rent of 40s. *Signed, wit, rec*: (as above).

Pages 397–400. 1 November 1771. Lease. Bet. **Thos. Ld. Fx.** and **Allan Guthridge** .. in Manor of Leeds .. cor. to **John Barton's** lott .. cor. to **Sullivan** .. 100 A. .. for his nat. life and lives of **Marget**, h. w. and **William Thatcher Guthridge**, their son .. yearly rent of 20s. sterling .. *Signed, wit, rec*: (as above).

Pages 400–403. 1 November 1771. Lease. Bet. **Thos. Ld. Fx.** and **Peter Laurence** .. in Manor of Leeds .. in **Sinklar's** Line .. 105 A. .. for his nat. life and lives of **Anne**, h. w. and **Mason Laurence**, their son.. yearly rent of 21s. sterling .. *Signed, wit, rec*: (as above).

Pages 403–405. 1 November 1771. Lease. Bet. **Thos. Ld. Fx.** and **Joseph Hitt** .. in Manor of Leeds .. cor. to **Wm. Walker** .. on the Beetree Branch, cor. to the sd. **Walker** .. cor. to **Wm. Corder, Sr.** .. 158 A. .. for his nat. life and lives of **Mary**, h. w. and **Elisha**, his son .. yearly rent of 31s. 7d. *Signed, wit, rec*: (as above).

Pages 405–407. 1 November 1771. Lease. Bet. **Thos. Ld. Fx.** and **Joseph Crimm** .. in Manor of Leeds .. cor. to **John Crimm**, dec'd .. line of **Joseph Grimsley** .. 157 A. .. for his nat. life and lives of **Peter & Elizabeth Crimm** .. yearly rent of 31s.4d. *Signed, wit, rec*: (as above).

Pages 407–409. 1 November 1771. Lease. Bet. **Thos. Ld. Fx.** and **John McQueen** .. in Manor of Leeds .. maple on Qnite Yard branch .. Hedgman's River .. mouth of Thumb Run .. 100 A. .. for his nat. life and nat. lives of **Elizabeth**, h. w. and **Zelah**, his son .. yearly rent of 20s. sterling ... *Signed, wit, rec*: (as above).

Pages 409–412. 1 November 1771. Lease. Bet. **Thos. Ld. Fx.** and **George Settle** .. tract in Manor of Leeds .. fork of the Beetree Br. .. 134 A. yearly rent of 26s.9d. .. for his nat. life and nat. lives of **Mary**, h. w. and **William**, his son .. *Signed, wit, rec*: (as above).

Pages 412–415. 1 November 1771. Lease. Bet. **Thos. Ld. Fx.** and **Benjamin Douglass** .. in Manor of Leeds .. large rock in bank of Hedgeman's River .. in the line of **Rich'd Crawley** .. 130 A. .. for his nat. life and lives of **Charity**, h. w. and **James**, h. s. .. yearly rent of 26s. sterling .. *Signed, wit, rec*: (as above).

Pages 415–418. 1 November 1771. Lease. Bet. **Thomas Lord Fairfax** and **William Hemmings** .. part of Manor of Leeds .. Cor. to Congrove .. 105 A. .. during his nat. life and nat. lives of **Elizabeth**, h. w.

and **Sarah,** their dau. .. yearly rent of 21s. sterling .. *Signed, wit, rec:* (as above).

Pages 418-420. 1 November 1771. Lease. Bet. **Thos. Ld. Fx.** and **William Allan** .. tract in Manor of Leeds .. cor. to **John Allan** .. 120 A. .. for his nat. life and nat. lives of **Martin & George Allan,** his nephews .. yearly rent of 24s. .. *Signed, wit, rec:* (as above).

Pages 420-424. 1 November 1771. Lease. Bet. **Thos. Ld. Fx.** and **Jesse Norman** .. in Manor of Leeds .. cor. to **Waller's Lott** .. 140 A. .. for his nat. life and nat. lives of **Elizabeth, h. w.** and **Martin Norman,** his nephew .. yearly rent 28s. *Signed, wit, rec:* (as above).

Pages 424-427. 1 November 1771. Lease. Bet. **Thos. Ld. Fx.** and **William Morgan** .. tract in Manor of Leeds .. oak by Crim's path .. 219 A. .. for his nat. life and the nat. lives of **E l i z a b e t h,** h. w. and **J a m e s,** his son .. yearly rent of 44s. ster. *Signed, wit, rec:* (as above).

Pages 427-429. 23 November 1771. Lease. Bet. **Lynaugh Helm** of Pr. Wm. Co. and **Benjamin Pope** .. 282 A. .. pur. of **John Gunnon** .. for his nat. life and nat. lives of **Behethland Pope, h. w.** and **Nathaniel Pope,** his son .. yearly rent of 1,000 lbs. crop tobacco in cask ... *Signed:* **Lynaugh Helm, Benjamin Pope.** *Wit:* **Henry Foote, John Wood, Griffin (X) Tullos.** *Rec:* 25 Nov. 1771, prov. by o. of wits.

Pages 429-430. 23 November 1771. Lease. Bet. **Lynaugh Helm** of Pr. Wm. Co., Gent. and **Enoch David Thomas** .. a certain tract of land purchased of **John Crump** .. on the n. side of the Road leading from the sd. **Crump's** to **Martin Hardins** .. for his nat. life and the nat. lives of **Anne, h. w. & John Thomas,** his son .. yearly rent of £4 and quit rents .. *Signed:* **Lynaugh Helm, Enoch David Thomas.** *Wit:* **Henry Foote, John Wood, Griffin (X) Tullos.** *Rec:* 25 Nov. 1771, prov. by o. of wits.

Pages 430-432. 25 November 1771. B & S. Bet. **Moses Arnold &** **Sarah, h. w.** of F'rick Co. and **William Jennings** .. £22 .. tract in Par. of Hamilton .. **Lyn Arnold's** fence .. line of **William Settle** .. cor. of **Bushrode Doggett** .. 50 A. .. *Signed:* **Moses Arnold.** *Wit:* **James Scott, Jr., Augustin Jennings, Sr., Wm. Pinkard.** *Rec:* 25 Nov. 1771, ack. by **Moses Arnold.**

Pages 432-433. 2 November 1771. B & S. Bet. **David Barton** of Leeds Par. and **Thomas Nelson** .. £60 .. Leasehold in Manor of Leeds .. from **Fairfax** to Barton .. 25 Sept. 1759 .. oak in **Ball's** line .. 150 A. .. *Signed:* **David Barton.** *Wit:* **J. Moffett, John Barton, Levin Powell, Peyton Harrison.** *Rec:* 26 Nov. 1771, prov. by o. of Moffett, Barton and Powell, wits.

Pages 433-435. 1 May 1771. B & S. Bet. **Wm. Churchill, Jno.** **Churchhill & Armistead Churchhill,** Exors. of Armistead Churchhill, dec'd and **William Bryan** and **James Bryan** .. £104 .. part of a large tract called Pageland .. desc. in plat. made by **Thomas Marshall** as Lotts 10,11,12 and part of 6 .. 805 A. .. *Signed*: **William Churchhill, John Churchhill, A. Churchhill.** *Wit*: **Churchill Jones, Benj'a. Churchhill, Joseph Hedger, George Nicholson, Jr.** *Rec*: 29 Oct. 1771, prov. by o. of **Benj. Churchill**, ack. by **Wm. & Armistead Churchhill** .. 26 Nov. 1771, prov. by o. of **George Nicholson** and by affirmation of **Joseph Hedger.**

Pages 436–437. 9 November 1771. Lease. Bet. **John Braxter** of Pr. Wm. Co. and **James Leach** of same co. .. for his nat. life and lives of **Sarah**, his wife .. tract .. situate on the northside of the Bull Run Mt. .. 280 a. .. part of larger tract granted to **Bradly Garner** from Prop. and by Garner sold to **Benjamin Stribling** and by sd. Stribling to **John Baxter** as by the sd. Stribling's will may more fully appear .. rent after 3 yrs. of 950 lbs. tobacco .. *Signed*: **John Baxter.** *Wits*: **Chas. Thornton, Thomas (X) Leach, Bartlett Leach.** *Rec*: 25 November 1771, prov. by o. of **Charles Thornton** and **Thos. Leach.** 23 Nov. 1772: prov. by o. of **Bartlett Leach.**

Pages 437–439. 20 November 1771. Lease. Bet. **Thomas Jackman** of Leeds Par. and **Thomas Maddux** .. tract on Cedar Run known by name of Jackman's Mountain .. east **Taylor's** land .. **Smith's** land .. northwest side of Smith's road on the Mountain .. **Baker's** line .. 250 a. .. for his nat. life and lives of **Elizabeth**, his wife and **John**, his son .. yrly rent of Ł3 .. *Signed*: **Thos. Jackman, Thos. Maddux.** *Wits*: **James Gray, Wharton Ransdell, Thos. Ransdell.** *Rec*: 23 March 1772, ack. by o. of parties.

Pages 439–441. 23 March 1772. B & S. Bet. **Joseph Martin** of Ham. Par. and **Philip Hufman** .. Ł50 .. part of greater tract .. cor. to Lewis .. 146 a. .. free of all claims of Joseph Martin & Cathoran, his wife. *Signed*: **Joseph Martin, Catheran (X) Martin.** *Rec*: 24 March 1772, ack. by **Joseph Martin** and **Catherine**, his wife.

Page 441. 28 September 1771. Bill of Sale. **Thomas Boggess** to **Martin Pickett** .. one Negro woman .. for Ł77 .. *Signed*: **Thos. Boggess.** *Wits*: **Thomas Maddux, Jr., Jacob Coons.** *Rec*: 23 March 1772, prov. by o. of wits.

Page 442. 24 March 1771. Apprentice's Bond. Bet. **Gerard Fowke** of Ham. Par. and **W. Phillips** of Staf. Co. .. sd. Fowke binds himself to W. Phillips for four years .. to learn carpentry .. *Signed*: **G. Fowke, Wm. Phillips.** *Rec*: 24 March 1772, ack. by parties.

Pages 443–445. 25 September 1771. B & S. Bet. **William Kesterson & Elizabeth**, his wife, and **William Blackwell, Jr.** .. Ł10 .. 64 acres .. adj. the lands of **George Crump, William Blackwell** and the land called Screens .. to **John Baylis** from Prop. *Signed*: **Wm. Kesterson.** *Wits*: **Thomas Keith, Joseph Blackwell, Jr., W. Nelson.** *Rec*: 24 March 1772, prov. by o. of wits.

END OF DEED BOOK 4

DEED BOOK NO. 5

1772 – 1774

Pages 1-6. 6 March 1772. Lease & release. Bet. **Judson Cooledge &
Mary,** his wife, of Maryland and **Thomas Bartlett** .. granted by Prop.
to **John Clark** of Salem in New England and by Clark conveyed to
James Campbell & by sd. Campbell & **Judith,** his wife, to sd.
Cooledge .. east side of main br. of Goose Creek called Hunger Run
[Little River] cor. to land of **John Fishback** and **Jacob Holtzclaw** ..
cor. to Major **James Ball** .. 2 small branches of Crummynses Run
[Cromwell's or Crummies' Run] .. land of **Dr. Thornton** .. 1,748 a. ..
Ł400 .. *Signed:* **Judson Cooledge, Mary Cooledge.** *Wits:* **Sanford
Carroll, Reubin Strother, William Yates.** *Rec:* 27 April 1772, prov.
by o. of wits.

Pages 6-10. 21 April 1772. Lease & release. Bet. **Thomas Bartlett
& Anne,** his wife, of Leeds Par. and **Minor Winn** .. same from Prop.
to **John Clark** of Salem (5 July 1740) .. same from **Cooledge** to
Bartlett .. cor. of **Thornton** & Clark .. flatt stone on Little River ..
mouth of the Whitewood Br. .. with **Josiah Fishback's** lines of the
land he bought of the sd. Clark's Tract .. Ł375 .. 1160 a. .. *Signed:*
Thomas Bartlett, Ann (X) Bartlett. *Rec:* 27 April 1772, ack. by grantors.

Pages 10-13. 1 April 1772. B & S. Bet. **Thomas Bartlett & Anne,**
his wife, of Leeds Par. and **John Hathaway** .. Ł200 .. part of larger
tract purchased of **Judson Cooledge** .. 514 a. .. cor. to **Gibson's** land ..
Signed: **Thomas Bartlett, Anne (X) Bartlett.** *Rec:* 27 April 1772, ack.
by Grantors.

Pages 13-15. 27 April 1772. B & S. Bet. **Thomas Bartlett & Anne,**
his wife, and **George Grant** of Ham. Par. .. Ł100 .. 227 a. .. in Par. of
Leeds .. joining land of **Wright, Hathaway, Barker** and **Bartlett** on
waters of Little River .. *Signed:* as above. *Rec:* 27 April 1772, ack.
by grantors.

Pages 15-17. 27 April 1772. B & S. Bet. **Thomas Bartlett & Anne,**
his wife, and **Josiah Fishback** .. Ł16.15s. .. 99 a. .. part of larger tract
pur. by Bartlett of **Cooledge** .. cor. to **Holtzclaw** standing on east side
of Hunger Run .. *Signed:* as above. *Rec:* 27 April 1772, ack. by grantors.

Pages 17-21. 26 April 1772. Lease & release. Bet. **Minor Winn &**
Margaret, his wife, of Leeds Par. and **James Winn** .. part of larger
tract from **Bartlett** to Winn .. Jesse's Branch .. River side ..
Fishback's line .. Whitewood Br. .. **Wright**'s line .. 424 a. .. Ł140 ..
Signed: **Minor (W) Winn, Margret (M) Winn**. *Rec*: 27 April 1772,
ack. by grantors.

Pages 21-23. 27 April 1772. B & S. Bet. **Minor Winn & Margaret**,
his wife, of Leeds Par. and **John Wright** .. Ł94.8.2. .. part of larger
tract Winn purchased of **Martin Pickett** .. which tract lays joining the
Dividing Line bet. **Thomas Bartlett** and the sd. **Pickett** .. cor. of
Fishback & Clark .. cor. for **Thornton & Clark** .. east side of
Whitewood Br. .. 292 a. .. *Signed*: **Minor (W) Winn, Margret (M)**
Winn. *Rec*: 27 April 1772, ack. by grantors.

Pages 23-27. 12/21 November 1771. Lease & release. Bet. **David**
Jenifer of Charles Co., Md. and **George Lamkin** .. following tracts of
land .. 17 a. on which George Lamkin had a mill & where there now
stands a mill and 225 a. bet. Chattin Run and Goose Creek contiguous
to the sd. Mill; 125 a. of which Lamkin pur. of **David Robinson** and the
remainder thereof from a certain **Thomas Furr** .. the sd. 225 a. of land
were conveyed to sd. Lamkin by **Simon Miller** .. and was sold by sd.
Lamkin & wife **Sarah** to David Jenifer .. 24/25 Feb. 1768 .. Ł151 ..
Signed: **David Jenifer**. *Wits*: **W. Ellzey, Danl McCarty, Chs.**
Eskridge. *Rec*: 25 May 1772, ack. by grantor.

Pages 28-31. 29/30 May 1771. Lease & release. Bet. **Joseph Delany**
and **John Stroud** of King Geo. Co. .. 162 a. .. in **Downman**'s Line ..
Ludwell's line .. part of tract given to sd. Delany by his father, dec'd
.. 1722 .. Ł10 .. *Signed*: **Joseph Delaney**. *Wits*: **W. Delaney, Jno.**
Smith, Chas. Murphey, Chas. Holdway. *Rec*: 26 August 1771, prov.
by o. of **William Delany and Charles Murphey**. 25 May 1772, by o. of
Charles Holdway.

Pages 31-32. September 1771. Bill of sale. **William Linton** of Pr.
Wm. Co. to **Daniel Shumate** .. one mare .. for 1000 lbs. crop tobacco
and 30s. *Signed*: **William Linton**. *Wit*: **Humphrey Brooke**. *Rec*.
25 May 1772, prov. by o. of wit.

Pages 32-34. 16 January 1772. B & S. Bet. **William Dulin &**
Clemence, his wife, of Leeds Par. and **Martin & William Pickett**,
Exors. of the last will of William Pickett, dec'd. .. Ł15 .. tract on NE
side of Carters Run .. 15a. .. small br. called Deep Ford .. cor. of
William McLanaham .. including the mill now called Pickett's Mill ..
being part of larger tract whereon the sd. Dulin now lives ... *Signed*:
William Dulin, Clamore Dulin. *Wits*: **Lazarus Hitt, William Dulin,**
George Pickett, Eve (X) Hitt, Thomas McClanaham. *Rec*: 25 May
1772, ack. by grantors.

Pages 34-35. 1 December 1771. Bill of sale. **Ephraim Hubbard** to
Martin Pickett .. tobacco, corn, cattle .. Ł88 .. *Signed*: **Ephraim**

Hubbard. *Wit*: Joseph Williams, Hurman (X) Utterback.
May 1772, prov. by o. of Joseph Williams.

Pages 35-38. 20 April 1772. B & S. Bet. Joseph Holtzclaw & Caty,
his wife, of Leeds Par. and Martin Pickett of same .. L10 .. tract
devised to sd. Holtzclaw by Jacob Holtzclaw his Grandfather .. 337 a.
.. by deed dtd. 1 Dec. 1742 from Prop., except 200 a. to be taken out
of sd. tract which was also devised by the sd. Jacob Holtzclaw to
Henry Holtzclaw and James Holtzclaw .. joining a tract before taken
up by Jacob Holtzclaw and near Little River .. n. side of br. of Hunger
Run, near line of Thomas Bartlett and Edward Feagan .. line of
Walker .. cor. to land surveyed for Thomas Barton .. *Signed*: Joseph
Holtzclaw, Caty Holtzclaw. *Wits*: John Likely, Joseph Blackwell,
George Pickett. *Rec*: 29 April 1772, ack. by Joseph Holtzclaw. 25
May 1772. ack. by Caty Holtzclaw.

Pages 38-41. 25 May 1772. B & S. Bet. Thomas Bartlett & Anne,
his wife, of Leeds Par. and Abraham Gibson of same .. L85 .. 204 a.
.. part of larger tract at the head of Little River .. part of tract pur. by
Bartlett of Coledge .. white oak on head of Little River ... *Signed*:
Thomas Bartlett, Anne Bartlett. *Rec*: 25 May 1772, ack. by grantors.

Pages 41-45. 1 November 1771. Lease. Bet. Thomas Lord Fairfax
and William Briggs .. tract in Manor of Leeds .. in Thos. Withers'
line .. river bank .. 200 a. .. for his nat. life and lives of J u d a , his
wife and David, his son .. yearly rent of 40s. .. *Signed*: Fairfax.
Wits: Jas. Scott, Jr., John (X) Pepper, John Chilton, Thomas Keith.
Rec: 25 May 1772, prov. by o. of James Scott, Thomas Keith and John
Chilton.

Pages 45-49. 1 November 1771. Lease. Bet. Thomas Lord Fairfax
and Dickerson Wood .. tract in Manor of Leeds .. cor. of Smootes &
H o p p e r s .. 100 a. .. for his nat. life and lives of Mary, his wife and
Mary Wood, his dau. .. yearly rent of 20s. *Signed*: Fairfax. *Wits*: as
above. *Rec*: 25 May 1772, prov. by o. of wits. listed above.

Pages 49-52. 1 November 1771. Lease. Bet. Thomas Lord Fairfax
and Jesse Thompson .. tract in Manor of Leeds .. line of Rd. Crawley
and near a line of Samuel Harris ... William Fletcher .. cor. of William Briggs .. large rock cor. to Briggs .. 140 a. .. for his nat. life and
the lives of Elizabeth, his wife and Fielding Jones .. yearly rent of
28s. *Signed*: Fairfax. *Wits*: as above. *Rec*: 25 May 1772, prov. by o.
of wits. as above.

Pages 53-57. 20 May 1772. Lease. Bet. Col. Richard Henry Lee of
W'land Co. and Alexander Bradford .. tract in Leeds Par. .. 185a...
Jones' Spring Br., cor. to Atwel .. cor. to Spicer and Price .. during
his nat. life and lives of Austin Bradford and Joseph Bradford ..
yearly rent of L11.2s. .. *Signed*: Richard Henry Lee, Alexander Bradford. *Wits*: Jos. Blackwell, Martin Pickett, Bennett Price. *Rec*: 25
May 1772, prov. by o. of wits.

Pages 57-60. 20 May 1772. Lease. Bet. **Richard Henry Lee** of W'land Co. and **Edmond Bayse** .. 118 a. .. in Hooe's line cor. to **Joseph Jeffries** .. **Bragg** .. cor. of **Arnold** in Turkey Run old field .. **Jones** .. during his nat. life and lives of **Nancy**, his wife, and **Jacob Bayse** .. yearly rent of Ł4.19s.5d. .. *Signed*: **Richard Henry Lee, Edmon Basye**. *Wits*: as above. *Rec*: 25 May 1772, prov. by o. of wits.

Pages 60-64. 20 May 1772. Lease. Bet. **Col. Richard Henry Lee** and **Humphrey Arnold** .. tract in Ham. Par. .. 141 a. .. Turkey Run .. cor. to **John Hathaway** .. cor. to **Taylor** .. cor. to **Joseph Jeffries** .. for his nat. life and lives of **Anne Arnold**, his wife and **Benjamin Arnold** ... yearly rent of Ł7.9s. *Signed*: **Richard Henry Lee, Humphrey Arnold**. *Wits*: **Jos. Blackwell, Martin Pickett, Randolph Spicer**. *Rec*: 25 May 1772, prov. by o. of wits.

Pages 64-69. 20 May 1772. Lease. Bet. **Richard Henry Lee** and **Martin Pickett** ... 123 a. .. in Leeds Par. .. cor. to **Kitson** and **Headley** .. Cattail Branch .. cor. to **Bell** .. cor. to **Grant** and **Bell** .. for his nat. life and lives of **Ann Pickett** and **Blackwell Pickett** ... yearly rent of Ł6.6s. *Signed*: **Richard Henry Lee, Martin Pickett**. *Wits*: **Jos. Blackwell, Francis Attwell, Bennett Price**. *Rec*: 25 May 1772, prov. by o. of wits.

Pages 69-74. 20 May 1772. Lease. Bet. **Richard Henry Lee** and **Martin Pickett** .. 27 a. .. in Leeds Par. .. cor. to **Kitson** .. cor. to **Jones** .. old peach tree stump in the Court old field .. **Robison's House** .. cor. of **Pickett's** garden and cor. to **Headley** .. including the sd. Pickett's houses, Pailings and gardens .. for his nat. life and the lives of **Ann**, his wife and **Blackwell Pickett** .. yearly rent of Ł3.12s.5d. .. *Signed*: **Richard Henry Lee & Martin Pickett**. *Wits*: **Bennett Price, Franc's Attwell, Randolph Spicer**. *Rec*: 25 May 1772, prov. by o. of wits.

Pages 74-78. 20 May 1772. Lease. Bet. **Richard Henry Lee** and **Randolph Spicer** ... 80 a. in Ham. Par. .. cor. to **Capt. Edmonds** .. Hathaways line .. TL [Thomas Lee] cor. to Main Tract .. for his life and lives of **Randolph** (son of **Wm. Spicer**) and **Randolph Smith** .. yearly rent of Ł4.16s. .. *Signed*: **Richard Henry Lee, Randolph Spicer**. *Wits*: **Jos. Blackwell, Franc's Attwell, Bennett Price**. Note: Randolph Spicer, nor any of the parties, to keep a public house or ordinary, without the permission of **R. H. Lee** in writing – the tenants on 1 1/2 a. near the Courthouse to use wood for fire purposes from this tenement and Spicer not to use any of the wood for coal for blacksmith purposes. *Rec*: 25 May 1772, prov. by o. of wits.

Pages 78-82. 20 May 1772. Lease. Bet. **Richard Henry Lee** and **Francis Attwell** .. 299 a. .. in Par. of Leeds .. cor. of **Bradford & Jones'** Spring branch .. cor. of **Ball** .. cor. to **Kitson** and **Hudnall** .. or his nat. life and lives of **Mary Attwell** and **Ludwell Lee** .. yearly rent of Ł17.18s.10d. .. *Signed*: **Richard Henry Lee, Francis Attwell**. *Wits*: **Jos. Blackwell, Martin Pickett, Bennett Price**. *Rec*: 25 May 1772, prov. by o. of wits.

Pages 82-87. 20 May 1772. Lease. Bet. **Richard Henry Lee** and **William Jones** .. 321 a. .. in Ham. Par .. Arnold's line .. cor. to **Arnold & Basye** .. cor. to **Pickett** .. cor. peach tree stump in the Courthouse old field .. cor. to **John Peake** .. cor. to **Peake and Taylor** .. for his nat. life .. yearly rent ₤14.18s.10d. *Signed*: **Richard Henry Lee, William (M) Jones.** *Wits*: **Bennett Price, Jos. Blackwell, Martin Pickett.** *Rec*: 25 May 1772, prov. by o. of wits.

Pages 87-93. 20 May 1772. Lease. Bet. **Richard Henry Lee** and **William Kitson** .. 95 a. in Leeds Par. .. cor. to **Ball** .. cor. of **Bell** and **Attwell** .. cor. of **Hudnall & Mr. Pickett** .. and **Headley** .. for his nat. life and lives of **Jane Kitson** and **James Birch Kitson** .. yearly rent of ₤5.14s. .. *Signed*: **Richard Henry Lee, William Kitson.** *Wits*: **Jos. Blackwell, Martin Pickett, Bennett Price.** *Rec*: 25 May 1772, prov. by o. of wits.

Pages 93-95. 14 May 1772. Trust. Bet. **Compton Williamson** of Calvert Co., Md. and **Richard Lingan Hall** of R'mond Co. .. marriage hath been had bet. sd. **Williamson** and **Mary Hall**, sister of R. L. Hall .. before marriage she was possessed of slaves .. given her by her mother, **Martha Hampton**, dec'd by deed before Martha m. **Richard Hampton**, dec'd .. in trust to R. L. Hall for his sister .. *Signed*: **Compton Williamson.** *Wits*: **Jas. Scott, Jr., Wm. Ransdell, Sam'l. Lingan.** *Rec*: 26 May 1772, prov. by o. of **James Scott** and **Samuel Lingan**, wits.

Pages 95-97. 7 June 1772. Mortgage. Bet. **William Courtney, Sr.** and **Richard Lewis** of King Geo. Co. .. ₤24 .. parcel whereon Courtney now lives .. 150 a. .. livestock .. on condition that sd. ₤24 is paid by 25 Oct. 1772 .. then to be void. *Signed*: **William (X) Courtney.** *Wits*: **Andrew Buchanan, James Robison, Alexander Wodrow.** *Rec*: 22 June 1772, prov. by o. of wits.

Pages 97-101. 30 November 1771. Lease. Bet. **Thomas Lord Fairfax** and **Sarah Ellis** .. tract in Manor of Leeds .. cor. to **Benj. Douglass** .. line of **Samuel Littrell** .. cor. to **John Marshall** .. 105 a. .. for her nat. life and the lives of **William**, her son and **Caty**, her dau. .. yearly rent of 21s. *Signed*: **Fairfax.** *Wits*: **J. Moffett, Thos. Barby, John Allan, Jr., Thos. Keith.** *Rec*: 25 May 1772, prov. by o. of **Thomas Keith** and **John Moffett.** 23 June 1772, prov. by o. of **John Allen, Jr.**

Pages 101-105. 30 November 1771. Lease. Bet. **Thomas Lord Fairfax** and **Roseanna Hurst** .. tract in Manor of Leeds .. 100 a. .. for her nat. life and lives of **Henry**, her son and **Delilah**, her dau. .. yearly rent of 20s. sterling ... *Signed*: **F a i r f a x.** *Wits*: as above. *Rec*: as above.

Pages 105-109. 30 November 1771. Lease. Bet. **Thos. Lord Fairfax** and **William Cooke** .. Manor of Leeds .. on Catemount Br. in the line of **Francis Payne** .. east side of Great Br. of South Run .. 120 a. for

fe and lives of **Ceccy**, his wife, and **Nancy Allen**, his niece
r year. *Signed*: **Fairfax**. *Wits*: as above. *Rec*: as above.

-114. 30 November 1771. Lease. Bet. **Thomas Lord Fair-**
.. ..u **James Glover** .. tenement in Manor of Leeds .. cor. of **John
Ellis** .. line of **Benjamin Piper** .. line of **John Robinson** .. 155 a. .. for
his nat. life and lives of **Benjamin** and **Richard Glover**, his brothers ..
yearly rent of 31s. sterling .. *Signed*: **Fairfax**. *Wits*: as above. *Rec*:
as above.

Pages 114-117. 30 November 1771. Lease. Between **Thos. Lord
Fairfax** and **Jacob Browning** .. tenement in Manor of Leeds .. Beg. at
oak on the Hedgman River near a large rock .. 100 a. .. during his nat.
life & lives of **Elizabeth**, his wife and **Thomas**, his son .. yearly rent
of 20s. .. *Signed*: **Fairfax**. *Wits*: as above. *Rec*: as above.

Pages 117-120. 30 November 1771. Lease. Bet. **Thomas Lord Fair-**
fax and **Thomas Payne** .. tenement in Manor of Leeds .. side of the
Naked Ridge .. 200 a. for his nat. life and the lives of **Sarah**, his wife,
and **Nancy**, his dau. .. yearly rent of 40s. sterling .. *Signed*: **Fairfax**.
Wits: as above. *Rec*: as above.

Pages 120-123. 30 November 1771. Lease. Bet. **Thomas Lord Fair-**
fax and **William Walker** .. tenement in Manor of Leeds .. Beetree
Branch .. fork of sd. branch .. cor. to **William Linager** .. 218 a. .. for
his nat. life and lives of **Elizabeth**, his wife and **William** his son ..
year rent of 43s.20d. *Signed*: **Fairfax**. *Wits*: as above. *Rec*: as
above.

Pages 124-127. 30 November 1771. Lease. Bet. **Thomas Lord Fair-**
fax and **John Grant** .. tenement in Manor of Leeds .. cor. to **Roseanna
Hurst** .. line of **Reuben Payne** .. cor. to said Payne and **Simon Hethl-**
ing .. 120 a. .. for his nat. life and lives of John and Daniel, his sons
.. yearly rent of 24s. sterling ... *Signed*: **F a i r f a x**. *Wits*: as above.
Rec: as above.

Pages 127-131. 30 November 1771. Lease. Bet. **Thomas Lord Fair-**
fax and **William Briggs** ... tenement in Manor of Leeds .. Large rock
cor. to **Sarah Ellis** .. line of **Benj. Douglass** .. large rocks on the
Hedgman River .. 163 a. .. during the nat. lives of **Thompson** and
Ebenezer, his sons, and **Isabel**, his dau. .. yearly rent of 22s.7d. ..
Signed: **Fairfax**. *Wits*: **John Moffett, Thos. Barbey, John Allen, Jr.,
Thos. Keith**. *Rec*: 25 May 1772, prov. by o. of **Thomas Keith** and **John
Moffett**. 23 June 1772, prov. by o. of **John Allen, Jr.**

Pages 131-134. 30 November 1771. Lease. Bet. **Thomas Lord Fair-**
fax and **William Corder** .. tenement in Manor of Leeds .. cor. to **John
McCormick** and in the line of **William Corder, Jr.** .. Beetree Branch
.. 137 a. .. year rent of 27s.4d. .. for his natural life and lives of
Joseph, his son, and **Eve**, his dau. .. *Signed*: **Fairfax**. *Wit*: as above.
Rec: as above.

Pages 134–138. 30 November 1771. Lease. Bet. **Thomas Lord Fairfax** and **John Jones** .. tenement in Manor of Leeds .. oak by **Crimm's** path cor. to **William Morgan** .. 170 a. .. for his nat. life and lives of **Elizabeth**, his wife, and **Reuben**, his son .. yearly rent of 34s. sterling. *Signed*: **Fairfax**. *Wits*: as above. *Rec*: as above.

Pages 139–143. 30 November 1771. Lease. Bet. **Thomas Lord Fairfax** and **James Hethling** .. tenement in Manor of Leeds .. cor. to **John Ellis** and in the line of **John Hopper** .. cor. to sd. **Hopper** and **Henry Jones** .. 140 a. .. yearly rent of 28s. ster. .. for his nat. life and lives of **Elizabeth**, his wife, and **Steuart**, his son .. *Signed*: **Fairfax**. *Wits*: as above. *Rec*: as above.

Pages 143–147. 30 November 1771. Lease. Bet. **Thos. Lord Fairfax** and **George Randall** .. tenement in Manor of Leeds .. cor. to **Peter Laurence's** lott .. in **Sinclair's** line .. **John Smith's** line .. 100 a. .. for his nat. life and lives of **Charity**, his wife, and **Caty**, their dau. .. yearly rent of 20s. sterling .. *Signed*: **Fairfax**. *Wits*: as above. *Rec*: as above.

Pages 147–152. 30 November 1771. Lease. Bet. **Thomas Lord Fairfax** and **John Hamrick** .. tenement in Leeds Manor .. cor. to **William Jett's** lot .. 134 a. for his nat. life and lives of **Nancy**, his wife, and **William Hamrick**, his son .. yearly rent of 26s.9d. *Signed*: **Fairfax**. *Wits*: as above. *Rec*: as above.

Pages 152–156. 30 November 1771. Lease. Bet. **Thos. Lord Fairfax** and **John Dearing** ..tenement in Manor of Leeds .. cor. to **Robert Bolt's** leased lot cor. to **Jett** .. **Narmon's** line .. with **Waller** .. to **Pinchard's** cor. .. 100 a. .. for his nat. life and lives of **Ann**, his wife and **George Dearing**, his brother .. yearly rent of 20s. sterling .. *Signed*: **Fairfax**. *Wits*: as above. *Rec*: as above.

Pages 157–161. 30 November 1771. Lease. Bet. **Thomas Lord Fairfax** and **John Jett** .. tenement in Manor of Leeds .. cor. to **Jesse Norman** .. with **William Jett's** Lott .. 238a. .. for his nat. life and lives of **Francis Jett** and **Daniel Jett**, his brothers .. yearly rent of 47s.7d. *Signed*: **Fairfax**. *Wits*: as above. *Rec*: as above.

Pages 161–165. 30 November 1771. Lease. Bet. **Thomas Lord Fairfax** and **Richard Randall** .. Tenement in Manor of Leeds .. **Robert Bolt's** line .. cor. to **Mrs. Oldham** .. 150 a. .. for nat. life of **John Randall** [sic] and lives of **Anne**, his wife, and **Richard Randall**, their son .. yearly rent of 30s. .. sd. **Richard**, his heirs & assigns shall and will well and truly pay .. *Signed*: **Fairfax**. *Wits*: as above. *Rec*: as above.

Pages 165–168. 30 November 1771. Lease. Bet. **Thos. Lord Fairfax** and **William Jett** .. tenement in Manor of Leeds .. beg. cor. to **Jesse Norman** .. 100a. .. for his nat. life and lives of wife **Sarah** and **Peter Jett**, their son .. yearly rent of 20s. ster. *Signed*: **Fairfax**. *Wits*: as above. *Rec*: as above.

Pages 169-172. 30 November 1771. Lease. Bet. **Thomas Lord Fairfax** and **Daniel Bennett** .. tenement in the Manor of Leeds .. to lot line of **John Crimm**, dec'd .. 100a. .. for the nat. life and lives of **Mary**, his wife, and **Sanford**, his son .. yearly rent of 20s. sterling .. *Signed*: Fairfax. *Wits*: as above. *Rec*: as above.

Pages 172-177. 7 July 1772. Lease. Bet. **H e n r y L e e** of Pr. Wm. Co. and **Uriel Crosby** of Staf. Co. .. on behalf of sd. Crosby, **Susannah**, his wife and **George**, his son .. 180a. .. lot No. 15 on survey made by **Thomas Marshall**, Surveyor of Fauquier County, part of tract granted to **Burgess** and from him descended to his grandson, **Burgess Smith**, who sold same to **James Ball** who sold to **Henry Lee** .. deed rec. in Fauq. Co. .. reserving the right to build a road to suit the tenants .. and the privilege of hunting and Fowling in or upon any part thereof .. yearly rent of 700 lbs. crop tobacco in one hogshead at some warehouse in Pr. Wm. Co. .. also 4 fat turkeys to be delivered at the Mansion house of the sd. Lee .. Quit rent & taxes .. *Signed*: **H e n r y Lee, Uriel Crosby**. *Wits*: Thos. Harrison, Howson Hooe, James Murrey, James (╀) Tolle. *Rec*: 27 July 1772, prov. by o. of all wits except **Howson Hooe**.

Pages 178-183. 7 July 1772. Lease. Bet. **Henry Lee**, of Pr. Wm. Co., and **James Murrey** .. for nat. life of Murrey and lives of **Lidia**, his wife, and **Reubin**, his son .. 180a. .. Lot No. 14, situate near Little River and being the place once called burns [sic] on the Long Branch in Leeds Par .. same granted to **Burgess**, descended to his grandson **Burgess Smith**, who sold to **Jas. Ball**, who sold to sd. Lee .. (same rent as above) .. during each life the rent to be raised 100 lbs .. *Signed*: James Murrey, Henry Lee. *Wits*: **Howson Hooe, Thomas Harrison, Uriel Crosby, James (╀) Tolle**. *Rec*: 27 July 1772, prov. by o. of all wits. except Hooe.

Pages 183-185. 22 July 1772. B & S. Bet. **John Rector, Sr.**, Planter & **Catherine**, his wife, and **James Stewart, Jr.** of Fx. Co. .. Ł90.8s. .. on waters of Goose Creek .. part of tract sold by **Burgess Ball**, Gent. of Lan. Co. to sd. Rector .. 7 Dec. 1770, for 4,874 a. .. 226 a. .. *Signed*: **John (R) Rictor, Katharine (CR) Rictor**. *Wits*: Henry Rictor, J. Moffett, Samuel Grigsby, John Hermons, Jacob (╀F) Fourbain. *Rec*: 27 July 1772, prov. by o. of **Henry Rector, Samuel Grigsby** and **John Hurmans**.

Page 186. 1772. Apprentice's Bond. Bet. **Barnard Dearing** and **John Dearing** .. Barnard apprentices himself to John Dearing .. until the age of 21 .. to learn the trade of a house carpenter .. *Signed*: **Barnett (+) Dearing, John Dearing**. *Rec*: 27 July 1772, ack. by **Barnett Dearing** and **John Dearing**.

Pages 186-189. 22 July 1772. Deed of Gift. Bet. **William Asbury** of Leeds Par., Planter, **Molly Leek [Lake ?]** dau. of the sd. **Wm. Asbury** .. for love and affection .. tract .. on the waters of Broad Run of Occoquan .. whereon **William Leek**, husband of sd. Molly now resides ..

cor. to **Robert Scott** .. to the late Rev. **Alex'r Scott's** line .. cor. to Capt. **Jas. Ball** .. along **Glascock's** line .. 76 a. .. *Signed*: **William (W) Asbury.** *Wits*: **J. Moffett, Henry Allen, Samuel Grigsby, Thomas Glascock.** *Rec*: 27 July 1772, prov. by o. of **Henry Allen, Samuel Grigsby, Thomas Glascock.**

Pages 189-191. 22 July 1772. Lease. Bet. **Harmon Hitt** of Leeds Par. and **Randolph Spicer** .. tract near the Watry Mountain .. red oak standing near the Bear Wallow .. 106 a. .. during his nat. life and lives of **John Attwell** (son of **Francis Attwell**) and **William Spicer** (son of Wm. Spicer) .. yearly rent of Ł5.6s. ... *Signed*: **Harmon Hitt, Randolph Spicer.** *Rec*: 27 July 1772, ack. by parties.

Pages 191-194. 24 March 1772. Mortgage. Bet. **John Churchhill** and **Andrew Cochrane, William Cunninghame, John Murdock, Peter Murdock, Robert Bogle** and **Alexander Cunninghame,** of Glasgow .. merchants .. grantor indebted to grantees in am't. of Ł1,039.12s.5d. by **James Robison** their Agent & Factor at Falmouth in K. Geo. Co. .. tract whereon John Churchhill lives .. which he pur. from **M a r t i n Pickett** .. 600 a. .. slaves .. to be void upon payment of sd. sum within two years .. *Signed*: **John Churchhill.** *Wits*: **Richard Chichester, W. Ellzey, John Likely.** *Rec*: 24 August 1772, ack. by **John Churchhill.**

Pages 194-195. 22 August 1772. Bill of Sale. **Burr Harrison** to **Russell & Lee** for Ł67.4s.9d. .. slaves .. cattle .. household furniture .. *Signed*: **Burr Harrison.** *Wits*: **P. Hammond, Henry Hammett, William Carr, John Neilson.** *Rec*: 24 August 1772, prov. by o. of last two wits.

Pages 195-198. 24 August 1772. B & S. Bet. **James Scott** of Leeds Par. & **Elizabeth,** his wife, and **William Edmonds** .. Ł237.15s. .. tract of 317a.1r. 5p. .. Beg. .. small island of the Mill Run about 60 poles above the parish Line and runs with a line of **William Ransdall** .. Cedar Run .. cor. with sd. **Ransdall** and **Stamps** Lott .. cor. to Stamps and **Stewarts** Lott .. part of tract whereon Scott now lives ... *Signed*: **James Scott, Jr., Eliz'a Scott.** *Rec*: 24 August 1772, ack. by Scott and wife.

Pages 198-199. 24 August 1772. Bond. **James Scott, Jr., Cuthbert Bullitt** and **Cuthbert Harrison** to **William Edmonds** .. For: Ł5,000 .. conditions: Scott to keep all covenants, etc. in abovementioned indenture .. *Signed*: **Jas. Scott, Jr., C. Bullett, Cuth't. Harrison.** *Wits*: **John Churchhill, A. Churchhill, John Eustace.** *Rec*: 27 August 1772, ack. by Scott, Bullett, & Harrison.

Pages 199-202. 10 June 1772. B & S. Bet. **Landon Carter & Charles Carter,** Esq's., Exors. of Charles Carter, Esq., dec'd. and **William W y a t t** .. recites Act of Assembly enabling them to sell lands of Charles Carter, dec'd. to pay his debts [See Hening:*Statutes at Large*, v. 8, p. 436]... 250 a. .. part of Kettle Run tract in Ham. Par. .. Ł125 .. cor. to **Chilton & Hughes** .. high knowl cor. to **McClaningham** ..

Hedger & Steel's line .. cor. to Shirley .. *Signed*: **Landon Carter,
Charles Carter**. *Wits*: **John Chilton, Catesby Woodford, Jeremiah
Wilson**. *Rec*: 24 August 1772, prov. by o. of wits.

Pages 202-205.　22 July 1772.　B & S. Bet. **John Rictor, Sr.** &
Catherine, his wife, and **John Harmons**, Doctor of Physic .. Ł38 .. on
waters of Goose Creek where Harmons now lives .. bet. the lands of
Joseph Robinson, William Fitzgerald, Alexander McPherson and the
sd. John Rector's own land whereon his son, **Benjamin Rector**, now
lives .. 151 a. .. pur. by sd. Rector of **Burgess Smith** .. *Signed*: **John
(R) Rictor, Katharine (CR) Rictor**. *Wits*: **John Moffett, Samuel
Grigsby, Jacob (HF) Faubion**. *Rec*: 27 July 1772, prov. by o. of wits.

Pages 205-210.　30-31 March 1772.　Lease & release.　Bet. **Bryan
Fairfax** of Fx. Co., Esq. and **Elizabeth**, his wife, and **Thomas Chinn**
of Loud. Co. .. tract on branches of Crummy Run .. cor. of Maj. **James
Ball's Horspen Tract** .. line of **Tilman Weaver** .. to **Burgess'** line ..
Crummy Run .. line of **Doct'r Thornton** .. line of the land of Mr. **John
Clarke** .. 680 a. .. Ł200. *Signed*: **Bryan Fairfax, Elizabeth Fairfax**.
Wits: **James Leith, John Rictor, George Brent, Charles West**. *Rec*:
22 June 1772, prov. by o. of **George Brent**. 24 Aug. 1772. prov. by o.
of **James Leith & Charles West**, wits.　Commission to examine
Elizabeth Fairfax, recorded.

Pages 210-212.　24 August 1772.　B & S. Bet. **Jeremiah Darnall** &
Catherine, his wife, of Ham. Par. .. and **Francis Southard** .. Ł25 ..
Surveyed by **John Moffett** .. cor. to **Morgan Darnall** .. line of **William
Smith** .. cor. **Corbin's** line .. 35 2/3 a. *Signed*: **Jeremiah Darnall,
Catherine (X) Darnall**. *Rec*: 24 August 1772, ack. by grantors.

Pages 212-213.　22 August 1772.　Agreement. Bet. **Mary Isham Keith**
of Leeds Par., widow & relict of the late **James Keith**, Clerk and
Thomas Keith, who paid her Ł150 for the paiment of her debts & to
maintain her .. slaves .. her dower in certain estate in possession of
Nicholas Davis, after Davis' death shall devolve to her the sd. Mary
Isham Keith, by the death of her mother, **Judith Davis** .. Thomas Keith
to become possessed of same after the death of Davis. *Signed*: **Mary
Isham Keith, Thomas Keith**. *Wits*: **John O'Bannon, William Morgan,
Burr (B) Barton**. *Rec*: 24 August 1772, .prov. by o. of O'Bannon and
Morgan.

Pages 213-214.　29 February 1772.　Bill of Sale.　**William Linton** of
Fauq. Co. to **John Waddle** .. cattle, household furniture .. for debt due
to Waddle of Ł10 .. and as security for debt of Ł2.11s.4 1/2d. ..
Signed: **William (X) Linton**. *Wits*: **John Likely, Charles Chilton**.
Rec: 24 Aug. 1772, prov. by o. of **John Likely**.

Pages 214-218.　20 May 1772.　Lease.　Bet. Col. **Richard Henry Lee**
of W'moreland Co. and **George Green** .. tenement in Ham. Par. ..
143a. .. cor. to **Peter Kamper** .. cor. to **Bragg** .. cor. to **Price** & Bragg
.. hiccory on Great Run, cor. to Price .. *Signed*: **Richard Henry Lee,**

George (X) Green. *Wits*: **Joseph Blackwell, Martin Pickett, Randolph Spicer.** *Rec*: 24 Aug. 1772, prov. by o. of wits.

Pages 218-220. 1772. B & S. Bet. **Daniel Bradford,** exor. of will of **Daniel Marr,** dec'd. and **Jemima Marr** .. both of Ham. Par .. Ł31 .. tract .. part of estate of Daniel Marr, dec'd .. south side of Horspen run .. **Hoppers Land** .. **McBees Line** .. 551a. .. *Signed*: **Daniel Bradford.** Receipt dated 4 Aug. 1772. *Rec*: 24 August 1772, ack. by Bradford.

Pages 220-221. 1772. B & S. Bet. **Daniel Bradford,** exor. of will of **Daniel Marr,** dec'd .. and **John Wheatley,** both of Ham. Par. .. Ł431 .. part of estate of Daniel Marr, dec'd .. in line of **Hedgman** and Wheatley .. near **Thornton's** cor. .. on east side of Tin Pott Run .. 581 a. .. *Signed*: **Daniel Bradford.** Receipt dated 24 August 1772. *Rec*: 24 August 1772, ack. by Bradford.

Page 222. 22 November 1769. Power of attorney. From **Pearson Chapman** of Charles Co., Md., Gent., appts. trusty friend, **John Moffett,** Gent. true and lawful attorney .. to give leases to lands in Culpeper and Fauq. Cos.. esp. to **Daniel Bradford, John Kemper, James Nelson** and **Samuel Grigsby** of Fauq. .. *Signed*: **Pearson Chapman.** *Wits*: **Gabriel Moffett, John Hitt, Isaac Foster, Jas. Nelson, George Ceneard.** *Rec*: 24 August 1772. prov. by o. of **John Hitt** and **George Ceneard** ...

Pages 223-225. 6 July 1772. B & S. Bet. **Hector Ross** of Fx. Co. and **Jarvis Cornwell,** Planter .. Ł52 .. parcel, on Pignut Ridge, part of larger tract granted to **Edward Washington** of Pr. Wm. .. 12 Dec. 1739 .. for 614a. .. oak in **Edmonds Line** .. Southside of Pignut Ridge .. 120 a. *Signed*: **H. Ross.** *Wits*: **James Craig, John Moffett, Whart'n Ransdell, Martin Pickett.** *Rec*: 27 July 1772, prov. by o. of **John Moffett & Martin Pickett.** 24 Aug. 1772. prov. by o. of **J. Craig.**

Pages 225-228. 6 July 1772. B & S. Bet. **Hector Ross** of Fx. Co. Merchant and **James Bashaw,** Bricklayer .. Ł18.5s. .. parcel at the Pignut Ridge, it being part of larger tract granted to **Edward Washington** of Pr. Wm. Co. .. 12 Dec. 1739 .. for 614a. .. cor to the late **Jeffrey Johnson** .. oak in **Jarvis Cornwell's** line .. 152a. .. *Signed*: **H. Ross.** *Wits*: **James Craig, John Moffett, Wharton Ransdell, Martin Pickett.** *Rec*:24 August 1772, prov. by o. of Craig, Moffett and Pickett, wits.

Pages 228-231. 24 August 1772. B & S. Bet. **J a m e s   B a s h a w** and **Frances,** his wife, and **Joseph Green** of Pr. Wm. Co. .. Ł75 .. 152a. .. (same as above). *Signed*: **James Bashaw, Frances Bashaw.** *Rec*: 24 August 1772, ack. by grantors.

Pages 231-234. 28-29 May 1772. Lease & release. Bet. **John Baxter** of Pr. Wm. Co. and **William Young** of same .. 283 a. .. bounded by **Thomas Baxter, George Berry, William Florence & Thomas Hogan, Jr.** .. sd. tract was beq. to sd. Baxter by will by his grandfather Ben-

141

jamin Stribling, dec'd .. L75 .. *Signed*: **John Baxter**. *Wits*: **Thomas Dawkins, R. Chinn, Henry Brett, Chs. Vivian, John Riddle, Thos. Athey, Wm. Hampton.** *Rec*: 23 September 1772, prov. by o. of **Thomas Dawkins, Charles Vivian, Thomas Athey.**

Pages 234-236. 1 June 1772. B & S. Bet. **Robert Thompson** of Loud. Co. and **Lewis Lemmert** of same .. lease from **George Washington** to Robert Thompson .. 17 March 1769 .. partly in Loud. and partly in Fauq. .. 150a. .. same to Thompson for his nat. life and lives of **Daniel McPherson**, son of **Richard McPherson** and **Alice Gibson**, dau. of **Joseph Gibson** .. L30 .. Lemmart to pay yearly rent to George Washington .. *Signed*: **Robert (C) Thompson**. *Wit*: **Thomas West, Obediah Oliphant, Daniel Jones.** *Rec*: 26 October 1772, prov. by o. of wits.

Pages 236-238. 23 April 1772. B & S. Bet. **William Wood, Jr.** of Loud. Co. and **Thomas West** of same .. lease from **G. Washington** to **W. Wood** .. 17 March 1769 .. tenement, partly in Fauq. and partly in Loud. .. 220a. .. L30 .. West to pay G. Washington the yearly rent .. *Signed*: **William Wood**. *Wits*: **Lewis Lemmert, John Dyer, Daniel Jones, Obadiah Oliphant.** *Rec*: 26 October 1772, prov. by o. of Oliphant and Jones, by affirmation of Lemmert.

Pages 238-240. 23 April 1772. B & S. Bet. **William Wood, Jr.** of Loud. Co. and **Obadiah Oliphant** .. lease from **George Washington** to Wood .. 17 March 1769 .. 220a. .. in Loud. and Fauq. .. L30 .. Oliphant to pay G. Washington yearly rent. *Signed*: **William Wood**. *Wits*: **Lewis Lemmert, Thomas West, John Dyer, Daniel Jones.** *Rec*: 26 October 1772, prov. by o. of West & Jones, by affirmation of Lemmert.

Pages 240-241. 23 November 1772. Deed of Gift. Bet. **Henry Martin** and **Samuel Martin** .. for nat. love and affection .. 50a. .. known by the name of the Old Plantation in the Germantown .. *Signed*: **H e n r y Martin**. *Rec*: 23 November 1772, ack. by Henry Martin.

Pages 241-244. 23 November 1772. B & S. Bet. **Jacob Rictor & Mary**, his wife, and **Henry Utterback** .. L55 .. 100a. .. in Ham. Par. .. on Licking Run it being part of a tract .. taken up by **John Fishback** and others of the Germans .. this piece was delivered by the sd. John Fishback unto his daughter, **Elizabeth**, which intermarried with **Peter C a m p e r** who conveyed sd. land to Jacob Rictor .. n. side of Licking Run being cor. of **John Spilman** .. *Signed*: **Jacob Rictor, Mary Rector**. *Wits*: **Harman Fishback, John Martin, John Utterback.** *Rec*:23 November 1772, ack. by grantors.

Pages 244-245. 30 September 1772. B & S. Bet. **Cuthbert Bullett** of Pr. Wm. Co. and **John Barker** .. **Henry Peyton**, Gent. of Pr. Wm. Co. .. by lease & release .. 1769 .. to C. Bullitt in trust for the benefit of his creditors .. 254a. .. L30 .. for and during the life of the sd. Henry Peyton .. *Signed*: **Cuth. Bullett**. *Wits*: **James Gray, George Boggett, Cuth't. Harrison.** *Rec*: 23 November 1772, ack. by grantor.

142

Pages 245-248. 30 May 1772. B & S. Bet. **John Rictor**, Planter, and **Catherine**, his wife, and **Isaac Nichols** of Loud. Co., Farmer .. £120 .. tract .. on or near Goose Creek .. being part of a tract formerly granted unto **Charles Burgess** and a deed to **Burgess Ball** and a deed from **John Rector** .. west cor. of lot surveyed for **Richard McPherson** .. cor. of **Stuart's** tract .. 325a. .. *Signed*: **John** (R) **Rector, Catherine** (CR) **Rector.** *Wits*: **Hez'h. Turner, Rich'd Mcpherson, John Clark, James Hatcher.** *Rec*: 23 November 1772, ack. by **John Rector.**

Pages 248-250. 29 May 1772. B & S. Bet. **Richard McPherson & Eliner**, his wife, and **Isaac Nichols** of Loud. Co., Farmer, .. £23.9s. .. part of lott .. from **John Rector** to sd. **McPherson** .. same from **Burges Ball** to **John Rector** .. cor. to **Isaac Nichols** .. 33 1/2a. .. *Signed*: **Richard McPherson, Eleanor McPherson.** *Wits*: **James Hatcher, John Clark, James Correy, Ann Clark.** *Rec*: 23 November 1772, ack. by grantors.

Pages 250-252. 26 October 1772. Lease. Bet. **Jeffery Johnson**, of Leeds Par .. and **Benjamin Stone**, of same .. cor. to **Anderson** .. oak in bottom in **Hudnall's** line .. 264a. .. during his nat. life and lives of **Ann Stone**, his wife and **Rhoda Stone**, his dau. .. yearly rent of £5 .. *Signed*: **Jeffrey** (X) **Johnson.** *Wits*: **George Bennett, Andrew Hume.** *Rec*: 23 November 1772, ack. by Johnson.

Pages 252-254. 5 December 1771. Lease. Bet. **James Scott**, of Leeds Par., Gent. and **William Holton** of same .. tract on waters of Carters Run .. part of tract granted to the late **Alex'r Scott**, Clerk, dec'd by a Prop. Deed .. 150a. .. to sd. **Holton** for nat. life of sd. **James Scott** .. yearly rent of 530 lbs. Tobacco with Cask and the Quitrents .. *Signed*: **James Scott, Jr., William Holton.** *Wits*: **Jno. McArtzham, R. Kenner, Brereton Jones.** *Rec*: 23 November 1772, ack. by parties.

Pages 254-257. 9 October 1771. B & S. Bet. **Landon Carter & Charles Carter**, Esqrs., exors of the will of Charles Carter, Esq., dec'd and **Robert Buchanon** of City of Anapolis, Md. .. by Act of Assembly, 1769, grantors empowered to sell lands to pay deceased's debts .. 800a. .. part of Kettle Run tract .. in Ham. Par. .. £400 .. east side of Carolina Road, cor. to **Warren and Morris** .. cor. to **Hedger, McClaninghames** line .. Kettle Run .. *Signed*: **Landon Carter, Charles Carter.** *Wits*: **Catesby Woodford, Jeremiah Wilson, Nathaniel Robinson.** *Rec*: 23 November 1772. Nov. by o. of wits.

Pages 257-260. 10 October 1772. B & S. Bet. (same as above) and **George Reeves** .. 420a. .. part of Kettle Run Tract .. being in Ham. Par., Pr. Wm. and Fauq. Cos. .. £210 .. Beg. red oak below the Cattail, cor. to **George Heal** .. cor. with **Robert Horner** .. hiccory on Burwells Road .. *Signed*: **Landon** and **Charles Carter.** *Wits*: (as above). *Rec*: 23 November 1772, prov. by o. of wits.

Pages 260-262. 10 October 1772. B & S. Bet. Carter's exors (as above) and **John Sullivant (Sullivan)** .. 200a. .. part of Kettle Run Tract .. Ł100 .. n. side of Mountain Road and near the same it being the place where the Broad Run Patent Intersects with the Kettle Run Patent .. cor. with **Foster** .. s. side Carolina Road ... *Signed*: **Charles** and **Landon Carter**. *Wits*: (as above). *Rec*: 23 November 1772, prov. by o. of wits.

Pages 263-264. 28 October 1772. B & S. Bet. **John Anderson &** **Elizabeth**, his wife, and **Joseph Jeffries** .. Ł112.10s. .. tract .. on s. side of Goose Creek .. being part of a tract belonging to sd. Anderson .. oak on s. side of Goose Creek in **Smith's** line .. down meanders of creek .. to mouth of small branch .. up sd. branch .. 225a. .. *Signed*: **John Anderson**. *Wits*: **Martin Pickett, John Duncan, Joseph Black-** **well, Jr., John Hathaway, Joseph Williams**. *Rec*: 23 November 1772, ack. by **John Anderson**.

Pages 264-266. 21 October 1772. Deed of Gift. Bet. **Thomas Conway** **& Elizabeth**, his wife and **William Conway** .. son of sd. Thos. & Elizabeth .. for nat. love and affection .. 200a. .. part of tract given by **Mary Waugh** to her dau., **Elizabeth Conway** .. 316 a. .. rec. in Pr. Wm. Co. .. cor. of main tract .. along Mr. **Thomas Bullitt's** line, to cor. white oak of the dividing line of **John Mosee [Mauzy ?]** .. to Furr's run .. to Mr. **Jonathan Gibson's** line .. along div. line of Maj'r. **Waggoner** down Elk Run to the beg .. *Signed*: **Thomas Conway,** **Elizabeth Conway**. *Wits*: **Jos. Blackwell, John Mauzy, George Con-** **way, Daniel Shumate**. *Rec*: 23 November 1772, ack. by **Thomas Con-** way and with Commission for the privy exam. of **Elizabeth** annexed.

Pages 267-269. 26 September 1772. Lease. Bet. **Henry Peyton** and **Silvester Welch** .. tract on the Main Br. of Broad Run of Occoquan .. cor. of **Brian Obannon** .. cor. of the land of **John Toward & Wm.** **McBee** .. to a path leading from **Edmonds** plantation to Broad Run .. 300a. .. for 99 years from above date .. yearly rent of 1,000 lbs of Crop tobacco & cask with quitrents and land taxes .. Welch not to build a mill.. to have timber from the "end of the Pignut tract of land" next to the 300a. above leased, if not enough on the 300a. .. *Signed*: **Henry** **Peyton, Silvester (X) Welch**. *Wits*: **Sanford Carrell, James Foley,** **John Obannon**. *Rec*: 23 November, 1772, ack. by parties.

Pages 269-270. 8 June 1772. B & S. Bet. **John Crump & Betty**, his wife, and **William Blackwell** .. Ł65 .. 300a. .. adj. the lands of **John** **Keas, William Eustace, Lynaugh Helm** .. reversion given to sd. Crump by his father John Crump, one other part bought of **William** **Eustace** .. *Signed*: **John Crump**. *Wits*: **W. Blackwell, Jr., Sam.** **Blackwell, Jos. Blackwell**. *Rec*: 24 August 1772, prov. by o. of **Joseph & Wm. Blackwell, Jr.** 23 Nov. 1772, by o. of **Samuel Black-** **well**.

Pages 271-273. 29 October 1772. B & S. Bet. **Thomas Stone &** **Mary**, his wife, and **William Nelson** .. Ł50 .. tract whereon sd. Stone now lives which was purch. of **John Dagg** .. 70a., more or less ..

Signed: **Thomas (X) Stone, Mary (X) Stone.** *Wits*: **John Wright, Joseph Blackwell, Jr., Sam. Blackwell, George (X) Creswell.** *Rec*: 23 November 1772, ack. by grantors.

Page 273. 7 August 1772. Bill of Sale. **Joseph Hudnall** to **Martin Pickett & Co.** .. ₤37 .. two Negroes, **Mareas & Lucy,** household furniture, livestock, crops, .. *Signed*: **Joseph Hudnall.** *Wit*: **Jos. Blackwell.** *Rec*: 23 November 1772, prov. by o. of **Joseph Blackwell, Jr.**

Pages 273-275. 23 November 1772. B & S. Bet. **William Hampton** and **Richard Hampton,** sons and devissees in trust of Richard Hampton, dec'd .. and Dr. **Richard Lingan Hall** of W'land Co. .. Richard Hampton devised in his Will, that after the death of his wife, Martha, the lands whereon he lived should be sold by his sons and the money paid out in land to be equally divided between his sons, Richard & **Gale,** the sd. Trustees to have right to live on the land for life .. **Martha Hampton** is dead and sd. Richard's debts nearly paid .. ₤150 .. 294a. .. Beg. at Mr. **Barbers** cor. in a line of the land granted to **Peter Lehue,** now Mr. **Jas. Scott's** land .. hiccory in the line of the land surveyed for **Col. Taply** .. lying in Leeds Par .. *Signed*: **William Hampton, Richard Hampton.** *Wit*: **Cuth. Bullett, H. Brooke, A. Buchanan.** *Rec*: 24 November 1772, prov. by o. of **Bullett, Brooke** and **Andrew Buchanan.**

Pages 276-277. 23 October 1772. B & S. Bet. **Isaac Adams** and **Elijah Glascock** .. ₤30 .. 70a. .. on Goose Creek .. part of tract taken up by Isaac Adams on the n. side of Goose Creek .. to **Carter's** line .. to the Gap Branch .. with sd. br. to Goose Creek. *Signed*: **Isaac (₤) Adams.** *Wits*: **Stephen Noland, James Noland, Aaron Drummond.** *Rec*: 24 November 1772, ack. by grantor.

Pages 277-280. 20 May 1772. Lease. Bet. **Col. Richard Henry Lee** of W'land Co. and **Charles Bell** .. 403a. .. Cattail Branch cor. to **Pickett** .. cor. to **Grant** .. thence with Grant's line .. stake on a nole in Bell's Plantation .. Stone marked TL standing on Towsers branch .. during his nat. life and lives of **Eliz'a Bell** and **James Bell,** the son of **Thomas Bell** .. yearly rent of ₤21.18s. *Signed*: **Richard Henry Lee, Charles Bell.** *Wits*: **Jos. Blackwell, Martin Pickett, Randolph Spicer.** *Rec*: 24 November 1772, prov. by o. of wits.

Pages 281-285. 31 Dec. 1772/1 Jan. 1773. Lease & release. Bet. **Thomas Turner & Jane,** his wife, of King Geo. Co. and **Thomas Marshall** .. tract granted to **Henry Turner** of King Geo. Co. by patent .. 18 Sept. 1740 .. and by him devised to Thomas Turner .. Beg. 3 red oaks cor. trees of **James Ball** and the land surveyed for **John Blowers** now **Mercers** .. crossing a br. of Goose Creek .. point near the foot of the North Cobler Mt. .. binding on lands surveyed for Blowers now **Mercer** .. 1,700a. .. ₤912.10s. .. *Signed*: **T. Turner, Jane Turner.** *Wit*: **L. Washington, Enoch Ashby, William Peake, B. Ashby, William Chapman.** *Rec*: 25 January 1773, prov. by o. of **William Peake, Ben & Enoch Ashby,** commission to examine **Jane Turner** returned.

Pages 285-287. 20 March 1773. B & S. Bet. **Nathaniel Rector &
Anne**, his wife, and **Harmon Button** .. Ł6 .. tract joining Button's own
land, part of tract taken up by the sd. Rector's mother .. cor. to **John
Kamper's** land .. 23a. *Signed*: **Nathaniel (O) Rector, Ann (I) Rector.**
Wits: **Martin Pickett, Joseph Blackwell**, Joseph Blackwell. *Rec*: 22
March 1773, ack. by grantors.

Pages 287-289. 20 March 1773. B & S. Bet. **Humphrey Brooke**, of
Leeds Par .. and **Robert Sanders** of same .. Ł12.10s. .. 10a. .. beg. at
Barkers Br. in the line of **Charles Carter**, Esq. *Signed*: **H. Brooke.**
Rec: 22 March 1773, ack. by **Humphrey Brooke.**

Pages 289-291. 1773. B & S. Bet. **Thomas Glascock & Agness**, his
wife, of Leeds Par .. and **William Turley** .. Ł74.16s. .. 191a. .. cor. to
George Glascock .. part of larger tract purch. by **John Rector**, dec'd.
of **Burgess Ball**, Gent. of Lan. Co. .. 7 Sept. 1770 .. *Signed*: **Thomas
Glascock, Agness (X) Glascock.** *Wits*: **George Glascock, Thomas
Neavill, William Murrey.** *Rec*: 22 March 1773, ack. by grantors.

Pages 291-293. 1 March 1773. Lease. Bet. **John Rector** and **Joseph
Neale** .. during his nat. life and lives of **Ann Neil** and **Thomas Neil**
his son .. 108a. .. near Goose Creek .. yearly rent of Ł5 .. *Signed*:
John (R) Rector, Joseph Neal. *Wits*: **James Thompson, William Turley, Thom. Marshall, Henry Rector, Charles Rector.** *Rec*: 22 March
1773, prov. by o. of **Turley, Henry Rector** and **Thomas Marshall**,
wits.

Pages 293-295. 9 March 1773. B & S. Bet. **John Rector, Sr.** and
Catherine, his wife, of Leeds Par. and **Robert Donaldson** of same .. Ł
56.2s.11d. .. 138a. .. heap of stones in Richard ---- Field, part of land
purch. by Rector of **Burgess Ball**, Gent. of Lan. Co. .. 7 Sept. 1770 ..
Signed: **John (R) Rector, Catherine (CR) Rector.** *Wits*: **John Glascock, William Murrey, John Hendren.** *Rec*: 22 March 1773, prov. by
o. of wits.

Pages 295-297. 9 March 1773. B & S. Bet. **John Rector &
Catherine**, his wife, and **John Hendren** .. Ł62.16s. .. near Goose Creek
being part of a large tract formerly granted unto **Charles Burgess**,
Gent. late of Lan. Co. dec'd .. cor. to **Jacob Rector, Jr.** .. cor. to **John
Rector, Sr.** .. cor. to **Charles Rector** .. 168a. .. *Signed*: **John (R) Rec-
tor, Catherine (CR) Rector.** *Wits*: **John Glascock, William Murrey,
Robert Donaldson.** *Rec*: 22 March 1773, prov. by o. of wits.

Pages 297-299. 9 March 1773. B & S. Bet. **John Rector, Sr. &
Catherine**, his wife, of Leeds Par .. and **William Murry** of same .. Ł
60.18s.10d. .. 159a .. cor to lot sold by Rector to **John Kincheloe**, cor.
to **John Squires** .. cor. at the old dividing line bet. **Burgess Ball &
Burgess Smith** .. oak in br. of Cromwell's Run, cor. to John Kincheloe
.. *Signed*: **John (R) Rector, Catherine (CR) Rector.** *Wit*: **John Glascock, George Glascock, Thomas (X) Priest.** *Rec*: 22 March 1773,
prov. by o. of wits.

Pages 299-301. 9 March 1773. B & S. Bet. **John Rector, S**
Catherine, his wife, .. and **Thomas Priest, Jr.** .. Ł87.1s. .. 18,..
cor to lot sold by Rector to **John Squires** .. old div. line .. cor to lot
sold to **Richard McFurson** .. part of tract from **Burgess Ball** to sd.
Rector .. *Signed*: **John (R) Rector, Catherine (CR) Rector.** *Wits*:
John Glascock, William Murrey, George Glascock. *Rec*: 22 March
1773, prov. by o. of wits.

Pages 302-304. 9 March 1773. B & S. Bet. **John Rector, Sr. &**
Catherine, his wife, .. and **John Glascock** .. Ł53.5s.6d. .. 139a. .. cor.
of **Jacob Rector** son of **Henry Rector** .. cor. of **George Glascock** ..
cor. of **Hezekiah Glascock's** lott .. part of larger tract to Rector by
Burgess Ball, Gent. .. *Signed*: **John (R) Rector, Catherine (CR) Rec-**
tor. *Wits*: **William Murrey, Thomas (X) Priest, George Glascock.**
Rec: 22 March 1773, prov. by o. of wits.

Pages 304-307. 19 March 1773. B & S. Bet. **William Robinson** of
Hanover Par., King Geo. Co., Gent. and **Rawleigh Downman** of Lan.
Co., Gent. .. Ł1200 .. tract in Ham. Par. on Tin Pot Run .. 1500a. ..
part of patent granted unto **William Thornton** of King Geo. Co., Gent.,
dec'd. who by his last will, etc. .. 3 Nov. 1742 .. gave the sd. 1500a.
to his grandson, the abovesd. Robinson and same was confirmed to
Robinson by his uncle, **William Thornton, Jr.** .. 13 Aug. 1743 .. rec.
in Pr. Wm. Co. .. *Signed*: **William Robinson.** *Wits*: **Wm. Ball, David**
Briggs, William Allason, Alex'r. Wodrow, James Robison, Robert
(R) Ashby. *Rec*: 22 March 1773 prov. by o. of Ashby, Ball & Allason.

Pages 307-309. 1 October 1771. B & S. Bet. **John Rector &**
Catherine, his wife, of Leeds Par. and **Jacob Rector** .. Ł40 .. 100a. ..
cor. to **Henry Rector** .. dividing line bet. **Ball & Smith** .. cor. to **Isaac**
Cundiff .. with **Kincheloe's** line .. part of tract Rector purch. of
Burgess Ball, Gent .. 7 Oct. 1771 .. *Signed*: **John (IR) Rector,**
Catherine (CR) Rector. *Wits*: **Thomas Marshall, Aaron Drummond,**
Daniel Brown. *Rec*: 22 March 1773, prov. by o. of wits.

Pages 309-312. 6 August 1772. B & S. Bet. **Thomas Middleton, Jr.**
and **Ann**, his wife and **Kimble Hicks** "in London" .. Ł200 .. 215a., part
in Fauq. and part in Loud. .. part of tract Middleton purch. of the Hon.
Robert Burwell, George Washington and **Fielding Lewis, Esq'rs.,**
Trustees of **George Carter,** dec'd .. bounded by lands now held by
Randall Morgan, Nath'l. Moss .. the sd. George Washington & Hon.
Thomas Lord Fairfax .. being the land where Middleton now lives ..
cont. 215a. .. *Signed*: **Thomas (X) Middleton, Ann (X) Middleton.**
Wits: **Francis Peyton, Leven Powell, J. P. Harrison, Rawleigh**
Chinn, Thomas Shore, Valentine Harrison. *Rec*: 23 March 1773,
prov. by o. of Powell & Chinn, with Commission to Loud. Court to ex-
amine Ann Middleton.

Pages 312-316. 22-23 September 1772. Lease & release. Bet. **W i l -**
liam Allason of Town of Falmouth, Merchant, & **Ann**, his wife, and
David Allason of same .. whereas **John Hooe**, Gent., late of Staff. Co.
dec'd by his last will .. 8 Oct. 1763 .. gave to his 3 daus. to wit, **Ann**

147

Allason, then **Ann Hooe, Sarah Hooe & Susannah Hooe,** all the land he held in Fauq. to be equally divided .. the devisees did before the death of sd. John Hooe purch. a tract adj. the above of **Rice Duncan,** which was granted by patent .. 13 Feb. 1743 to Rice Duncan .. 189a. .. neither parcel has been divided .. to David Allason all of Ann Allason's part in both tracts .. £500 .. *Signed:* **William Allason, Anne Allason.** *Wits:* **A. Buchanan, John Eustace, Robert T. Washington, James Scott, Jr., William Peake, James Robison.** *Rec:* 23 March 1773, prov. by o. of **Andrew Buchanan, Scott and Eustace.**

Pages 317-319. 10 December 1772. B & S. Bet. **James Robinson,** of Falmouth, King Geo.Co., Merchant Factor & Atty. for **A n d r e w Cochrane, William Cuninghame, John Murdock, Peter Murdock, Robert Bogles, Alexander Cuninghame** and **John Stewart** of Glasgow, merchants & partners, and **William Blackwell the Younger** .. £60 .. tract on branches of Browns Run .. cor. to land of **Henry Calfee** and tract surveyed for **Owen Grinan** .. Hudnall's land .. crossing sd. run .. saplin on main road .. 253a. .. same to sd. Robinson as factor by **Thomas Matthews & Elizabeth,** his wife .. 5 Dec. 1768 .. *Signed:* **James Robison.** *Wits:* **A. Buchanan, Thos. Keith, W. Nelson, John Eustace.** *Rec:* 23 March 1773, prov. by o. of **Andrew Buchanan, Keith** and **William Nelson,** wits.

Pages 319-320. 27 April 1772. Mortgage. Bet. **John Twentyman** and **Payne, Moor & Co.,** merchants .. £60 .. 226a. .. sd. £60 to be repaid, with int., by 1 Jan. 1773 .. if done, this to be null and void .. *Signed:* **John (X) Twentyman.** *Wits:* **Thos. Obannon, And. Buchanan, Joshua Meals, William Payne.** *Rec:* 24 Nov. 1772, prov. by o. of **Andrew Buchanan.** 23 March 1773, ack. by **Twentyman.**

Page 321. 2 July 1772. Bill of Sale. **James Dennison** for £20 .. paid by **Leven Powell** .. livestock, farming equip., household furniture .. crops .. *Signed:* **James Dennison.** *Wit:* **Peyton Harrison.** *Rec:* 25 August 1772, prov. by o. of **John Peyton Harrison.**

Pages 321-323. 26 April 1773. B & S. Bet. **Josiah Holtzclaw** and **Susannah,** his wife, and **Joseph Martin** .. £34 .. tract in Hambleton Par .. part of larger tract whereon sd. Holtzclaw lives .. cor to **Boswell** .. cor. to **B u n b e r y's** on a branch .. 34a. (+/-). *Signed:* **J o s i a h Holtzclaw, Susannah (X) Holtzclaw.** *Wits:* **Martin Pickett, Joseph Blackwell, Jr., William Blackwell, Jr.** *Rec:* 26 April 1773, ack. by grantors.

Pages 323-328. 28 September 1772. Lease & release. Bet. **J a m e s Seaton & Elizabeth,** his wife, of Barkley Co., **Howson Kenner & Margaret,** his wife, of Hambleton Par., **James Seaton, Jr.** and **James Gillison** .. tract in Ham. Par. .. on the Marsh Run in the line of **Corbin's** tract .. 183a. .. £132.10s. .. *Signed:* **James Seaton, James Seaton, Jr., Eliza Seaton, Howson Kenner, Margaret Kenner.** *Wits:* **Jos. Blackwell, William Nelson, Jos. Blackwell, Jr., Wm. Blackwell, Jr.** *Rec:* 26 April 1773; prov. by o. of **Joseph Blackwell, Joseph Blackwell, Jr.** and **Wm. Nelson.** Commission to examine **Elizabeth Seaton** to **Thomas Rutherford, James Strode, Robert Stephens,** Justices in Berkeley Co., annexed.

Page 328. 22 June 1770. Bond. **William Ball to James Foley.** For: L400. *Sec*: **John Moffett & Thomas Keith.** For good title to Negroes sold to Foley. *Signed*: **William Ball, John Moffett, Thomas Keith.** *Wit*: **Joseph Blackwell, Jr.** *Rec*: 26 April 1773, prov. by o. of wit.

Pages 329–330. 24 September 1772. B & S. Bet. **David Allason** of Falmouth and **William Allason** of Falmouth, Merchant .. **John Hooe,** Gent., late of Staff. Co. dec.d by his will dated 8 Oct. 1763, devised to his 3 daus., **Ann, Sarah & Susannah Hooe,** all the land he held in Fauq. Co. to be equally divided bet. them .. before his death the 3 daus. purchased of **Rice Duncan** a tract adj. their father .. same to Duncan by grant dtd. 7 Feb. 1743 .. for 189a. .. Wm. Allason m. Ann Hooe and they sold their right in the above tracts to David Allason .. for L500 .. sd. David conveys same to William .. i.e. Ann Allason's third part .. *Signed*: **David Allason.** *Wits*: **A. Buchanan, Robert Washington, Martin Pickett, A. Churchill.** *Rec*: 26 April 1773, prov. by o. of Buchanan, Pickett and Churchill.

Pages 330–332. 26 April 1773. B & S. Bet. **John Churchill** and **Sarah,** his wife, **Armistead Churchill & Elizabeth,** his wife and **James McClanahame** .. L150 .. oak on the Carolina or Jersey road .. line of **Benjamin Morris** .. line of James McClanahame .. crossing Kettle Run .. line of **George Steeles** .. line of **John Tomlin** .. 178a. .. *Signed*: **John Churchhill, Sarah Churchhill, Armistead Churchhill.** *Rec*: 26 April 1772, ack. by **John, Sarah and Armistead Churchhill.**

Pages 333–334. 5 May 1773. Deed of Gift. Bet. **Thomas Conway &** **Elizabeth,** his wife, and **William Conway** and **George Conway,** sons of sd. Thos. and Elizabeth .. for nat. love and affection .. 316 a. .. lying on Elk Run .. tract orig. given to Elizabeth Conway by deed of gift from **Mary Waugh,** her mother .. and rec. in Pr. Wm. Co. .. all that land on w. side of Furrs Run .. 200a. to William, where he now lives .. the remainder, or 116a. on e. side of Furrs Run to George .. *Signed*: **Thomas Conway, Elizabeth Conway.** *Wits*: **Thomas Smith, John Smith, William Brooke.** *Rec*: 24 May 1773, ack. by grantors, **Elizabeth** examined by Commissioners of the Court, Wm. and Joseph Blackwell.

Pages 335–337. 24 May 1773. B & S. Bet. **Jacob Rector** and **Mary,** his wife, and **Jeremiah Darnall** .. L70 .. 100a. .. whereon **Peter Hitt,** dec'd. lived .. being one of the lotts of land in the German Town .. *Signed*: **Jacob Rector, Mary (X) Rector.** *Rec*: 24 May 1773, ack. by grantors.

Pages 337–338. 24 May 1773. Lease. Bet. **Richard Covington** and **Sarah Benjar** .. 40a. .. in Ham. Par. .. for her nat. life .. yearly rent of 5s. .. the first payment to come due 5 Dec. 1776 .. *Signed*: **R i c h a r d Covington.** *Rec*: 24 May 1773, ack. by grantor.

Pages 338-339. 25 May 1773. B & S. Bet, **John Duncan & Elizabeth**, his wife, and **Benjamin Holtzclaw** .. Ł16.10s. .. tract in Ham. Par., part of larger tract Duncan purch. of **Joseph Hitt** .. oak in **Russell's** line .. 16 1/2a. *Signed*: **John Duncan, Elizabeth (X) Duncan**. *Wits*: **Joseph Holtzclaw**. *Rec*: 24 May 1773 [sic] ack. by grantors.

Pages 340-343. 26-27 October 1772. Lease & release. Bet. **J a c o b Holtzclaw and Susanna**, his wife, of Culp. Co. and **Evan Griffiths** .. Ł 40 .. 163a. .. 50a. lying bet. the lines of **John Mercer** .. and another tract of Holtzclaw's in Leeds Par. .. cor. of **John Mercer** .. old cor. hiccory of **Thomas Barton's** old deed .. cor. to John Glascock .. 213a. .. *Signed*: **Jacob Holtzclaw, Susanna Holtzclaw**. *Wits*: **John Rust, Samuel Rust, John Mitchell, John (X) Twentyman**. *Rec*: 24 May 1773, ack. by grantors.

Pages 343-347. 16-14 [sic] October 1772. Lease & release. Bet. **George Lamkin** of Fx. Co. and **George Conway** .. Ł250 .. 500a. .. cor. to **Thomas Chattin** and the sd. **Jenifer** .. cor. on the side of Chattins Mt. thence along a line of marked trees being the dividing line bet. **Daniel Florence [Flowerree ?]** and the sd. **Jenifer** .. a hill near Chattins run .. oak in the fork of the road .. from Rectors Mill .. *Signed*: **George Lamkin**. *Wits*: **William Carr, Thomas Chapman, William Phillips, Alexander Campbell**. *Rec*: 24 May 1773. prov. by o. of Chapman, Phillips and Campbell.

Pages 347-350. 20 May 1772. Lease. Bet. Col. **Richard Henry Lee** of W'land Co. and **John Peake** .. tract in Ham. Par. .. 174a. .. cor. of the original tract (stone marked T) .. cor. of **Jones** .. cor. to **Taylor** in the line of **Arnold** near Turkey Run .. during the nat. lives of sd. Peake, **Mary Peake and William Harrison Peake** .. yearly rent: Ł 7.10d. *Signed*: **Richard Henry Lee, John Peake**. *Wits*: **Bennett Price, Francis Attwell, Joseph Blackwell**. *Rec*: 25 Nov. 1772, prov. by o. of Blackwell and Attwell; 24 May 1773, by o. of Price.

Pages 350-351. 18 May 1773. Bill of Sale. **Durk Bennear** to **John Likely** on acc't of Messrs. **Wm. Cunningham & Co.** of Glasgow, merchants .. bed & furniture, horse, crops, debt of Ł12.17s.11d. *Signed*: **Durk (X) Bennear**. *Wit*: **Wm. Nelson**. *Rec*: 25 May 1773, prov. by o. of Nelson.

Page 351. 11 January 1773. Bill of Sale. **James Barton** to **John Likely** on acc't of Messrs. **Wm. Cuninghame & Co.** .. sorrel mare .. for debt of Ł4.10s.7d. *Signed*: **James (X) Barton**. *Wits*: **Randolph Spicer, Robert Sanders**. *Rec*: 25 May 1773, prov. by o. of Spicer.

Page 352. 2 March 1773. Bill of Sale. **Alexander Campbell** of Pr. Wm. Co. to **John Likely** on acct. of Messrs. **William Cuninghame & Co.** .. cattle, horses, furniture .. for debt of Ł12.13s.4d. .. *Signed*: **Alex'r Campbell**. *Wit*: **Peter Grant**. *Rec*: 25 May 1773. ack. by Campbell.

Pages 352-353. 25 May 1773. Bill of Sale, **Joseph Morehead** of Hallifax Co. to **Charles** and **John Morehead** .. Negroes .. for debt due sd. Moreheads of Ł30 .. *Signed*: **Joseph Morehead**. *Wit*: **John Likely**. *Rec*: 25 May 1773, ack. by **Joseph Morehead**.

Pages 353-355. 8 May 1773. B & S. Bet. **William Kearns** of Ham. Par. and Messrs. **Wm. Cuninghame & Co.** of Glasgow, mearchants .. Ł44.6s. .. tract on the branches of Licking Run and the Marsh Run binding on the lands of **Augustin Smith, John Rector, Tilman Wever, John Ashby** and **Martin Hardin** .. 182a. .. more or less .. after 50a. of the same be laid off to **John Kearnes** including his house & plantation and 50a. to **Benjamin Horton** incl. his house and plantation .. *Signed*: **William Kearnes**. *Wits*: **Martin Pickett, William Nelson, Randolph Spicer**. Receipt to **John Likly** for Cuninghame & Co. *Rec*: 28 June 1773, ack. by **William Kearnes**.

Pages 355-357. 22 March 1773. B & S. Bet. **John Anderson & Elizabeth**, his wife, & **Thomas Cummings** .. Ł60 .. llla. .. in Leeds Par. on Goose Creek, being part of a larger tract belonging to sd. Anderson .. oak on the br. in **Smith's** line .. to Goose Creek & up the meanders .. *Signed*: **John Anderson, Elizabeth Anderson**. *Wits*: **Elijah Glascock, William McDaniel, Matthew Adams, James Atchison**. *Rec*: 28 June 1773, prov. by o. of McDaniel, Adams and Atchison.

Pages 357-358. 17 October 1772. B & S. Bet. **Daniel Jenifer** of Chas. Co., Md., Esq. and **George Lamkin** of Fx. Co. .. Ł250 .. 500a. .. cor. to **Thomas Chattin** and the sd. Jenifer thence along a line of marked trees being the dividing line bet. **Daniel Florence** [**Flowerree** ?] and sd. Jenifer .. fork of the road that leads from Rectors Mill .. *Signed*: **Daniel Jenifer**. *Wits*: **John Riddell, Alex'r Campbell, Thomas Chapman, Riginald Graham, Evan Williams**. "D. Jenifer is to have present years rent." *Rec*: 24 May 1773, prov. by o. of Campbell, Chapman; 28 June 1773, prov. by Graham.

Pages 358-362. 31 March 1773. B & S. Bet. **Jesse Ewell & Charlotte**, his wife, of Pr. Wm. Co. **James Ewell & Mary**, his wife, of Lan. Co. and **Solomon Jones** of Pr. Wm. Co. .. Ł40 .. tract .. on upper side of Leather Coat Mt. and n. side of the Broad Run of Occoquan .. oaks on side of sd. run below the mouth of the Cabbin br. being the beg. of **Capt. Cockes** land .. chesnut on side of the mt. thence along sd. mt. .. lower end of the first meadow within the thoroughfare thence up the run side .. 270a. .. which was taken up by **Charles Ewell** in the year 1741 and divided by him to his sons Jesse and James .. *Signed*: **Jesse Ewell, Charlotte Ewell, James Ewell, Mary Ewell**. *Wits*: **James Scott, Henry Lee, James Ewell, Jr., Alex'r Campbell, Wm. Carr, Thos. Chapman**. *Rec*: 24 May 1773, prov. by o. of Campbell, Chapman; 28 June 1773, prov. by o. of Carr. Rec. with Commissions and ack. of signatures of Charlotte and Mary Ewell.

Pages 362-364. 27 February 1773. Lease. Bet. **John Rector** and **John Clark** .. lease .. 161a. .. for Clarke's nat. life and lives of **Ann**

Clarke his wife and **Daniel Clarke,** his son .. lying on Goose Creek ..
yearly rent of Ł5 .. *Signed*: **John (R) Rector, John Clarke.** *Wits*:
Henry Rector, Frederick Rector, Benjamin Robinson. *Rec*: 28 June
1773, prov. by o. of wits.

Pages 364–365. 8 June 1773. B & S. Bet. **Charles Rector &
Elizabeth,** his wife, of Leeds Par. and **Benj**ᵃ **Rector** .. Ł71.13s. ..
128a. .. on the branches of Goose Creek .. cor. to **Henry Rector, Sr.** ..
part of tract given to Charles Rector by the will of **John Rector,** dec'd
.. *Signed*: **Charles Rector, Elizabeth (X) Rector.** *Rec*: 28 June 1773,
ack. by grantors.

Pages 365–367. 28 June 1773. B & S. Bet. **Benjamin Rector & Sally,**
his wife, of Leeds Par. and **John Kerr, Jr.** of Ham. Par. .. Ł100 ..
168a. .. near Goose Creek .. *Signed*: **Benjamin Rector, Sally Rector.**
Rec: 28 June 1773, ack. by grantors.

Pages 367–368. 20 May 1773. Mortgage. **John Orear** of Fauq. Co.,
Planter, to **James Robison** of Falmouth, merchant, on behalf of
Messres. **Andrew Cochrane, Wm. Cuninghame & Co.** of Glasgow,
merchants & partners .. for Ł106.4d. .. slaves .. to be void by payment
of above sum, with interest .. *Signed*: **John Orear.** *Wits*: **Adam
Newall, Waller Colquhoun.** *Rec*: 28 June 1773.

Pages 368–369. 8 January 1773. Release of Mortgage. **William
Ellzey** of Pr. Wm. Co. to **Thomas Chinn,** formerly of Fauq. now of Pr.
Wm. .. who mort. tract of 820 a. to Ellzey as security for several
sums which Ellzey paid .. hereby releases sd. mortgage .. *Signed*:
William Ellzey. *Wits*: **Cuth**ᵗ **Harrison, Chas. Gallahue, James
Lewis, James Crump.** *Rec*: 28 June 1773, ack. by Ellzey.

Pages 369–372. 27–28 June 1773. Lease & release. Bet. **Bryant
Breeding** of Dunmore Co. and **James Thompson** .. tract in Ham. Par.
part of tract cont. 200a. .. part of large tract taken up by **S a m u e l
E a r l e ,** 22 Oct. 1743, in Pr. Wm. Co. and on branches of Deep Run ..
in line of **Alexander Beach** .. line of **John Barber** .. **Thomas Eaveses**
line .. **Blagrow Hoppers** line .. to **William Blackwell's** line ..
Signed: **Bryant (X) Breeding.** *Wits*: **Joseph Blackwell, Joseph Blackwell, Jr., Wm. Nelson.** *Rec*: 28 June 1773, prov. by o. of **J. Blackwell, Jr.** and **William Nelson.**

Page 373. 26 June 1773. Mortgage. Bet. **John Cockshutt** & others,
trustees of Mr. **John Bland** of London, merchant and **John Holden** .. for
Ł27.17s.10d.1f. .. Holden to trustees: one Negroe girl **P r i s c i l l a ,**
horses, cattle .. to be void upon Holden's payment of above with interest .. *Signed*: **John (+) Holden.** *Wits*: **David Briggs, Charles Ashby,
William Wright, Lauch**ⁿ **Mackintoush.** *Rec*: 26 July 1773, ack. by
Holden.

Pages 374–375. 13 February 1773. B & S. Bet. **William Bryant &
Elizabeth,** his wife, and **James Bryant** and **Joseph Martin** .. for Ł40 ..
tract in Ham. Par. .. being part of greater tract sd. Bryants purch. of

Wm., John & Armistead Churchhill .. in line of William Bryant ..
cor. to **Basswell & Holtzclaw** .. cor. to **Burnbury** on a branch .. 38a. ..
Signed: **William Bryan, Elizabeth Bryen, James Brien.** *Wits*: **Martin Pickett, John Duncan, John Likly, Joseph Blackwell.** *Rec*: 26 July
1773, ack. by **William Bryan** and wife.

Pages 375-377. 9 July 1773. Lease. Bet. **George Conway** of Leeds
Par., Gent. and **Thomas Furr** of same .. tract in Par. of Leeds ..
spring branch called Thomas Furr's Spring branch .. to **John Rector's**
cor .. to **Thomas Chattin's** old line .. cor. tree formerly mark't on a
Division of the sd. land bet. **Thomas Chattin, Jr.** and **George Lamkin**
.. 125a. .. for Furr's nat. life and lives of **Elizabeth Furr** the now wife
of Thos. Furr .. yearly rent of ₤2.3s.1 1/2d. .. *Signed*: **George Conway, Thomas (X) Furr.** *Wits*: **William (X) Smalwood, Susanna (X)
Suttle, John Goddard, Aaron Drummond, John Rust.** *Rec*: 26 July
1773, prov. by o. of Rust, Goddard and Drummond.

Pages 377-380. 7-8 June 1773. Lease & release. Bet. **George Conway & Ann, his wife, and Traverse Downman** of Par. of Dittingen, Pr.
Wm. Co. .. tract on Goose Creek .. 500a. .. same purch. by **George
Lamkin** of **Thomas Chattin** and by Lamkin mortgaged to Mr. **Dan'l.
Jenifer** and by them conveyed to Conway .. ₤200. *Signed*: **George
Conway, Ann Conway.** *Wits*: **John Coppedge, Jos. Taylor, Alexander
Jeffries.** *Rec*:26 July 1773, prov. by o. of **John Coppedge, Joseph
Taylor** and **Alexander Jeffries.**

Pages 380-381. 26 July 1773. Lease. Bet. **Henry Rector, Jr.** of
Leeds Par. and **John Goddard** .. after decease of mother, **Catherine
Rector** .. let parcel .. Beg. at the spring branch from the Road joining
Jacob Rector's land .. to Chattins Run .. to the mouth of a sm. br.
joining the land whereon **Gerard McDaniel** now lives .. 100 a. .. for
Goddard's nat. life and lives of **Mary Goddard** his now wife, and John
Goddard, son of John Goddard .. yearly rent of 600 weigh of Crop
Tobacco .. *Signed*: **Henry Rector, John Goddard.** *Wits*: **James
Thomson, Zachariah Linton.** *Rec*: 26 July 1773, ack. by parties.

Pages 381-386. 17 October 1772. Lease & release. Bet. **T h o m a s
Hay & Frances,** his wife, of Staff. Co. and **William Grigsby** .. tract in
Cos. of Staff. & Fauq. and on head branches of Aquia ..oaks about 1
po. East of **Markham's** line .. cor. to **Tobias Woods** land .. oak by the
sawpitt br. .. 350a. .. ₤87.10s. .. *Signed*: **Thomas Hay, Frances Hay.**
Wits: **Joshua Brown, William Mullin, Walter Anderson, James
Buchanan, William Love, A. Buchanan, Edward Moor, David Briggs.**
Rec: 28 June 1773, prov. by o. of **Andrew Buchanan** and Briggs; 26
July 1773, prov. by o. of **Moor.** Commission to examine **Frances
Hay** from **Bailey Washington** and **Yelverton Peyton,** Gent. of Staff.
Co., annexed.

Pages 386-388. 4 December 1772. B & S. Bet. **Waugh Darnall,
Morgan Darnall,** of Culp. Co., planters, and **Alexander Williamson** of
Ham. Par., Breeches maker .. ₤42 .. tract in Ham. Par. .. part of tract
.. oak in **Whitley's** line .. 84a. .. *Signed*: **Waugh Darnall, Morgan**

(MD) Darnall. *Wits*: John Blackwell, Sam'l. Blackwell, Ann Blackwell, Joseph Blackwell. *Rec*: 26 July 1773, prov. by o. of John, Samuel and Joseph Blackwell.

Pages 388-390. 26 July 1773. B & S. Bet. **Jemima Marr** of Ham. Par. and **Jaila Marr** of same .. Ł65 .. part of tract bought of the exor. of **Daniel Marr**, dec'd .. pine in line of **Daniel Bradford** .. 333a. .. *Signed*: Jemima (X) Marr. *Wits*: **Daniel Bradford, John Wheatley, Cossum Day**. *Rec*: 26 July 1773, ack. by Jemima Marr.

Pages 390-392. 26 July 1773. B & S. Bet. **John Wheatley & Ann**, his wife, of Ham. Par. and **Mary Marr** .. Ł100 .. part of tract bought by Wheatley of Exors. of **Daniel Marr**, dec'd .. 175a. .. *Signed*: **John Wheatley, Ann** (X) **Wheatley**. *Wits*: **Daniel Bradford, William Pinchard, Francis Day**. *Rec*: 26 July 1773, ack. by grantors.

Pages 392-394. 26 July 1773. B & S. Bet. **John Wheatley and Cossom Day**, both of Ham. Par .. Ł100 .. trees in line of **Hedgman & Wheatley** .. oak near **Maj'r. Thornton's** cor .. 170 1/2a. .. *Signed*: **John Wheatley, Ann** (X) **Wheatley**. *Wits*: **Daniel Bradford, William Pinckard, Francis Day**. *Rec*: 26 July 1773, ack. by grantors.

Pages 394-396. 20 May 1772. Lease. Bet. **Col. Richard Henry Lee** of W'land Co. and **Isaac Arnold** .. tract in Ham. Par. .. 122a. .. now in his actual possession .. stone in Turkey Run Old field cor. to Arnold and in the line of **Joseph Jeffrys** .. cor. of **Edmond Bayse** .. in the line of **Jones** .. chesnut by a path the cor. of **Taylors** line .. for his nat. life & lives of **Mary**, his wife and **George Arnold** .. yearly rent of Ł 6.6s.5d. .. *Signed*: **Richard Henry Lee, Isaac Arnold**. *Wits*: **Joseph Blackwell, Martin Pickett, Bennett Price**. *Rec*: 26 July 1773, prov. by o. of wits.

Pages 397-398. 1773. B & S. Bet. **John Smith & Mary**, his wife, of Ham. Par. and **Augustin Jennings, Sr.** of same .. Ł105 .. west side of branch of Elk Marsh .. cor. of **Thornton's** .. cor. of **James Duff's** .. 182a. *Signed*: **John** (X) **Smith, Mary** (X) **Smith**. *Wits*: **John Hudnall, George Calvert, Augustin Jennings, John Likly**. *Rec*: 23 August 1773, ack. by grantors.

Pages 398-400. 20 August 1773. B & S. Bet. **John Anderson & Elizabeth**, his wife, of Leeds Par. and **Nathaniel Moss** .. Ł130 .. 248a. .. Beg. at the mouth of a Branch above the piney hill at **Joseph Jeffrys** Cor. on the s. side of Goose Creek .. Jeffry's Cor. in the line of a tract of Land formerly belonging to **Burgess Ball** .. from Jeffry's Cor. to **Thomas Cummins** Cor. .. up meanders of Goose Creek .. part of tract taken up by Mr. **William West** of Fx. Co. *Signed*: **John Anderson**. *Wits*: **Thos. Williams, George Williams, John Glascock, Daniel** (X) **Adams**. *Rec*: 23 August 1773. prov. by o. of **Thomas and George Williams and Adams**, wits.

Pages 401-403. 24 May 1773. B & S. Bet. **Thomas Bartlett**, planter, & **Ann**, his wife, and **Thomas Marshall, John Moffett, Martin Pick-**

ett, John Obannon, James Scott, Henry Peyton, William Edmonds and Charles Chinn, Gent., vestrymen for Leeds Par .. Ł31.5s. .. [names added:] Humphrey Brooke, Samuel Grigsby, John Chilton, William Pickett .. tract for the use of the Par. as a Glebe .. on the waters of Little River .. oak on the sd. Little River cor. to Fishback .. 25a. .. Signed: Thomas Bartlett, Ann Bartlett. Rec: 23 August 1773, ack. by grantors.

Pages 403-406. 24 May 1773. B & S. Bet. John Fishback, planter, & Sarah, his wife, and Vestry of Leeds Par. (as above) .. Ł145.5s. .. tract to be used as a Glebe for Leeds Par on the waters of Little River .. marked saplin by a cor. called and known by the name of the burnt corner .. 83a. .. Signed: John Fishback, Sarah Fishback. Rec: 23 August 1773, ack. by grantors.

Pages 406-409. 20-21 August 1773. Lease & release. Bet. Andrew Barbee & Jane, his wife, and Landon Carter, Jr., Gent. .. 145a. .. in Ham. Par. .. bounded by land of sd. Carter, Benj. Crump, Adie & Moses Hayes and was conveyed by Benj. Crump to sd. Barbee by deeds rec. in Pr. Wm. Co. .. Ł21.10s. .. Signed: Andrew Barbey, Jane Barbey. Rec: 23 August 1773, ack. by grantors.

Pages 409-413. 16-17 April 1773. Lease & release. Bet. Bertrand Ewell, John Gunyon and Jesse Ewell of Pr. Wm. Co. and George Ash of same co. .. 463a. .. on Goose Creek, part of a tract which the sd. Bertrand Ewell purch. formerly of Col. James Ball of Lan. Co. .. 10 March 1738 .. who conveyed to John Gunyon who by deed of mort., 27-28 Aug. 1764 conveyed the same to Robert Scott, who assigned the same to John Knox who by deed of assignment assigned the same to Jesse Ewell, except 100a. formerly sold to Nimrod Ashby by the sd. Bertrand Ewell .. Ł225 .. Signed: Bertrand Ewell, John Gunyon, Jesse Ewell. Wits: William Carr, Thomas Chapman, Phil. Rd. Fras. Lee, Alex'r. Campbell, Henry Rector. Rec: 28 June 1773, prov. by o. of Carr & Rector; 23 Aug. 1773, prov. by o. of Alex'r Campbell.

Pages 413-414. 23 August 1773. B & S. Bet. John Duncan & Elizabeth, his wife, and Messrs. William Cuninghame & Co. of Glasgow, merchants .. Ł61.6s. .. tract in Ham. Par. .. part of larger tract .. old dividing line to Hitt's .. red oak marked HH .. 146a. .. Signed: John Duncan, Elizabeth (X) Duncan. Wits: George Pickett, Randolph Spicer, Henry (X) Newby. Rec: 23 August 1773, prov. by o. of grantors.

Pages 415-417. 24 August 1773. B & S. Bet. Jeremiah Darnal & Catherine, his wife, and Tilman Weaver .. Ł100 .. right & title to tract of 100a. whereon Peter Hitt, dec'd. lived .. being one of the Lotts of Land in the German Town .. Signed: Jeremiah Darnall, Catherine (X) Darnall. Rec: 24 August 1773, ack. by grantors.

Pages 417-420. 21-22 August 1773. Lease & release. Bet. Jeremiah Darnall & Catherine, his wife, and William Brent of Town of Dumfries, Pr. Wm. Co. .. 280a. the upper part of a larger tract of the sd. Darnall and where he formerly lived .. cor. to **James Sinclair** .. Ł 250 .. *Signed*: **Jeremiah Darnall, Catherine (X) Darnall**. *Rec*: 24 August 1773. ack. by grantors.

Pages 420–422. 24 August 1773. B & S. Bet. **Jeremiah Darnall & Katherine**, his wife, and **John Shanks** .. Ł25 .. 50a. .. being a Lott of land in German Town .. Wt. side of Licken Run .. *Signed*: **Jeremiah Darnall, Catherine (X) Darnall**. *Rec*: 24 August 1773, ack. by grantors.

Pages 422–423. 4 January 1773. Lease. Bet. **Joseph Combs** of Loud. Co. and **Peter Wood** .. cor. of Homes on Falmouth road .. down sd. road to **John Peters** line .. to **Lynaugh Helm's** line .. to Darrells Run .. to **Homes** .. 100a. .. for 30 years from 25 Dec. .. yearly rent of 530 lbs. transfer tobacco on Quantico or Acquia warehouses .. *Signed*: **Joseph Combs**. *Wits*: **O. Young, James (X) Holms, John (X) Martin**. *Rec*: 26 July 1773, prov. by o. of **James Holmes, John Martin**; 25 Oct. 1773, prov. by o. of **Originald Young**.

Pages 423–425. 1773. Lease. Bet. **Joseph Combs** of Loud. Co. and **Edward Wood** .. **John Peter's** line thence to **Original Young's** line thence to Brenttown road .. to **Carter's** road .. to Peter's .. 100a. .. for 30 years from 25 Dec .. yearly rent of 530 lbs. transfer tobacco in one note on Quantico or Aquia Warehouse .. *Signed*: **Joseph Combs**. *Wits*: **O. Young, James (X) Holmes, John (X) Martin**. *Rec*: 26 July 1773, prov. by o. of **Holmes & Martin**; 25 Oct. 1773, prov. by o. of **Original Young**.

Pages 425–427. 25 October 1773. B & S. Bet. **John Glascock** of Pr. Wm. Co. and **Margaret**, his wife, and **William Berry** .. Ł150 .. tract at the Bull Run Mt. on the waters of Broad Run of Occoquan being the remainder of a tract of land granted to sd. Glascock .. 22 April 1728 for 633a. 130 per. .. oak by a br. of Fornication Branch a cor. to **Edward Fagin** .. cor. to **Henry Berry**, with his and **John Willoughby** .. to the old mill on the branch .. 300a. .. *Signed*: **John (J) Glascock**. *Wits*: **J. Moffett, Peter Tait, Thomas Glascock, George Glascock**. *Rec*: 25 October 1773, ack. by **John Glascock**.

Pages 427–429. 25 October 1773. Lease. Bet. **Samuel Grigsby** of Leeds Par., Gent. and **Peter Tate** .. part of larger tract leased of **Pearson Chapman** of Md., Gent. .. cor. to **John Fishback and Henry Peyton**, Gent. .. cor. of sd. Tate's dwelling house .. 100a. .. for his nat. life and life of **Elizabeth**, his wife .. yearly rent of Ł7 .. *Signed*: **Samuel Grigsby, Peter Tait**. *Rec*: 25 October 1773, ack. by **Grigsby & Tait**.

Page 429. 15 October 1773. Deed of Gift. **Elizabeth Marshall** of Leeds Par. to **Charles Burrus** .. for nat. love and affection .. in consideration of his marriage with my granddaughter .. one Negroe woman named Sarah .. *Signed*: **Elizabeth Marshall**. *Wits*: **W. Grant, Joseph Smith, James Smith, Augustine Smith**. *Rec*: 25 October 1773, prov. by o. of **Augustin and James Smith**.

Pages 429-432. 6-7 April 1773. Lease & release. Bet. **Daniel Jenifer** of Chas. Co., Md., Gent. and **Thomas Maddux, Jr.** .. tract at the Thoroughfare at the Pignut Ridge .. 100 a. .. same which sd. Jenifer purch. of a certain **George Lamkin** late of Fauq. Co. .. Ł75 .. *Signed*: **Dan'l. Jenifer**. *Wits*: **Thomas Maddux, Elias Edmonds, Henry Hammitt**. *Rec*: 26 July 1773, prov. by o. of **Maddux & Edmonds, Jr.**; 25 Oct. 1773, by o. of **Hammitt**.

Pages 432-434. 14 September 1770. B & S. Bet. **William Nalls** and **Sarah**, his wife, and **Alexander Ewen** of Dumfries, Pr. Wm. Co., merchant .. Ł350 .. 93 1/2a. .. on the Broad Run of Occoquan and the Wolf Trap Branch, residue of a larger tract which Capt. **William Grant** sold to **William Nalls** .. on the Broad Run in the Thoroughfare of the Mother Leathercoat and Bisket Mountains .. cor. to **Nelm's** Patent .. crossing Wolf Trap Br. to a rock of Stone on the top of the Bisket Mt. .. *Signed*: **William Nalls, Sarah (X) Nalls**. *Wits*: **Jas. Scott, Wm. Ransdell, John Chilton**. *Rec*: 25 October 1773, prov. by o. of wits.

Pages 435-437. 25 October 1773. B & S. Bet. **Henry Rector, Jr.** & **Mary**, his wife, of Leeds Par. and **Henry Rector, Younger**, of Ham. Par. .. Ł64.16s. .. 108a. .. cor. to **John Rector** and **Jacob Rector** .. **Isaac Cundiff's** line .. *Signed*: **Henry Rictor, Mary (X) Rictor**. *Wits*: **James Thomson, John Churchhill, George Glascock** (**John Squires**, wit. to receipt). *Rec*: 25 October 1773, ack. by grantors.

Pages 437-439. 25 October 1773. B & S. Bet. **John Squires** & **Elizabeth**, his wife, of Leeds Par. and **Edward Lawrence** (and **Larrance**) .. Ł60 .. 100a. .. cor. to **Thomas Priest** .. cor. to **William Murrey** .. part of tract purch. by **John Rector, Jr.**, dec'd. of **Burgess Ball**, Gent. of Lan. Co. .. 7 Sept. 1770 .. *Signed*: **John Squires, Elizabeth (X) Squires**. *Wits*: **Bailey Johnson, Beede Johnson**, receipt wit. by **Alex'r. Campbell**. *Rec*: 25 October 1773, ack. by grantors.

Pages 439-440. 25 October 1773. Bond. **Charles Burrus** to **Elizabeth Marshall** .. in sum of Ł500 .. that Sarah, a slave, formerly given to sd. Burrus, to remain with sd. Elizabeth during her lifetime and that sd. Elizabeth is to have any child born to Sarah during Elizabeth's lifetime .. Burrus obligated to abide by sd. conditions .. *Signed*: **Charles Burruss**. *Wits*: **W. Ellzey, Thomas Marshall**. *Rec*: 25 October 1773, prov. by o. of wits.

Pages 440-444. 25-26 October 1773. Lease & release. Bet. **Martin Pickett** & **Ann**, his wife, and **Minor Winn, Jr.** .. all that tract (except 200a. devised out of the same by the last will & test. of **Jacob Holtzclaw**, dec'd. to two of his grandsons, viz. **James** & **Henry Holtzclaw**) .. joining upon **Gilson Syars** & another tract of the sd. Jacob Holtzclaw upon Hungar Run the whole cont. 337a. out of which the sd. 200a. are to be deducted .. n. side of a br. of Hungar Run & near the line of **Thomas Barton** & **Edward Feagan** .. line of **Walker** .. the same being orig. surveyed by one **George Binn** & granted 1 Dec. 1742 to **Jacob Holtzclaw** .. Ł30 .. *Signed*: **Martin Pickett, Ann Pick-**

ett. *Wits*: Cuthbert Bullitt, Joseph Blackwell, John Hawkins. *Rec*: 26 October 1773, ack. by grantors.

Pages 444-446. 26 October 1773. B & S. Bet. John Hendron & Margaret, his wife, of Leeds Par. and William Young of Pr. Wm. Co. .. Ł 120 .. 168a. .. cor. to Jacob Rector .. dividing line bet. Burgess Smith & Burgess Ball .. cor. to Charles Rector .. part of larger tract purch. by John Rector, dec'd. of Burgess Ball of Lan. Co. and sold to Hendron .. 9 Mar. 1773 .. *Signed*: John Hendron, Margaret (M) Hendron. *Wits*: John Chilton, Bryant Young, Hez'h Turner, John (X) Bristol. *Rec*: 26 October 1773. ack. by grantors.

Pages 446-448. 26 October 1773. B & S. Bet. Jacob Rector & Jane, his wife, of Leeds Par. and William Young of Pr. Wm. Co. .. Ł100 .. 130a. .. cor. to Henry Rector .. cor. in dividing line bet. Burgess Ball & Burgess Smith .. cor. to Isaac Cundiff .. line of Henry Rector .. part of tract purch. by John Rector, dec'd of Burgess Ball, Gent. *Signed*: Jacob Rector, Jane (X) Rector. *Wits*: Hez'h Turner, John (X) Bristol, John Chilton. *Rec*: 26 October 1773, ack. by grantors.

Pages 448-449. 11 September 1773. B & S. Bet. Thomas Marshall and John Webb of N'land Co. .. Ł200 .. tenement whereon Marshall now lives .. 330a. being lands devised to sd. Marshall by Thomas Ludwell Lee, Esqr. & Molly Lee, his wife, & Col. Richard Henry Lee & Ann, his wife .. 12 Oct. 1765. *Signed*: Thom Marshall. *Wits*: Martin Pickett, John Likly, John Lee. *Rec*: 26 October 1773.

Pages 449-454. 25-25 September 1773. Lease & release. Bet. Joseph Combs & Elizabeth, his wife, of Loud. Co. and James Holms .. tract .. in Ham. Par. .. part of tract given by Joseph Combs, Sr. to his son Joseph Combs, Jr. party to these presents by deeds of lease & release, in Pr. Wm. Co. .. 22 Nov. 1756 .. Beg. at the foard of Dorells Run where the Brenttown road crosses cor. tree to Stark .. to forks of road, thence down Fall Road .. 105a. .. Ł50 .. *Signed*: Joseph Combs, Elizabeth Combs. *Wits*: O. Young, Peter Wood, John (X) Marton, Richard Luttrill, Richard Luttrill, Jr. *Rec*: 22 November 1773, prov. by o. of Original Young, Luttrells, with Commission to William Smith and Thomas Lewis, Gent. of Loud. Co. to examine Elizabeth Combs.

Pages 454-455. n.d. Bond. Bond of Thomas Harrison, for Sheriff of Fauq. Co. For: Ł500. *Sec*: Jonathan Gibson and William Harrison. Commission dated 25 October 1773. *Rec*: 22 November 1773, ack. by T. Harrison and securities.

Pages 455-456. 22 November 1773. Bond. (same as above).

Page 456. 22 November 1773. Bond. Bond of Thomas Harrison, as Sheriff to collect taxes. (same as above) For: Ł1,000.

Pages 457-459. 1 October 1771. Lease. Bet. Thomas Lord Fairfax and Thomas Harris .. tenement in Manor of Leeds .. cor. to Benj.

Neale .. 150a. .. for his nat. life and nat. lives of **Rachel Harris**, his sister and **Samuel**, his brother .. yearly rent of 30s. *Signed*: Fairfax. *Wits*: **Samuel Harris, John Marshall, William Smith.** *Rec*: 22 November 1772, prov. by o. of wits.

Pages 459–462. 1 October 1771. Lease. Bet. **Thomas Lord Fairfax** and **James Harris** .. tenement in Manor of Leeds .. cor. to **Samuel Harris** .. cor. to **Jesse Thomson** & in the line of **R'd. Crawley** .. cor. to **Benj. Douglass** .. 30 a. .. for his nat. life and lives of **Susanna**, his wife and **C a t y**, his daughter .. yearly rent of 6s. sterling .. *Signed*: Fairfax. *Wits*: **Samuel Harris, John Marshall, William Smith.** *Rec*: 22 November 1773, prov. by o. of wits.

Pages 463–465. 22 November 1773. B & S. Bet. **Thomas Glascock** and **Agnes**, his wife, of Leeds Par. and **John Leake [Lake]** .. Ł60 .. tract .. on branches of Goose Creek being part of a tract .. devised to **John Rector** by **Burgess Ball** of Lan. Co. .. cor. to **John Squires** and **Thomas Priest** .. cor. to **James Stewart** .. 100 acres .. *Signed*: **Thomas Glascock, Agnes (X) Glascock.** *Wits*: **William Turley, John Glascock, John Barker.** *Rec*: 22 November 1773, ack. by Grantors.

Pages 465–467. 22 November 1773. B & S. Bet. **Michael Marr** and **Mary**, his wife, of Culp. Co. and **John Bethell** .. Ł25 .. land on branches of Summerduck run .. The first is a tract cont. 75a., which was purch. by **Thomas Toms** of **John Henry** and by him conveyed to sd. Marr .. the other tract of 50a .. was purch. by **Joseph Sebastian** of John Henry and by sd. Sebastian conveyed to sd. Marr & joins first mentioned tract. *Signed*: **Michael Marr, Mary Marr.** *Rec*: 22 November 1773, ack. by Grantors.

Page 467. 19 August 1773. Bill of Sale. **Ann Owens** of Pr. Wm. Co. to Messrs. **William Cuninghame & Co.** .. livestock, crop of tobacco .. in consideration of a debt due of Ł28.8s.10d. .. to **John Likly** in behalf of Cuninghame & Co. *Signed*: **Ann Owens.** *Wits*: **Peter Grant, William Nelson.** *Rec*: 22 November 1773, prov. by o. of Nelson.

Pages 467–468. 22 June 1773. Bill of Sale. **Robert Kairns** to **John Likly** on acct. of Messrs. **Wm. Cuninghame & Co.** .. livestock, household furniture and crops .. in consideration of a debt of Ł 32.10.6d.3f. *Signed*: **Robert (X) Kairns.** *Wits*: **James Craig, Samuel Holliday.** *Rec*: 22 November 1773, prov. by o. of James Craig.

Page 468. 24 August 1773. Bill of Sale. **Rubins Cochram** to **John Likly** .. in behalf of **Wm. Cuninghame & Co.** .. horse purch. of **Jacob Minter**, dec'd, share in crop of corn and tobacco that I will make this season with **William Kirk** .. debt of Ł15.1.6 .. being my security to **William Settle**, Exor. of Jacob Minter. *Signed*: **Reubens Cockram.** *Wits*: **Samuel Porter, John Lee.** *Rec*: 22 November 1773, prov. by o. of **John Lee.**

Page 469. 23 August 1773. Bill of Sale. **Valentine Flynn** to **John Likly** in behalf of Messrs **Wm. Cuninghame & Co.**, Merchants of

Glasgow .. cattle, servant woman named **Agnes Smith**, feather bed & furn. .. crop of corn & tobacco .. for debt of Ŀ23.10.3 1/2d. *Signed*: **Valentine Flynn**. One hat delivered in the name of the whole. *Wit*: **John Lee**. *Rec*: 22 Nov. 1773, prov. by o. of **John Lee**.

Page 469. 27 August 1773. Bill of Sale. **Samuel Connor** to **John Likly** in behalf of Messrs. **Wm. Cuninghame & Co.** .. debt of Ŀ 19.18s.10d. .. furniture .. cattle .. *Signed*: **Stephen (X) Connor** [sic]. *Wit*: **John Lee**. *Rec*: 22 November 1773, prov. by o. of **John Lee**.

Pages 470-471. 28 April 1773. B & S. Bet. **Obadiah Oliphant** of Loud. Co. and **Joseph Miller** of sd. Co. .. whereas **George Washington** of Fx. Co., Esq. by lease of 17 March 1769 unto **William Wood** of Loud. Co. .. partly in Loud. and partly in Fauq. .. 220a. .. for nat. lives of William Wood, **John Wood**, his Brother and **Wm. Young**, son to **John & Margaret Young** .. Wm. Wood to **Obadiah Oliphant** .. rec. in Fauq. Co. .. for Ŀ35 paid by sd. Miller .. one part or moiety of sd. Lott .. *Signed*: **Obadiah Oliphant**. *Wits*: **Thomas West, Isaac Milner, Edward Milner, John Oliphant**. *Rec*: 23 November 1773, prov. by o. of **West, Isaac** and **Edward Milner**.

Page 472. 28 April 1773. Bill of Sale. **William Walker** to **Martin Pickett & Co.** .. in consideration of Ŀ26.5.10 1/2d. .. cattle, household goods .. *Signed*: **William (X) Walker**. *Wits*: **Joseph Blackwell, Jr., Randolph Spicer**. *Rec*: 23 November 1773, prov. by o. of **Blackwell**.

Pages 472-473. 26 February 1773. Bond. **Peter Kamper, Jr. & Peter Kamper, Sr.** to **King** .. for 1,000 lbs. Tobacco .. Peter Kamper, Sr. has undertaken to Erect and build a good & sufficient Bridge over Carters Run at a place already agreed on by **Wm. Edmonds & John Moffett**, Gent., the sd. bridge to be strongly built .. at least 12 ft. wide and the same to be completely finished in a good and workman-like manner on or before 26 Aug. next and if it shall be carried away Kamper to have same rebuilt sufficiently within 6 months .. and to keep the same in good repair as often as need require for 7 years from 26 Aug. .. for 4,500 lbs. tobacco .. *Signed*: **Peter Kamper, Jr., Peter Kamper, Sr.** *Wit*: **William Edmonds**. *Rec*: 23 November 1773, prov. by o. of **Edmonds**.

Page 473. 30 June 1773. Bill of Sale. **William Brown** to **Martin Pickett**, in consideration of sum of Ŀ47.2.10d. .. one Negro boy named **Richard Nick**, nam'd **Dick**, household furniture .. cattle. The horse and saddle delivered for the whole .. *Signed*: **William Brown**. *Wit*: **Joseph Blackwell**. *Rec*: 23 November 1773, prov. by o. of **J. Blackwell**.

Pages 473-474. 24 November 1773. Bond. **John Moffett**, appointed Coroner of Fauq. Co. .. for Ŀ500 .. *Security*: **Cuthbert Bullitt**. *Signed*: **J. Moffett, Cuth'bt. Bullitt**. *Rec*: 25 November 1773, ack. by parties.

Pages 474-475. 24 January 1774. Bond. **William Edmonds** as Sheriff of Fauq. Co., Commission from Governor dated 11 January .. For: Ŀ

1,000. *Security*: John Blackwell and Charles Morehead. *Signed*: William Edmonds, John Blackwell, Charles Morehead. *Rec*: 24 January 1774, ack. by parties.

Page 475. 24 January 1774. Bond. Same as above .. For: £500 .. to collect Quitrents, fines .. *Signed*: William Edmonds, John Blackwell, Charles Morehead. *Rec*: 24 January 1774, ack. by parties.

Page 475. 24 January 1774. Bond. Same as above .. For: £1,000 .. to collect land taxes. *Signed*: as above. *Rec*: 24 January 1774, ack. by parties.

Pages 476-477. 18 August 1773. Division, with Plat. At the request of Messrs. Martin Pickett (who purch. Land of Henry Holtzclaw and Joseph Holtzclaw) and by the consent of Jeremiah Darnall, Gent. (who is appt. gdn. to James Holtzclaw for this purpose) in the presence of John Fishback, Philip Fishback and Josiah Fishback, the Comm'rs. mentioned in an order of the Wor. Court of Fauq. dated Nov. Court 1772, I proceeded to survey and Divide the Land mentioned in the said order according to the above plat .. near the line of Thomas Barton & Edward Feagans .. to the line of Walkers now Bartlett's .. near a line of a former Tract of land of the Holtzclaws now Jeremiah Darnall's .. up the side of the mountain to a great rock .. 340a. .. *Signed*: J. Wright, Surveyor, John Fishback, Philip Fishback, Josiah Fishback, Edward Neale and Samuel Wigenton, Chainmen. *Rec*: 24 November 1773, returned and ordered recorded.

Pages 477-480. 21 October 1773. Lease. Bet. Thomas Ludwell Lee, Esq. & Molly, his wife, of Staf. Co. and Col. Richard Henry Lee of W'land Co. and Thomas Kenneday .. for the nat. lives of the grantors .. 150a. .. on Goose Creek .. Beg. at Smith's cor. in Seaton's line .. side of the Red Oak Mt. .. cor. to Kennedy's other lott .. cor. of sd. Lott & lott of William Seaton .. yearly rent of 50s. *Signed*: Grantors. *Wits*: Thos. Lewis, James Key, Matthew Smith. *Rec*: 28 March 1774, prov. by o. of wits. Rec. with commission to examine Molly Lee.

Pages 480-483. 21 October 1773. Lease. Between [grantors above] and William Seaton .. 100a. .. on Goose Creek .. Beg. at a cor. standing in the old line of Col. Lee's tract on the mountainside and cor. to Keith's lott .. to the line of Kennedy's lott, .. cor. of Kenndedy's two lotts .. during natural lives of grantors .. yearly rent of 33s.4d. .. *Signed*: Thomas Lud. Lee, Molly Lee, Richard Henry Lee. *Wits*: Thomas Lewis, Matthew Smith, James Key. *Rec*: 28 March 1774, with Commission to examine Molly Lee .. prov. by o. of wits.

Pages 484-488. 21 October 1773. Lease. Bet. [above Lees] and Matthew Smith .. 150a. .. on Goose Creek .. Beg. at James Searces cor. Col. Lee's old line on the side of the Blue Ridge .. the side of the Goose Creek Mt. .. to Earls Cor. .. for nat. lives of grantors .. yearly rent of 50s. *Signed*: [all above Lees]. *Wits*: Thos. Lewis, William Seaton, James Key. *Rec*: 28 March 1774, with Comm. for exam. of Molly Lee .. prov. by o. of wits.

Pages 488-491. 21 October 1773. Lease. Bet. [above Lees] and James Searse .. 150a. .. on Goose Creek .. cor. of **William Hill's** in **Col. Lee's** old line .. cor. of **Matthew Smith** .. for nat. lives of grantors .. yearly rent of 50s. .. *Signed*: [all above Lees]. *Wits*: **Thos. Lewis, James Key, William Seaton.** *Rec*: 28 March 1774, with Comm. for exam. of **Molly Lee** .. prov. by o. of wits.

Pages 492-495. 21 October 1773. Lease. Bet. [above Lees] and **Samuel Earl** of F'rick Co. .. 150a. .. lying on Goose Creek .. Beg. at **Matthew Smith's** cor. and cor. to **Colo. Lee's** tract .. chesnut trees in a hollow near the head of Goose Creek, beg. trees to Col. Lee's original tract .. for nat. lives of grantors .. yearly rent of 50s. *Signed*: [all above Lees]. *Wits*: [as above]. *Rec*: [as above].

Pages 495-499. 21 October 1773. Lease. Bet. [above Lees] and **James Key** .. 300a. .. Col. Lee's old line near a large Branch of Goose Creek .. on the side of Red Oak Mt. .. top or near it of Red Oak Mt. cor. to a lot belonging to **Samuel Moore** .. for nat. lives of grantors .. yearly rent of Ł5 .. *Signed*: **Thomas Lud: Lee, Molly Lee, Richard Henry Lee.** *Wits*: **Thos. Lewis, Matthew Smith, William Seaton.** *Rec*: 28 March 1774, prov. by o. of wits., with Comm. to examine **Molly Lee.**

Pages 499-501. 28 March 1774. B & S. Bet. **John Smith** and **Harmon Button** .. Ł16 .. tract in Ham. Par. being one equal third of a larger tract of land, a deed for which **Henry Kamper, Catharine** and **Mary Kamper** obtained from the Proprietor .. 22 Jan. 1741 .. the tract mutually divided bet. the sd. Kempers .. **Catherine Kempers** third cont. 120a. .. in line of **Peter Kemper** standing at the end of the sd. Kampers Mill Dam .. crossing the Main Road .. a stone in **Harmon Kamper's** plantation .. Spanish oak on the Great Run .. which tract the sd. **John Smith** (being heir of the body of the sd. Catherine Kamper) (now Button) devises .. *Signed*: **John Smith.** *Rec*: 28 March 1774, ack. by **John Smith.**

Pages 501-504. 9 December 1773. Lease. Bet. **Henry Peyton** of Leeds Par., Gent. and **Sanford Carroll** and **Sylvester Welch** .. tenement at the Pignut Ridge and on the waters of Broad Run of Occoquan, being part of a tract devised to the sd. Henry, by his father, **John Peyton**, Gent., late of Staf., dec'd .. cor. to **Bryant O'Bannon** .. cor. of the land of **John Toward** and **William McBee** .. to a path leading from Edmonds' plantation to Broad Run .. 300 a. .. during nat. lives of sd. **Sylvester Welch**, and sons Sylvester and **Demsey Welch** .. yearly rent of 1,000 lbs. crop tobacco and cask .. *Signed*: **Henry Peyton, Sanford Carroll, Sylvester (X) Welch.** *Wits*: **John Fishback, John Barker, George Glascock, Josiah Fishback.** *Rec*: 28 March 1774, prov. by o. of **Barker, Glascock** and **Josiah Fishback.**

Pages 504-506. 22 September 1773. B & S. Bet. **John Thompson** and **Richard Watts** of Loud. Co. .. Whereas **George Washington** of Fx. Co. by lease, 17 March 1769, to **George Russell** of Loud. Co., parcel in Loud. & Fauq. Cos. .. 106a. .. George Russell for Ł30 to **John Thompson**, wit. by **David Keays, Thomas West, Edward Wisely**, .. Thompson to Watts for Ł30 .. and rents to George Washington .. *Signed*: **John Tompson**. *Wits*: **William Tompson, David Kease, Joseph (X) Thompson**. *Rec*: 28 March 1774, ack. by **John Thompson**.

Pages 506–508. 26 November 1773. B & S. Bet. **John Dyer** of Loud. Co. and **George Heald** of Christiana Hundred, New-Castle Co., Pa. .. Whereas **George Washington** of Fx. Co., by lease, 17 March 1769, to John Dyer, tract in Fauq. & Loud. Cos. .. 227a. .. for Ł50 Dyer to Heald .. lott adj. **Col. Fitzhugh**'s and **Thomas West**'s lott & the Great Road .. 100a. .. part of the 227a. *Signed*: **John Dyer**. *Wits*: **Lewis Lemert, Thomas West, Daniel Jones, David Keas**. *Rec*: 28 March 1774, ack. by **John Dyer**.

Pages 508–509. 21 February 1774. Servant's Bond. Bet. **Graves Wapshott** and **Charles Hammond** .. Wapshott to serve Hammond for 7 years in the employment of a servant .. Hammond agrees to set free **John Hamilton** (now servant to the sd. Charles Hammond) and Hammond agrees to set free Wapshott when Hamilton pays him Ł50 sterling .. *Signed*: **Graves Wapshott**. *Rec*: 28 March 1774, ack. by Wapshott.

Pages 509–511. 28 March 1774. B & S. Bet. **John Hudnall & Jimmina**, his wife, of Leeds Par. and **Charles Morehead** of same .. Ł190 .. 127a. part of tract of 250a. obtained by **Joseph Hudnall** from **John Hudnall**, dec'd. of N'land Co., grandfather to the aforesaid John Hudnall .. *Signed*: **John Hudnall, Jemima Hudnall**. *Wits*: **John Blackwell, Edward Humston, Chs. Chinn**. *Rec*: 28 March 1774, ack. by grantors.

Pages 511–512. 28 March 1774. Lease. Bet. **Pearson Chapman** of Charles Co., Md., Gent. and **Robert Turn Bull**, planter .. tenement .. joining the lands rented to John Kamper, the lands belonging to **Jacob** and **John Kamper**, Mr. **Pickett Jordine** & the Main Road .. 272a. .. during the nat. lives of the sd. Robert Turnbull, **Betty**, his wife & **Charles Kamper**, son of John .. yearly rent of Ł3 and the quitrents .. *Signed*: **Pearson Chapman**, by **John Moffett**, his Attny. **Robert (X) Turnbull**. *Rec*: 28 March 1774, ack. by **John Moffett**, attorney for **Pearson Chapman** and **Robert Turnbull**.

Pages 513–514. 22 March 1774. Lease. Bet. **William Champe**, Esq. of K. G. Co., Par. of Brunswick and **Wm. Jones** of Ham. Par. .. 100a., part of greater tract .. joining the lands of the late **Charles Carter**, Esq., dec'd and **Richard Lewis** .. being that part whereon the sd. Jones now lives .. to be laid off in such a manner as to join the land of Richard Lewis and include that part of the Main Road that runs thro' the sd. tract .. for his nat. life & lives of S a r a h, his wife and his son **Joe Jones** .. yearly rent of 50s. *Signed*: **William Champe, Wm. (X) Jones**. *Wits*: **Joseph Emmons, Henry Hurst, James (X) Emmons**. *Rec*: 29 March 1774, prov. by o. of wits.

Pages 514-515. 28 March 1774. Lease. Bet. **Pearson Chapman** of Charles Co., Md., Gent. and **John Kamper,** Planter .. included by the lands of sd. Kamper, **Bushrod Dogett, Augustine Jennings & Jardine &** the Main Road .. 100 a. .. for his nat. life & nat. lives of **Anne,** his wife & **Elias Kemper,** their son .. yearly rent of 40s. *Signed*: **Pearson Chapman,** by **John Moffett** his atty., **John (X) Kemper.** *Wits*: The Court *Rec*: 28 March 1774, ack. by **John Moffett & John Kamper.**

Pages 515-517. 29 March 1774. B & S. Bet. **Wm. Demsy & Jane,** his wife, of F'rick Co. and **Joseph Emmons** .. Ł21 .. 139a. .. branch in **Ludwell's** line, now **Knox** .. dividing line bet. **Charles Carter & Joseph Delany** .. Delanies line .. *Signed*: **William (X) Demsy, Jane (X) Demsey.** *Wits*: **Joe Blackwell, John Kirk.** *Rec*: 29 March 1774, ack. by Grantors.

Pages 517-518. 1 September 1773. Bill of Sale. **Joshua Lampton** to **James Robison,** of K. G. Co., Merchant in behalf of Messrs. **Wm. Cuninghame & Co.** .. for Ł19.13s.7d. .. household furniture .. horses (one with a glass eye purch. of **Max'm. Berryman**) .. and farm utensils .. *Signed*: **Joshua Lampton.** *Wits*: **John Likly, Adam Newal.** *Rec*: 28 March 1774, ack. by **Joshua Lampton.**

Pages 518-519. 28 January 1774. Bill of Sale. **Daniel Pendleton** [sic] of Leeds Par. to **John Waddle** of same Par. .. for Ł11, indebtedness .. wagon .. horse. *Signed*: **Daniel Penington** [sic]. *Wits*: **Thomas Edwards, Eliz'a (X) Edwards.** *Rec*: 28 March 1774, prov. by o. of **Thomas Edwards** to be the act of **Daniel Peninton.**

Pages 519-522. 12 November 1773. B & S. Bet. **Lindey Opie,** Gent., and **Elizabeth,** his wife, of St. Stephens Par., N'land Co. and **William Downing** of same .. L71.18s.4d. .. 232 acres .. in Leeds Par. on south side of Broad Run, part of tract given by **Samuel Nelms,** dec'd to **Hannah Shapliegh Nelms, Elizabeth Nelms** and **William Nelms,** by will dated 3 Dec. 1759 .. sd. Hannah Shapliegh Nelms who married **Joseph Blackwell,** dying leaving issue two children, a daughter and a son, both of whom departed this life in their infancy, whereby the land descended to **Elizabeth Opie,** wife of aforesaid **Lindsy Opie,** sister of **Hannah Shapliegh Blackwell** and surviving heir by the whole blood .. cor. tree between this land & land of Mr. **William Nelms** & the land of Mr. **Thomas Keith** .. trees marked I̶F. S N .. oaks on south side of Broad Run .. 232a. .. according to a div. of sd. land made by Mr. **Thos. Marshall,** Surveyor of Fauq. Co., 26 April 1767 .. *Signed*: **Lindsy Opie, Elizabeth Opie.** *Wits*: **Williby (X) Marefield, John Owens, George Blackwell, Sam'l (X) Jones.** *Rec*: 22 November 1773, with Comm. to examine **Elizabeth Opie,** prov. by o. of **Willoughby Marefield** and **John Owens,** to be act & deed of **Lindsey Opie;** 28 March 1774, prov. by o. of **Samuel Jones.**

Page 522. 7 September 1773. Lease. Bet. **Jannet Chinn,** widow & relict of **Thomas Chinn,** late of Pr. Wm. Co. and **James Lewis,** farmer .. her Dower in lands Lewis purch. of Thomas Chinn in his lifetime, during the nat. life of **Janet Chinn** .. for annual rent of Ł10 .. *Signed*:

Jannet Chinn. *Wit*: W. Ellzey, Whart'n Ransdell, Alex'r. Campbell. *Rec*: 25 April 1774, prov. by o. of wits.

Pages 522-524. 25 October 1773. B & S. Bet. John Glascock of Pr. Wm. Co. and Margaret, his wife, and Thomas Marshall, John Moffett, Martin Pickett, John Obanon, James Scott, Henry Peyton, William Edmonds, Humphrey Brooke, Samuel Grigsby, John Chilton, William Pickett and Charles Chinn, Gent., Vestrymen of Leeds Par. .. Ł67.4s. .. tract .. on the waters of Hungar Run alias Little River .. Beg. .. saplin on Sier's Road .. burnt cor. being the Beg. cor. of the land sold by John Fishback &c to the Vestrymen .. Bartletts Cor. .. 112a. *Signed*: John (Ł) Glascock. *Rec*: 24 April 1774, ack. by John Glascock.

Pages 525-526. 23 April 1774. Deed of Trust. Bet. Peter Kemper, Catherine Kamper and Arthur Morson and Martin Pickett & Co. .. Ł 95.9s.11d. .. said Kampers are indebted to Morson & Pickett & Co. in above sum .. tract whereon they now live, part of which was granted to Harman Kamper, dec'd. and the remainder purch. of Jordan heirs and joining Peter Kamper, Harmon Button, Charles Williams and Hoes [H o o e] Tract .. one mare .. household furniture .. stock .. to be sold after Dec. 1774 if debt is unpaid with interest, for best price, overplus to be paid the Kampers .. *Signed*: Peter Kamper, Catherine (K) Kamper. *Wits*: William Pickett, Richard Lee, Willis Green, Armistead Churchill. *Rec*: 25 April 1774, prov. by o. of Pickett, Lee & Green.

Pages 526-527. 23 September 1773. Bill of Sale. Charles Waller to John Morehead for Ł19.13s.10d.1f. .. furniture, horse, cattle, slaves, whole crop of Corn and Tobacco .. *Signed*: Charles (C) Waller. *Wits*: Bailey Johnson, Thomas Massey. *Rec*: 25 April 1774. prov. by o. of wits.

Pages 527-529. 14 February 1774. Deed of Trust. Bet. Daniel Brown and Martin Pickett & Co. .. Brown indebted to Pickett in amount of Ł 91.14s. .. tract purch. of James Taylor .. joining Hampton's Line, Daniel Floweree's Line and Charles Taylor's Line .. furniture .. Upon Trust .. after 20 Oct. 1774 to sell for debt .. *Signed*: Daniel Brown. *Wits*: Geo. Cordell, Samuel Blackwell, Richard Lee. *Rec*: 25 April 1774, prov. by o. of wits.

Pages 529-532. 22-23 April 1774. Lease & release. Bet. Andrew Cochrane, Wm. Cuninghame & Co., Merhants of Glasgow and Hugh Brent of Pr. Wm. Co. .. tract in Cos. of Fauq. and Pr. Wm. .. 370a. .. granted to sd. Cochrane & Co. by Proprietor .. 23 July 1773 .. cor. to Shackelford, Parker & Thornberry .. cor. to Burgess .. cor. to Col. H a r r i s o n .. white oak marked A P in Shackelford's line .. stone by Burwell's Road. *Signed*: Andrew Cochrane, Wm. Cuninghame by James Robison, their attorney. *Rec*: 25 April 1774, ack. by Robison.

Pages 532-533. 26 April 1774. B & S. Bet. William Morehead and Presley Morehead .. Ł50 .. the reversion of 100a. being part of tract whereon **John Morehead** dec'd formerly lived, Father to the aforesaid Wm. and by him beq. to William .. *Signed*: **William Morehead.** *Wits*: **Joseph Blackwell, Samuel Blackwell, Charles Morehead.** *Rec*: 26 April 1774, ack. by said **William Morehead.**

END OF DEED BOOK 5

Pages 1-4. 27 June 1774. Lease & release. Bet. **Samuel Porter &
Eve**, his wife and **William Porter** .. 100a. .. part of tract formerly
belonging to **Denis Conyers**, dec'd .. saplins on west side of the north
branch of Licking Run .. **James Bailey's** plantation .. Ł50 .. *Signed*:
Samuel Porter, Eve Porter. *Rec*: 27 June 1774, ack. by **Samuel
Porter.**

Pages 4-6. 27 June 1774. B & S. Bet. **James Bailey** and **Hannah**,
his wife, of Ham. Par. and **Robert Fisher** .. Ł76.14s. .. 118a. whereon
sd. Bailey now lives .. part of greater tract belonging to sd. Bailey ..
hiccory on west side of main branch of Licken Run .. *Signed*: **J a m e s
(B) Bailey, Hannah (X) Bailey.** *Rec*: 27 June 1774, ack. by Grantors.

Page 7. 20 June 1774. Bill of Sale. **William Grubbs** to **Alexander
B r o w n** of Pr. Wm. Co. .. for .. Ł28.10s. .. goods and chattels ..
Signed: **William Grubbs.** *Wit*: **Robert Brown.** *Rec*: 27 June 1774.

Page 8. June 1774. Renunciation of Will. **Mary Neavil**, widow and
relict of **George Neavil**, dec'd, of Fauquier County .. *Signed*: **Mary
Neavill.** *Wits*: **Ambrose Barnett, James Hathaway.** *Rec*: 27 June
1774, prov. by o. of wits.

Pages 8-11. 13-14 April 1774. Lease & release. Bet. **C h u r c h h i l l
Jones** and **John Bryant** .. 305a. .. cor. south side of Turkey Run ..
land sd. Jones purchased of **G e o r g e B o s w e l l** .. Ł400. *Signed*:
Churchhill Jones. *Wits*: **Wm. Ransdell, Jr., James Robison, Hubbard Prince.** *Rec*: 25 June 1774, ack. by grantor.

Pages 12-14. 21 May 1774. B & S. Bet. **Thomas Chilton**, Gent. of
W'land Co. and **George Heale**, Gent. .. Ł470.5s. .. tract in Ham. Par.
which **Stephen Chilton** of W'land Co. purch. of Exors. of **Charles
C a r t e r**, Esq., dec'd. and upon death of Stephen Chilton descended to
Thomas Chilton as his eldest brother and heir-at-law .. 519a. .. Kettle
Run Patent line .. cor. with **Wm. Watkins** .. cor. of aforesd. Heale ..
crossing south branch of Kettle Run .. **Buchanan's** line (under **Horner**)
.. cor. to **McClanahan** near an Ivy Clift near Kettle Run .. cor. of
Wyatts .. near a drain of Mawl Branch .. *Signed*: **Thos. Chilton.**
Wits: **William Omohundro, Charles Chilton, William Claxone, Phill.
Heale, John Blackwell, Jr.** *Rec*: 25 June 1774, ack. by **Thos. Chilton.**

Pages 14-19. 22-23 May 1774. Lease & release. Bet. Richard Lewis & Ann, his wife of Brunswick Par., K. G. Co. and Robert Stringfellow of St. Paul's Par., Staf. Co. .. tract purch. of Robert Allason .. 500a. .. east side of Rock Run cor. to land of Charles Travers and John Courtney .. Col. Charles Carter's line .. east side of Main Road cor. to William Brooks .. cool spring branch .. L150 .. Signed: Richard Lewis, Ann (X) Lewis. Wits: Jos. Blackwell, John Blackwell, John Eustace, George Conway, Thomas Skinker, Thomas Marshall, A. Wodrow, David Briggs. Rec: 22 August 1774, prov. by o. of Joseph Blackwell, John Eustace, David Briggs.

Pages 20-21. 1 February 1774. B & S. Bet. William Pickett Sanford and William Bartlett .. tract whereon Bartlett now lives on hungar run .. cor. to Wm. Pickett Sanford's land in Mercer's line .. to Walker's Patent line .. cor. to Jacob Holtzclaw .. mouth of Branch of Hungar Run .. to the mouth of long branch to a maple marked W B .. 277a. Signed: Wm. Pickett Sanford. Rec: 22 August 1774, ack. by grantors.

Pages 21-23. 22 August 1774. B & S. Bet. Thomas Glascock & Agnas, his wife of Leeds Par. .. and John Kincheloe .. L60 .. 100a. .. cor. to John Leak [Lake?] .. oak in line of Edward Laurence .. Signed: Thomas Glascock, Agnas (X) Glascock. Wits: J. Markham, Richard Rixey, Jr., Samuel Grigsby. Rec: 22 August 1774, ack. by Thomas and Agnes Glascock.

Pages 24-26. 22 August 1774. B & S. Bet. Thomas Glascock & Agnas, his wife, of Leeds Par. .. and John Monday .. L60 .. 100a. .. cor. to William Turley .. oak in the line of Edward Laurance .. Signed: Thomas Glascock, Agnas (X) Glascock. Wits: J. Markham, Wm. Ransdall, Jr., Thos. Ransdall. Rec: 22 Aug. 1774, ack. by Grantors.

Pages 26-28. 22 August 1774. B & S. Bet. George Grant & Mary, his wife and Edward Feagan .. L120 .. tract in Leeds Par. .. on head branches of little river, part of larger tract known as Clerks [Clark's ?] land .. cor. marked T cor. of Thomas Thornton's now John Barkers .. line of the sd. Clerk which a line of the Grand Patent .. oak marked in the orig. I C K for John Clerk .. Lott line bet. this and John Hathaway .. saplins in the line of Bartlett and Hathaway .. 277a. .. Signed: George Grant, Mary (X) Grant. Rec: 22 Aug. 1774, ack. by Grantors.

Pages 29-31. 1 January 1773. B & S. Bet. Moses Hayes, Planter and John Gibson of Staf. Co. merchant .. L68.17s.11d. .. tract of land which descends to me in right of my wife .. bet. Town Run and Negro Run .. 80a. .. another tract of land which I now live on purch. of B e n - jamin Crump and have since sold 32a. to Mr. Wm. Grant which lies on the lower end of the tract, the whole cont. ca. 132a. .. bounded by Fishg Run and Ludwels line .. Signed: Moses Hayes. Wits: Nicholas (X) Spring, John Murray, George Balfoier. Rec: 23 August 1773, prov. by o. of Nicholas Springs; 25 July 1774, by o. of John Murray; 22 Aug. 1774, by o. of Geo. Balfour.

168

Pages 31-34. 21 February 1774. B & S. Bet. **James Slaughter &** **Susanna**, his wife, of Culp. Co. and **Gawin Lawson** of same county .. whereas **Nathaniel Hedgman** being seized in fee simple of a tract by virtue of letters patent, dated 21 Aug. 1724, from the Proprietor on a branch of Tin Pot Run on north side of Rappahannock River adj. to tract of **Peter Hedgman**, cont. 2,025a. .. N. Hedgman did by deed, 27 Jan. 1738, convey one moiety of sd. tract unto **James Jones** .. 500a. .. which descended to Jones's son & heir, **Joseph Jones**, who, on 11 Aug. 1763, conveyed same to **Francis Whiting**, said Whiting conveyed same to **James Slaughter** of Culp. Co. .. Ł140 paid by Lawson .. 260a. being part and parcel from Whiting to Slaughter .. east side of Tin Pot Run to the cor. of **John Duncan** and joining the lands of **John Black-well, Samuel Fox, Hancock Lee** and the land which belonged to the late **Catesby Cocke**, dec'd .. *Signed*: James Slaughter, Susanna Slaughter. *Wits*: **Robert Patton, William Williams, Aug. Slaughter, George Hamilton, William Knox**. *Rec*: 22 August 1774, with Comm. to examine **Susanna Slaughter** from Culp. Co. signed by **John Slaugh-ter & William Walker**, prov. by o. of **Hamilton & Knox**, wits; 26 Sept. 1774, prov. by o. of **Robert Patton**.

Pages 34-36. 23 May 1774. B & S. Bet. **John Duncan & Elizabeth**, his wife of Culp. Co. and **Joseph Duncan, Sr.** .. Ł30 .. tract in Ham. Par. .. bought by sd. Duncan of **Joseph Hitt** .. 53a. .. oak on Marsh Road, joining **Benj. Holtzclaw**'s land .. saplins in **Bumberry**'s line .. oak on sd. road near Turkey Run Church .. *Signed*: John Duncan, Elizabeth (X) Duncan. *Wits*: **Jos. Blackwell, Thos. Keith, Samuel Blackwell**. *Rec*: 26 Sept. 1774, ack. by Grantors.

Pages 36-38: xxxth August 1774. B & S. Bet. **James Foley** of Pr. Wm. Co. and **Edmund Homes** of same county .. Ł27 .. tract in Ham. Par. .. on branches of little Summer Duck Run .. 200a., being part and the lower end of a tract of 800a. granted **Elizabeth White** of Staf. Co. by the Prop., 10 May 1725 and by her sold to James Foley, 23 Oct. 1746 .. Beg. in **Ludwell**'s Line .. cor. to **John Foley** and others thence to divide these 200a. from John Foley's .. *Signed*: James Foley. *Wits*: **William Parker, Jr., Geo. Lowry, James Hume, John Chilton, Jas. (X) Homes, J. Moffett**. *Rec*: 26 Sept. 1774, prov. by o. of Lowry, Chilton and Hume.

Pages 38-40. xxviith August 1774. B & S. Bet. **John Foley** of Hampshire Co. and **Milly**, h. w. and **Edmund Homes** of Pr. Wm. Co. .. Ł21.10s. .. tract in Ham. Par., on branches of Persimon Run, joining the lands of **John Kelly**, cont. 200 a., part of 800 a. tract granted **Elizabeth White** of Staf. Co. by the Prop., 10 May 1725 and by her conveyed to sd. Foley, 23 Oct. 1746 .. cor. to Ludwell .. cor. with **James Foley** .. cor. to John Kelly .. *Signed*: John Foley, Milly Foley. *Wits*: **J. Moffett, John Chilton, Wm. Parker, Jr., George Lowry, James (X) Homes, James Hume**. *Rec*: 26 Sept. 1774, prov. by o. of Chilton, Lowry and Humes.

Pages 40-43. 31 August 1774. Lease. Bet. **Thomas Lord Fairfax** and **Edward Humston** .. tenement in Manor of Leeds .. cor. to

Hamrick's lott .. to a stake in **Dixon's** Quarter tract .. 150 a. .. for his nat. life & lives of **Susanna**, h. w. and Edward, his son .. yearly rent of 30s. sterling .. *Signed*: **Fairfax**. *Wits*: **Andrew Barbee, John Barton, Garner Burgess**. *Rec*: 26 Sept. 1774, prov. by o. of wits.

Pages 43-45. 24 September 1774. Div. of Land. Bet. **James Young** and **John Thornberry**, who purch. in partnership of **Burgess Ball & M a r y**, h. w. of Lan. Co., 23 March 1771, the moiety of a tract upon Kettle Run & for the most part in Fauq. Co., the other in Pr. Wm. Co., line where it crosses Burwell's Rd., oak marked BB. RL in the **Brenton** Line .. oak said to be **Harrison's** Cor. .. Cor. with **Hugh Brent** .. Cor. to **Samuel Thornberry** .. Cor. of **Heale's** and **Carter's** bet. sd. run and **Adams's** Horsepen Lick .. 2100 a. .. tract divided between Young and Thornberry .. *Signed*: **John (W) Young, John Thornberry**. *Wits*: **John Tomlin, Wm. Ransdell, Jr., George Lowry**. *Rec*: 26 Sept. 1774, ack. by parties.

Pages 46-47. 9 February 1774. Bill of Agreement. Bet. **Walker Taliaferro** of Car. Co. and **Samuel Love** of Loud. Co. .. Taliaferro has sold to Love a tract of land on Broad Run .. 1200a. .. 50 a. more or less not to be noticed, but to be accounted for in proportion to the price given the Mill that is erected on the aforesd land, in the like good order and condition that they now are in together with Dickersons Pretentions .. to be delivered to Love when he pays Taliaferro £1375, as follows: a bill of exchange of £200 sterling at the next meeting of Merchants at Williamsburgh for which the sd. Taliaferro is to allow the exchange that is then given, £500 Current Money of Virginia, the next Oct. General Court .. the remaining the next Oct. General Court 1775 .. *Signed*: **Walker Taliaferro, Sam'l Love**. *Wits*: **Landon Carter, Jr., William Fitzhugh**. Receipt signed by **Taliaferro** with **Catesby Woodford** and **Joseph Rogers**, wits. *Rec*: 24 Oct. 1774, prov. by o. of **Woodford & Rogers**.

Pages 47-50. 22 October 1774. B & S. Bet. **Walker Taliaferro**, Gent. of Car. Co. and **Samuel Love** of Charles Co., Md., Gent. .. notes above article of agreement bet. Taliaferro and Samuel Love of Loud. Co., son of Sam'l. Love of Md. .. tract in Fauq. and Pr. Wm. Cos. .. tract of 1200 a., mill, mill dam and appurtenances .. agreement above made by **Sam'l. Love the Younger** for **Sam'l. Love the Elder** .. part of tract called Broad Run in Par. of Ham. and Leeds in Fauq. & Pr. Wm .. from **Charles** and **Landon Carter**, Esqrs, exors. of Charles Carter, dec'd to Walker Taliaferro .. 1771 .. together with mill, mill lands, etc. erected thereon .. **Sally Taliaferro** to relinq. her dower rights .. *Signed*: **Walker Taliaferro**. *Wits*: **Catesby Woodford, Charles Love, Jeremiah Wilson, Robt. Gilchrist, Wm. Buckner, James Taliaferro, Wily Roy, Joseph Walker**. *Rec*: 24 Oct. 1774, with performance bond, and prov. by o. of Rogers, Woodford and Wilson.

Pages 50-55. 20-21 September 1774. Lease & release. Bet. **J o h n Wright, Jr.** and **Ann**, h. w. and **Peter Grant** .. tract on branches of Little River called "Whitewood" same purch. by Wright of **M i n o r Winn** .. cor. to tract formerly belong. to **Clark** now a cor. of **Thomas**

Bartlett .. oak on south side of Whitewood Br. near a large r[c]
crossing br. at the mouth of Jesse's Branch .. cor. to John Barke.. ..
292 a. .. Ł200. *Signed*: **John Wright, Jun'r, Ann Wright**. *Wits*: **John
Peake, Minor (W) Winn, James Winn**. *Rec*: 24 October 1774, ack. by
John Wright.

Pages 56-57. 21 July 1774. Lease. Bet. **John Oar & Mary**, h. w. of
Ham. Par. and **James Wheatley** .. tenement to be entered 13 Oct. ..
whereon Oar now lives .. 212 a. .. 1/2 of undivided tract bet. Oar and
Benj. Turner .. for 21 years .. annual rent of Ł6.13s.4d. *Signed*: **John
(X) Oar, Mary (X) Oar**. *Wits*: **James Garner, Vincent Garner, Vin-
cent Garner, Sr**. *Rec*: 24 Oct. 1774, ack. by **John Ore**.

Pages 57-58. 29 May 1773. Bill of Sale. **William Felkins** to **John
Likly** on acc't of Messrs. **Wm. Cuninghame & Co**. .. household furni-
ture .. stock .. crops L37.4s.3d. *Signed*: **William (X) Felkins**. *Wit*:
Benj'a Robinson. *Rec*: 24 Oct. 1774, prov. by o. of witness.

Pages 58-61. 20 October 1774. Lease. Bet. **Thomas Lord Fairfax**
and **Benjamin Piper** .. tenement in the Manor of Leeds .. part of line
of **Simon Hethling's** Lott .. Pipers old Lott .. crossing Thumb run ..
135 a. for his nat. life and lives of **Robert**, his son and **Mary** and
Nancy, his daus. .. yearly rent of 27s. sterling .. *Signed*: **Fairfax**.
Wits: **Samuel Harris, William Briggs, Spencer Smith**. *Rec*: 24 Oct.
1774, prov. by o. of wits.

Pages 61-64. 20 October 1774. Lease. Bet. **Thomas Lord Fairfax**
and **Samuel Harris** .. tenement in Manor of Leeds .. cor. to **Thomas
Harris's** lott .. cor. to **Benj. Fletcher's** lott .. cor. to **Wm. Smith's**
lott .. 235 a. .. for nat. life of Samuel Harris his son and lives of
Zephaniah and **Zachariah Harris**, his grandsons .. yearly rent of 47s.
sterling .. *Signed*: **Fairfax**. *Wits*: **William Briggs, Spencer Smith,
William Smith**. *Rec*: 24 October 1774, prov. by o. of wits.

Pages 64-67. 20 October 1774. Lease. Bet. **Thomas Lord Fairfax**
and **William Strother** .. tenement in Manor of Leeds .. side of Piny
Mt. .. 110 a. .. for his nat. life and lives of **Milly** h. w. and **Elizabeth**
his dau. .. yearly rent of 22s. sterling .. *Signed*: **Fairfax**. *Wits*: **William Briggs, Samuel Harris, Spencer Smith**. *Rec*: 24 Oct. 1774,
prov. by o. of wits.

Pages 67-69. 22 October 1774. B & S. Bet. **Edward Wiseley**, car-
penter, and **Robert Thomson** of Loud. Co. .. lease fr. **George
Washington**, Esq. .. 15 March 1774 to **Edward Wisly** for 130 a. .. for
his nat. life and lives of **Mary**, h. w. and **William Thomson** and **John
Thomson** .. for Ł6 .. assigns lease. *Signed*: **Edward Wisly**. *Rec*: 24
Oct. 1774, ack. by **Edward Wisly**.

Pages 69-71. 24 October 1774. B & S. Bet. **Catherine Kemper** of
Ham. Par., widow, **Peter Kamper & Alice**, h. w. and **John Kamper** of
Culp. Co. .. Ł90 .. there part in tract formerly belonging to **H a r m a n
Kamper**, dec'd .. dividing line bet. **Peter Kamper, Sr.** and Harman

Kamper, dec'd by the road side .. oak cor. in the line of Mess'rs Williams's .. line of John Hooe .. 130 a. .. *Signed*: Catherine (3) Kemper, Peter (X) Kemper, Alice (X) Kemper. *Rec*: 24 October 1774, ack. by Kampers.

Pages 71–73. 24 October 1774. B & S. Bet. Peter Kamper & Alice, h. w., Catherine Kamper, of Ham. Par. and Harman Button .. Ł10 .. tract whereon he now lives, which was formerly owned by Harman Kamper, dec'd .. 28 a. .. oak in Williams's line on the road .. *Signed*: Catherine (X) Kemper, Peter (X) Kemper, Alice (X) Kemper. *Rec*: 24 Oct. 1774, ack. by Kampers.

Pages 73–77. 15 March 1774. Lease. Bet. George Washington of Mount Vernon, Fx. Co., Esq. and William Dulin, farmer .. tenement for his nat. life and lives of Elizabeth, h. w. and Lewis Dulin their son 120 a. .. near Lost Mt., part of tract of 3,112 a. .. called Springfield .. in line of Lott No. 3 .. side of the lost mountain .. formerly leased to one B a l l e n g e r and by him forfeited by non payment of rent .. yearly rent of Ł5 .. *Signed*: G.° Washington, Wm. Dulin. *Wits*: Edward Wisly, James Dermont, Isaac Milner. *Rec*: 24 Oct. 1774, prov. by o. of wits.

Pages 77–82. 15 March 1774. Lease. Bet. George Washington, .. Fx. Co. .. and Isaac Milner .. for his nat. life and lives of Bathia Milner, h. w., Isaac and Nicholas Milner, his sons .. 120 a. .. part of Springfield .. cor. to William Wood's lot no. 12 in line with John Dyer's lott .. on south by lotts No. 16 & 17 leased to John Glascock and Thomas Loyd on the West by lot No. 19 leased to Deal Clyman .. on north by lot No. 12 leased to Wm. Wood but now in the tenure of Joseph Milner son to sd. Isaac Milner .. yearly rent of Ł4 .. *Signed*: G.° Washington, Isaac Milner. *Wits*: William Dulin, James Dermont, Edward Wisely. *Rec*: 24 Oct. 1774, prov. by o. of wits.

Pages 82–86. 15 March 1774. Lease. Bet. George Washington .. Fx. Co. .. and Edward Wisely, Carpenter .. for his nat. life and lives of Mary, his wife, Wm. Thompson, son of John Thompson .. 130 a. .. near Lost Mt. .. called Springfield .. NW cor. of Lott No. 19, leased to Deal Clyman, SW cor. of sd. lott & cor. to the reserved Lott .. to Lotts 4 & 5 leased to two of the Ballengers line of Lot No. 5 (now in the possession of Thomas Slator) .. Lotts 7 & 8, in poss. of Wm. Thompson and Richard Watts .. *Signed*: G. Washington, Edward Wiseley. *Wits*: William Dulin, James Dearmont, Isaac Milner. *Rec*: 24 Oct. 1774 prov. by o. of wits.

Pages 87–91. 15 March 1774. Lease. Bet. George Washington of Mt. Vernon, Fx. Co., Esq. and William Thompson, Farmer .. for his nat. life and lives of Sarah, h. w. and Hannah, dau. .. 115a. near the lost mountains .. being a part of Springfield .. cor. to Lot No. 6 leased to James Wood, now in poss. of David Keas .. yearly rent of Ł4 to be paid to sd. Washington at his house in Fx. Co. on 25 Dec. each year .. *Signed*: G. Washington, Wm. Thompson. *Wits*: James Dearmont, Isaac Milner, Peter Romine. *Rec*: 24 Oct. 1774, prov. by o. of wits.

Pages 91-96. 15 March 1774. Lease. Bet. **George Washington** .. and **Peter Romine** .. for the lives of **Abel, Layton** and **Zachariah,** his three sons, by **Susannah** his present wife .. part of tract known as Springfield near the lost mountains .. 120 a. .. oak on the Bent Branch .. along patent line .. along side of lost mt. .. near a spring in a hollow .. yearly rent of Ł3. *Signed:* **G. Washington, Peter Romine.** *Wits:* **James Dearmont, Isaac Milner, William Thompson.** *Rec:* 24 Oct. 1774, prov. by o. of wits.

Pages 96-97. 28 November 1774. B & S. Bet. **John Likly,** Factor for Messrs. **Wm. Cuninghame** & Co., merchants of Glasgow and **Francis James** .. Ł17 .. part of larger tract in Ham. Par. .. cor. to **Jas. Duncan** joining **John Hitt's** land on the Falmouth road .. to Hampton's road .. to Turkey Run Church .. 30 a. .. *Signed:* **J o h n L i k l y.** *Rec:* 28 Nov. 1774, ack. by **John Likly.**

Pages 97-99. 28 November 1774. B & S. Bet. **John Likly,** Factor .. and **William Russell** .. Ł25 tract in Ham. Par. part of larger tract .. cor. to **John Stewart's** land and William Russell's old tract .. to Dumfries Road .. to Turkey Run Church then down Hampton's Road .. 60 a. *Signed:* **John Likly.** *Rec:* 28 Nov. 1774, ack. by **John Likly.**

Pages 99-101. 16 November 1774. B & S. Bet. **Wm. Nelms** of N'land Co. and **John Owens** .. Ł66 .. tract in Leeds Par .. 232 a. .. cor. dividing sd. land from **Lindy Opie's** .. line dividing sd. land from **Keith** .. cor. to dividing line by **Lindsy Opie** .. cor. tree standing on Broad Run .. *Signed:* **William Nelms.** *Wits:* **William Downing, Andrew Cottrill.** *Rec:* 28 November 1774, ack. by grantor.

Pages 101-103. 21 November 1774. B & S. Bet. **Benj. Crump** of Ham. Par. and **Benj. Bradford** of same .. Ł26.5s. .. hic. in Ludwell's line .. hic. on banks of Marsh Run .. 59 1/2 a. *Signed:* Benjamin **Crump.** *Wits:* **Joseph Allen, W. Sturdie, Charles Day.** *Rec:* 28 Nov. 1774, prov. by o. of wits.

Pages 103-105. 6 October 1774. B & S. Bet. **William Wyatt & Lettice,** h. w. of Pr. Wm. Co. and **George Heale** .. Ł170 .. 170 a. .. part of land Wyatt bought of the Exor. of **Charles Carter,** Esq., Dec'd .. bounded on the lands of **William Watkins, Thomas Shirley, James McClanahan** and **Stephen Chilton,** now the property of the afsd. Heale .. *Signed:* **William Wyatt, Lettice (X) Wyatt.** *Wits:* **John Coppedge, George Lowry, Phil Heale.** *Rec:* 28 Nov. 1774, ack. by grantors.

Pages 105-107. 26 November 1774. B & S. Bet. **William Wiatt & Lettice,** h. w. of Pr. Wm. Co. and **Thomas Shirley** .. Ł50 .. 102 a. .. part of tract from Exors. of **C h s. C a r t e r,** Esq. dec'd .. bounded by: **Watkins** line, Kettle Run, **McClannahan** .. stony hill in **Steele's** line .. cor. with **John Shirly** .. *Signed:* **William Wyatt, Lettice (X) Wyatt.** *Rec:* 28 November 1774, ack. by grantors.

Pages 107-108. 28 November 1774. B & S. Bet. **John Likly**, Factor for Messrs. **Wm. Cunninghame & Co.**, merchants of Glasgow and **Benjamin Holtzclaw** .. Ł23.8s. .. part of larger tract in Ham. Par .. oak in **Russell's** ancient line .. oaks on Falmouth Rd. .. cor. to **Duncan** .. Turkey Run Church then down the Dumfries Road .. 56 a. .. *Signed*: **John Likly**. *Rec*: 28 Nov. 1774, ack. by **John Likly**.

Pages 108-111. 28 November 1774. B & S. Bet. **Thomas Glascock & Agnes**, h. w. of Leeds Par. and **William Turley** .. Ł74.16s. .. 191 a. .. Beg. at a red oak & Span. oak cor. to **George Glascock** & running thence .. part of larger tract purch. by **John Rector**, dec'd of **Burges Ball**, Gent. of Lan. Co., 7 Sept. 1770 .. *Signed*: **Thomas Glascock, Agnes (X) Glascock**. *Wits*: **Robt. Dobson, Elias Edmonds, John Chilton**. *Rec*: 28 Nov. 1774, ack. by grantors.

Pages 111-113. 11 August 1774. Lease. Bet. **Jaily Marr** of Ham. Par. and **Benj. Bradford** .. 330 a. .. for 20 years .. yearly rent of Ł5 .. *Signed*: **Jaily** (her X mark) **Marr, Ben Bradford**. *Wits*: **Dan'l. Bradford, John Wheatly, Alex'r Bradford**. *Rec*: 22 Aug. 1774, prov. by o. of **Daniel & Alexander Bradford**, wits .. 28 Nov. 1774, prov. by o. of **J. Wheatley**.

Page 113. 11 February 1774. Bill of Sale. **Henry Allen & Betty**, h. w., Admrs. of Estate of **James Nelson**, dec'd, in consideration of a judgment of Ł63 obtained by **Wm. Carr** agst. the estate, which judgment **Henry Peyton** and **John Obanon** are bound to pay .. to Peyton & Obanon .. house hold furniture .. horses .. cattle .. servant man named **Nicholas Ball**, one named **Robert Dunn**, do: named **Mary Jones**. *Signed*: **Henry Allen, Betty Allen**. *Wits*: **Sanford Carrell, Samuel Obannon, Thomas Allen**. *Rec*: 23 January 1775, prov. by o. of Carrell and Obanon, wits.

Pages 113-114. 27 February 1775. Bond. Of **John Chilton**, appointed Surveyor of Fauq. Co. by Commission from the Pres. & Masters of the College of Wm & Mary. For: Ł500. *Sec*: **William Blackwell** and **Humphrey Brooke**. *Signed*: **John Chilton, W. Blackwell, H. Brooke**. *Rec*: 27 Feb. 1775, ack. by parties.

Pages 114-115. 9 August 1775. Lease. Bet. **William Wright** of Staf. Co. and **Feathergail Adams** .. 40 a. .. cor. of **John Hudnall's** land .. poplar in Wm. Wright's land .. **Charles Martin's** line .. large spring, cor. to **Mrs. Baylie** .. for his nat. life and lives of **Elizabeth**, h. w. and **Anne**, his dau. .. yearly rent of 1s. per acre. *Signed*: **William Wright, Feathergail Adams**. *Wits*: **Edward Ball, James Ball, Reubin Smith**. *Rec*: 28 Nov. 1774, prov. by o. of **Edward & James Ball**; 27 Feb. 1775, prov. by o. of **R. Smith**.

Pages 115-116. 27 Feb. 1775. Deed of Gift. Bet. **James Stewart** of Ham. Par. and James Stewart of Fx. Co. .. for nat. love and affection .. part of a tract purch. by sd. Jas. Stewart of **Richard Grubbs** .. cor. to **B e l l** and **H i t t** on the Parsons Branch .. cor. of **R a n s d e l l** ..

Ransdell's line cor. with **John Stewart** .. 85 acres .. *Signed*: James Stewart. *Rec*: 27 Feb. 1775, ack. by grantor.

Pages 116-117. 19 July 1774. Bill of Sale. **George Conway** to **Charles Chilton** .. ₤30 .. horse .. riding chair .. household furniture. *Signed*: **George Conway**. *Wits*: **John Coppage, John Blackwell**. *Rec*: 27 Feb. 1775, prov. by o. of **John Blackwell**.

Page 117. 8 August 1774. Bill of Sale. **James Gray** to **John Chilton** and **Martin Pickett** .. one servant named **Thomas Harrison**, one Negro woman named **Shillis** .. horse .. cattle .. real estate & pers. est. ₤100 .. articles to **James Scott** and Martin Pickett and whole of Est., real and personal, to John Chilton and Martin Pickett .. *Signed*: **James Gray**. *Wits*: **Charles Chilton, John Blackwell, Jr.** *Rec*: 27 Feb. 1775, prov. by o. of Blackwell.

Pages 117-120. 21 November 1774. B & S. Bet. **George Mercer** of Virginia and presently of City of London, Esq. of lst part, **M a r y Wroughton** of City of Bath, Spinster, 2nd pt. and **John Tayloe & George Washington**, Esqs., attys in Fact of sd. Geo. Mercer and Mary Wroughton of 3rd pt. and **John Peyton Harrison** of Loud. Co. of 4th part .. sd. Mercer is tenant in common with **James Mercer** and **John Francis Mercer** an infant of 1/4th part of undivided tract in Fauq. and Pr. Wm. called the Bull Run and Battle River tracts .. about 16,000 acres .. put the same in Mortgage to Mary Wroughton, 15 May 1773 .. **George Mason**, Esq. refused to be one of the attys. in Fact .. to divide tract and sell George Mercer's part .. it was decreed to sell George Mercer's part at public auction .. 4,157 a. .. of the larger tract was allotted to Geo. Mercer which falls in Fauq. Co. .. John Peyton Harrison purchased 306 a. .. ₤132 .. in line of Lot No. 5 .. foot of the mt. .. cor. to Lot No. 4 .. to Beg., Lot No. 6 .. *Signed*: George Mercer, Mary Wroughton, George Washington. *Wits*: Francis Peyton, Leven Powell, George (X) Sullivan, John Monday, William Owens. *Rec*: 27 March 1775, prov. by o. of Powell, Sullivan and Owens.

Pages 120-123. 21 November 1774. B & S. Bet. **George Mercer, Mary Wroughton, John Tayloe** and **George Washington** and **John Monday** .. 470 a. .. ₤99 .. Lot No. 6 at foot of mt. .. Being Lot No. 7 in survey .. *Signed*: **George Mercer, Mary Wroughton, G. Washington**. *Wits*: **Francis Peyton, Leven Powell, Geo. (X) Sullivan, Peter Bryant**. *Rec*: 27 March 1775, prov. by o. of Powell, Sullivan, and Bryant.

Page 123. 13 February 1775. B & S. Bet. **Thomas Elliott** of Leeds Par. and **William Elliott** of same .. lease held under the Rev'd Mr. **James Scott** .. one Negroe man slave, **James**, all personal estate .. for the maintenance of **Mary Elliott**, wife of sd. Thomas and their following children .. **Ellis, Martin**, and **Curtis** and good Clothing for sd. Thomas and at his death the "working tools" to belong to said Wm. .. *Signed*: **Thomas Elliott, William Elliott**. *Wits*: **J. Moffett, John Powe, Thomas Maddux**. *Rec*: 27 March 1775, prov. by o. of wits.

ge 124. 13 February 1775. Bond. **William Elliott to Thomas Elliott, Sr.** for Ł200 .. to carry out provisions of foregoing deed. *Signed*: **William Elliott.** *Wits*: **J. Moffett, John Powe, Thomas Maddux.** *Rec*: 27 March 1775, ack. by **Wm. Elliott.**

Pages 124-126. 10 October 1774. Lease. Bet. **Martin Hardin** of Augusta Co. and **Mark Hardin** of same and **Hubbard Prince** .. tract adjoining land leased by Martin Hardin to **Charles Wickliffe** and to the lands of Capt. **John Ashby** and **Humstead** and contains land Martin Hardin purch. of Col. **William Eustace** .. 300 a. .. for his nat. life and lives of **Betsy Prince**, h. w. and **John Prince** son of sd. Hubbard .. yearly rent of Ł8 .. *Signed*: **Martin Hardin, Mark Hardin, Hubbard Prince.** *Wits*: **Thornton Farrow, Robt. Wickliffe, Chas. Wickliff, Dan'l. Kincheloe, Sam. Blackwell, Jno. Shumate.** *Rec*: 27 March 1775, prov. by o. of Blackwell and two Wickliffs.

Pages 126-127. 27 March 1775. Apprentice Bond. Bet. **William English** and **Robert Sanders** .. English binds himself to Sanders until he becomes 21 years of age .. to learn the carpentery and joiner trade .. *Signed*: **Wm (X) English, Robert Sanders.** *Rec*: 27 March 1775, ack. by parties.

Page 127. 29 November 1774. Bill of Sale. **Henry Lee** of King George Co. to **John Lee** of Pr. Wm. Co.. slaves .. *Signed*: **Henry Lee.** *Wit*: **Edward Leavel.** *Rec*: 27 March 1775, prov. by o. of wit.

Pages 127-129. 8 October 1774. Lease. Bet. **Martin Hardin** and **Mark Hardin** of Augusta Co. and **Charles Wickliffe** of Pr. Wm. Co. .. 200 a. .. lower end of tract willed to me by my father Mark Hardin, dec'd. and part of tract I purch. of Col. **William Eustace**, same where I formerly lived .. for his nat. life and lives of **Lidia**, h. w. and **Mary Wickliffe** his dau. .. yearly rent of Ł10 .. *Signed*: **Martin Hardin, Mark Hardin, Charles Wickliffe.** *Wits*: **Robert Wickliffe, Dan'l. Kincheloe, Mary Wickliffe.** *Rec*: 27 March 1775, prov. by o. of wits.

Pages 129-130. 27 March 1775. Lease. Bet. **Harman Hitt** of Leeds Par. and **John Smith** of same .. saplin in **Lee's** line .. 100 a. .. for 99 years .. yearly rent of Ł4.2s.6d. .. *Signed*: **Harman Hitt, John Smith.** *Rec*: 27 March 1775, ack. by parties.

Pages 130-132. 27 March 1775. Lease. Bet. **Harman Hitt** of Leeds Par. and **John Low** of same .. marked cor. of Harman Hitt's in **Lee's** line near a branch .. to **Smith's** cor. .. 100 a. .. for his nat. life and lives of **Judah**, h. w. and **William Low**, his son .. yearly rent of Ł 5.2s.6d. .. *Signed*: **Harman Hitt, John Low.** *Rec*: 27 March 1775, ack. by parties.

Pages 132-133. 27 March 1775. B & S. Bet. **Catherine Kamper (Elder), Peter Kamper**, younger and **Alice**, h. w. and **Peter Greenleaves** .. Ł65 .. tract in Ham. Par. .. part of larger tract, a deed for which **John**, Peter and **Harman Kemper** obtained from the Prop., 4 March 1726 for 264 a. and Harman Kempter died without will, the

176

premises devolved to the dower of sd. Catherine his wife and property of the sd. Peter Kamper his eldest son which sd. tract the sd. Catherine Kamper and Peter Kamper and Alice, h. w. do sell .. Beg. at 2 maples on a br. of Great Run called Mackelty's Branch and in line of Mr. **William Allason** .. to cor. of sd. Allason, **Chas. Williams** and **Hudnall** .. to the main road leading from the Manor to Falmouth .. 60 acres .. *Signed*: **Peter (X) Kamper, Catherine (X) Kamper, Alice (X) Kamper.** *Rec*: 27 March 1775, ack. by grantors.

Page 134. 26 September 1774. Power of Attorney. **William Winn** of Craven Co., S. C. appts. his son-in-law **Matthew Smith** of Fauq. Co. his "true and lawfull attorney" .. to represent him in all things, esp. to recover certain slaves in the poss. of **Thomas Lingam** of Baltimore Co., Md., which Winn claims in the name of his dau., **Martha**, wife of Matthew Smith, who is the sole heiress to **Ann Lingam**, former wife of Wm. Winn. *Signed*: **W. Winn.** *Wits*: **James Winn, Minor Winn, Minor (W) Winn, Jr.** *Rec*: 27 March 1775, prov. by o. of **James Winn, Minor Winn** and **Minor Winn, Sr.**

Pages 134-135. 26 December 1775 [sic] Apprentice Bond. Bet. **Chandler Fowke** of Ham. Par. and **Wharton Ransdall** of Leeds Par., house carpenter & joiner .. Fowke by his mother's consent & approbation of the Court binds himself for 5 years an apprentice to Ransdall .. Fowke agrees not to frequent tipling houses nor taverns nor play at cards Dice or any unlawful game .. *Signed*: **Chandler Fowke, Wharton Ransdall.** *Rec*: 26 Dec. 1774, ack. by parties.

Pages 135-137. 21 November 1774. B & S. Bet. **George Mercer, Mary Wroughton, John Tayloe** and **George Washington** and **George Sullivan** .. 522 a. .. part of the 4,157-acres of sd. Mercer's portion for ₤355 .. according to a survey made by **Francis Peyton**, Gent. .. cor. to Lot No. 4 thence with the line of that lot and Lots No. 9 and 15 .. cor. of Lot No. 7 .. line of Lot 6 .. heap of Stones in **John Mondays** field in the lower line of the sd. Dividend & cor. to Lot No. 6 .. being two lots: Nos. 5 and 8 .. *Signed*: **George Mercer, Mary Wroughton, Geo. Washington.** *Wits*: **Francis Peyton, Leven Powell, John Monday, Peter O'Bryant.** *Rec*: 27 March 1775, prov. by o. of **Powell & O'Bryant**; 27 May 1775, prov. by o. of **John Monday.**

Pages 138-140. 21 November 1774. B & S. Bet. **George Mercer, Mary Wroughton, John Tayloe, Geo. Washington** and **Peter Bryant** .. 143 a. for ₤81 .. cor. to Lot No. 3 .. being Lott No. 4 .. *Signed*: **George Mercer, Mary Wroughton, Geo. Washington.** *Wits*: **Francis Peyton, Levin Powell, Geo. (X) Sullivan, John Monday.** *Rec*: 27 March 1775, prov. by o. of **Powell & Sullivan**; 22 May 1775, prov. by o. of Monday.

Pages 140-142. 21 November 1774. B & S. Bet. **George Mercer, Mary Wroughton, John Tayloe, George Washington** and **William Owens** .. 126 3/4 a. for ₤111 .. cor. to Lot No. 9 .. Being Lot No. 10 .. *Signed*: (as above). *Wits*: **Francis Peyton, Leven Powell, George (X)**

Sullivan, John Monday. *Rec*: 27 March 1775, prov. by o. of Powell & Sullivan; 27 May 1775, prov. by o. of Monday.

Pages 143-144. 22 May 1775. B & S. Bet. **John Monday** of Leeds Par. and **John Kincheloe**, of same .. L58 .. 103 a. .. Beg. at a Span. oak cor. to **Wm. Turley** .. in line of **Edward Laurence** .. to Wm. Turley .. same purch. of **Thomas Glascock** .. *Signed*: **John Monday**. *Wits*: **John Barker, John Macmillian, James (X) Toole (Tolle)**. *Rec*: 22 May 1775, ack. by Monday.

Pages 144-145. 1 January 1775. Lease. Bet. **Thomas Maddux** of Leeds Par. and **John Dugard** of same 1/2 tract of land on Cedar Run whereon Dugard now lives .. 100 a.. for Maddux's nat. life ..for yearly rent of L5 .. *Signed*: **Thomas Maddux, Jr., Dugard**. *Wits*: **Elias Edmonds, Jr., Ben Harrison, James Scott, Jr.** *Rec*: 22 May 1775, ack. by parties.

Pages 145-147. 22 May 1775. B & S. Bet. **John Green** of Leeds Par. and **James Scott** of Same .. L68.10s. .. 100 a. .. part of tract Green lives on .. **Tarpley and Blowers** line on western side .. Baldwin's Ridge .. to road on top of that ridge .. crossing main road to an oak on the side of Stewart's Cart path .. to a fork of the path, thence down the mill path and an arm of Baldwin's Ridge .. in line of **Lehugh [LeHew?]** cor. to Lehew .. cor. to Lehew & Blowers .. *Signed*: **J. Green, Jr.** *Wits*: **Alex'r Keith, John Likly, J. Moffett**. *Rec*: 27 May 1775, ack. by Green.

Pages 147-149. 22 May 1775. B & S. Bet. **James Scott & Elizabeth**, h. w., and **John Green, Jr.** .. L64 .. oak on top of Baldwin's Ridge and on eastern side of a cart path leading from the main road to **James Stewart's** in the line of **Lehew & Blowers** .. Stewart's lot cor. .. 32 a. *Signed*: **Jas. Scott, Jr.** *Wits*: **Alex. Keith, John Likly, John Moffett**. Receipt wit. by **Dugard** and **Alex Keith**. *Rec*: 22 May 1775, ack. by **James Scott**.

Pages 149-151. 28 April 1775. B & S. Bet. **John Green, Jr.**, son & heir at law of **Duff Green**, Gent., late of Fauq. Co., dec'd and **Ann Green**, widow & relict of Duff Green, dec'd .. according to an agreement bet. the parties, Ann Green was to relinquish certain of her dower slaves to **John Green** and also her dower to lands in Fauq. Co. .. John Green had agreed to give her good deeds for that part of the Manor plantation lying on the south side of the South Run of Broad Run, with a Negro woman slave **Jenny** & her child **Betty** .. 300 a. .. *Signed*: **J. Green, Jr.** *Wits*: **William Haydon, Joseph Minter, Willis Green**. *Rec*: 22 May 1775, ack. by **J. Green**.

Pages 151-154. 28 April 1775. Mortgage. Bet. **John Green, Jr.** son, etc. of **Duff Green**, Gent., etc. and **Ann Green**, widow, etc. .. John mortgages to Ann Green 400 a. being the land the said Duff Green purch. of **John Mercer**, known as the Quarter Tract .. provided nevertheless that **John Green** makes good his agreement with Ann Green, then this indenture to be void .. *Signed*: **J. Green, Jr.** *Wits*:

William Haydon, Willis Green, Joseph Minter. *Rec*: 22 May 1775, ack. by **John Green.**

Pages 154-155. 22 May 1775. Lease. Bet. **George Reeves** and **Ambrose Legg** .. 75 a. .. in Ham. Par. .. on Kettle Run .. line of **Robert Buchanan, Thomas Foster**, it being part of a tract which sd. Reeves purch. of the Exors. of **Chs. Carter**, Esq., dec'd .. during Legg's nat. life .. yearly rent of Ł3 .. *Signed*: **Geo. Reeves, Ambrose Legg.** *Rec*: 22 May 1775, ack. by parties.

Pages 155-159. 27 April 1775. B & S. Bet. **John Hathaway** and **Sarah**, h. w. of Leeds Par. and **Joseph Blackerby** .. Ł110 .. tract on head br. of Little River .. part of land from Prop. to Mr. **John Clark** .. in Chinn's line thence with line of the orig. survey .. Bartlett's line .. 200 a. *Signed*: **John Hathaway, Sarah (X) Hathaway.** *Wits*: **John Metcalf, John Orear, Sanford Carrell, Josiah Fishback.** *Rec*: 22 May 1775, ack. by grantors.

Pages 158-159. 22 May 1775. B & S. Bet. **John Barker** and **Jemima**, h. w. and **John McMilliam** of Loud. Co. .. Ł77.10s .. part of larger tract whereon sd. Barker now lives .. line of **Burgess** .. cor. of **Wm. Fitzjerrel, John Hurmans** and **James Allen** .. line of **William Faulin** .. 155 a. *Signed*: **John Barker, Jemima Barker.** *Rec*: 22 May 1775, ack. by grantors.

Page 160. 22 May 1775. Bet. **James Scott** and **Henry Peyton**, Gent., Church wardens of Leeds Par. and **Peter Grant** .. Court ordered that the Churchwardens bind **William Tyrrel**, aged 2 years, on 17 Oct., .. to serve Grant until he becomes 21 years of age, for which Grant is to provide Tyrrel with clothing, food and a years schooling and to pay the accustomed freedom dues .. *Signed*: **Jas. Scott, Henry Peyton, Peter Grant.** *Wit*: **Ben. Harrison.** *Rec*: 22 May 1775, ack. by parties.

Pages 160-162. 10 July 1775. Mortgage. Bet. **Peter Grant** of Leeds Par. and **Thomas Marshall** of same .. Ł68.11s.8d. which sum the sd. Grant is indebted to Marshall for .. in trust, the land purch. by Grant of **John Wright** .. 292 a. .. until 1 July 1777 .. after which to be sold after 10 days notice .. *Signed*: **Peter Grant.** *Wits*: **Dugard, Joseph Blackwell, John Turner, William Nelson.** *Rec*: 24 July 1775, ack. by **Peter Grant.**

Pages 162-165. 3 February 1773. B & S. Bet. **Thomas Chinn & Jane**, h. w. of Pr. Wm. Co., **Robert Scott**, of same, **James Hunter** of K. G. Co., Merchant, and **James Lewis** of Fauq. .. Thos. Chinn being indebted to Robert Scott in the sum of Ł192 did deed to him an estate of 829 a. on 2-3 Oct. 1764 in Fauq. to be void by payment of the sum; Scott, in order to secure to debt to James Hunter, in 1764, endorsed the deed from Chinn to sd. Hunter, by decree of Court, Chinn was ordered to pay James Hunter Ł192, plus int. from Dec. 1764, til paid. The sum was paid and all parties agreed to sell the tract to James Lewis .. near Wolf Trap Branch of Broad Run .. foot of the Mountain .. *Signed*: **Thomas Chinn, Jennett Chinn, James Hunter.** *Wits*: **Benj.**

Robinson, Dan'l. Penington, Chichester Curtis, John (X) Tomlin, Charles Chilton, Jno. (X) Thornberry. *Rec*: 27 March 1775, prov. by o. of **Robinson, Penington, Tomlin; Andrew Buchanan** as to **James Hunter;** 24 July 1775, prov. by o. of **Chilton** and **Thornberry.**

Pages 165–169. 28 Feb./1 Mar. 1775. Lease & release. Bet. **B r y a n Fairfax & Elizabeth,** h. w. of Fx. Co., Esq. and **George Washington** of same .. tract on lower side of Goose Creek and on a branch thereof called Chattin's Run .. 600 a. .. granted by the Hon. **W m . F a i r f a x ,** Agt. .. 4 Aug. 1742 to his youngest son, Mr. **Wm. Henry Fairfax** .. who d. intestate, fell to his bro. & heir at law, Bryan Fairfax .. cor. to **Thomas Ashby** .. line of the land surveyed for **Charles Taylor,** now **Col. Turner's** .. cor. of late **Mr. Burgess's** Goose Creek Tract .. by Chattins Run .. down the run to the mouth at Goose Creek .. Ł150 .. *Signed*: **Bryan Fairfax.** *Wits*: **W. Smith, Benjamin Clark, Jas.** (X) **Betson, Samuel Pearle, Joseph Jackson.** *Rec*: 24 July 1775 pro. by o. of **Smith, Pearle** and **James Betson.**

Page 170. 13 August 1774. Bond. **Burr Harrison** of Leeds Par. to **William Harrison** for Ł500 .. to sell Wm. Harrison a tract of land beq. to him by Col. **Thos. Harrison,** dec'd. and jointly held by Burr with sd. William .. sd. Burr's part to contain 225 a. .. to be void if deed is made by last of October. *Signed*: **Burr Harrison.** *Wits*: **Thos. Keith, William Blackwell, Elias Edmonds.** *Rec*: 24 July 1775, ack. by **Burr Harrison.**

Pages 170–172. 1 December 1774. B & S. Bet. **Burr Harrison & Elizabeth,** h.w. of Leeds Par. and **William Harrison** of same .. Ł 112.10s. .. 225 a. .. land devised by **Thos. Harrison,** Gent., dec'd. to Burr Harrison which Thomas had a quarter on at the time of making his will, purch. of **Elias Edmonds** and also a small piece on the right hand side of the road leading thro' Ashby's Gap, being part of land purch. of **Mr. Mercer** .. *Signed*: **Burr Harrison, Elizabeth Harrison.** *Wits*: **Thomas Harrison, Sr., Thos. Nelson, Wm** (X) **Congrove, Price** (x) **Hambruck.** *Rec*: 24 July 1775, ack. by **Burr Harrison.**

Pages 172–173. 13 August 1774. Bond **Burr Harrison** to **William Harrison,** for Ł500 .. (same bond, etc. as on page 170, above).

Pages 173–175. 24 July 1775. B & S. Bet. **Harman Fishback** of Culp. Co. and **Harman Fishback,** his son, of Fq. Co. .. and **Cristinah,** h. w. of one part and **John Martin** .. Ł65 .. part of a Lott of the Germantown .. NE side of Licking run .. cor. to **Jeremiah Darnall** .. cor. to sd. Martin .. **P a g e** line .. SW side of Licking run .. 60 a. (+/–) .. *Signed*: **Harman** (x) **Fishback, Harman Fishback, Cristinah** (X) **Fishback.** *Rec*: 24 July 1775, ack. by grantors.

Pages 176–177. 3 January 1775. B & S. Bet. **James Garner** and **Martin Pickett & Co.** .. Ł35.3s.9 1/2d. which Garner is indebted to Pickett for .. tract whereon Garner now lives joining the land of **Thos. Withers, Joseph Duncan & John Jeffries** .. 214 a. *Signed*: **James**

Garner. *Wits*: **Joseph Blackwell, David Blackwell, Joseph Williams.** *Rec*: 28 Aug. 1775, prov. by o. of wits.

Pages 178-180. 24 July 1775. B & S. Bet. **Harman Fishback** of Culp. Co. and **Harman Fishback,** his son & **Cristinah,** h. w. and **John Shanks** .. Ł12 .. part of lott of land in German Town on SW side of Licking Run .. **Jeremiah Darnall's** line .. cor. to **John Shanks** .. 40 a. .. *Signed*: **Harman** (x) **Fishback,** Harman Fishback, **Cristinah** (X) **Fishback.** *Rec*: 24 July 1775, ack. by grantors.

Pages 180-182. 7 April 1775. Mortgage. Bet. **William Lane** and **John Likly** in behalf of Cunninghame & Co., merchants .. Ł28.8s.6d. .. indebtedness of Lane to **Cunningham** .. one Lott of land belonging to **Lord Fairfax** & bought by him of **Peter Lawrence** joining **Robert Sinclair** and **John Sinclair** .. horse bought of **Henry Rogers** .. cow & calf bot of **William Asberry** .. household furniture .. upon trust .. *Signed*: **William Lane.** *Wits*: **Wm. Grigsby, Thos. Maddux, Jr., William Gillico, Thos. Keith.** *Rec*: 28 August 1775, prov. by o. of Maddux, Gillico and Keith.

Pages 182-185. 25 August 1775. Lease. Bet. **Henry Peyton,** Gent. of Leeds Par. and **William Kidwell** .. east side of Millars Spring br. .. down to Broad Run .. for his nat. life and for lives of Mary, h. w. and **John Kidwell,** his son .. yearly rent of 530 lbs. tobacco, quitrents & land tax .. *Signed*: **Henry Peyton, William Kidwell.** *Wits*: **James Foley, William Foley.** *Rec*: 28 Aug. 1775, prov. by o. of **Sanford Carrell, James** and **William Foley.**

Pages 185-187. 2 June 1775. Lease. Bet. **Solomon Jones** of Pr. Wm. Co. and **Charles Chadduck** .. part of greater tract belong. to Jones .. on the n. end of the Leathercoat Mt. in Fauq. Co. .. Beg. at ridge of rocks on sd. mt. .. with **Mercer's** line .. to **Feagans** line .. along **Baxters** line thence up the mt. .. with **Coleman's** line .. for his nat. life, **W i n i f r e d**, his wife and of the first child if there should be any born to them .. yearly rent of Ł5 .. *Signed*: **Solomon** (S) **Jones, Charles Chadduck.** *Wits*: **Thos. Evans, George Jones.** *Rec*: 25 Sept. 1775, ack. by parties.

Pages 187-190. 2 September 1775. B & S. Bet. **Charles Taylor & Judith,** h. w. and **James Taylor & Sarah,** h. w. of Leeds Par. of 1st part, and **Joseph Smith** .. Ł41 .. cor. to **Ball** and **Weaver** .. Burgesses line .. **Thornton's** line .. 75 a., part of larger tract sold by **Samuel P o r t e r** to sd. Charles and James Taylor, 23 March 1767 .. *Signed*: **James** (X) **Taylor, Sarah** (X) **Taylor, Charles Taylor, Judith** (X) **Taylor.** *Wits*: **Thos. Marshall, Chas. Chinn, Daniel Brown, Harman Hitt.** *Rec*: 25 Sept. 1775, prov. by o. of Chinn, Brown and Hitt.

Pages 190-191. 22 February 1775. Mortgage. Bet. **John Peake** and **Martin Pickett & Co.** .. Ł186.15s.1/2d. indebtedness of Peake to Pickett .. 2 lotts of land - one in Fauq. purch. of **John Hathaway** which Hathaway leased of Col. **Richard Henry Lee** for 3 lives, the other in Loud. Co. which Peake rented of **Robert Carter,** Esq., ca. 250

Negroes .. in trust .. *Signed*: **John Peake**. *Wits*: **W. Blackwell,** **Pickett, Thos. Keith, David Blackwell, Isaac Arnold**. *Rec*: 25 Sept. 1775, prov. by o. of **David Blackwell, George Pickett** and **Thomas Keith**.

Pages 192-193. 23 January 1775. Mortgage. Bet. **Samuel Conyers** and **Martin Pickett & Co.** .. for indebtedness of £62.2s.11d. .. tract taken up by his father, joining **Hooes** tract, **Balls** and **Porters** .. 120 a. .. upon trust .. *Signed*: **Samuel (X) Conyers**. *Wits*: **George Cordell, David Blackwell, Joseph Williams, John Dulin**. *Rec*: 25 Sept. 1775, prov. by o. of **Blackwell, Williams** and **Dulin**.

Pages 193-194. 17 February 1775. Bill of Sale. **William Hall** to **Martin Pickett & Co.** .. £20 .. horses, household furniture .. *Signed*: **Wm. Hall**. *Wits*: **Samuel Blackwell, Jr., David Blackwell**. The mare delivered in the name of the whole. *Rec*: 25 Sept. 1775, prov. by o. of **David Blackwell**.

Page 194. 7 June 1775. Bill of Sale. **Thomas White** to **Thomas Massey** .. £7.19s.11d. .. cow from **Allen Guttridge**, horse from **George Randall** .. sum to be paid by 25 Dec. next .. *Signed*: **Thomas (X) White**. *Wits*: **Charles Delaney, John Morehead**. *Rec*: 25 Sept. 1775, prov. by o. of **Delany & Morehead**.

Pages 195-196. 23 October 1775. B & S. Bet. **Charles Delany**, Schoolmaster, and **Richard Lewis**, of K. G. Co. .. £3 .. 100 a. .. near Summerduck Run joining the land of **Richard Lewis, Rawleigh Downman**, and **Robert Knox** .. land beq. to him by his father, **Joseph Delany** .. that within the next 10 years the sd. **Delany** to give Richard Lewis a good deed .. *Signed*: **Charles Delaney**. *Wits*: **Jos. Blackwell, Bailey Johnson, William OBanon**. *Memo*: 22 Oct. 1775, **Delany** gave a "quiet" deed for the property to **Richard Lewis**. *Rec*: 23 Oct. 1775, ack. by **Charles Delaney**.

Pages 196-198. 23 October 1775. B & S. Bet. **Henry Rector & Mary**, h. w. and **Benjamin Rector** .. £100 .. 94 a. in Leeds Par. on Goose Creek and Chattins Run .. cor. to **Henry Rector** .. to the mouth of Chattins Run .. *Signed*: **Henry Rector, Mary (X) Rector**. *Rec*: 23 Oct. 1775, ack. by **Henry Rector**.

Pages 198-201. 21-22 October 1775. Lease & release. Bet. **James Young** of Ham. Par. and **Benjamin Neale** .. tract in Ham. Par., part of larger tract purch. in partnership with **John Thornberry** of **Burgess Ball**, Esq. of Lan. Co. .. **Ball's** Patent line .. lower line joining **Parker** now **Hugh Brent** .. cor. of **John Thornberry** .. 350 a. .. *Signed*: **James Young**. *Rec*: 23 Oct. 1775, ack. by **Young**.

Pages 201-205. 20-21 October 1775. Lease & release. Bet. **Charles Rector & Elizabeth**, h. w. of Leeds Par. and **Thomas Owsley** of Loud. Co. .. tract on Goose Creek (branches of) .. **Chattins** line .. cor. of **William Finch** .. line of **John Rector**, dec'd .. **Henry Rector's** line .. 257 a. .. same to sd. **Rector** from his father **John Rector** and remaining part by will from his father .. L300 .. *Signed*: **Charles Rector, Elizabeth (X) Rector**. *Wits*: **John Rust, James Metcalf, John Metcalf**. *Rec*: 23 Oct. 1775, ack. by Grantors.

Pages 205-207. 20 October 1775. B & S. Bet. **Francis Jett** of Leeds Par. & **Mary**, h. w. and **John Pinckard** .. L100 .. tract at the Cobler Mt. .. 100 a. same purch. by Jett of **Thomas Turner**, Gent., 9-10 Nov. 1754 .. rec. in Pr. Wm. Co. .. *Signed*: **Francis Jett, Mary Jett**. *Rec*: 23 Oct. 1775, ack. by grantors.

Pages 207-208. 23 October 1775. Deed of Gift. **Francis Jett**, for nat. love & affection for granddau. **Jane Pinckard**, dau. of **John Pinckard**, who married dau. **Jane** .. Negroe **Bob** .. to son-in-law, **John Pinckard**, Negroe girl **Sall** .. and house-hold furniture in his possession .. *Signed*: **Francis Jett**. **John Pinckard** agreed to accept the above in lieu of any further claim on Jett's estate. *Wit*: **Martin Pickett**. *Rec*: 23 Oct. 1775, ack. by parties.

Pages 208-210. 23 October 1775. B & S. Bet. **Benjamin Rector & Sarah**, h. w. of Leeds Par. and **William Finch** .. L100 .. 128 a. on branches of Goose Creek .. cor. to **Henry Rector, Sr.** .. same given to **Charles Rector** by will of **John Rector**, dec'd .. *Signed*: **Benjamin Rector, Sally Rector**. *Rec*: 23 Oct. 1775, ack. by grantors.

Pages 210-211. 10 June 1775. B & S. Bet. **Henry Rector & Mary**, h. w. and **Daniel Floweree** .. L20 .. one lott of ground in the Town of Maidstone .. No. 1 and all houses, etc. *Signed*: **Henry Rector, Mary Rector**. *Rec*: 23 Oct. 1775, ack. by grantors.

Pages 211-217. 13-14 June 1775. Lease & release. Bet. **Armistead Churchhill**, Esq. & **Elizabeth**, h. w. and **Cuthbert Bullitt** of Pr. Wm. Co. .. tract .. for the most part between the road leading from Falmouth to Fauquier Courthouse and the road commonly called the Jersey Road .. line of **Charles Carter**, Esq. of Corotoman .. cor. to **Fitzhugh** on Turkey Run .. cor. to one **Bryant** .. 793 1/2 a., purch. by sd. Churchhill out of tract of land called Pageland .. L1190.5s. *Signed*: **A. Churchill**. *Wits*: **Elias Edmonds, Martin Pickett, W. Blackwell, Cuth. Harrison, Will. Heth**. *Rec*: 27 Nov. 1775, ack. by grantor.

Pages 217-218. 23 September 1775. B & S. Bet. **Charles Waller & Hester**, h. w., **Jesse Norman** and **Andrew Buchanan** .. slaves .. same from Charles Waller to Norman on 4 Oct. 1768 .. sd. Indenture recites the marriage of Chas. Waller to **Hester Norman**, sister of Jesse Norman and conditions of transfer .. for L200 to Waller & Norman from Buchanan .. the sd. slaves .. *Signed*: **Charles (X) Waller, Hester (X) Waller, Jesse Norman**. *Wits*: **Edward Moor, John Blackwell, William Love, David Briggs, George Lobb**. *Rec*: 27 Nov. 1775, prov. by o. of Blackwell, Love and Lobb.

Pages 218-219. 25 September 1775. B & S. **Andrew Buchanan** to **Charles Waller** .. recites the transfer of slaves to **Jesse Norman** by

Waller, who had married the <u>Daughter</u> (Hester) of Jesse Norman .. 4 Oct. 1768 .. this deed recites that the previous deed was made in 23 Sept. <u>1773</u>, not 1775 as written in the deed. Buchanan sells the slaves to Waller for £200 .. *Signed*: Andrew Buchanan. *Wits*: Martin Pickett, David Briggs, George Lobb, Edward Moor, J. Blackwell, Charles Ashley, W. Blackwell. *Rec*: 27 Nov. 1775, prov. by o. of Pickett, Lobb and William Blackwell.

Pages 219-222. 24 November 1775. B & S. Bet. John Peters & Betty, h. w. and James Peters .. £100 .. part of larger tract belonging to James Peters, Sr., dec'd and beq. to sd. John, his son .. Carters Road where a path crosses where James Peters, dec'd. formerly lived to a place where Edward Wood formerly lived .. Joseph Combs' line .. cor. to sd. Combs by Edward Woods old field .. lick branch .. edge of John Peters's old field .. 120 a. .. *Signed*: John Peters, Betty Peters. *Rec*: 27 Nov. 1775, ack. by grantors.

Pages 222-225. 3 August 1775. Lease. Bet. Thomas Lord Fairfax and James Armstrong .. tenement in Manor of Leeds .. road in Samuel Nicholas's line .. 100 a. .. for his nat. life and lives of Martha, h. w. and Elijah, his son .. yearly rent of 20s. *Signed*: Fairfax. *Wit*: Francis Payne, William Payne, C. Morgan. *Rec*: 27 Nov. 1775, prov. by o. of Wits (Charles Morgan).

Pages 225-227. 3 August 1775. Lease. Bet. Thomas Lord Fairfax and William Payne .. tenement in Manor of Leeds .. cor. to Francis Payne .. 166 a. .. for his nat. life and lives of Ann, h. w. and Frank Payne his son .. yearly rent of 33s.2d. .. *Signed*: Fairfax. *Wits*: James Armstrong, Francis Payne, C. Morgan. *Rec*: 27 Nov. 1775, prov. by o. of wits.

Pages 228-230. 3 August 1775. Lease. Bet. Thomas Lord Fairfax and Francis Payne .. tenement in Manor of Leeds .. branch of South Run .. 233 a. .. for his nat. life and lives of Susanna, h. w. and William Payne, his son .. yearly rent of 46s.7d. .. *Signed*: Fairfax. *Wits*: William Payne, James Armstrong, C. Morgan. *Rec*: 27 Nov. 1775, prov. by o. of wits.

Pages 230-231. 4 November 1775. Commission. Commission from Court to Joseph Blackwell, John Moffett, Martin Pickett and Charles Chinn, Gent. .. to examine Elizabeth Harrison, wife of Burr Harrison, as to her signature on a deed dtd. 1 Dec. 1774 to William Harrison for 225 a., since she cannot conveniently come to the Court to verify same .. *Signed*: H. Brooke. Cert. signed by J. Moffett and Chas. Chinn. *Rec*: 28 Nov. 1775.

Page 232. 8 December 1775. Power of Attorney. From Jeffry Johnson of Surry Co., N. C. to his son George Johnson of Fauq. .. to sell all real estate in Fauq. Co. .. *Signed*: Jeffrey (////) Johnson. *Wits*: John Johnson, Samuel Johnson. *Rec*: 22 Jan. 1776, prov. by o. of wits.

Pages 233-235. 26 February 1776. B & S. Bet. Frederick Rector & Elizabeth, h. w. of Leeds Par. and Hugh Morrison of same .. Ł8 .. one certain corner or strip of land .. 12 a. .. side of road called Furrs Road, cor. to Morrison .. in P e a r l e s line .. part of tract beq. to sd. Rector by his father John Rector, dec'd. *Signed*: Frederick Rector, Betty Rector. *Rec*: 26 Feb. 1776, ack. by grantors.

Pages 235-239. 24-25 August 1775. Lease & release. Bet. Benjamin T u r n e r & A n n, h. w. of Culp. Co., Bromfield Par., planter, and Nicholas Newport of Ham. Par., planter .. 7 a. .. adj. tract now in tenure & occupation of Thomas Drummonds .. cor. to William Withers, Sr. and Benj. Garner .. Muddy Br. .. Ł7 .. *Signed*: Benjamin (X) Turner, Ann (X) Turner. *Wits*: John Bragg, Mary Bragg, Peter Newport. *Rec*: 26 February 1776, prov. by o. of wits.

Pages 239-242. 16 November 1775. B & S. Bet. William Wood, Jr. of Ham. Par. & Elizabeth, his wife and John Dooling of Staff. Co. .. 80 a. .. part of tract taken up by Wm. Wood. Sr. and conveyed to Wm. Wood, Jr. .. Beg. on west side of Br. called Wm. Woods Br. .. both sides of Poplar Br. .. 5s. .. *Signed*: William Wood, Elizabeth (X) Wood. *Wits*: Daniel Harrill, Nehemiah (N) Wood, Samuel Harrill. *Rec*: 26 Feb. 1776, prov. by o. of wits.

Pages 242-244. 6 February 1776. B & S. Bet. Peter Beech and John Humphries .. Ł85 .. 200 a. .. on branches of Deep Run, part of tract taken up by Robert Jones and by him sold to Alexander Beech, father to Peter .. lower end of larger tract on east side of deep run .. *Signed*: Peter (B) Beach. *Wits*: Jos. Blackwell, Joseph Blackwell, Jr., Will. Eustace, Jr., Isaac Eustace. *Rec*: 26 Feb. 1776, prov. by o. of Blackwells and William Eustace, Jr.

Pages 244-246. 26 February 1776. B & S. Bet. Martin Pickett & Ann, h. w. and John Duncan of Culp. Co. .. Ł200 .. part of great tract of land commonly called Pageland .. cor. to Josiah Holtzclaw .. cor. to Holtzclaw and Samuel Porter and Thomas Porter .. cor. to sd. Thos. Porter and John Bryan .. cor. to sd. Bryan and William Bryan .. 250 a. .. *Signed*: Martin Pickett, Anne Pickett. *Rec*: 26 Feb. 1776, ack. by grantors.

Pages 247-249. 26 February 1776. B & S. Bet. Jeffry Johnson of Surry Co., N. C. and Moses Johnson of Fq. Co., devissees of Jeffry Johnson, dec'd and J o h n M o f f e t t .. Jeffry Johnson, dec'd was possessed of large tract, which by his will, dated 1750, rec. in Pr. Wm. Co., devised all his estate, real & personal .. Ł100 .. survey & plat included to tract on north side of the Piney Branch .. cor. to land of the Rev'd Mr. Scott .. cor. to Wm. Johnson .. gum in O'banon's line .. cor. to O'banon & Ford .. side of the Rappahannock Mt in the line of William Fairfax, Esq. .. 513 a. according to survey by Thomas Davis, 17 Jan. 1774 .. *Signed*: Jeffry Johnson by George Johnson, his atty., Moses Johnson. *Rec*: 26 Febr. 1776, ack. by grantors.

Pages 249-251. 25 March 1776. B & S. Bet. **Abraham Gibson & Ann**, h. w. of Leeds Par. and **W i l l i a m Y a t e s** .. L40 .. tract near head of Little River, part of tract purch. from **Thomas Bartlett** and **Martin Pickett**, whereon Gibson now lives .. 100 a. .. cor. to land of **John Clark** .. down Little River .. line of **John Hathaway** .. *Signed*: **Abraham (X) Gibson, William (P) Yates**. *Wits*: **Aaron Drummond, John Hathaway**. *Rec*: 25 March 1776, ack. by grantor.

Pages 251-253. 25 March 1776. B & S. Bet. **Nehemiah Wood & Abishai**, h. w. and **John Dooling** and **Isaac Judd** AND **Thomas Massey** .. L80 .. 3 parcels of land: 1) 80 a. in line of **George Crosby** .. Woods Br. .. to dividing line bet. the sd. land & a piece conveyed by **W m. Wood the Older** to **Wm. Wood the Younger** .. purch. of **John Wood** by Nehemiah Wood, part of tract taken up by Wm. Wood father to John & Nehemiah .. Another tract, adj. above tract .. 80 a. .. sold by Wm. Wood to John Dooling, west side of Wcods Br. .. One other piece, 33 a., patented by sd. Isaac Judd, adj. above sd. 80 a. also adj. **John Perse** .. *Signed*: **John (X) Duling, Isaac Judd, Nehemiah (N) Wood, Abisha (X) Wood**. *Wits*: **Martin Pickett**. *Rec*: 25 March 1776, ack. by grantors.

Pages 253-256. 4 January 1776. Lease. Bet. **Ambrose Barnett** and **James Muschett** of Dumfries, Pr. Wm. Co. .. 250 a. .. 2/3rds of tract on which **Mary Neavil**, widow of **George Neavil**, dec'd now dwelleth & beq. by Geo. Neavil to Ambrose Barnett .. the remaining 1/3rd part now in poss. of Mary Neavil for her dower .. for 11 years .. yearly rent for first 5 year, L10 and for the remainder L12 per annum. *Signed*: **Amb's Barnett, James Muschett**. *Wits*: **Reginald Graham, Evan Williams, Alexander Campbell, Thomas Chapman, Traverse Nash, William Warren**. *Rec*: 25 March 1776, ack. by parties. *Memo*: **Ambrose Barnett** can extend the mill race as it now exists.

Pages 256-259. 4 March 1776. B & S. Bet. **James Bashaw** and **Frances**, h. w. and **Thomas Maddux** .. L25 .. tract at the Pignut Ridge & granted to sd. Bashaw by the Prop, 28 Nov. 1772 .. cor. to **J a m e s Warren** and **Edward Washington** .. cor. to Warren and **George Neavill** .. 60 a. .. *Signed*: **James Bashaw, Frances Bashaw**. *Wits*: **Joel Weedon, John Weedon, Josias Basye, Alexander Patton**. *Rec*: 25 March 1776, prov. by o. of **Joel & John Weedon** and **Alex. Patton**.

Pages 259-262. 9 October 1771. B & S. Bet. **Landon & Charles Carter**, Esqs., Exors. of **Charles Carter**, dec'd, and **Robert Buchanan** of Annapolis, Maryland .. 800 a. .. part of a tract called Kettle Run .. in Ham. Par. .. L400 .. s. side Carolina Rd. .. cor. to **W a r n e r** and **Morris** .. Hedgers Cor. in **McClanahan's** line .. **Hale** .. *Signed*: **Landon Carter, Chas. Carter**. *Wits*: **Catesby Woodford, Jeremiah Wilson, Nath. Robinson**. Receipt wit. by **Wm. Warren, Robert Cleaveland, William Roach**. *Rec*: 25 March 1776, prov. by o. of wits.

Pages 262-264. 18 September 1775. Power of atty. **Robert Buchanan** appts. **William Carr** of Dumfries, his attorney to execute a deed for the above 800 a. to **Traverse Nash**, Gent. .. **Wm. Warren** was empowered to receive a good deed from the Exors .. **Chas. Carter**, one of the Exors, signed **Landon's** name and incorrectly dated the deed .. sold same to **Traverse Nash**, Gent. for Ł500 .. *Signed*: **Robert Buchanan**. *Wits*: **Alex'r. Campbell, James Muschett, Thomas Chapman, Robt. Dobson, William Cunninghame, James Weir, Thomas Aithen, James Dunlop**. *Rec*: 25 March 1776, prov. by o. of Muschett, Chapman and Weir, wits.

Pages 264-267. 22 March 1776. B & S. Bet. **Robert Buchanan** of Annapolis, Maryland, Merchant and **Traverse Nash** of Fauq. Co., Gent. .. same from **Carter's** Exors. to **Buchanan** .. *Signed*: **Robert Buchanan**. *Wits*: **Thomas Chapman, James Muschett, James Wier, Alexander Campbell, Daniel Anderson, William Cunninghame**. *Rec*: 25 March 1776, prov. by o. of Muschett, Chapman and Wier.

Pages 268-270. 25 December 1775. B & S. Bet. **John Dyer** and **Ezekiel Phillips** of Loud. Co. .. parcel from **George Washington**, Esq. to **Dyer**, partly in Fauq. & partly in Loud. .. 227 a. .. to sd. **Dyer** & his 2 sons **Wm.** and **Abraham Dyer** or the longer liver of them .. for Ł80 one moiety of sd. lott .. 127 a. .. on lower side of the great road leading from Ashby's Gap to Alexandria .. *Signed*: **John Dyer**. *Wits*: **David Keas, Isaac Milner, Robert (R) Ashby**. *Rec*: 25 March 1776, prov. by o. of wits.

Pages 270-271. 25 March 1776. Deed of Gift. Bet. **Caleb Smith** of Pr. Wm. Co. and **Joseph Smith** .. for nat. love & affection Caleb has for his son **Joseph** .. tract whereon Joseph now lives .. 75 a. .. same Caleb purch. of **Wm. Durham** .. *Signed*: **Caleb Smith**. *Rec*: 25 March 1776, ack. by grantor.

Pages 271-272. 25 March 1776. Lease. Bet. **John James** of Ham. Par. and **Marmaduke Brown** of same .. tenement on Elk Run cor. to **Coppedge & Crump** .. Tullos's Path .. 200 a. .. for his nat. life and life of **Sarah Brown** his wife .. yearly rent of Ł3 .. *Signed*: **John James**. *Rec*: 25 March 1776, ack. by James.

Pages 273-276. 9 November 1775. Lease. Bet. **Henry Smith** and **James Markham** .. tenement .. 126 a. lying on Jones's road, part of larger tract cont. 336 a. which was granted by patent by Prop. to Henry Smith of Staff. Co. .. 2 Jan. 1751 .. cor. to **Richard Young's** land .. **Robert Jones's** line .. **Thomas Jones's** line .. branch of Middle Run .. to the line of the land of Capt. **James Markham**, dec'd .. for 20 years, yearly rent of Ł12 .. *Signed*: **Henry Smith, James Markham**. *Wits*: **Brereton Jones, George Seaton, Thomas Railey**. *Rec*: 22 April 1776, prov. by o. of wits.

Pages 276-277. 15 April 1776. Lease. Bet. **John James** and **Adam Fox** .. tenement .. in line of **Samuel Earle** at a path known by the name of the Ridge Path .. br. by the old road to Aquia .. top of a ridge where Tullos's Path crosses old rd. to Aquia .. 200 a. .. for his nat. life and lives of **Margaret** and **Mary Fox** .. yearly rent of 450 lbs lawful Tobacco and the quit rents and taxes .. *Signed*: **John James**. *Rec*: 26 August 1776, ack. by James.

Pages 277-278. 15 April 1776. Lease. Bet. **John James** and **John Peter Fox** .. parcel.. .. Box oak by Russell's Path and near the waggon Road .. line of **Samuel Earle's** land .. to the Ridge Path .. along said Path to where it crosses Tullos's Path .. 200 a. for his nat. life and lives of his sons **Joseph** and **Martin Fox** .. yearly rent of 500 lbs lawful Tobacco .. *Signed*: **J o h n J a m e s**. *Rec*: 26 August 1776, ack. by **John James**.

Pages 278-290. 30 January 1775. B & S. Bet. **James Lewis & Mary**, h. w. of Leeds Par. and **David Thomas** of same .. £55.10s. .. tract on Wolf Trap Br., being part of tract purch. by Lewis of **Thomas Chinn**, dec'd, patented by Lambert .. cor. of **Peyton & John Thomas** .. cor. to **Keith, Lambert** .. 111 a. *Signed*: **James Lewis, Mary Lewis**. *Wits*: **Edward Broadus, Joseph Carter, Kimber Barton**. *Rec*: 22 April 1776, ack. by grantors.

Pages 291-295. 25-26 May 1776. Lease & release. Bet. **Roger Tolle** of Leeds Par. farmer and **Thomas Owsley** of Shelburn Par., Loud. Co., farmer .. 100 a. cor. of **Wm. Fitzgerald** and **Edward Turner** and near head of a drain of Crummels Run .. cor. to **Turner** and **Crosby's** lease from Col. **Henry Lee** .. part of a tract or parcel of land sold by **Burgess Smith** to the sd. Roger Tolle .. 28 Sept. 1767 .. £100 .. *Signed*: **Roger Tolle, Sarah Tolle**. *Wits*: **Uriel Crosby, Nathaniel Weedon, James (Ʇ) Tolle, Susanna (S) Tolle**. *Rec*: 27 May 1776, ack. by Tolle.

Pages 295-296. 27 May 1776. B & S. Bet. **William Fitzgerald** of Leeds Par. & **Kitty**, h. w. and **John McMillian** .. £44 .. 56 a., part of a tract formerly belonging to Mr. **Charles Burgess** .. an oak in the line of land sold by **Roger Tolle** to **Thos. Owsley** .. a road at the mouth of a lane in the dividing line bet. Mr. **Burgess** and **Mr. Stamps** cor. to Burgess, Stamps and **Doctor Thornton** .. Burgess' grand patent .. *Signed*: **William (X) Fitzgerald, Kitty (X) Fitzgerald**. *Rec*: 27 May 1776, ack. by grantors.

Pages 297-299. 27 May 1776. Lease & release. Bet. **John Morehead** of Leeds Par. & **Mary**, h. w. and **Samuel Morehead** of Ham. Par. .. tract in Ham. Par. .. part of tract by deed of gift from John Morehead, father of aforesd. John Morehead, 2 Mar. 1764 .. 124 a. .. £27 .. *Signed*: **John Morehead, Mary Morehead**. *Rec*: 27 May 1776, ack. by grantors.

Pages 300-301. 24 June 1776. Deed of Gift. Bet. **Thomas Jackman, Sr.** of Leeds Par. and **Richard Jackman**, his son, of Dunmore Co., for nat. love & affection .. tract at Pignut Ridge and Watry Mt. .. by grant from Prop., 1 Dec. 1742, to sd. **Thomas Jackman** for 157 a. .. except a parcel sold to **Elias Edmonds**, Gent. .. *Signed*: **Thos. Jackman**. *Wits*: **Thos. Stone, Thomas Jackman, James Neavil**. *Rec*: 24 June 1776, prov. by o. of wits.

Pages 301-302. 24 June 1776. Deed of Gift. Bet. Thomas Jackman, Sr. of Leeds Par. and Adam Jackman, his son of Dunsmore Co. .. for nat. love & affection .. tract .. at the Watry Mt., same from Prop. by deed dated 28 June 1728 .. for 419 a. .. except 119 a. sold to Charles Baker .. Signed: Thos. Jackman. Wits: Thos. Jackman, Thomas Stone, James Neavil. Rec: 24 June 1776, prov. by o. of Thomas Stone, Thomas Jackman and James Neavil.

Pages 302-303. 23 August 1776. Marriage contract. Bet. Samuel Love of Maryland & Ann Brunskill who have agreed to unite in matriomony and to prevent any difference in question of fortune ..if she should outlive Love she would claim no part of his estate, real or personal, except what he wills to her .. she reserves the right to dispose of her property at anytime, before or after his death .. as if she was a feme sole .. Signed: Samuel Love, Ann Bruinskill. Wits: John Ashby, Jean Ashby, Francis (X) Weatherall. Rec: 26 Aug. 1776, prov. by o. of John Ashby, Jane Ashby and Francis Weatherall.

Pages 303-304. 15 April 1776. Lease. Bet. John James and George Brown .. tract .. cor. to Brereton Jones .. to the waggon road .. Tulloss' path .. to the old rolling road .. 300 a. .. for his life and lives of Elizabeth his wife and Joshua, his son .. yearly rent of ₤3 .. Signed: John James. Rec: 26 August 1776, ack. by John James.

Pages 304-306. 22 April 1776. Lease. Bet. Harmon Hitt and Wm. Spiser, Mary Spiser and Randolph Spiser .. tract in Leeds Par. .. now in the tenure of sd. Spicers .. 100 a. .. on the Watry Mt. adj. the lines of Randolph Spiser, John Smith .. during their nat. lives .. yearly rent of ₤3 .. Signed: Harman Hitt, William (X) Spiser. Wit: Jos. Blackwell, Jeremiah Darnall, George Cordell. Rec: 26 Aug. 1776, ack. by parties.

Pages 306-309. 23-24 August 1776. Lease & release. Bet. John Cantwell of Leeds Par. and John Baxter & Amelia, h. w. .. to John Cantwell, tract in Par. of Leeds, part of tract belonging to John Baxter .. cor. to George Berry and Edward Feagins .. 40 a. .. ₤37.10s. .. Signed: John Baxter, Amelia (X) Baxter. Rec: 26 Aug. 1776, ack. by grantors.

Pages 309-311. 23 September 1776. B & S. Bet. Thomas Keith & Judith, h. w. and Edward Matthew .. ₤13.10 .. part of tract in Leeds Par. whereon Keith now lives .. adj. the land of Samuel Nelms .. on the main Trap Br. .. 9 a. Signed: Thomas Keith, Judith Keith. Rec: 23 Sept. 1776, ack. by grantors.

Pages 312-313. 20 September 1776. Clear title. Bet. James Ewell, Jr. of Lan. Co., C'wealth of Virginia and John Thomas Chunn .. James Ewell on behalf of James Ewell, Jr., 25 July 1767 .. who was to be 21 yrs. of age in 6 mos. .. conveyed to John Adams, Zephaniah Turner, a tract, which they have assigned to J. T. Chunn .. Chunn has agreed to convey a part of this to John Ashby agreeable to a div. by them made .. for £250 rec'd. from James Ewell .. tract devised to Jas. Ewell, Jr. by Maj. **James Ball**, dec'd late of Lan. Co. .. cor. of Col. **Landon Carter's** land .. near the main road which leads from **Robert Ashby's** now dwelling house to that part of the Blue Ridge called Ashby's Gap .. Crooked Run .. 1000 a. now in the tenure of Chunn and Ashby .. *Signed*: **Jas. Ewell, Jr.** *Wits*: **Robert Warren, Phil. Heale, Jas. Ewell, Charles Thornton, John Thornberry.** *Rec*: 23 Sept. 1776, prov. by o. of Warren, Thornton and Ewell, wits.

Pages 314-315. 21 September 1776. B & S. Bet. **John Thomas Chunn & Martha**, h. w. and **John Ashby, Jr.** .. £125 .. part of lot of 1000 a. conveyed by **Jas. Ewell, Jr.** of Lan. Co. to J. T. Chunn .. cor. tree of **John Adams, Hezekiah Turner** and **George Adams** .. 230 a. *Signed*: **John Thos. Chunn, Martha Chunn.** *Wits*: **Hez'h Turner, John Adams, George Adams.** *Rec*: 23 Sept. 1776, ack. by grantors.

Pages 315-316. 21 September 1776. B & S. Bet. **John Thomas Chunn & Martha**, h. w. and **George Adams** .. £125 .. 1/2 lot of 1000 a. from Jas. Ewell, Jr. to Chunn .. Beg. at cor. tree to **John Adams, Hezekiah Turner** and **John Ashby, Jr.** .. oak marked LC standing near Ashby's Gap Road, being cor. of Col. **Landon Carter** .. 500 a. .. *Signed*: **John Thos. Chunn, Martha Chunn.** *Wits*: **Hez'h. Turner, John Adams, Mary Ashby.** *Rec*: 23 Sept. 1776, ack. by grantors.

Pages 316-319. 26-28 October 1776. Lease & release. Bet. **Stephen Pritchard & Peggy**, h. w. and **David Wickliffe** of Pr. Wm. Co. .. 190 a. granted by patent from Prop. to **Daniel Newland**, 17 Jan. 1764 .. n. side of Town Run in **Mr. Mauzy's** line .. **Fowke's** line .. **Righly's** line .. down sd. run .. £200 .. *Signed*: **Stephen Pritchard, Peggy Pritchard.** *Rec*: 28 Oct. 1776, ack. by grantors.

Pages 320-322. 28 October 1776. B & S. Bet. **Benjamin Turner** of Culp. Co. & **Ann**, h. w. and **Wm. Allason** of Fauq. Co., Merchant .. the Turners and **John Orr & Mary**, h. w. were lately seised in fee simple in right of Ann and Mary of tract in Ham. Par. .. from Prop. to **Francis Jackson & Thomas Jordan** .. 11 Aug. 1741 .. was recovered by judgmt. from Fauq. Co. Court from **John Hooe** late of Staff. Co., Gent., by ejectment in suit brought by Turner & wife and sd. Mary and a certain **Martin Settle** her former husband and divided bet. Turner and Orr, April 1776 and Turner was allotted the share next to Wm. Allason .. and the Turners, for £100 .. tract .. adj. where Allason now resides and dwells .. *Signed*: **Benjamin (X) Turner, Ann (X) Turner.** *Wits*: **James Williams, Robt. Hinson, Thos. James, Wm. Vaughan.** *Rec*: 28 Oct. 1776, ack. by grantors.

Pages 322-323. 28 October 1776. B & S. Bet. **John Ennis**, Planter and **Mary**, h. w. and **Morias Hansbrough** of Staff. Co. .. £30 .. 105 a. .. part of tract taken up by **Isaac Judo** .. on head br. of Cannons Run .. cor. to **John Savage** .. line of **Joseph Wood**, now in poss. of **John Nelson** .. line of **William Bethels** .. *Signed*: **John Enness, Maryan (X) Enness.** *Rec*: 28 Oct. 1776, ack. by grantors.

Pages 323-325. 22 April 1776. B & S. Bet. James Lewis & Mary, h. w. of Leeds Par. .. and James Sanders .. ₤66.15s. .. part of tract Lewis purch. of Thomas Chinn, dec'd .. cor. of Lewis' whole tract (or Lambert's Patent) .. cor. to Keith .. hic. near the top of a mt. .. 89 a. *Signed*: James Lewis, Mary Lewis. *Wits*: Jos. Blackwell, Jere. Darnall, Fras. Atwell. *Rec*: 28 Oct. 1776. ack. by grantors.

Pages 326-327. 20 March 1776. B & S. Bet. Joseph Smith & Ann, h. w. and John Smith .. ₤32.10s. .. part of larger tract purch. of George Neavil .. 25 Oct. 1765 .. 103 a., one half of the whole .. down the hollow to Rowley Smith's fence where the run makes a turn from thence a direct course into the Pignut line .. 1/2 of the whole – the residue after that half which Rowley Smith holds and and lives on comes out .. *Signed*: Jos. Smith, Ann Smith. *Wits*: Martin Pickett, John Cooke, John Blackwell, Jr. *Rec*: 28 Oct. 1776, ack. by grantors.

Pages 327-329. 20 March 1776. B & S. Bet. Joseph Smith & Ann, h. w. and Rowley Smith .. ₤32.10s. .. part of tract purch. from George Neavil, 25 Oct. 1765 .. 103 a. .. being 1/2 of the whole .. (same description as above) whereon Rowley Smith now lives .. *Signed*: Jos. Smith, Ann Smith. *Wits*: Martin Pickett, John Cooke, John Blackwell, Jr. *Rec*: 28 Oct. 1776, ack. by grantors.

Pages 329-333. 21 September 1776. B & S. Bet. James Scott, Gent. and Elizabeth, h. w. of Leeds Par. and Samuel Pepper .. ₤210 .. tract on waters of Carter's Run and the Piney Branch of Broad Run of Occoquan, part of larger tract granted to the late Rev. Alex. Scott for 2,823 a. by the Prop., 10 July 1727 .. to a road commonly called Rectors Road .. to fork of sd. road and Main Rd. to Winchester .. 300 a. *Signed*: Jas. Scott, Jr., Eliz'a Scott. *Wits*: Phil. Heale, H. Peyton, H. Brooke, Thos. Digges. *Rec*: 27 Jan. 1777, ack. by Grantor.

Pages 333-334. 17 October 1776. Deed of Gift. John Carr, Sr. of Ham. Par. for nat. love & affection .. for my beloved Son, John Carr .. to him.. one Negro N a n .. cattle .. crops .. furniture .. on plantation whereon I now live .. for which John Carr, Jr. delivered to John Carr, Sr. one pewter dish .. *Signed*: John (X) Carr, Sr. *Wits*: John Matthews, John James, William Conway, Thomas Shumate, Bailey Shumate, Daniel Shumate. *Rec*: 27 January 1777, prov. by o. of James and Conway, wits.

Pages 334-338. 19-20 November 1776. Lease & release. Bet. Thomas Bronaugh & Betty, h. w. and William Gibson .. part of larger tract purch. of Thomas Walsh by Bronaugh's father .. cor. to Francis Bronaugh & in John Wither's line .. line of James Withers .. Corbin's corner .. 152 a. .. for ₤65 .. *Signed*: Thos. Bronaugh, Betty Bronaugh. *Wits*: Wm. Grant, Thomas Helm, David Blackwell, Vincent (X) Garner, Sr., John Blackwell, Jeremiah Darnall. *Rec*: 27 Jan. 1777, ack. by grantors.

Pages 339-343. 24-25 November 1776. Lease & release. Bet. John Duncan, Jr. & Elizabeth, h. w. and Alexander Lithgow & John Lithgow of Dumfries, merchants .. cor. to **Josiah Holtzclaw** .. cor. to sd. **Holtzclaw, Samuel Porter** and **Thomas Porter** .. cor. to sd. T. Porter and **John Bryan** .. cor. to sd. J. Bryan and **Wm. Bryan** .. 250 a. .. part of tract called Pageland, which sd. Duncan purch. of **Martin Pickett** .. Ł200 .. *Signed*: **John Duncan, Elizabeth** (X) **Duncan.** *Wits*: **H. Brooke, John Blackwell, John Bryan.** *Rec*: 27 January 1777, prov. by o. of wits.

Pages 343-344. 5 November 1776. Relinquishment. **Sarah Ann Cornwell** relinquishes her right to any part of deceased husband's estate - **Peter Cornwell.** *Signed*: **Sarah Ann** (X) **Cornwell.** *Wits*: **W. Grant, Dugard.** *Rec*: 27 Jan. 1777, prov. by o. of **John Dugard.**

Pages 345-346. 14 January 1774. B & S. Bet. **Richard McPherson** of Leeds Par. & **Eleanor**, h. w. and **Edwin Furr** of Shelbourne Par., Loud. Co. .. Ł63 .. tenement cont. 150 a. (except 30 a. sold to **I s a a c Nichols**) being part of the land purch. by **John Rector** of **Burgess Ball,** Gent. of Lan. Co. & by Rector conveyed to sd. McPherson, 28 Oct. 1771 .. Beg. at 3 red oak saplins in the dividing line formerly run bet. **Smith** & **Ball** being James Murrays Beg. cor. to **Thomas Priest** .. cor. to **Ephraim Furr** .. cor. to **James Murray** .. *Signed*: **Rich'd McPherson, Eleanor** (E) **McPherson.** *Wits*: **Thos. Lewis, John Kincheloe, Jerem'h** (x) **Furr, Moses** (C) **Cummings, John McCarty, Isaac** (Ɨ) **Cundiff.** *Rec*: 27 March 1775, prov. by o. of **John Kincheloe** and **Jeremiah Furr** and 27 Jan. 1777, prov. by o. of **Isaac Cundiff.**

Pages 346-349. 28 April 1777. B & S. Bet. **Samuel Conyers & Keziah**, h. w. and **Martin Pickett** and **John Ball** .. Ł115.10s. .. paid to Conyers & Pickett .. 107 a. .. red oak in **Samuel Porter**'s line .. NE side of br. of Licking Run .. white oak in **Hooe**'s line .. cor. to Porter by road to Fauq. C. H. .. part of larger tract conveyed to **Denis Conyers**, dec'd. by Prop., 9 April 1723 .. *Signed*: **Samuel** (X) **Conyers, Heziah** (X) **Conyers, Martin Pickett.** *Rec*: 28 Apr. 1777, ack. by grantors.

Pages 349-351. 24 March 1777. B & S. Bet. **James Gillison & Ann**, h. w. and **John Berryman** .. Ł7 .. land in Ham. Par. .. cor. to sd. Gillison .. 8 a. 1 r. 17 po. .. *Signed*: **James Gillison, Anne Gillison.** *Wits*: **Augustin Jennings, Joseph Whitley, William Watson.** *Rec*: 24 March 1777, ack. by grantors.

Pages 351-353. 24 March 1777. B. & S. Bet. **Reubin Wright & Mary**, h. w. and **John Quisenberry** .. Ł36 .. parcel in Ham. Par .. line of Mr. **John Alexander** .. 122 a. .. *Signed*: **Reubin Wright, Molly** (X) **Wright.** *Wits*: **Augustin Jennings, James Monroney, Elisha Arnold.** *Rec*: 24 Mar. 1777, ack. by grantors.

Pages 353-356. 24 March 1777. B & S. Bet. **Augustin Jennings the Elder** of Ham. Par. and **Hannah**, h. w. and **Augustin Jennings the Y o u n g e r** .. all their moiety or half part of a tract of land .. formerly sold by Nathaniel Hedgman to **John Duncan** for 200 a. .. oak in dividing line bet. **Peter** and **Nathaniel Hedgman** .. south end of tract .. 100

a. ... 5 shillings .. *Signed*: **Augustine Jennings, Hannah Jennings.** *Wits*: **Martin Pickett, William Jennings, Joseph Wheatley.** *Rec*: 24 March 1774, ack. by grantors.

Pages 356-358. 15 March 1777. Deed of Gift. Bet. **Thomas Jackman, Sr.** of Leeds Par. and **Thomas Jackman, Jr.** .. for love, goodwill and affection for his son .. part of larger tract granted sd. Thomas, Sr. for 419 a. by the Prop., 22 Nov. 1740 .. hiccory on Carters Run, near the mouth of a br. cor. to sd. Patented tract .. to Crooked Tree Branch .. 150 a. .. *Signed*: **Thomas Jackman.** *Wits*: **J. Neavill, Wm. Jackman, Joseph Jackman.** *Rec*: 24 March 1777, prov. by o. of wits.

Pages 358-359. 20 March 1777. Deed of Gift. Bet. **Thomas Jackman, Sr.** of Leeds Par. and **William Jackman** .. for love & affection .. part of larger tract of 419 a. granted to sd. Thos. 22 Nov. 1740 .. with **Michael Mildiams** the out line .. 100 a. .. *Signed*: **Thomas Jackman.** *Wits*: **J. Neavill, Thomas Jackman, Jr., Joseph Jackman.** *Rec*: 24 Mar. 1777, prov. by o. of **James Neavil, Thomas** and **Jos. Jackman.**

Pages 359-361. 11 March 1777. B & S. Bet. **James Gillison** and **Ann,** h. w. and **Peter Bower** of K. G. Co. .. Ł333.10s. .. par. in Ham. Par. .. red oak on bank of Marsh Run .. with **C o r b i n** 's line .. edge of the Main road .. 333 1/2 a. .. *Signed*: **James Gillison, Anne Gillison.** *Wits*: **William Watson, Joseph Morgan, Joseph Wheatley, Jonathan Gibson.** *Rec*: 24 March 1777, ack. by grantors.

Pages 361-363. 24 March 1777. B & S. Bet. **John Pinckard** of Leeds Par. and **Jane,** h. w. and **Eli Thompson** .. Ł175 .. tract at the Cobler Mt. .. 100 a. .. being the land purch. by **Francis Jett** from **Thomas Turner,** Gent. by deed of lease & release 9-10 Nov. 1754, prov. in Pr. Wm. Co. .. *Signed*: **John Pinckard, Jane Pinckard.** *Rec*: 24 March 1777, ack. by grantors.

Pages 363-365. 29 October 1776. B & S. Bet. **John Waddle & Betty,** h. w. and **Joseph Blackwell, Jr.,** son of Joseph .. Ł60 .. 60 a. .. at the Pignut Ridge, part of tract formerly belong. to **William Wright** and by him sold to Waddle .. 14 Oct. 1762 .. in **Simon Miller's** line .. *Signed*: **John (I) Waddle, Betty (X) Waddle.** *Wits*: **W. Grant, Thos. Keith, Joseph Blackwell, A. Churchill, John Blackwell.** *Rec*: 26 May 1777, ack. by grantors.

Pages 365-368. 16 May 1777. B & S. Bet. **Bryant Fairfax** of Fx. Par., Fx. Co. & **Elizabeth,** h. w. and **John Craine** of St. Stephen's Par., N'land Co. .. Ł156 .. 260 a. .. known & bounded by the lands formerly taken up by **Mr. Chinn** and **Stamp** and by a lot of the sd. Fairfax now settled by **Samuel Pearle** and also by Little River .. upper cor. of Sam'l Pearle's lot on Little River .. line of Chinn's land .. cor. to Stamp's land .. *Signed*: **Bryan Fairfax, Elizabeth Fairfax.** *Wits*: **Joseph Jackson, Edward Turner, Stanley Singleton.** *Rec*: 26 May 1777, prov. by o. of wits.

Pages 368-371. 22 April 1777. Lease. Bet. **Henry Peyton** of Leeds Par. and **John Kibble** .. tenement .. Beg. tree of tract of land formerly **Denis Coniers** now **Simon Miller** and **James Foley's** .. cor. to Foley & Miller .. cor. to Foley in the line of **Henry Watkins** .. line of **Wm.** and **Samuel Nelms** .. cor. of **William O'bannon** .. cor. of **Mr. Eustace** .. 287 a. .. for his life and nat. lives of **Grace**, his wife and **Anderson Kibble**, his son .. 530 lbs. Tobacco and quitrents and taxes .. *Signed*: **Henry Peyton, John Kibble**. *Wits*: **A. Churchill, W. Edmonds, Edward Digges**. *Rec*: 26 May 1777, ack. by grantor.

Page 372. 24 May 1777. Bill of Sale. **Richard Gregory** to **James Bailey** .. cattle, crops, furniture and utensils .. in consideration of debt of Ł20.5s. .. *Signed*: **Richard** (x) **Gregory**. *Wits*: **Charles Morehead, John** (+) **Allen**. *Rec*: 26 May 1777, prov. by o. of wits.

Pages 372-373. 26 May 1777. Apprentice Bond. Bet. **James Davis** and **George Grasty** .. Davis, an illegitimate child, son of **Sarah Davis**, dec'd., binds himself to Grasty for 7 years, being 14 years of age. Grasty to teach the Apprentice to read & write and the Trade or mistery of a Shoemaker .. *Signed*: **George Grasty, James** (X) **Davis**. *Rec*: 26 May 1777, ack. by parties.

Pages 373-375. 26 May 1777. B & S. Bet. **John Basye** and **George Carter** .. Ł250 .. tract adj. **Charles Morehead** and **Charles Martin's** land .. **John James's** line .. 200 a. *Signed*: **John Basye**. *Wits*: **Geo. Cordell, J. James, James Genn**. *Rec*: 26 May 1777, ack. by grantor.

Pages 375-376. 28 July 1777. Bond. Bond of **Jeremiah Darnall** as Sheriff, apptd. by the Governor, 6 June 1777. For: Ł1000. *Sec*: **Armistead Churchhill, Martin Pickett**, to Justices of the County Court: **Joseph Blackwell, William Grant, James Bell, Henry Peyton,** Gent. *Signed*: **Jeremiah Darnall, A. Churchhill, Martin Pickett**. *Rec*: 28 July 1777, ack. by parties.

Pages 376-377. 28 July 1777. Bond. **Jeremiah Darnall**. Sheriff. For: Ł500. To Justices listed above and securities .. *Rec*: 28 July 1777.

Page 377. 28 July 1777. Bond. Bond of **Jeremiah Darnall**, Sheriff, to Justices of Fauq. Co. Court, listed above. *Sec*: **A r m i s t e a d Churchhill, Martin Pickett**. For: Ł1000. *Rec*: 28 July 1777.

Pages 377-379. 28 July 1777. B & S. Bet. **Henry Rector, Jr.** of Leeds Par. & **Mary**, h. w. and **Henry Rector, Youngest** .. Ł12.7s.6d. .. 9 a. part of tract purch. by **John Rector** of **Burgess Ball** of Lan. Co., 7 Sept. 1770 .. part of tract owned by Henry Rector, Jr. ... *Signed*: **Henry Rector**. *Rec*: 28 July 1777, ack. by grantor.

Pages 379-381. 28 July 1777. B & S. Bet. **Henry Rector & Mary**, h. w. of Leeds Par. and **George Glascock** .. Ł70 .. tract on branches of Goose Creek .. part of purch. of **John Rector**, dec'd. of **Burgess Ball** of Lan. Co. .. 104 a. .. except a lease now in possession of **Joseph Neale** .. *Signed*: **Henry Rector**. *Rec*: 28 July 1777, ack. by grantor.

Pages 381–383. 28 July 1777. B & S. Bet. **William Bartlett** of Leeds Par. and **William Pickett Sanford** [sic, **William Sanford Pickett**] .. Ł20 .. where **William Pickett Sanford** now lives on Hungar Run [Little River] .. Beg. at the mouth of Long Branch, on Hungar Run or Little River .. **Mercer's** new made line .. 297 a. .. *Signed*: **William Barkley**. *Rec*: 28 July 1777, ack. by **William Barkley** [sic].

Pages 383–385. 28 July 1777. B & S. Bet. **William Pickett Sanford** of Leeds Par. and **William Barkley** .. Ł5 .. tract adj. lands of sd. Barkley, being part of the land Wm. Pickett Sanford purch. of **Wauker** on Little River .. cor. bet. Wm. P. Sanford and Wm. Barkley .. **Mercers** new made line .. 5 acres .. *Signed*: **William Pickett Sanford**. *Rec*: 28 July 1777, ack. by **William Pickett Sanford**.

Page 385. 23 December 1776. B & S. **Peter Grant** to **John Hull** of N'land Co. .. Ł120 .. all that tract to Peter Grant from **Richard Henry Lee**, Esq. by lease for three lives .. *Signed*: **Peter Grant**. *Wits*: **James Bell, Sam'l. Boyd, W. Edmonds**. *Rec*: 28 July 1777, ack. by grantor.

Pages 385–386. 17 July 1777. Acknowledgment. To every reader .. hereof .. we the Subscribers, **Benjamin Ganer** and **Mary Ganer**, do hereby ack. (and are willing the public should be advertised) that all and every report by us expressed either by word or words .. injurious to the Character or reputation of Capt. **John Moffett** were without foundation .. but spoken in heat of passion and Anger and we desire the publick to take notice of this our sincere recantation. *Signed*: **Bryant (X) Gainer, Mary (X) Gainer**. *Wits*: **J. Neavil, Tho. Nelson, Jos. Neavil**. *Rec*: 28 July 1777, prov. by o. of wits.

Pages 386–387. 28 July 1777. B & S. Bet. **John McBee** and **Fanny**, h. w. and **John Shumate** .. Ł25 .. tract in Ham. Par. .. same beq. to McBee by his grandfather .. piece of cleared land called by some McBee's folly and by some the dogs battle yard .. **Hardins** line .. 56 a. .. *Signed*: **John (X) McBee, Fanny (X) McBee**. *Rec*: 28 July 1777, ack. by grantors.

Pages 387–389. 7 June 1777. B & S. Bet. **James Young** and **Thomas Digges** .. Ł300 .. 300 a. cor. (formerly) to **Killy Jenings** and **James Genn** .. cor. to **John Neavil** .. line of **Charles Carter**, Esq. .. Cedar Run lowgrounds .. cor. to **John Wood** .. land Young purch. of **William Hackney** .. *Signed*: **James (()) Young**. *Wits*: **H. Brooke, James Bell, Edward Digges**. *Rec*: 28 July 1777, ack. by grantor.

Pages 390–391. 26 May 1777. B & S. Bet. **James Young** of Ham. Par. and **Benjamin Neale** of same .. Ł120.12s. .. tract in Ham. Par. sd. Young and **John Thornberry**, purch. of **Burgess Ball**, Esq. of Lan. Co. .. line adj. **Parker** now **Hugh Brent** .. 350 a. *Signed*: **James (())**

Young. *Wits*: **George Grant, John Stone, Alexander Parker, James Hathaway, Richard Parker.** *Rec*: 28 July 1777, ack. by grantors.

Pages 392-393. 6 August 1777. B & S. Bet. **Bushrode Dogget** of Culp. Co. & **Ann,** h. w. and **Jacob Burger** .. Ł100 .. 304 a. .. same Dogget purch. on two separate times from **Thomas Mitchell** and is part of larger tract from the Prop. to **Thomas Welch** of Pr. Wm. Co., 14 Nov. 1740 .. present survey made by **Charles Morgan** .. line of **John Kemper** .. cor. to **John Arnold** .. *Signed*: **Bushrode Doggett, Ann Doggett.** *Wits*: **R'd. Doggett, Gavin Lawson.** *Rec*: 25 Aug. 1777, ack. by grantors.

Pages 393-395. 25 August 1777. B & S. Bet. **Jesse Williams & Mary,** h. w. and **George Calvert** of Culp. Co. .. Ł80.15s. .. cor. to **Kemper** .. Courthouse Road .. 161 1/2 a. .. *Signed*: **Jesse Williams, Mary Williams.** *Wits*: **George Williams, John P. Williams, Thos. OBanon.** *Rec*: 25 Aug. 1777, ack. by grantors.

Pages 395-396. 8 March 1777. Lease. Bet. **Ephraim Hubbard** and **Richard Stage,** both of Leeds Par. .. rents to Stage the plantation he now lives on with the remainder of 150 a. .. for his nat. life and lives of **Sarah Stage,** h. w. .. yearly rent of Ł5 per 100 acres .. *Signed*: **Ephraim Hubbard, Richard Stage.** *Wits*: **John Edmonds, Silvester** (o) **Welch.** *Rec*: 25 Aug. 1777, ack. by parties.

Pages 396-398. 20 August 1777. B & S. Bet. **James Burditt** and **Frederick Burditt** .. Ł35 .. tract on Great Run .. 190 a. .. saplin on N. side of **Peter Kemper's** mill dam .. line of **Col. Lee** .. cor. to sd. Kemper .. line of Maj. **Richard Buckner,** dec'd .. meanders of Great Run .. part of tract taken up by jt. tenancy by **Henry Kemper, Catherine Kemper** and **Mary Kamper** .. 1741 .. where sd. Frederick Burditt now lives on ... *Signed*: **James Burditt.** *Wits*: **John Blackwell, John Ball, Martin Pickett.** *Rec*: 25 Aug. 1777, ack. by grantor.

Pages 398-400. 15 April 1777. B & S. Bet. **Nathaniel Williams,** Blacksmith, of Staff. Co. and **John Pope Williams** .. Ł100 .. tract on branches of Great Run, part of larger tract .. 199 a. .. cor. to **Charles Williams** and **Jesse Williams** .. cor. to **William Jennings** .. *Signed*: **Nath'a Williams.** *Wits*: **Jesse, Charles, Lewis** and **George Williams.** *Rec*: 25 August 1777, ack. by grantor.

Pages 400-401. 16 April 1777. B & S. Bet. **Nathaniel Williams,** Blacksmith, of Staff. Co. & **Charles Williams** .. Ł100 .. 197 a. on branches of Great Run .. part of Larger tract .. cor. to **Jesse & John Pope Williams** .. oak standing in an Anchant line called **Hooe's** line .. cor. to **Thomas Airs** land .. *Signed*: **Nath'a Williams.** *Wits*: **Jesse, J. P., Lewis** and **Geo. Williams.** *Rec*: 25 Aug. 1777, ack. by grantor.

Pages 401-402. 7 April 1777. B & S. Bet. **Nathaniel Williams,** Blacksmith, of Staff. Co. and **Jesse Williams** .. Ł100 .. 162 a. on br. of Great Run, pt. of larger tract .. cor. to **John Kamper** .. Courthouse

Road .. *Signed*: Nath'a Williams. *Wits*: John P., Charles, Lewis, Geo. Williams. *Rec*: 25 August 1777. ack. by grantor.

Pages 403-404. 1 November 1777. Lease. Bet. John James of Ham. Par. and Bailey Shumate .. tenement in Ham. Par. .. line of Capt. Howsin Kenner .. oak on the old rolling road .. 192 a., .. for his nat. life and lives of his wife Mary and his dau. Susannah .. paying one in 2 years, 1000 lbs. Merchantile Tob., prized and one hogshead .. inspected at a warehouse in Falmouth or Dumfries .. *Signed*: John James. *Wits*: W. Grant, Dan'l. Shumate, John Kerr, Jonathan Gibson, Rodham Tullos, William Wright. *Rec*: 24 Nov. 1777, prov. by o. of Grant, Shumate and John Kear, wits.

Pages 404-406. 11 October 1777. Lease. Bet. John James of Ham. Par. and Lazarus Mattox of same .. tenement in Ham. Par. .. Housen Kenner's line and near the old rolling road .. Rodham Tullos's line .. 200 a. .. for his nat. life and lives of Frances Mattox and his son Thomas Mattox .. paying once in 2 yrs. 1000 lbs. Tobacco, prized in one hogshead .. *Signed*: John James. *Wits*: Dan'l. Shumate, James Luttrell, John Luttrell. *Rec*: 24 Nov. 1777, prov. by o. of wits.

Pages 406-410. 23-24 October 1777. Lease & release. Bet. Edwin Furr and Ann, his wife of Loud. Co. and Samuel Bayly [also spelled: Bailey] .. part of larger tract .. which was purch. by John Rector of Burgess Ball, Gent. of Lan. Co., 17 Sept. 1770 .. Beg. at 3 red oaks in the div. line bet. Ball and Smith being James Murray's .. cor. to Thos. Priest .. cor to Ephraim Furr .. cor to James Murray .. 150 a. .. Ł 100 .. *Signed*: Edwin (X) Furr. *Wits*: William Stephens, John Cantwell, Benjamin Richards, Moses (X) Furr, James Glascock. *Rec*: 25 Nov. 1777, ack. by grantors.

Pages 410-415. 5-6 May 1777. Lease & release. Bet. Lynaugh Helm of Pr. Wm. Co. and Esther, h. w. and William Pope .. tract in Pr. Wm. & Fauq. Cos. .. cor. to Richard Tidwell .. oak on Goose Run .. cor. of John Catlett .. 275 a. .. also another tract .. cor. to sd. Helm's land bought of Gunyon and to land of Lewis .. cor. to John Catlett, also to sd. Helm's land bought of Coppedge .. cor. to John Ralls .. Acquia Road .. large Chestnut oak called the Royal Oak .. 233 a. .. 508 a. .. *Signed*: Lynaugh Helm, Hester Helm. *Wits*: Benjamin Pope, James Dowdall, John Franklin. *Rec*: 24 Nov. 1777, ack. by grantors.

Pages 415-417. 24 November 1777. B & S. Bet. Margaret Reynolds and Robert Hopper of Culp. Co. .. Ł15 .. part of tract granted to sd. Reynolds by patent, 12 May 1777 .. Routs Cor .. on n. side of Hedgman's River .. cor. to Col. Corbin .. 25 a. .. *Signed*: Catherine (X) Reynolds. *Rec*: 24 Nov. 1777, ack. by sd. Catherine Reynolds.

Pages 417-419. 6 May 1777. B & S. Bet. Lynaugh Helm and Hester, h. w. of Pr. Wm. Co. and Benjamin Pope .. tract. containing 282 a. which was purch. from John Gunyon .. oak on Dorrells Run cor. to John Catlett's .. up Dorrells Run .. 5s. .. *Signed*: Lynaugh Helm,

Hester Helm. *Wits*: **John Franklin, William Pope, James Dowdall.** *Rec*: 24 Nov. 1777, ack. by grantors.

Pages 420-421. 24 November 1777. B & S. Bet. **Benjamin Neale** and **Robert Luttrell** .. Ł16 .. 80 a. .. part of 240 a. tract first granted to **John Crump,** 29 July 1745, who gave it to his son **George Crump** and by him conveyed to **Richard Luttrell,** dec'd who gave it to his dau. **Anstis** .. oak on W. side of Rocky Run in **Michael Dearmont's** line .. **Joseph Wood's** line .. along **John Forsyth's** line .. *Signed*: **Benjamin Neale, Anstis Neale.** *Wits*: **John Luttrell, John Medlay, James Luttrell, Lazarus Maddux.** *Rec*: 24 Nov. 1777, ack. by grantors.

Pages 422-424. 7 October 1777. B & S. Bet. **Thomas Digges,** Gent. & **Elizabeth,** h. w. and **William Fitzhugh the Younger** of K. G. Co. .. Ł500 .. 300 a. .. oak a cor. (formerly) to **Kelly Jenings** and **James Genn** .. cor. to **John Neavil** .. line of **Charles Carter,** Esq. .. Cedar Run lowgrounds .. cor. to **John Wood** .. land Digges purch. of **James Young** .. *Signed*: **Thomas Digges, Elizabeth Digges.** *Wits*: **H. Brooke, Fran's Whiting, George Fitzhugh.** *Rec*: 24 Nov. 1777, ack. by grantors.

Page 425. 4 December 1776. Rent adjustment. Bet. **Pearson Chapman** of Charles Co., Md., Gent. and **Samuel Grigsby** .. by indenture dated March 1770 Grigsby was to pay to Chapman the annual rent of Ł 10 .. for 378 1/2 a. on S. side of North Run of Broad run of Occoquan, since which time sd. Chapman has sold 100 a. to **William Stewart** .. rent adjusted to Ł6.10s. .. *Signed*: **Pearson Chapman, Samuel Grigsby.** *Wits*: **J. Moffett, William O'Bannon, William Stewart.** *Rec*: 24 Nov. 1777, prov. by o. of **O'Bannon** and **William Stewart,** wits.

Pages 426-428. 24 November 1777. B & Ś. Bet. **Joseph Smith** and **Leanna,** h. w. and **Benjamin Neale** of Pr. Wm. Co. .. Ł110 .. 75 a. .. **Carter's** line, now **Heale's** .. Cor. of **James Genn** .. cor. formerly belong. to **William Coleclough** .. *Signed*: **Joseph Smith, Leanna (X) Smith.** *Rec*: 24 Nov. 1777, ack. by grantors.

Pages 428-432. 20 May 1772. Lease. Bet. Col. **Richard Henry Lee** of W'land Co. and **Wm. Jones** .. tenement in Parishes of Ham. & Leeds 321 a. .. cor. to **Arnold & Bayse** .. cor. to **Pickett** .. to a Peach tree stump in the Courthouse Old fields another cor. of Pickett .. cor. to **John Peake** .. cor. to **Peake & Taylor** .. for his nat. life and lives of **Mary,** h. w. and **Nathan Jones,** his son .. yearly rent of Ł14.18s.10d. .. *Signed*: **William (W) Jones, Richard Henry Lee.** *Wits*: **Bennett Price, Jos. Blackwell, Martin Pickett.** *Rec*: 23 Feb. 1778, prov. by o. of Blackwell and Pickett.

Pages 432-435. 23 February 1778. B & S. Bet. **William Watkins** & **Anne,** h. w. and **John Cooke** .. 119 1/2 a. .. in Ham. Par. .. Ł250 .. Beg. in **Stephen Chilton's** cor. on the patent line .. cor. to **Shirley** .. *Signed*: **William Watkins, Anne (X) Watkins.** *Rec*: 23 Feb. 1778, ack. by grantors.

Pages 435-438. 14 June 1777. B & S. Bet. **James Genn** and **Nat Matthew** .. £90 .. part of an Antient Survey called **Bell's** .. bet. the lines of **Waugh Darnall** now **Simon Morgan, William Norris, John James** and **Peter Bashaw** .. 148 a. .. *Signed*: **James Genn**. *Wits*: **Joseph Carter, John Norris, Edward Matthew, James Kelly**. *Rec*: 24 Nov. 1777. prov. by o. of **Edward Matthew** & **John Norris**, wits; 23 Feb. 1778, prov. by o. of **Joseph Carter**.

Pages 438-439. 23 February 1778. Article of Agreement. Bet. **Cuthbert Bullitt** and **William Tilson Buttress**, his servant .. sd. servant agrees to serve Bullitt for 2 years after his Indenture .. to learn the trade of fuller & dyer at Bullitt's fulling mill .. also learn the trade of a shoemaker .. if Bullitt should erect a grist mill to work there and manage any slave or servant put under him .. Bullitt to furnish £10 per year and other supplies. *Signed*: **Cuth't Bullitt, W. Buttries**. *Wits*: **John Bryan, Alex'r. H. Bullitt, Alex'r. Stephen**. Buttries also agrees to teach the man put under him to read and write. *Rec*: 23 Feb. 1778, ack. by parties.

Pages 439-441. 1 October 1777. B & S. Bet. **Richard Covington** & **Winifred**, h. w. of Ham. Par. and **Wm. Love** of Town of Falmouth, merchant .. £46.5s. .. 185 a., part of larger tract where Covington lives .. Main Road .. cor. to **Carter** .. Brown's Field .. cor. to **Morehead** .. *Signed*: **Richard Covington, Winifred Covington**. *Wits*: **J. Moffett, Alex'r. Bradford, Fran's. Attwell, Thomas Helm, Geo. Cordell**. *Rec*: 23 Feb. 1778, prov. by o. of Moffett, Attwell and Helm, wits.

Pages 442-444. 2 November 1777. B & S. Bet. **Thomas Bryan Martin** of F'rick Co. and **Thomas Lord Fairfax** .. £100 .. tract on Rappahannock Marsh in Fauq. Co. .. survey made by Mr. **John Mauzey** .. cor. to **Morgan Darnal** .. cor. to Thornton's Patent .. **Thornton** at Mount Pleasant, then joining Allen .. Beg. of **Prince's** Patent .. 255 a. .. granted to Martin, 1 Nov. 1777. *Signed*: **T. B. Martin**. *Wits*: **David Allason, Jas. Scott, Jr., Robert Scott**. *Rec*: 23 March 1778, prov. by o. of wits.

Pages 444-446. 1 March 1778. B & S. Bet. **John Hall** & **Elizabeth**, h. w. and **William Matthis** [also **Matthews**] .. £75 .. for nat. life of **Chichester Matthews** .. 1/2 of tract containing 300 a. as by a div. line made and agreed to by the parties .. which **Robert Matthis**, dec'd. held by lease from the Rev. **Wm. Stewart** of Staff. Co., 1764 .. same terms as agreed upon by the late Robert Matthis .. *Signed*: **John Hall, Elizabeth (X) Hall**. *Wits*: **James McClanahan, Joseph Minter, Robert Cleveland**. *Rec*: 23 March 1778, prov. by o. of wits.

Pages 446-447. 17 September 1777. Agreement. **Robert Dinwiddie Fowke** ack. his indebtedness to **Elizabeth Fowke**, widow of **Gerard Fowke**, Esq. late of Staff. Co. .. £5000 .. 17 Sept. 1777 .. R. D. Fowke entered into the above bond with Elizabeth, Executrix of the est. of Gerard Fowke, dec'd. for the am't. rec'd. to be his share of his father's estate .. however, he has since become discontented with his bargain and in order to keep peace in the family they entered into a new agreement. The above agreement to be void, if he receives 5 slaves, 13 cows & calves, feather bed & furniture. *Signed*: **Robert Dinwiddie Fowke.** *Wits*: **Wily Roy, William Baker, William Bradford, Gerard Fowke, Thomas Respress, Jr.** *Rec*: 23 Mar. 1778, prov. by o. of Roy & Fowke, wits.

Pages 447-448. 21 February 1778. B & S. Bet. **Robert Hopper &** **Sarah, h. w.** and **Gavin Lawson** of Culp. Co. .. Ł30 .. tract occupied by Hopper purch. of **Margaret Reynolds** .. 25 a. .. Routs cor. .. n. side Hedgman River .. cor. to **Col. Corbin** .. *Signed*: **Robert Hopper, Sarah (X) Hopper.** *Wits*: **John Graham, George Williams, Elias Barbee.** *Rec*: 25 May 1778, ack. by grantors.

Pages 449-450. 22 May 1778. B & S. Bet. **Samuel Luttrell** of Leeds Par. and **Robert Luttrell** of Ham. Par .. Ł100 .. 70 a. .. part of 354 a. grant to Robert Luttrell's father from the Prop., 12 March 1722 .. on Town Run and by him conveyed to Samuel Luttrell and by him conveyed to his brother Robert Luttrell .. Cabin Branch .. post in **Michael Dearmont's** line .. down Town Run .. to the mouth of Cabin Br. *Signed*: **Samuel Luttrell.** *Wits*: **Benjamin Neale, James Luttrell.** *Rec*: 25 May 1778, ack. by grantor.

Pages 450-452. 18 March 1778. Bond. **Bushrod Doggett** of Culp. Co. and **Ann Doggett** of Fauq. Co. bound to each other in sum of Ł1000 .. Ann Doggett never held any part of her father's est. till since the death of her husband, **Benjamin Doggett,** leaving 3 children, and Ann thinks she should have a slave named **Hannah** and her child, but they not agreeing have bound themselves to the judgment of Mr. **Wm. Morgan,** who is to decide what to settle on the children and whether Ann is to keep the slave. ... *Signed*: **Bushrode Doggett, Nanny Doggett.** *Wits*: **John Mauzy, Betty Kelly.** *Award*: 18 March 1778 – **Ann Doggett** ought to give her dau. **Mary** a slave named **David,** to be delivered at age of 18 or marriage or Mother's death, to son **Thomas Bushrode Doggett** one negro named **George,** to dau. **Susanna,** a Negro Boy named **Dick** .. Bushrode Doggett to allow Ann to live on the land during her nat. life, but not to sell or rent to anyone working more than 2 tithables .. Ann to have her Dower out of the slave Hannah & child after debts are paid .. if she mistreats the children, they and the slaves are to be taken away from her. *Signed*: **William Morgan.** *Wits*: **John Mauzy, Betty Kelly.** *Rec*: 25 May 1778, prov. by o. of wits.

Pages 452-454. 27 April 1778. B & S. Bet. **Reuben Wright & Mary,** **h. w.** and **James Tutt Dickerson** of Culp. Co. .. Ł90 .. part of tract of 422 a. granted to Reuben Wright .. (122 a. already conveyed to **John Coosenberry**) .. 300 a. .. *Signed*: **Reuben (X) Wright, Mary (X) Wright.** *Wits*: **Augustin Jennings, John Wheatley, William Jennings, John Morehead, John Blackwell.** *Rec*: 25 May 1778, prov. by o. of Blackwell, Wheatley and A. Jennings, wits.

Pages 455-457. 15 December 1777. B & S. Bet. **Joseph Duncan** and **Lydia, h. w.** and **Tunis Johnson** .. Ł157 .. 214 a. .. cor. to sd. Duncan

.. land Duncan purch. of **James Garner** .. 28 Nov. 1776. *Signed*: **Joseph (X) Duncan, Lydia (X) Duncan.** *Wits*: **A. Churchhill, William Bryant, Charles Bell, James Duncan, Samuel Johnson.** *Rec*: 25 May 1778, ack. by grantors.

Pages 457–458. 2 December 1777. Power of Atty. **Alexander Keith** of the 10th Virginia Regiment appts. his trusty and well-beloved friend, **Isham Keith,** his Lawful attorney .. *Signed*: **Alex. Keith.** *Wits*: **Tho. Blackwell, John Rust, Clough Shelton.** *Rec*: 25 May 1778, prov. by o. of **John Rust,** wit.

Pages 458–462. 16 December 1777. Lease & release. Bet. **Wm. Grigsby & Elizabeth, h. w.** and **John Grigsby** of K. G. Co. .. tract in counties of Fauq. & Staff. and upon head branches of Aquia .. **Markham's** line .. cor. to **Tobias Woods** land .. Saw Pitt Branch .. 350 a. .. Ł70 .. *Signed*: **Wm. Grigsby, Elizabeth Grigsby.** *Wits*: **Samuel Grigsby, William Stewart, John Bullitt, James White.** *Rec*: 22 June 1778, ack. by grantors.

Pages 462–463. 17 January 1778. B & S. Bet. **John Hall & Elizabeth** and **George Grubbs & Elizabeth, h. w.** and **Henry Griffin** .. the Rev. **Wm. Stewart** leased 300 a. to **Robert Matthews** in 1764 for 3 lives, and by his will, dated 30 Nov. 1764, devised the land to his wife **Elizabeth Matthews** for her life and then to be divided among his 3 youngest daus: **Elizabeth, Anna & Nancy** .. the last two died before Elizabeth, the widow, who has since married John Hall and Elizabeth, the dau., has married said Grubbs .. Ł65 .. 150 a., part of the tract .. where Geo. Grubbs now lives .. and which was formerly leased by Stewart to one **E d w a r d s** .. for the residue of the term of the lease .. *Signed*: **John Hall, Elizabeth (X) Hall, George Grubbs, Elizabeth (X) Grubbs.** *Wits*: **George Rogers, Jr., George (X) Dodson, Reuben George.** *Rec*: 25 May 1778, prov. by o. of Dodson and George; 22 June 1778, prov. by o. of Rogers.

Pages 463–466. 22 June 1778. B & S. Bet. **U r i a h R e c t o r &** **Elizabeth, h. w.** of Leeds Par and **George Glascock** of same .. Ł70 .. on waters of Goose Creek, part of purch. of **John Rector,** dec'd, of **Burgess Ball** .. sd. Glascock's land .. cor. of sd. Glascock, **Wm. Turley & John Kincheloe** .. Lick Branch .. line of **John Peyton Harrison** .. 48 a. .. *Signed*: **Uriah Rector, Elizabeth Rector.** *Rec*: 22 June 1778, ack. by grantors.

Pages 466–469. 22 June 1778. B & S. Bet. **U r i a h R e c t o r &** **Elizabeth, h. w.** of Leeds Par. and **Thomas Neavil** .. Ł81 .. on waters of Goose Creek .. part of tract purch. by **J o h n R e c t o r,** dec'd of **Burgess Ball** of Lan. Co. .. line of **John Peyton Harrison** and cor. of **Geo. Glascock** .. in line of **John Kincheloe** .. Lick Branch .. 154 a. .. *Signed*: **Uriah Rector, Elizabeth Rector.** *Rec*: 22 June 1778, ack. by grantors.

Pages 469–471. 1 January 1777. B & S. Bet. **J o h n** [sic] **A d a m s &** **Jemima, h. w.** and **Benjamin Rust** .. Ł130 .. in Rust's possession by virtue of B & S to him from said <u>Isaac</u> Adams .. taken up by **I s a a c** **Adams**, 12 June 1766 ..near the mouth of Ashby's Bent Branch and cor. to **Landon Carter**, Esq. .. to Goose Creek .. **Lamkins** corner .. 170 a. .. *Signed*: Isaac (X) **Adams**, Jemima (X) **Adams**. *Wits*: **J. Moffett, Eppa Timberlake, Samuel Rust, John Garlington, Benjamin Rector, Thomas Nelson**. *Rec*: 22 June 1778, prov. by o. of **Nelson, Rust** and **Rector**, wits.

Pages 471–473. 23 March 1778. Trust. Tripartite bet. **J a m e s G i l - lison & Ann**, h. w., 1st part; **Benjamin Harrison** and **Jonathan Gibson**, Gent. of 2nd part and **John Gillison, Margaret Gillison, James Gillison, Jr., Benj. Harrison Gillison** and **Mary Gillison**, children of sd. James & Ann Gillison ... Ł220 from **Harrison** & **Gibson** as for the nat. love for his wife & children and any other child he might have by sd. Anne .. slaves .. in trust for the support & education of sd. children & any others .. *Signed*: **James Gillison, Benjamin Harrison, Jonathan Gibson**. *Wits*: **Jas. Markham**, Thomas (x) **Brooks**, Benjamin (x) **Newell**. *Rec*: 22 June 1778, ack. by parties.

Pages 473–475. 26 December 1777. Deed of Gift. **Brereton Jones** of Ham. Par. for nat. love and affection for son **Henry Brereton Jones** .. tract of land whereon H. B. Jones now lives .. in line of **Hackney** and **Robert Jones** .. cor. to **Hackney, Jones** and **Blackman** .. 172 a. *Signed*: **Brereton Jones**. *Wits*: **John Matthews, Rodham Tullos, Charles Jones, Joseph Hopper**. *Rec*: 22 June 1778, ack. by grantor.

Page 475. 6 November 1777. Power of Attorney. **John Stone** of Craven Co., 96 Dist., S. C., appoints **John Ashby**, lawful atty. .. *Signed*: **John Stone**. *Wits*: **William Russell, Susann Darnall, Leannah Darnall, Jeremiah Darnall**. *Rec*: 22 June 1778, prov. by o. of **Russell** and **Jeremiah Darnall**.

Page 476. 25 May 1778. Bond. Bond of **Jeremiah Darnall** as duty and tax collector. For: Ł3000. *Sec*: **William Grant** and **Thomas Bronaugh**, held unto **George Webb**, Esq., Treas. of Virginia. *Signed*: **Jeremiah Darnall, W. Grant, Thos. Bronaugh**. *Rec*: 25 May 1778, ack. by parties.

Pages 476–479. 27 July 1778. B & S. Bet. **James Bailey** and **Hannah**, h.w. and **Robert Fisher** .. Ł162 .. 181 a. .. oak on W. side of North branch of Licking Run and cor. to **John Ball's** land .. **Hoe's** line .. cor. to **Ann Barrett** .. *Signed*: James (x) **Bailey**, Hannah (x) **Bailey**. *Wits*: **H. Brooke, Willis Green**. *Rec*: 27 July 1778, ack. by grantors.

Pages 479–486. 11–12 June 1775. Lease & release. Bet. **P e t e r Wagener**, Gent. of Fx. Co. & **Sinah**, h. w. and **Benjamin Harrison** .. tract on branches of Elk Run and Licking Run .. 235 a. .. glade of Licking Run, cor. of Original Patent .. Owl Run .. road to Falmouth .. Elk Run by Capt. **Thomas Bullitt's** plantation .. same purch. by late Peter Wagener of Fx. Co. of **Richard McGraw** then of K. G. Co., 24–25 May 1745 .. for 200 a. .. which became the property of the grantor on the death of sd. Peter Wagener .. Ł235 .. *Signed*: **Pet Wagener**,

Sinah Wagener. *Wits*: H. Ross, Alex. Henderson, W. Thompson, James Nisbett, Jr. *Rec*: 27 July 1778, ack. by grantor.

Pages 486-488. 25 June 1778. Deed of Gift. Bet. Henry Mauzy, Sr. of Ham. Par. and John Mauzy, Jr., son of sd. Henry Mauzy .. for nat. love and affection .. and 5s. .. a Negro boy named J a m e s (commonly called Pickett) .. tract on Great Run, adj. the lands of Thomas Ayres, James Withers, Sr., Benj. Garner and Wm. Withers, Sr. .. 200 a. .. same formerly the prop. of my father-in-law, James Withers, Elder, dec'd. and dev. to me and my former wife Nanney .. *Signed*: Henry Mauzy. *Rec*: 27 July 1778, ack. by grantor.

Pages 488-489. 30 June 1778. Bond. John Mauzy, Jr. to Henry Mauzy, Sr. .. Ł1000 .. Henry Mauzy and his father John Mauzy of Staff. Co. are seized in Fee Tail of a tract of land .. *Signed*: J o h n Mauzy. *Wits*: John Withers, Charles Ayres, John Anderson. *Rec*: 27 July 1778, ack. by John Mauzy.

Pages 489-493. 28 May 1778. B & S. Bet. Thomas Chinn of Loud. Co. & Sarah, h. w. and James Winn .. Ł263.15s. .. Beg. ancient cor. of John Clark's land, known now by Edward Feagans and Joseph Blackebee's cor. .. line of Thomas Thornton .. line of Mr. Charles Burgess .. 211 a. *Signed*: Thomas Chinn, Sarah Chinn. *Wits*: Wm. Heale, John Barker, Minor Winn, Phil. Heale, John Macmillain. Cert. of Exam. of Sarah Chinn from Loud. Co. signed by Thomas Lewis and Wm. Smith, Gent., returned. *Rec*: 27 July 1778, prov. by o. of John Barker, John McMillian and Minor Winn.

Pages 493-496. 27 July 1778. B & S. Bet. John Barker & Jemima, h. w. and James Winn .. Ł164 .. one moiety of a piece of land lately purch. by Barker & Winn of Elizabeth Fallin and her dau. Agatha Fallin .. part contains 127 a. .. cor. to Barker & Winn line of John McMillian .. line of Thomas Thornton. *Signed*: John Barker, Jemima Barker. *Rec*: 27 July 1778, ack. by grantors.

Pages 496-499. 27 July 1778. B & S. Bet. James Winn & Hannah, h. w. of Leeds Par. and J o h n B a r k e r .. Ł164 .. other half of above cited purchase .. cor. of Winn in John McMillian's line .. land of Burgess now William Fitzgerald .. Burgess's antient cor. .. Burgess's, Stamp's & Thornton's antient cor. at foot of a Small Mt. .. 127 a. .. *Signed*: James Winn, Hannah Winn. *Rec*: 27 July 1778, ack. by grantors.

Pages 499-503. 10 August 1778. B & S. Bet. William Sutton & Margaret, h. w. of Leeds Par. and William Dulin(g), Jr. .. Ł300 .. 209 a. .. part of larger tract granted to Dennis Conyers .. 13 Nov. 1742 .. cor. to Mr. Thos. James .. cor. to Capt. Wm. Pickett's part of sd. tract .. *Signed*: William (M) Sutton, Margaret (X) Sutton. *Wits*: J. Moffett, Wm. Pickett, Thos. James, Benj'a Ball, Reuben Bramlett, Edward Dulin. *Rec*: 24 August 1778, prov. by o. of John Moffett, Thomas James and Benjamin Ball, wits.

Pages 503–506. 10 August 1778. B & S. Bet. **Benjamin Morris** and **Travers Nash** .. Ł400 .. same tract Morris purch. from **Landon &** **Chas. Carter**, Exors. of Charles Carter, Esq.. dec'd, part of larger tract known as Kettle Run .. cor. on Kettle Run .. drain near the road that leads from **Thornton's** to **Neavils** where **Warren** corners .. 131 a. *Signed*: **Benjamin (X) Morris**. *Wits*: **James McClanahan, William Warren, Carr Bailey**. *Rec*: 24 August 1778, ack. by grantor.

Pages 506–509. 3 February 1778. B & S. Bet. **Thomas Bunberry, Jr.** of K. G. Co. and **Wily Roy**, now of Loud. Co. .. Ł1400 .. tract in Ham. Par .. 713 a. .. bounded by lands of **Richard Henry Lee**, Esq. and Mrs. **Elizabeth Bunberry** (widow) .. given to sd. Bunberry by **William Bunberry**, dec'd. by his last will & testament rec. in Staff. Co. .. cor. of **Humphrey Arnold's** Lott .. *Signed*: **Thos. Bunberry, Jr.** *Wits*: **Thos. Roy, Chan: Fowke, Stephen Chandler, Chandler Fowke, Jr., James Payne**. *Rec*: 24 August 1778, prov. by o. of **Wm. Fowke, Roy** and **Payne**.

Pages 509–512. 4 December 1776. B & S. Bet. **Pearson Chapman**, Gent. of Charles Co., Md. & **Susannah**, h. w. and **William Stewart** of Leeds Par. Ł100 .. where Stewart now lives .. part of tract granted to **John Toward**, 10 June 1731 for 751 a., head of a br. cor. to the Rev. Mr. **James Scott** .. cor. bet. sd. Scott and Mr. **Robert Scott** .. run commonly called the North Run .. 100 a. .. *Signed*: **Pearson Chapman**. *Wits*: **J. Moffett, William Obannon, Samuel Grigsby**. *Rec*: 27 Nov. 1777, prov. by o. of **Grigsby** and **Obannon**; 24 Aug. 1778, prov. by o. of **John Moffett**.

Page 513. 26 August 1776. Deed of Gift. Bet. **George Berry** of Leeds Par. and **John Cantwell** of Craven Co., S. C. for love and affection .. tract at the Bull Run Mountains .. cor. to **Edward Feagan** and sd. Cantwell .. land of **Wm. Young** .. 60 acres .. *Signed*: **George Berry**. *Wits*: **J. Moffett, John Baxter, Peter Grant, H. Brooke**. *Rec*: 27 Jan. 1777, prov. by o. of **Grant & Brooke**; 24 Aug. 1778, prov. by o. of **John Moffett**.

Pages 514–515. 24 August 1778. B & S. Bet. **John Thomas Chunn** & **Martha**, h. w. and **John Hickman** of Loud. Co. .. Ł750 .. tract whereon sd. Chunn now lives .. cor. tree of Capt. **John Ashby's** in line of Mr. **John Adams** .. oak on side of Crooked Run .. in line of Col. **Landon Carter** .. cor. tree of Mr. **George Adams** (marked: ᛏAZT)... 260 a. *Signed*: **John Thos. Chunn, Martha Chunn**. *Rec*: 24 Aug. 1778, ack. by grantor.

Pages 515–519. 17–18 February 1778. Lease & release. Bet. **James Bryan, Wm. Bryan & Elizabeth**, h. w. and **Alexander Lithgow** of Pr. Wm. Co. .. oak in Bunberry's line .. cor. to **William Lynn** near a br. of Licking Run .. 265 a. .. another tract: in line of tract sd. Lithgow purch. of **John Duncomb** .. **Joseph Martin's** line .. 50 a. .. Ł447.10s. *Signed*: **James Bryan, William Bryan, Elizabeth Bryan**. *Wits*: **Cuthbert Bullitt, John Mizner, Jesse Smith**. *Rec*: 24 Aug. 1778, ack. by grantors.

Pages 519–521. 24 August 1778. B & S. Bet. Chichest
and **Charles Chilton**, Gent. .. Ł290 .. 127 a. .. on s. side (
of Broad Run of Occoquan .. bounded by lands of Col. Ch
the Rev. **Wm. Stewart, William Duff, Lawrence Debutts** .
sold by **Benj. Morris** to **Robert Matthis**, dec'd and by him ̣ ̣ ̣
Chichester Matthis. *Signed*: **Chichester Matthis.** *Wits*: **W. Edmonds,
John Stone, Henry Thornberry.** *Rec*: 24 Aug. 1778, ack. by grantor.

Page 522. 23 March 1778. Election. The freeholders of Fauquier
County chose **John Blackwell, Thomas Keith** and **James Hathaway,**
Commissioners for appointing assessors .. *Signed*: **Jas. Scott, Wm.
Pickett, Jeremiah Darnall,** Sheriff. *Retc*: 23 Mar. 1778, ret. made by
Jeremiah Darnall, Sheriff, **James Scott & William Pickett,** Gent.,
Justices.

Pages 522–525. 8 September 1778. Keith's Division. Whereas by the
last will & Testament of the Rev. **James Keith,** dec'd. amongst other
things he devised a tract of land to his sons, Thomas, Alexander and
Isham Keith, to be equally divided. They being of proper age, met and
agreed to the division as surveyed: **Thomas Keith** to have Huntly ..
543 a. .. on Battle Branch, cor. of **Hugh Lampert** (now **David
Thomas's**) also cor. of **Benjamin Thomas** and the heirs of **John
Peyton,** dec'd .. to cor. of sd. Lampert (now **James Sanders**) .. cor. to
Isham Keith .. line of the **Rev. Mr. Scott** .. side of one of the main
springs of Trap branch Scott's antient cor. .. cor. of Isham Keith's on
main Trap Branch .. up meanders where sd. Battle Br. falls into Trap
Branch .. less 5 a. sold **Edward Matthew. Alexander Keith** to have 2
lotts: Roslin & Stony Wood .. 552 a. cor. of Rev. Mr. Scott on main
prong of Trap Br. .. Thos. Keith's line .. foot of the Pignut Ridge by 4
rocks in the line of **Samuel Nelms** .. lines of **Joseph Gibson** .. s. side
of Pignut .. to cor. of **Samuel Skinker** .. from Skinker's line to the line
of Rev. Mr. Scott .. 386 a. part of land left me by Rev. Jas. Keith, the
other part: beg. at cor. of **John Frogg**'s, now Isham Keith's .. John
Peyton's cor, now the land of **Wm. Kirk** .. Kirk's and Hugh Lampert's
(now **James Lewis**) cors .. cor. of Isham Keith .. 166 a. .. **Isham Keith**
to have 2 lotts, the Soldiers Retreat and South Run. cont. 552 a. ..
Beg. at foot of Pignut Ridge in the line of Samuel Nelms (now **Wm.
Downing**) near Four Rocks cor. bet. Isham Keith & Alex. Keith's land
.. cor. of Edward Matthews 9 a. sold him by Thomas Keith .. Matthews cor. on the Wolf Trap Br. .. cor. to Thos. Keith's div. .. 386 a.
.. the other Beg. at cor. former John Frogg's now Alex. Keith's .. line
of Dr. **Alex. Bell** .. cor. of Rev. Mr. Scott .. line of Hugh Lampert, now
James Sanders .. 166 a. .. *Signed*: **Thomas Keith, Alex. Keith, Isham
Keith.** *Wits*: **John Barker, William Courtney, Burr (B) Barton,
Elizabeth (X) Ball.** *Rec*: 28 Sept. 1778, prov. by o. of Barker,
Courtney and Barton, wits.

Pages 525–527. 22 June 1778. Lease. Bet. **Thomas Lord Fairfax** ✗
and **William Briggs** .. in Manor of Leeds .. cor. to **John Deering** ..
along **Wm. Jett**'s lott line .. cor. to sd. Jett and **William John
Hamrick**'s Lotts .. 245 a. .. for his nat. life and lives of **Thomson,**

enezer and John, his sons .. yearly rent of 49s. sterling .. *Signed*: _airfax, **William Briggs**. *Wits*: **Jesse Thompson, David Briggs,** Nathaniel (X) Ellis. *Rec*: 28 Sept. 1778, prov. by o. of wits.

Pages 527–531. 1–2 May 1778. Lease & release. Bet. **William Cat-lett** of Fred'k. Co. & **Lettice, h. w. and James Dowdall** .. 179 a. .. n. side of road commonly called Brent Town Road .. br. of Goose Run .. cor. tree to Glebe Land of Ham. Par. .. e. side of the Rolling Road that comes fr. Cedar Run and falls into the above mentioned Brent Town Rd. and commonly called the Glebe Rd. .. part of larger tract granted to **John Catlett**, which was dev. by will, rec. in Staff. Co. to John Catlett, father of sd. William .. £358 .. *Signed*: **William Catlett, Lettice Catlett**. *Wits*: **Winnifred Williams, Thomas** (X) **Dowdall, Jeremiah** (X) **Northcut, Alex'r. Catlett, Lewis** (X) **Pritchett**. *Rec*: 28 Sept. 1778, prov. by o. of Williams, Dowdall and Northcut.

Pages 532–534. 1–2 May 1778. Lease & release. Bet. **Alexander Catlett & Susannah, h. w.** of Loud. Co. and **James Dowdall** .. 179 a. .. e. side of Dorrells Run, ca. 1/4 mile above where Brent Town Rd. crosses Dorrells Run .. £360 .. *Signed*: **Alex. Catlett, Susannah Catlett**. *Wits*: **Lewis** (x) **Pritchet, Jeremiah** (X) **Northcut, Thomas** (X) **Dowdall, Winnefred Williams, William Catlett**. *Rec*: 28 Sept. 1778, prov. by o. of Dowdall, Williams and Northcutt, wits.

Pages 534–535. 7 February 1777. Bond. Bond of **Nathaniel Williams** of Staff. Co. to **John Mauzy** for £200, to convey, with wife **Elizabeth**, a good deed to Mauzy for land adj. **George Calvert, Mr. John & Peter Kamper, Jr.**, formerly Jordan's land, **John Pope Williams** .. 195 a. *Signed*: **Nath'a Williams**. *Wits*: **John Withers, Uriah Knight, Carles Harding, Francis Harding**. *Rec*: 28 Sept. 1778, prov. by o. of **John Withers**.

Page 535. 10 September 1778. Deed of Gift. Bet. **Susannah Drum-mond** and **Sally Drummond**, eldest dau. to sd. Susannah .. for nat. love & affection .. Negro boy named **Lancaster** .. *Signed*: **Susanah Drum-mond**. *Wits*: **Richard Wiatt Shipp, Mary Turner, Mary Shipp, Betsey Shipp**. *Rec*: 28 Sept. 1778, prov. by o. of wits, **Mary, Betsey** and **R. W. Shipp**.

Pages 535–536. 10 September 1778. Deed of Gift. Bet. **Susanah Drummond** and **Molly Drummond**, youngest dau. of sd. Susanah .. all the money due from late husband **Richard Drummond**, dec'd to me and all money due me from est. of late father, **John Shipp**, dec'd. *Signed*: **Susanah Drummond**. *Wits*: **Richard Wiatt Shipp, Mary Turner, Mary Shipp, Betsey Shipp**. *Rec*: 28 Sept. 1778. prov. by o. of **Mary, Betsey** and **R. W. Shipp**.

Pages 536–537. 28 September 1778. B & S. Bet. **John Leachman** and **William Skinker** of Pr. Wm. Co. Leachman obtained a grant of waste land, 27 Nov. 1772 .. for 83 a. .. for £120 .. branch of Broad Run and cor. to **Wm. Flowrence** .. cor. to **Thomas Barton** .. red oak in **John**

Glascock's line .. cor. to **Baxter** (formerly **Garner**) .. *Signed*: **John L) Leachman**. *Rec*: 28 Sept. 1778, ack. by grantors.

Pages 537-538. 28 September 1778. B & S. Bet. **Jacob Burger** and **Nanny**, h. w. of Ham. Par. and **William Jennings** of same .. £25 .. part of larger tract sold by Mr. **Richard Doggett** of Culp. to sd. Burger .. 20 a. .. beg. in Wm. Jennings' Cornfield .. *Signed*: **Jacob Burger, Nanny (x) Burger**. *Wits*: **John Mauzy, Chas. (x) Garner**. *Rec*: 28 Sept. 1778, ack. by grantors.

Pages 538-540. 28 September 1778. B & S. Bet. **John Baxter** of Leeds Par. & **Amelia**, h. w. and **Edward Feagan** .. £163 .. part of tract laid off by Capt. **John Moffett** for **Thomas Baxter**, 15 Sept. 1762 .. cor. of **Bradley Garner's** tract .. mouth of lane cor. of E. Fegan's & **Berry** also cor. of 40 a. sold **John Cantwell** by sd. Baxter .. cor. to Garner and **Benjamin Stripling** at the foot of the Leathercoat Mt. .. 163 a. .. *Signed*: **John Baxter**. *Wits*: **John Feagins, William Berry, Thomas (x) Laws, Evan Griffiths**. *Rec*: 28 Sept. 1778, prov. by o. of wits.

Pages 540-542. 28 April 1778. B & S. Bet. **George Calvert** & **Lydia**, h. w. of Culp. Co. and **Martin Pickett** .. £323 .. land which Calvert purch. of **Jesse Williams** .. bounded by **Kamper** & **Hooe, Chas. Williams, Pope Williams** & **Nathaniel Williams** .. 161 1/2 a. .. *Signed*: **George Calvert, Jr., Lydia Calvert**. *Wits*: **Jos. Blackwell, W. Ellzey, Thos. Keith, Judith Keith, Thos. Maddux, Jr**. *Rec*: 28 Sept. 1778, ack. by grantors.

Pages 542-543. 3 June 1775. Lease. Bet. **Rawleigh Downman**, Gent. of Lan. Co. and **George Threlkeld** .. part of tract Downman purch. of **Thos. Randell** lying on the Rappahannock River & on Summer Duck Run sd. tract having been divided into 3 parcels .. this parcel is in the upper end .. 204 a. .. divided by a line from **Joseph Odor's Lott** .. for his nat. life and lives of wife **Elizabeth** and son **William** .. yearly rent of 530 lbs. tobacco .. *Signed*: **Raw'h. Downman, George Threlkeld**. *Wits*: **Jos. Blackwell, Sam'l. Blackwell, Jr., Joseph Odor, Sr**. *Rec*: 26 Feb. 1776, prov. by o. of **Joseph Blackwell** and Odor; 28 Sept. 1778 by o. of **Samuel Blackwell**.

Pages 543-545. 8 December 1774. Deed of Trust. Bet. **William Dulin, Sr**. and **Martin Pickett & Co**. .. £55.15s.6d. debt to be secured .. 150 a. on Carters Run & Dags line also 150 a. leased from Lord Fairfax on Carters Run .. to be sold for best price after 8 Dec. 1775 to pay above debt plus interest .. *Signed*: **William Dulin**. *Wits*: **John Peake, David Blackwell, Humphrey Jones**. *Rec*: 22 May 1775, prov. by o. of Blackwell and Peake; 28 Sept. 1778, same ordered to be recorded.

Pages 545-547. 28 September 1778. B & S. Bet. **Charles Chilton** of Ham. Par. and **Betty** (or **Elizabeth**), h. w. and **Francis McMeckin** .. £ 230 .. tract adj. **George Rogers, Ambrose Barnett** & sd. Chilton ..

east side of Rogers' spring branch .. 15 acres .. *Signed*: **Charles Chilton, Betty Chilton**. *Rec*: 28 Sept. 1778, ack. by grantors.

Pages 547-549. 26 September 1778. B & S. Bet. **Wharton Ransdell** and **Robert Sanders** .. Ł10 .. 113 a. on the N. side of the Pon Mt. cor. **Wm. Hunton** & sd. Sanders .. stake in **Presley Coxes** line .. **Peyton's** line .. cor. bet. this Land sold the sd. Sanders and the land sold to **Jonathan Newhouse**. *Signed*: **Wharton Ransdell**. *Rec*: 28 Sept. 1778, ack. by grantor.

Pages 549-550. 28 September 1778. B & S. Bet. **Wharton Ransdell** and **Joseph Smith** of Pr. Wm. Co. .. Ł137 .. 274 a. .. cor. to **Presley Cox** and **Robert Sanders** .. **John Thomas's** line .. **Peyton's** line .. *Signed*: **Wharton Ransdell**. *Rec*: 28 Sept. 1778, ack. by Ransdell.

END OF DEED BOOK 6

INDEX

ACRESAYERS, Thomas 39
ADAMS, 170 Anne 174 Daniel 154
Elizabeth 174 Feathergail 174
George 87 190 204 Isaac 145
202 Jemima 201 John 74 78 79
87 110 111 189 190 201 204
Matthew 151
AIRS, Thomas 196
AITHEN, Thomas 187
ALEXANDER, Jesse 31 52 John
192
ALLAN, Abigail 121 Arch'd 61
Archibald 49 50 92 120 121 Ar-
chibald Jr 126 Archibald Sr 126
Elizabth 126 George 128
James 93 John 91 100 126 128
John Jr 135 Martain 126 Martin
128 Nancy 126 William 20 128
ALLASON, Ann 147 148 David
147–149 199 Robert 168 Wil-
liam 93 147–149 177 Wm 190
ALLEN, 34 199 Abigail 121 Ar-
chibald 63 70 121 Betty 174
Henry 139 174 James 179 John
49 50 194 John Jr 135 136
Joseph 173 Mary 50 Moses 70
Nancy 136 Thomas 174 Wil-
liam 20 70 110
ALLENSWORTH, Philip 96
ALLIN, Thos 7
ALLIS, John 80 John Jr 80
ANDERSON, 122 143 Cyprain 29
Daniel 187 Elizabeth 144 151
154 John 112 122 123 144 151
154 203 Mary 29 Walter 4 7 29
77 153
ARISS, Elizabeth 65 Jno 65 John
55 57 58 65
ARMSTRONG, Elijah 184 James
40 48 64 184 Martha 184
ARNOLD, 75 135 150 198 Ambros

ARNOLD (continued)
95 Anne 40 134 Benjamin 134
Elisha 192 George 154
Humphrey 40 41 94 134 204
Isaac 154 182 James 12 15 46
52 72 81 88 John 196 John Jr
38 John Sr 38 Lutishea 38 Lyn
128 Mary 154 Moses 38 128
Samuel 40 Sarah 15 128
ASBERRY, William 17 23 181
ASBURY, Henry 112 William 23
138 139
ASH, George 155
ASHBY, B 97 145 Ben 145 Ben-
jamin 6 Charles 152 Enoch 145
Hannah 6 Jean 189 John 3 13
18 23 26 43 87 111 151 176 189
202 204 John Jr 116 190 Mary
190 Nimrod 6 8 18 155 Robert
5 6 62 78 82 87 96 97 109 147
187 190 Thomas 180 Thomas
Bryan 86 Wm 62
ASHLEY, Charles 184
ASHWORTH, Alice 33 34 John 33
Joseph 33 34
ATCHISON, James 151
ATHEY, Thomas 142
ATTWELL, Francis 61 107 134
139 150 John 139 Mary 107 134
ATWEL, 135 Fran's 199 Fran-
cis 55 79 89 Fras 191
ATWELL, 135 Fran's 199 Fran-
cis 55 79 89 Fras 191
AYRES, Charles 203 Milly 103
Thomas 50 103 203
BACK, John 98
BAILEY, Carr 90 204 Hannah 167
202 James 66 167 194 202
Samuel 197 William 34
BAILY, James 72 96 98
BAKER, 129 Charles 93 112 189
William 200

209

BALENDINE, John 62 63
BALEY, James 72 John 77 90
BALFOIER, George 168
BALFOUR, Geo 168
BALL, 69 122 126 128 134 135
    181 182 Benjamin 12 203
    Burges 75 77 82 112 115 121
    Burgess 73 90 111 123 126 138
    143 146 147 154 157–159 170
    174 182 192 194 195 197 201
    Edward 12 65 87 118 174 Ed-
    ward Jr 87 Elizabeth 87 205
    Frances 78 James 4 8 12 21 34
    47 51 65 76 77 79 82 98 100
    107 110 111 131 138 140 145
    155 174 190 James Jr 8 Jas 38
    75 77 82 139 Jesse 8 78 100
    111 112 John 87 100 113 192
    196 202 Lettice 82 Major 23
    Mary 111 112 115 170 Nicholas
    174 Sarah 117 Sinah 78 Sineh
    111 William 82 85 86 89 91 98
    108 114 117 118 149 Wm 107
    147
BALLARD, Benjamin 61
BALLENDINE, John 49 50 Mary
    49
BALLENGER, 172 Dorcas 99 Ed-
    ward 99 Frances 99 Francis 99
    James 99 John 99
BALLERTER, William 6
BALMAIN, Alex'r 90
BANISTER, William 25
BANKS, Gerrard Jr 39
BANNISTER, William 25
BARBAY, 86
BARBE, And'w 2
BARBEE, 86 Andrew 41 155 170
    Elias 200 Jane 155 John 19
BARBER, 101 Col 53 Colo 22
    John 52 94 152 Mr 2 12 56 145
    Robert 22 Thomas 69 121
BARBEY, Andrew 63 70 155 Jane
    70 155 John 18 Joseph 70 84
    Thos 136
BARBY, Thos 135
BARKER, 131 Jemima 179 203
    John 12 82 83 142 159 162 168
    171 178 179 203 205 Mary 82
    83 108 William 33 62
BARKLEY, William 123 195
BARNARD, Ambrose 124 125

BARNES, John 37 95 115 Rebecca
    115
BARNETT, Ambrose 125 167 186
    207
BARNS, 6
BARRETT, Ann 202
BARRY, Geo 74 Mary 74
BARTLETT, 161 165 168 179 Ann
    155 Anne 131 133 Thomas 131
    132 133 154 155 170 171 186
    William 168 195
BARTON, 107 Benjamin 86 126
    Bur 14 Burr 74 140 205 David 4
    86 107 109 116 126 128
    Elizabeth 4 James 150 John 86
    109 116 126–128 170 Kimber
    188 Rhoda 126 Ruth 4 Thomas
    82 133 150 157 161 206 Valen-
    tine 82 100 101 121 Vall 100
    William 40
BASEY, Edmund 116 Winnifred
    116
BASHAW, Frances 62 123 141
    186 James 15 18 23 62 123 141
    186 Mary 22 Peter 123 199
BASSWELL, 153
BASYE, 135 Edmond 7 116 Ed-
    mund 27 John 18 24 194
    Joseph 123 Josias 186 Win-
    nefred 116
BATHENEY, Thomas 25
BAXTER, 181 207 Amelia 189
    207 John 129 141 142 189 204
    207 Thomas 141 207
BAYLES, William 120
BAYLIE, Mrs 174
BAYLIS, Jno 16 John 13 129
BAYLY, Samuel 197
BAYSE, 198 Edmond 134 154
    Hannah 27 Jacob 134 Nancy
    134 Winifred 27
BEACH, Alexander 6 16 152 Peter
    5 6 185 William 5 6
BEALE, Thos 104
BEECH, Alexander 185 Peter 185
BELL, 101 134 135 174 199 Alex
    205 Alexander 18 77 112
    Charles 145 201 Doctor 22 Dr
    93 Eliz'a 145 Eliza 78
    Elizabeth 12 77 Frances 18 77
    Frankey 2 7 77 89 George 30
    31 James 2 12 18 53 78 89 117

BELL (continued)
145 194 195 John 2 7 15 18 20
22 39 45 50 62 77 78 89 112
117 123 Thomas 12 18 77 145
Thos 78
BENETT, John 69
BENJAR, Sarah 149
BENNEAR, Durk 150
BENNEHAN, Alex'r 82
BENNETT, Daniel 138 G 61
George 61 118 143 Mary 138
Sanford 138 Thomas 81
BENNITT, Ge 90 George 63
BERNARD, William 17
BERRIMAN, Mr 42
BERRY, 207 George 74 117 141
189 204 Henry 117 156 Jos 99
Joseph 99 117 Mary 74 William 156 207
BERRYMAN, John 192 Mamimillian 37 Mary 47 Max'm 164
Maximilian 45 Robert 47
BESHAW, James 15
BETHELL, John 159
BETHELS, William 190
BETSON, James 180 Jas 180
BILLINGS, Jasper 83 Jesper 7
BINN, George 157
BLACK, Stewart 48
BLACKBURN, Edwd 63
BLACKEBEE, Joseph 203
BLACKEMORE, 70 John 12
BLACKERBY, Joseph 179
BLACKLEY, John 16
BLACKMAN, 202 John 44 55
BLACKMORE, Ann 3 65 John 3
10 65
BLACKWELL, Ann 82 154 David
181 182 191 207 Eliz'h 106
Elizabeth 106 George 164
George Steptoe 79 Hannah
Shapliegh 164 J 43 44 184
James 82 95 115 Joe 164 John
26 35 49 63 64 67 71 72 76 77
105 109 115 154 161 163 168
169 175 183 191 193 196 200
205 John Jr 167 175 191 Jos 15
38 40 41 42 56 61 63 64 66 67
71 73 74 76 77 79 81 84 88 91
92 94 99 100 102 133 134 135
144 145 148 169 182 185 189
191 198 Jos'h 14 Joseph 1 3 5

BLACKWELL (continued)
16 19 33 35 37 38 47 48 60 61
66 71 74 77 81 84 90 93 94 98
99 105 108 110 111 115 116
133 141 144 146 149 150 152–
154 158 160 164 166 168 179
181 184 193 194 207 Joseph Jr
114 129 144 145 148 149 152
160 185 193 Lucy 71 Mary 85
Mr 85 Sam 144 145 176 Sam'l
99 100 104 Sam'l Jr 207
Samuel 30 88 98 99 144 154
165 166 169 207 Samuel Jr 182
Thos 201 W 47 52 63 64 66 71
78 87 90 93 95 100 104 106 110
174 182 183 184 W Jr 144 William 1 3 5 15 20 30 34 37 42
47 52 55 56 60 61 66 71 72 90
95 106 108 114 115 117–119
129 144 152 174 180 184 William Jr 43 52 61 65 90 95 106
113 121 129 148 William the
Younger 148 Willm Jr 90 Wm
6 7 13 83 94 99 108 149 Wm Jr
30 95 99 104 144 Wm Sr 104
BLAIN, James 49 52
BLAKEMORE, John 29 Thomas 4
BLAND, James 17 23 24 John 152
Mary 17
BLOWER, John 28
BLOWERS, 178 John 38 62 77
107 121 145
BOATMAN, Henry 100 Margaret
100
BOGGESS, Thomas 129
BOGGETT, George 142
BOGLE, Robert 139
BOGLES, Robert 148
BOLEY, John 74 76 Simon 45
BOLT, Elizabeth 24 John 24
Robert 24 61 116 137
BONIS, William 82
BOOTH, William Aylett 90
BOSWELL, 148 G 101 George 101
105 108 110 125 167 Judith 125
William 116 Wm 125
BOWER, Peter 193
BOYD, Sam'l 195 Samuel 117
BOYLE, Robert 94
BRADFORD, 107 134 Alex'r 53
199 Alexander 6 39 133 174
Austin 133 Ben 62 83 Benj 173

BULLITT (continued)
T 45 Thomas 66 144 202
BUMBERRY, 169
BUNBERRY, 148 Elizabeth 204
Thomas Jr 204 William 204
BURDETT, Frederick 105 John
105 Mary 105
BURDITT, Frederick 196 James
196
BURGER, Jacob 196 207 Nanny
207
BURGES, Charles 75
BURGESS, 107 122 138 140 165
179 181 203 Charles 8 67 69 73
76 77 90 97 107 110 112 143
146 188 203 Chas 75 76
Elizabeth 107 Garner 126 170
Mr 5 29 69 76 180
BURNBULL, Betty 163
BURNBURY, 153
BURRELL, Mr 71
BURRUS, Charles 156 157
BURRUSS, Charles 157
BURTON, Rachael 41 Samuel 41
William 41
BURWELL, 111 125 Lewis 52
108 113 114 115 Robert 25 104
147
BUSH, Squire 45
BUSHROD, John 17
BUTLER, Benjamin 17
BUTT, George 16
BUTTLER, John 16
BUTTON, Harman 172 Harmon 46
146 162 165
BUTTRESS, William Tilson 199
BUTTRIES, W 199
BYRAM, George 62
BYRUM, Peter 56
CAEL, David 106
CAFLY, Henry 64
CAIL, 106 David 106 David Jr 106
Jacob 106 John 106 Peter 106
William 106
CALFEE, Henry 148 John 72
CALVERT, George 154 196 206
207 George Jr 207 Lydia 207
CAMPBELL, Alex'r 151 155 157
165 187 Alexander 150 186
Isaac 124 James 51 131 John
66 Judith 51 131
CAMPER, Peter 142

CANTWELL, John 189 197 204
207
CARR, John Jr 191 John Sr 191
William 13 25 29 49 54 69 78
79 88 89 94 108 120 139 150
155 186 Wm 16 45 78 151 174
CARRELL, Sanford 144 174 179
181
CARROLL, Sanford 131 162
CARTER, 3 14 60 72 109 145 170
198 199 Charles 24 52 61 65 95
96 112 114 123-125 139 140
143 144 146 163 164 167 168
170 173 183 186 195 198
Charles Jr 24 Chas 65 187 204
205 Chs 179 Col 28 46 69 75
87 93 95 Colo 2 6 George 96
105 112 147 194 Joseph 188
199 L Jr 124 Landon 78 112
123-125 139 140 143 144 170
186 190 202 204 Landon Jr 124
125 155 170 Mr 95 Norris 100
Peter 49 65 100 101 Robert 22
181 Secretary 75 Thom's 65
Thomas 3 4 26 49 79 110 William 13
CATLETT, Alexander 206 John
15 21 75 197 206 Lettice 206
Robert 15 Susannah 206 William 206
CAVE, William 74
CENARD, George 105
CENEARD, George 141
CHADDUCK, Charles 181
Winifred 181
CHALFEE, Henry 94
CHALPEE, Henry 87
CHAMBERS, 17 Joseph 12 83 108
119
CHAMPE, Ann 23 William 163
CHANDLER, Stephen 204
CHAPMAN, 118 Pearson 101 102
105 107 141 156 163 164 198
204 Susannah 204 Thomas 47
49 54 78 79 88 89 94 98 106
108 121 150 151 155 186 187
Thos 151 William 145
CHATTIN, 75 123 Thomas 34 52
112 150 151 153 Thomas Jr
153
CHEVES, David 114
CHEW, Larkin 54

213

CONYERS, Alice 38 109 110
  Denis 110 167 192 Dennis 203
  Heziah 192 John 38 78 109 110
  Keziah 192 Peggy 109 110
  Samuel 38 182 192 William
  109 110
COOK, Geo 1
COOKE, Jno 112 John 101 191
  198 William 135
COOLEDGE, Judson 131 Mary
  131
COOLIDGE, Judson 51
COONS, Jacob 129
COOSENBERRY, John 200
COPAGE, Jane 42 Moses 15 42
COPEDGE, Moses 15
COPPAGE, 84 Isaack 15 John 117
  175 William 94 117
COPPEDGE, 187 197 Elizabeth
  45 Isaac 45 Jane 42 John 16 45
  153 173 Moses 16 42 William
  45 118
CORBIN, 5 72 81 98 140 148 191
  193 Col 197 200 Garwin Jr 125
  Gavin 52 Gawin 1 Gawin Jr 124
  Gowen 57
CORDELL, Geo 165 194 199
  George 182 189
CORDER, Elizabeth 10 Eve 136
  James 10 John 3 Joseph 136
  Mary 55 William 3 10 35 136
  William Jr 136 Wm Sr 127
CORNWELL, 105 Jarvis 141
  Peter 83 192 Sarah Ann 192
CORNWILL, Obed 69
CORREY, James 143
COTTRILL, Andrew 173
COULSON, George 39
COURTNEY, John 7 37 47 71 91
  93 168 Mary 91 William 37 71
  91 95 135 205 William Sr 135
COVINGTON, Rich'd 8 9 15 63
  Richard 87 149 199 Winifred
  199
COX, Presley 208
CRAIG, J 141 James 21 40 41 50
  54 79 111 141 159
CRAIK, James 79 87
CRANDON, Abraham 16
CRAP, J 71 James 70 James
  Jun'r 21 Thomas 93
CRAWFORD, Thomas 42 48

CRAWLEY, James 127 R'd 159
  Rd 133 Rich'd 127 Richard 80
CREEL, John 69 Rosannah 69
CREELL, John 56
CRESWELL, George 145
CRIM, Jacob 83 John Jr 83 Mary
  83
CRIMM, 137 Elizabeth 127 John
  Jr 83 John Sr 83 Joseph 127
  Mary 83 Peter 83 127
CRITTENDEN, John 103
CROSBY, 188 George 63 104 138
  186 Susannah 138 Uriel 138
  188
CRUMP, 187 Benj 155 Benjamin
  8 9 56 168 173 Betty 95 104
  144 Elizabeth 95 Geo 7 30 64
  George 1 11 30 64 129 198
  James 152 John 7 8 11 64 95
  104 128 144 198 Joseph 64
CUMMING, Malica 77
CUMMINGS, Hannah 64 John 62
  64 Moses 192 Simon 44 62 64
  Thomas 151
CUMMINS, Thomas 154
CUNDIFF, Benjamin 98 Isaac 121
  122 126 147 157 158 192
CUNINGHAM, 181 Alexander 41
  69
CUNINGHAME, Alex 54 Alex'r 28
  Alexander 47 48 148 William
  57 148 150 155 159 Wm 150
  151 152 160 164 165 171 173
  174
CUNNINGHAM, 98 Wm 150
CUNNINGHAME, A 73 Alex'r 73
  Alexander 45 94 139 William
  45 94 98 139 187 Wm 94 101
CURRELL, Nicholas 38
CURTIS, Chichester 180
DADE, Francis 8 16
DAGG, John 12 78 83 108 110 119
  144 Thomas 12
DAGS, 207
DALTON, Catherine 14 John 14
DALYELL, David 110
DAMKINS, Thos 101
DANIEL, Peter 54 58 Travers 28
  Traverse 54
DARNAL, Catherine 155 David 10
  Jeremiah 18 155 John 57 Mary
  10 65 Morgan 199 Morgan Jun'r

DARNAL (continued)
10 Raughley 10
DARNALL, 77 Catharine 53
Catherine 53 54 140 155 156
David 29 42 48 49 55 65 79 85
Dianah 15 Jane 81 98 Jean 72
Jere 191 Jeremiah 1 5 8 9-11
15 18 20 39 47 53-55 61 77 88
107 109 114 117 140 149 155
156 161 180 181 189 191 194
202 205 John 5 11 57 72 81 98
101 Katherine 156 Leannah 202
Mary 45 Morgain 111 Morgan
11 12 45 49 57 72 76 98 101
111 140 153 154 Morgan Jr 70
Russell 202 Sarah 111 Susann
202 Waugh 11 18 23 26 33 40
42 45 62 101 105 111 153 199
William 57 72 81 98
DARNEL, Waugh 123
DARNELL, John 5 Morgan 5
DAVIS, Ankram 103 Eli 103
James 194 John 103 112 Judith
140 Nicholas 140 Sarah 84 194
Thomas 19 185 William 69
DAWKINS, Thomas 142
DAY, Charles 173 Cossom 154
Cossum 154 Francis 154 Jane
85 Joannah 85 John 85 William 9 85
DEARING, Ann 137 Barnard 138
Barnett 138 George 137 John
137 138
DEARMONT, James 172 173
Michael 198 200
DEBITY, John 41
DEBUT, 3
DEBUTT, 59 60 124
DEBUTTS, 90 John 119 120
Laurance 63 119 Laurence 17
120 121 Lawrence 49 50 61 120
205 Mr 46 Sam'l 50 Samuel 63
120
DEERING, John 205
DELANEY, Charles 9 37 182
Josep 41 Joseph 41 W 132
William 9 71 132
DELANIE, 164
DELANY, Charles 8 20 71 182
Joseph 19 20 132 164 182
Joseph Jun'r 20 William 20 95
DELASHUMATE, John 20

DELENY, Charles 2 Joseph 2
Joseph Jun'r 2
DEMOVEL, Sampson 57 Samson
19 57
DEMSEY, Jane 164
DEMSIE, William 19
DEMSY, Jane 164 William 164
DENNISON, James 148
DERMON, Michael 11 55
DERMONT, James 172 Michael
44
DICKENS, Henry 36
DICKENSON, Edward 48
DICKERSON, James Tutt 200
DICKINS, Henry 36
DICKINSON, Edw'd 69 John 69
DIGGES, Edward 194 195
Elizabeth 198 Thomas 195 198
Thos 191
DIXON, 38 126 170
DOBBIE, William 88
DOBSON, Robt 174 187
DOD, Nathaniel 15
DODD, Nathaniel 72 111
DODSON, 45 Abraham 22 66 69
Ann 69 92 Anna 60 Elisha 22
Elizabeth 59 60 Geo'e 14
George 14 59 60 92 201 Greenham 22 Joseph 3 14 47 55 56
59 60 66 69 Joshua 22 Lazarus
69 Mary 59 Sarah 98 Thomas 3
22 60 61 66 69 96 Thomas Jr
56 59 66 Thomas Jun'r 14
Thomas Sen'r 14 Thomas Sr 59
60 66 69 Thos 14 William 14
Wm 14
DOGETT, Bushrod 164
DOGGET, Ann 196 Bushrod 64
Bushrode 196
DOGGETT, 65 Ann 196 200 Benjamin 200 Bushrod 39 75 200
Bushrode 2 38 50 128 196 Mary
200 Nancy 50 Nanny 200 R'd
196 Richard 207 Susanna 200
Thomas Bushrode 200
DONALDSON, Andrew 97 John 92
Mary 97 Robert 146 William
97 Wm 97
DONIPHAN, Mary 66
DOOLING, John 185 186
DOOMIS, John 16
DORGAIN, Timothy 75

DORGAN, Timothy 2
DOUGLAS, Edward 80 Effirella 80
Joseph 64 Menoh 80 Sarah 48
64 William 48 Wm 64
DOUGLASS, Benj 27 135 136 159
Benjamin 47 127 Charity 127
Sarah 47 William 47
DOWDALL, James 197 198 206
Thomas 206
DOWNING, Mr 119 William 164
173 Wm 205
DOWNMAN, 132 Rawleigh 147
182 207 Rawleigh Jr 82 Robt
82 Robt P 29 Traverse 116 153
DREGHORN, Allan 35 36 41 47
Allen 46
DRUMMOND, Aaron 121-123 126
145 147 153 186 Benjamin 74
James 25 28 Molly 206
Richard 47 206 Sally 206
Susannah 206
DRUMMONDS, Thomas 185
DUFF, James 43 63 113 154
Sarah 113 William 45 61 205
DUGARD, 179 John 178 192
DULANEY, Anna 43 Charles 43
Joseph 37 42 43 William 37 43
DULANY, Charles 9 21 William
21
DULIN, Clamore 132 Clemance
86 Clemence 132 Edward 203
Elizabeth 119 172 John 86 182
Lewis 172 William 12 86 119
132 172 207 William Jr 119
203 William Sr 207
DULING, John 186 Wiliam Jr 203
William 108
DUNCAN, 174 Anne 46 Caty 60
Charles 63 64 Dinah 81
Elizabeth 20 21 101 150 155
169 191 192 James 72 201 Jas
173 John 2 7 12 19-21 39 57 72
73 81 101 105 108 119 120 144
150 153 155 169 185 192 John
Jr 72 81 98 191 Jos 69 Joseph
19 21 45 60 73 180 200 201
Joseph Jr 45 Joseph Sr 169
Lydia 73 200 201 Rice 29 148
149 Robert 46 Robert Jr 46
Robert Sr 46 Wilkey 57
DUNCOMB, John 204
DUNLOP, James 187 John 42 48

DUNLOP (continued)
49 73
DUNLOPS, John 27
DUNN, Robert 174
DURHAM, William 72 Wm 9 187
DUTY, Caty 19 101 William 19
101
DYER, Abraham 96 187 John 96
142 163 172 187 William 96
Wm 187
EADE, John 95
EARL, 161 Samuel 162
EARLE, Elizabeth 14 Sam'l 23
Samuel 14 25 152 187 188
EAVES, Thomas 93 Thomas Jr 93
William 16
EAVESES, Thomas 152
EDGE, John 14 62
EDMONDS, 141 144 162 Betty 38
107 Capt 134 E 65 Eli's 54 92
Elias 1 20 21 27 34 38 54 56
62 63 89 107 111 112 117 157
174 180 183 188 Elias Jr 178
Elis 92 John 196 W 39 71 107
194 195 205 William 1 2 7 39
40 48 89 111 114 115 118 139
155 160 161 165 Wm 12 53 117
EDMONDSON, James 43
EDWARD, Benjamin 69
EDWARDS, 201 Andrew 19 Eliz'a
164 Elizabeth 123 Garrard 63
Gerrard 23 30 John 38 103
Thomas 23 164 Thos 43
EGAN, Barnaby 50 63
ELKINS, William 71
ELLETT, Reuben 77 Ruth 77
ELLIOTT, Curtis 175 Elizabeth
103 Ellis 175 John 43 Martin
175 Mary 175 Reubin 105
Robert 43 103 Thomas 24 36
43 44 82 175 Thomas Sr 176
William 175 176
ELLIS, Caty 135 John 136 137
Nathaniel 206 Sarah 135 136
William 135
ELLISON, Henry 109
ELLISTON, Eleanor 93 Jacob 93
Robert 93 Robt 93
ELLIT, Rubin 69
ELLZEY, Alice 16 W 21 47 54 61
84 88 89 106 120 121 132 139
157 165 207 William 16 26 29

ELLZEY (continued)
34 51 57 58 84 106 108 120 121
152 William Jr 106
ELLZSY, W 51
EMBRY, Robert 95
EMMONS, James 163 Joseph 163
164
ENGLISH, William 176
ENNESS, John 190 Maryan 190
ENNIS, John 190 Mary 190
ESKRIDGE, Charles 108 109 110
Chas 110 Chs 132 George 33
36
ETHERINGTON, Elizabeth 92
John 92
EUSTACE, Agatha 56 Ann 7 Anne
6 Isaac 56 185 John 139 148
168 Mr 194 W 104 Will Jr 185
William 1 3 6 34 56 95 98 104
118 144 176 Wm 6 7 12 13 16
98 100 104
EVANS, Thos 181
EVES, William 110
EWELL, Bertrand 5 8 46 47 51 78
89 100 155 Charles 88 151
Charlotte 88 151 Eve 74 78 79
87 Frances 8 James 74 78 79
87 88 111 151 James Jr 151
189 Jas 190 Jas Jr 190 Jesse
79 82 87–89 151 155 Mary 78
151 Solomon 74
EWEN, Alexander 157
FAGIN, Edward 156
FAIRFAX, 77 85–87 91 98 105
126 128 133 135–137 159 170
171 184 206 Brian 55 Bryan
118 140 180 Bryant 193 Col 4
83 Elizabeth 140 180 193
George Wm 77 William 29 53
55 57 185 Wm 180 Wm Henry
180
FAIRFAXE, Rt Hon Lord 29
FALKNER, 14 Ralph 16 Thomas
14
FALLIN, Agatha 203 Elizabeth
203
FARGURSON, John 15
FARROW, Alex'r 37 43 61 63
Alexander 22 36 61 63 Ann 43
Anna 61 Anne 61 Thornton 176
Wm 43
FAUBION, Jacob 140

FAULIN, 107 William 107 179
FEAGAN, 181 Edward 74 133 157
168 204 207
FEAGANS, Edward 161 203
FEAGIN, Daniel 104 Violety 104
FEAGINS, Daniel 104 Edward 189
John 207 Violety 104
FELKINS, John 85 Sarah 85 William 85 171
FERGUISON, John 9 Martha 9
FERGUSON, Nehemiah 6
FIELD, 2 8 Henry Jr 108 John 107
FIELDING, Edwin 64 116 120
Edwr 119
FINCH, William 182 183
FINDLAY, Robert 48
FINEY, John 64
FISHBACK, 118 132 Cristinah 180
181 Elizabeth 142 Frederick 55
Harman 22 114 142 180 181
Harmon 53 Herman 114 John
16 34 40 49 51 90 131 142 155
156 161 162 165 Josiah 131
161 162 179 Philip 161 Sarah
155
FISHER, Matthew 30 Robert 167
202
FITZGARRALD, Wm 76
FITZGARREL, Will'm 73
FITZGARRELL, Will'm 77 William 77
FITZGARRIL, Will'm 73
FITZGERALD, Kitty 1 188 William 1 2 140 188 203 Wm 188
FITZHUGH, Col 14 163 George
198 Henry 58 John 26 Thomas
21 William 113 170 William
Jr 52 William the Younger 198
FITZJERREL, Wm 179
FLETCHER, Benj 171 Elizabeth
80 James 23 Jas 17 Spencer 80
William 80 133
FLORENCE, Daniel 150 151 William 141
FLOURENCE, William Jr 82
FLOWEREE, Daniel 105 165 183
FLOWERREE, Daniel 106 107
150 151
FLOWREE, Daniel 74
FLOWRENCE, Wm 206
FLYND, Maxwell 101
FLYNN, 85 Hannah 4 Michael 4

FLYNN (continued)
  Valentine 3 159 160
FOLEY, James 103 144 149 169
  181 194 John 169 Milly 169
  William 181
FOOTE, 76 George 24 27 53 Gil-
  son 21 24 26 27 35 53 61 Henry
  24 28 128 John 27 Margaret 24
  Richard 26 27 28 Richard Jr 24
  Richard Jun'r 21 Richard Sr 25
  William 21 28 Wm 45
FORD, 185
FORGUESON, John 72 Martha 72
FORGUSON, John 72 Martha 72
FORSYTH, John 11 198
FOSTER, 144 Isaac 141 Thomas
  179
FOURBAIN, Jacob 138
FOWK, 95
FOWKE, 190 Chan 204 Chandler
  177 Chandler Jr 204 Elizabeth
  199 Gerard 129 199 200 Robert
  Dinwiddie 199 200 Wm 204
FOX, Adam 187 John Peter 188
  Joseph 188 Margaret 187 Mar-
  tin 188 Mary 187 Samuel 88
  169
FRANKLIN, John 197 198
FRAZIER, James 24
FREEMAN, Jas 17
FRENCH, James 108 John 51 91
FRISTOE, Robert 111
FROG, John 64
FROGG, Elizabeth 13 John 13 50
  62 119 205
FURNEL, James 63
FURR, Ann 197 Edwin 192 197
  Elizabeth 71 153 Ephraim 122
  192 197 Jeremiah 192 Moses
  197 Thomas 71 79 132 153
  William 29
GAINER, Bryant 195 Mary 195
GALLAHUE, Chas 152
GANER, Benjamin 195 Mary 195
GARDNER, Jane 3 Jeane 3 John
  Jun'r 3 John Sen'r 3 Thomas
  Jun'r 3
GARLINGTON, John 202
GARMAN, Thomas 69
GARNER, 31 44 207 Benj 185 203
  Benjamin 106 Bradley 207
  Bradly 82 129 Charles 21 Chas

GARNER (continued)
  207 Elinson 71 James 87 171
  180 181 201 John 44 71 72
  Margaret 42 Parish 2 42 71
  Thomas 44 64 71 72 Thomas
  Jr 71 Thomas Sen'r 2 Thos 15
  Thos Jr 57 Thos Jun'r 2 Vin-
  cent 2 42 171 Vincent Sr 171
  191 Vinson 17
GENN, James 2 75 120 123 194
  195 198 199
GENT, Mary 26
GEORGE, 35 70 Moses 10
  Nicholas 20 110 Parnack 98
  108 Parnak 60 Reuben 201
  Susanna 10 Thomas 10 70
GERRARD, Jacob 35 John 35
  Mary 35
GIBBINS, John 27
GIBSON, 107 131 Abraham 133
  186 Alice 97 142 Ann 186 John
  168 Jonathan 144 158 193 197
  202 Joseph 14 142 205 Mr 66
  William 69 191
GILCHRIST, Robt 170
GILLICO, William 181
GILLISON, Ann 192 193 202 Anne
  82 192 193 Benj Harrison 202
  James 116 148 192 193 202
  James Jr 202 Margaret 202
  Mary 202
GILSON, George 28
GINN, James 69
GINNINS, Joshua 39
GINSTEAD, Elizabeth 108 James
  108
GLASCOCK, Agnas 168 Agnes
  122 123 159 168 174 Agness
  146 Elijah 75 145 151 George
  82 122 123 146 147 156 157
  162 174 194 201 Gregory 75
  Hezekiah 122 147 James 197
  John 4 54 146 147 150 154 156
  159 165 172 207 John Jr 96 97
  Margaret 156 165 Thomas 91
  121-123 125 139 146 156 159
  168 174 178
GLASSCOCK, Elizabeth 97
  Hezekiah 97 John 97
GLASSELL, John Jr 54
GLEEK, William 16
GLOVER, Benjamin 136 James

219

GLOVER (continued)
136 Richard 136
GODDARD, John 153 Mary 153
GORDON, John 113 Lucy 113
GRAHAM, Geo 81 John 47 51 89
200 Reginald 98 186 Richard
13 Riginald 151
GRANT, 134 145 Capt 34 Christian 36 Dan'l 17 Daniel 33 36
44 45 136 George 36 39 44 45
51 116 118 131 168 196 John 5
33 36 51 87 116 136 John Jr 51
John Sr 51 Judith 13 118 Margaret 88 Mary 168 P 88 Peter
87 99 150 159 170 179 195 204
Susannah 99 W 7 43 46 50 156
192 193 197 202 William 5 13
20 33 37 43 44 47 49 51 83 99
109 113 115 118 157 194 202
Wm 16 60 83 92 94 100 168
191
GRASTY, George 194
GRAY, Elizabeth 118 James 118
129 142 175
GRAYSON, Benjamin 8 Willm 89
GREEN, 119 120 Ann 178 Duff 12
28 47 51 59 178 George 100
140 141 J Jr 178 James 72
John 178 179 John Jr 178
Joseph 141 Richard 88 Willis
165 178 179 202
GREENLEAVES, Peter 176
GREGORY, Richard 194
GRIFFIN, Henry 201 Thomas
Bertrand 79 William 104
GRIFFITHS, Evan 4 150 207
GRIGSBY, Aaron 102 Elizabeth
201 John 201 Samuel 101 102
138-141 155 156 165 168 198
201 204 Susannah 102 Talliaferro 102 William 153 Wm
181 201
GRIMSLEY, Joseph 127 Nimrod
85 William 85
GRINAN, Owen 148 Thomas 47
GRINHAM, Elizabeth 95 Thomas
94 95
GRINING, Thomas 37 47
GRINNAN, Owen 87 94
GRINNEN, Owen 7 William 12
GRINNING, Owin 17 Thomas 71
GRINSTEAD, James 82 119

GRUBBS, Darius 40 Elizabeth 201
George 201 Rich'd 105 Richard
12 78 101 174 Sarah 40 Susannah 101 Thomas 26 35 40 46
William 167
GUNNON, John 128
GUNNYON, John 78 79 89
GUNYON, 197 John 29 46 51 74
155 197
GUTHRIDGE, Allan 127 Marget
127 William Thatcher 127
GUTTRAY, Hugh 21 29
GUTTRIDGE, Allen 182
GUTTRIGE, 126
HACKLEY, Elizabeth 94 Fran's
84 Francis 83 95 James 94 95
Joseph 94 Lott 46 84 Richard
94 95
HACKLY, Elizabeth 95 James 95
Richard 95
HACKNEY, 202 Joseph 19 101
Sarah 19 101 William 44 69 72
95 120 195
HADDOX, Sam'l 42 William 118
HAILY, Honor 49 Richard 49
HALE, 186
HALL, Elizabeth 199 201 John
199 201 Mary 135 Richard Lingan 135 145 William 182
HAMBRUCK, Price 180
HAMILTON, George 169 Hugh 42
48 Jesse 36 John 163 William
36
HAMMETT, Catherine 28 Henry
139 John 56 Nathaniel Jones
10 Rosanna 10 William 9 10
28
HAMMITT, Catherine 28 Henry
157 William 28
HAMMOND, Charles 163 P 139
HAMPTON, 165 Gale 145 Martha
135 145 Richard 33 135 145
William 145 Wm 142
HAMRICK, 170 John 137 Nancy
137 William 137 William John
205
HANEY, Catherine 117 Charles
117
HANSBROUGH, Jane 89 Morias 6
24 28 89 190 Morrias 89 Smith
104
HARDIN, 7 195 Mark 6 26 176

221

HITT (continued)
Joseph 20 60 105 127 150 169
Mary 20 60 105 127 Nath'l 105
Peter 26 114 149 155
HODO, Peter 103
HOE, 165 202
HOGAIN, Ann 46 Daniel 35 46
William 46
HOGAINS, Ann 46 Daniel 46 114
HOGAN, Ann 22 Charles 22
Daniel 22 Thomas 39 Thomas
Jr 141
HOLDEN, John 152
HOLDWAY, Charles 132
HOLLIDAY, Samuel 159
HOLMES, Anne 59 George 59
James 156 John 59
HOLMS, James 156 158
HOLTON, William 143
HOLTZCLAW, 107 153 Benj 169
Benjamin 150 174 Catherine 24
25 Caty 132 Henry 24 133 157
161 Jacob 34 40 51 123 131
133 150 157 168 James 133
157 161 John 20 71 Joseph 25
84 87 132 150 161 Josiah 57 58
112 114 148 185 192 Susanna
24 112 150 Susannah 148 Wil-
liam 24
HOMES, 156 Edmund 169 James
169
HOOE, 100 134 165 182 192 196
207 Ann 29 148 149 Howson
138 John 147-149 172 190 Rice
90 110 Sarah 29 148 149
Susannah 29 148 149
HOOPER, Thomas 89
HOOS, John 29
HOPPER, 34 133 141 Ann 15 62
63 Anne 80 93 Blagro 84 93
Blagrow 152 Elizabeth 10 93
George 84 91 John 15 17 23 62
63 79 87 137 John Jun'r 10 Jos
91 Joseph 84 91 93 202 Mary
10 24 Robert 197 200 Sarah 200
Thomas 38 84 91 93 Thos 91
HORD, Thomas 42 Thomas Jr 27
Thos 39
HORGAIN, Daniel 35 James 35
HORNER, 124 167 Robert 125 143
HORTON, Benjamin 151
HUBBARD, Ephraim 94 132 133

HUBBARD (continued)
196
HUDNAL, John 6
HUDNALL, 134 135 143 148 177
Jemima 163 Jimmina 163 John
18 25 56 57 76 94 154 163 174
Jos 72 75 90 Jos Jr 99 Jos'h Jr
18 Joseph 2 15 31 56 72 145
163 Joseph Jr 99 Mary 27 99
Richard 99 Thomas 23 30 37
52 62 64 95 106 115 William
23 30 52 64
HUFFMAN, John 40 55 Phillip 15
HUFMAN, Philip 129 Phillip 71
HUGHES, 139
HUGHS, Ralph 46
HULL, John 195
HUME, Andrew 143 Charles 13
Eliz'h 64 F 104 Francis 104 G
2 George 7 9 21 50 James 169
Jno 63
HUMPHRIES, John 185
HUMSTEAD, 176
HUMSTON, 104 Edward 8 38 41
45 163 169 170 Edward Jr 8
Susanna 170
HUNTER, James 50 93 179 180
William 93
HUNTLY, 205
HUNTON, Judith 60 William 12
18 20 58-61 66 69 96 119 Wm
47 60 61 66 120 208
HURMANS, John 138 179
HURMONT, John 91
HURST, Delilah 135 Henry 135
163 Roseanna 135 136
INGRAM, Archibald 93
INNAS, John 89
JACKMAN, Adam 189 Joseph 193
Richard 66 188 Thomas 93 112
129 188 193 Thomas Jr 193
Thomas Sr 189 193 William
193
JACKSON, Ann 118 Francis 190
George 118 Joseph 118 180 193
Samuel 83
JACOBS, Morace 20 Morris 46 95
JAMES, Churchill 117 Elizabeth 8
Francis 173 Hannah 8 J 194
John 62 76 123 187-189 191
194 197 199 Thomas 8 78 87
93 99 119 203 Thos 190

222

JAMESON, Alex'r 28
JAONES, Joseph 36
JAPHRASS, Joseph 55 Margaret 55
JARDINE, 164
JEFFRIES, Alexander 40 118 153 George 40 41 94 John 180 Joseph 134 144 Sarah 40
JEFFRIS, John 98
JEFFRY, Joseph 154
JENIFER, 150 Dan'l 153 Daniel 79 151 157 David 132
JENINGS, Kelly 198 Killy 195
JENKENS, Ezekel 99
JENKINS, Ezeken 99
JENNIFER, Daniel 34
JENNINGS, A 200 Augustin 154 192 200 Augustin Sr 128 154 Augustin the Elder 192 Augustin the Younger 192 Augustine 39 57 62 88 101 103 164 193 Augustine Jr 101 Augustine Sr 101 Hannah 192 193 William 6 62 128 193 196 200 207
JETT, 70 Daniel 9 137 Elizabeth 13 35 Francis 9 13 137 183 193 Francis Jr 9 Franics Jun'r 14 James 35 126 Jane 183 John 90 91 137 Mary 183 Peter 137 Sarah 137 Thomas 43 William 1 35 137 Wm 205
JOHNSON, 27 105 Bailey 157 165 182 Beede 157 Benj'a 6 Debar 73 George 16 184 185 Jafery 2 Jefery Jr 53 Jeffery 42 65 143 Jeffrey 2 3 39 141 143 Jeffry 6 7 57 83 184 185 Jeffry Jr 83 Jefry Sr 53 John 39 42 57 98 104 184 Moses 2 3 6 83 185 Rachael 83 Rachel 83 Samuel 184 201 Sarah 42 Tunis 200 William 7 23 46 Wm 185
JOHNSTON, G 3 4 George 15 52 74 William 17
JONES, 134 150 154 Bereton 14 Brereton 44 143 187 189 202 Charles 10 70 202 Chas 126 Churchhill 73 95 167 Churchill 115 125 129 Daniel 142 163 Elizabeth 10 137 189 Fielding 133 Gabriel 88 113 George 181 Henry 10 79 137 Henry

JONES (continued)
Brereton 202 Humphrey 207 James 36 40 169 Joe 163 John 12 137 Joseph 15 36 54 79 108 169 Joshua 189 Lermah 80 Mary 12 36 40 54 174 198 Nathan 198 Reuben 137 Robert 9 14 55 185 187 202 Samuel 164 Solomon 151 181 Thomas 187 Thos 55 William 9 40 54 73 94 95 115 135 198 Wm 163
JORDAN, 165 206 Thomas 190
JORDINE, Anne 46 Pickett 163 Thomas 46
JOURDAN, Thomas 62
JUDD, Isaac 6 23 186 Lettis 6
JUDO, Isaac 190
JUSTISE, John 67
KAIRNS, Robert 159
KAMPER, 100 207 Alice 176 177 Anne 164 Catharine 162 Catherine 20 60 165 176 177 Charles 163 Elizabeth 18 62 Harman 20 60 165 171 172 Harmon 162 172 Henry 6 18 162 Jacob 163 John 6 64 146 163 164 171 196 206 Lettice 6 Mary 162 196 Peter 18 46 62 114 140 165 171 172 176 177 Peter Jr 112 160 206 Peter Sr 160 171
KEAR, John 197
KEARNE, 71
KEARNES, John 151 William 151
KEARNS, William 151
KEAS, David 163 172 187 John 144
KEASE, David 163
KEAYS, David 163
KEIRNES, William 51 Wm 7 22
KEIRNS, William 26 52
KEITH, 161 173 188 191 Alex'r 178 Alexander 58 201 205 Isham 58 119 201 205 J 59 James 1 140 205 John 58 59 Judith 189 207 Mary Isham 140 Thomas 93 108 110 117 129 133 135 136 140 149 164 182 189 205 Thos 15 88 92 148 169 180 181 193 207
KELLY, Betty 200 James 199 John 169

MILLARD, Elizabeth 62 William 62
MILLER, Joseph 160 Simon 19 25 29 30 34 38 61 71 79 103 112 132 193 194 Symon 71 William 53
MILLS, George 67
MILNER, Bathia 172 Edward 160 Isaac 160 172 173 187 Joseph 172 Nicholas 172
MINTER, Jacob 90 159 Joseph 51 103 178 179 199
MITCHELL, John 150 Richard 79 Susannah 44 Thomas 44 71 196 Thos 2
MIZNER, John 204
MOFFET, John 6
MOFFETT, Gabriel 141 Hannah 29 106 Henry 29 106 J 76 77 85 86 91 98 102 105 107 119 128 135 138 139 156 169 175 176 178 184 198 199 202 203 204 John 8-11 21 24 29 30 82 94 95 102 105-107 116 119 135 136 140 141 149 154 160 163-165 178 184 185 195 203 204 207 Mary 29 Walter 25
MONCURE, J 28 John 26 29
MONDAY, Catherine 116 John 116 123 168 175 177 178 Robert 116 117 William 123
MONRONEY, James 192
MOOR, 148 153 Edward 153 183 184
MOORE, Frances 65 Peter 112 Samuel 162
MORDOCK, 4
MOREHEAD, 199 Alexander 113 Betty 64 Charles 33 43 56 161 163 166 194 Chas 22 64 Elizabeth 64 John 13 15 23 25 38 62 64 71 90-92 116 151 165 166 182 188 200 John Senr 91 Joseph 30 37 64 151 Mary 188 Presley 165 Samuel 91 188 William 91 165 166
MORESON, Arthur 114
MORGAN, 76 Alice 72 Anthony 36 C 184 Charles 26 39 79 103 126 184 196 Charles Jr 26 50 Charles Sr 39 50 Chas 84 104 Chas Jr 39 48 53 Chas Jun'r 5

MORGAN (continued) Elizabeth 17 27 39 54 72 76 126 128 James 17 54 128 John 25 26 55 65 76 79 84 Joseph 193 Phebe 72 Randall 147 Randle 116 Rosannah 72 Simon 3 23 26 123 199 Spencer 102 Sukey 126 William 18 27 50 72 73 79 128 137 140 200 Wm 2 126 200
MORLESS, Henry 37 47 62 Sarah 62
MORRICE, Benj 22
MORRIS, 124 143 186 Benj 205 Benjamin 61 123 124 149 204 Elizabeth 61 Israel 96
MORRISON, Hugh 73 185
MORSON, Arthur 165
MOSES, John 144
MOSS, Mathew 54 Matthew 4 Nath'l 147 Nathaniel 116 154 Sarah 4 54
MOUNTJOY, Thomas 63
MULLIN, William 153
MUNDAY, Robt 76
MURDOCK, John 94 139 148 Peter 94 139 148
MURPHEW, Ann 11 Gabriel 11 Mary Anne 11
MURPHEY, Charles 132 Peter 67
MURRAY, James 103 192 197 John 168
MURREY, James 76 138 Lidia 138 Reubin 138 William 146 147 157
MURRY, James 103 107 122 William 122 146
MUSCHETT, James 89 121 186 187
MUSKETT, Patt 69
MYNATT, Rich'd 6 15 45 47 62 63 Richard 64
NALLS, Sarah 119 157 William 118 119 157
NARMON, 137
NASH, Elijah 82 Francis 104 James 82 Mary 101 Travers 204 Traverse 186 187
NEAL, 35 Joseph 146 Ju'r 35
NEALE, Anstis 197 Benj 158 Benjamin 9 182 195 198 200 Benjamin Jun'r 9 Edward 161 Elizabeth 9 James 9 Joseph

NEALE (continued)
146 195 Mary Ann 9 Matthew 9
70
NEAVIL, 118 204 George 57 114
120 167 186 191 George Jr 57
61 J 195 James 188 189 193
John 69 120 195 198 Jos 195
Joseph 57 Joseph Sr 77 Mary
167 186 Rachel 57 61 Thomas
120 201
NEAVILE, John 69
NEAVILL, 124 George 3 4 25 31
78 186 J 193 Jesse 10 Joseph
25 Mr 35 Thomas 120 146 Wil-
liam 10 29 31 34 Winifred 10
34 Yelverton 34
NEAVILLE, James 94
NEAVILS, 124
NEIL, Ann 146 Thomas 146
NEILES, Matthew 70
NEILSON, John 41 45 48 49 52 98
110 139
NELLSON, James 105
NELM, 157
NELMS, 118 Elizabeth 164 Han-
nah Shapliegh 164 Samuel 164
189 194 205 William 164 173
Wm 194
NELSON, Betty 107 James 49 54
61 107 112 141 174 John 20 67
72 190 John Jr 67 72 Mr 55
Tho 195 Thomas 128 202 Thos
119 180 W 129 148 William 65
107 144 148 151 152 159 179
Wm 150
NEVILE, John 69
NEWAL, Adam 164
NEWALL, Adam 152
NEWBY, Henry 155 Oswald 77
NEWELL, Benjamin 202
NEWGENT, Edward 81
NEWHOUSE, Jonathan 208
NEWLAN, Daniel 52 95
NEWLAND, Daniel 190
NEWLIN, Daniel 52
NEWMAN, James 52
NEWPORT, Nicholas 185 Peter
18 65 185
NEWTON, Benj 75 Benjamin 2
William 93 Willoughby 1
NICHOLAS, Samuel 184
NICHOLS, 29 Isaac 143 192

NICHOLSON, George 129 George
Jr 113 114 115 117 129
NISBETT, James Jr 203
NOLAND, James 145 Stephen 145
NORMAN, Clement 35 Elizabeth
128 Hester 90 183 184 Hugh 90
Isaac 35 Jemimah 35 Jesse 90
128 137 183 184 Martin 128
William 70
NORRIS, John 199 William 62
123 199
NORRISS, William 12 18 26
NORTHCUT, Jeremiah 206
O'BANNON, John 23 Mary 23
Sarah 23 William Jun'r 23 Wm
Sen'r 23
O'BRIANT, Peter 123
O'BRYANT, Peter 123 177
OAR, John 171 Mary 171
OBANION, Elizabeth 45 William
45 60
OBANNION, William Sr 45
OBANNON, 107 Brian 144 Bryan
23 36 37 61 Bryant 92 162
Elizabeth 45 119 John 37 62 63
71 77 107 140 144 155 165
John Jr 36 61 119 John Sr 36
61 Mary 22 36 Samuel 174
Sarah 37 107 Thomas 36 37 45
61 101 Thos 148 William 22
23 36 45 61 69 119 194 198 204
William Jr 107 William Sr 119
William the Younger 61
OBANON, 185 Bryant 119
Elizabeth 119 John 174 John Sr
119 Mary 34 Thos 196 William
34 119 182
OBRYANTS, Peter 116
ODER, Joseph 3
ODOR, Joseph 83 207 Joseph Sr
207 Thomas 84
OLDER, Thos 22
OLDHAM, Mrs 137 Samuel 1 Wm
15
OLIPHANT, John 160 Obadiah
160 Obediah 142
OMOHUNDRO, William 167
OPIE, Elizabeth 164 Lindey 164
Lindsey 164 Lindsy 164 173
Lindy 173
OREAR, John 152 179
ORISS, John 40 41

POWELL (continued)
175 177 Levin 128 177 William 19 Wm 57
POWNAL, John 15
PRICE, 133 140 Benitt 71 Bennett 35 36 45 48 57 69 81 102 108 133-135 150 154 198 Bennitt 89 92
PRICHET, Lewis 62 Mary 62
PRICHETT, Lewis 62 Mary 62
PRIEST, John 70 Mason 70 Thomas 122 146 147 157 159 192 Thomas Jr 147 Thos 197
PRIM, Wm 91
PRIMM, William 91
PRINCE, 199 Betsy 176 Hubbard 29 167 176 John 176
PRITCHARD, Peggy 190 Stephen 95 190
PRITCHET, Lewis 206
PRITCHETT, Lewis 206 William 38
QUARLES, Betty 82
QUISENBERRY, John 192
RAILEY, Thomas 187
RAILY, Thomas 95
RALEY, Thomas 100
RALL, 75
RALLS, 85 John 28 44 197 Margaret 44
RAMEY, Absalom 46 Absolem 28 Sarah 46
RAMY, John 52
RANDALL, Anne 137 Caty 137 Charity 137 George 137 182 John 137 Richard 137
RANDELL, Thos 207
RANDSDELL, Edward 17
RANDSELL, Edwd Jr 17 Wharton 33
RANKINS, George 41
RANSDALE, William 5
RANSDALL, Edward 103 Margaret 117 Thos 168 Wharton 117 177 William 98 139 Wm Jr 168
RANSDELL, 63 174 175 Capt 119 Edward Jun'r 17 Eliza'th 17 Margarett 117 Scott 120 Thos 129 Wharton 5 50 62 78 117 119 120 121 129 141 165 208 William 6 84 91 Wm 33 43 46 50 85 86 112 120 135 157 Wm

RANSDELL (continued)
Jr 167 170
READ, William 83
READING, Mary 15 William 15 71
RECTOR, Ann 8 Anne 85 146 Benjamin 140 152 182 183 202 Betty 185 Catherine 73 91 121 122 123 125 126 138 143 146 147 153 Charles 121 146 152 158 182 183 Conway 85 Daniel 7 8 85 86 Elizabeth 152 182 183 185 201 Frederick 152 185 Henry 73 121-123 138 146 147 152 153 155 158 182 183 194 195 Henry Jr 121 153 157 194 Henry Jun'r 8 Henry Sr 152 183 Henry the Younger 157 194 Jacob 91 122 123 147 149 153 157 158 Jacob Jr 121 146 Jane 158 John 52 63 64 67 71 73 75-77 79 91 112 121-123 125 126 143 146 151-153 157-159 174 182 183 185 192 194 197 201 John Jr 123 157 John Sr 138 146 147 Mary 149 157 182 183 194 Nathaniel 46 64 146 Rebecka 64 Sally 152 183 Sarah 183 Uriah 201
REDDING, Mary 23 26 Timothy 55 William 23 26 71 William Jr 65
REDING, William 71
REEVE, George 72 John 72
REEVES, George 72 124 143 179 John 72 Mary 79
RENO, Thomas 45
RENOE, Jane 72 Thomas 72
RESPRESS, Thomas Jr 200
REXAY, Rich'd 47
REYNOLDS, Catherine 197 Margaret 197 200
RICHARDS, Benjamin 197
RICTOR, Catherine 140 143 Henry 138 157 Jacob 142 John 138 140 143 John Sr 140 Katharine 138 140 Mary 142 157
RIDDELL, John 45 78 79 88 98 121 151
RIDDILL, John 26
RIDDLE, John 142 William 47
RIGHLY, 95 190

SPANN, Priscilla 113
SPICER, 133 Randall 102 Randolph 89 92 102 107 108 121 134 139 141 145 150 151 155 160 William 102 139 Wm 134
SPILLER, Jeremiah 35
SPILMAN, John 26 142
SPINCER, Lawrence 33
SPISER, Mary 189 Randolph 92 94 102 189 William 189
SPRING, Nicholas 168
SQUIERS, John 112
SQUIRES, Elizabeth 157 John 121 122 146 147 157 159
ST CLAIR, Mr 17
STAGE, Richard 196 Sarah 196
STAMP, 203
STAMPS, 139 Ann 56 91 Anne 56 91 Catharine 47 John 60 66 Leanna 60 Mary 5 Mr 188 Thomas 2 5 56 60 75 Timothy 3 5 47 William 5 55 56 66 84 91 92 101
STANTON, William 21
STARK, 158 Catharine 94 Jeremiah 94
STEEL, 140 George 124
STEELE, George 124 Samuel 124
STEELES, George 149
STEPHEN, Alex'r 199
STEPHENS, Robert 149 William 197
STEUART, Adam 49 52
STEVENSON, Betty 119 James 119
STEWARD, 14
STEWART, 139 Adam 49 52 Allan 101 James 5 81 84 159 174 175 178 James Jr 138 John 1 148 173 175 Joseph 14 William 103 198 201 204 Wm 199 205
STONE, Ann 143 Benjamin 143 John 2 18 196 202 205 John Jun'r 18 Mary 78 144 145 Rhoda 143 Thomas 12 78 83 108 119 144 145 189
STRAWDER, 77 105
STRIBLING, Benjamin 129 141
STRICKLAN, Abigail 103 Joseph 103
STRICKLAND, J 103

STRINGFELLOW, Robert 168
STRIPLING, Benjamin 207
STRODE, James 149
STROTHER, 74 Elizabeth 171 James 67 Milly 171 Reubin 131 William 103 171
STROUD, John 132
STUART, James 92 101 John 94 Mr 60 66 Rev'd Mr 61 Reverend Mr 59 William 16 24 27 28 45 49 51
STURD, 76
STURDIE, W 173 William 39 Wm 15
STURDY, Will'm 12 William 40 42 44 Wm 7 45 57 81
STURMAN, Fox 17 Foxhall 17
SUDDOTH, Francis 98
SULLIVAN, David 126 George 175 177 178 John 144 Jonathan 127 Mary 127
SULLIVANT, John 144
SURDIE, 14
SUTHARD, John 109
SUTTEN, William 110
SUTTLE, Susanna 153
SUTTON, John 120 Margaret 203 William 203
SYARS, Alice 107 James 107
SYAS, John 120
TAIT, Peter 156
TALIAFERRO, James 170 Sally 170 Walker 124 170
TAPLY, Col 145
TARPLEY, 178 Col 28 John 47
TATE, Elizabeth 156 Peter 156
TAYLOE, John 104 175 177
TAYLOR, 129 134 135 150 154 198 Benjamin 27 54 116 Charles 18 69 126 165 180 181 Elizabeth 22 27 54 Henry 60 James 69 116 165 181 Jos 112 Joseph 22 27 45 64 116 153 Judith 55 181 Laz's 3 Lazarus 25 30 Milly 126 Peter 18 22 53 57 Richard 27 53 55 112 116 Sarah 126 181 W R 18 William Robertson 18
TEBBS, Foushe 88 89 George 47 William 16
TEMPLEMAN, William 109
TENNELL, Francis 27 57 Mar-

TENNELL (continued)
garet 27
TENNIEL, John 47
THOMAS, Anne 128 Benjamin 205
Catey 87 Catherine 24 25 Caty
87 David 22 188 205 Enoch
David 128 Jacob 25 James the
Younger 82 121 John 113 119
128 188 208 Joseph 87 Judith
25 Margret 113 Peyton 188
Robert 9
THOMPSON, Debar 73 Dekar 54
Eli 193 Elizabeth 133 Hannah
172 James 146 152 Jesse 133
206 John 162 163 172 Joseph
163 Robert 97 142 Sarah 172 W
203 William 172 173
THOMSON, James 107 111 153
157 Jesse 159 John 171 Robert
171 William 52 171
THORNBERRY, 165 Henry 205
Jno 180 John 111 115 125 170
182 190 195 Samuel 111 170
William 75 120
THORNBURY, Samuel 22
THORNSBERRY, Samuel 75
THORNTON, 124 132 141 154 181
199 203 204 Anne 107 Charles
129 190 Doctor 188 Dr 131 140
Elizabeth 43 Maj 29 Maj'r 154
Major 42 Mr 33 Thomas 83 88
107 168 203 Timothy 52 Wil-
liam 22 43 53 147 William Jr
147
THOS, 45
THRELKELD, Elizabeth 207
George 41 42 50 207 Stephen
72 William 207
TIDWELL, Richard 15 42 197
TIDWILL, Richard 15
TILLOS, Rodham 16
TIMBERLAKE, Eppa 202
TOLLE, James 138 178 188
Roger 188 Sarah 188 Susanna
188
TOLLOS, Rodham 37
TOMLIN, John 36 61 124 149 170
180
TOMPSON, John 163 William 163
TOMS, Thomas 7 50 159
TOOLE, James 178
TOWARD, 107 Anne 102 John 17

TOWARD (continued)
101 102 144 162 204
TOWLS, Roger 75
TRAVERS, Charles 168 Giles 93
TRIPLETT, 29 Francis 121 John
43 Mary 114 Simon 83 William
46 114
TRIPPLETT, John 14
TULLOS, Griffin 128 John 104
Joshua 100 106 Rodham 6 14
16 45 46 95 100 197 202
Susannah 100 104
TULLOSS, Joshua 100 Rodham 87
Susannah 100
TURLEY, William 146 159 168
174 Wm 178 201
TURNBULL, Robert 163
TURNER, 6 11 95 Ann 185 190
Benj 171 Benjamin 185 190
Col 180 Edward 97 188 193
Henry 145 Hez'h 87 111 143
158 Hezekiah 87 190 Jane 145
John 94 109 179 Mary 7 206
Thomas 29 145 183 193 Thos
10 Zeph 74 87 Zephaniah 74 77
79 189 Zephenia 87 Zepheniah
87
TWENTYMAN, Edw'd 2 Edward
21 John 21 148 150 Sarah 21
TYLER, Benjamin 53 John 51
Mary 53
TYRREL, William 179
UNDERWOOD, W 100 William
53 Wm 9 42
UTTERBACK, Elizabeth 86 Henry
76 142 Hurman 133 Jacob 86
John 76 142 Martin 86
VAUGHAN, William 103 Wm 190
VAULX, 120 Robert 17 43 103
VAUX, Robert 119
VIVIAN, Charles 142
VOWLES, Thomas 111
WADDELL, John 77 100
WADDLE, Betty 193 John 26 77
140 164 193
WAGENER, Pet 202 Peter 202
Sinah 202 203
WAGGONER, Maj'r 144 Mr 66
WAITE, William 104
WALKER, 107 133 157 161 168
Elizabeth 136 James 62
Joseph 170 Samuel 19 46

WALKER (continued)
Thomas 25 57 William 19 25
123 136 160 169 Wm 15 16 126
127
WALLER, 128 137 Charles 67 84
89 90 126 165 183 Easther 126
Hester 183 184 John 126 William 93
WALSH, Thomas 191
WAPSHOTT, Graves 163
WARD, Miles 18
WARNER, 186 John 2 16 75 88
Lewis 73
WARREN, 143 James 186 Robert
190 William 124 186 204
WASHINGTON, Augustine 17 93
Bailey 153 Edward 141 186 G
96 97 99 142 George 96 99 104
105 116 142 147 160 162 163
171-173 175 177 180 187 L 145
Robert 148 Robert T 148
WATKINS, Anne 198 Henry 194
William 173 198 William Jr
125 Wm 167
WATSON, William 192 193
WATTS, Richard 162 172 Thomas
47 48
WAUGH, 42 Gowrey 58 Joseph
106 Mary 66 144 149 William
73
WAUKER, 195
WEADON, Nathaniel 107
WEATHERALL, Francis 189
WEAVER, 181 Ann Elizabeth 20
60 Benjamin 90 Tilman 12 20
23 52 69 74 140 155
WEBB, George 202 John 158
WEBBS, Lazarus 77
WEEDON, Joel 186 John 186
Nathaniel 188
WEIR, James 187
WELCH, 44 Alice 31 44 Benjamin 31 44 Daniel 31 44
David 2 31 44 54 Demsey 162
Elizabeth 31 44 Frances 31 44
John 31 44 Joshua 31 38 44
Silvester 144 196 Sylvester 162
Thomas 31 44 71 196 William
31 38 44
WELSH, Benjamin 19 Daniel 19
David 2 18 19 John 18 19
Joshua 19 Thomas 19 William

WELSH (continued)
18 19
WEST, Charles 140 Edward 64 95
115 Thomas 142 160 163 William 112 154
WEVER, Jac'b 15 Jacob 19 114
Tilman 15 114 151
WHALEY, James 119
WHEATLEY, Ann 154 Betty 25
Dinah 39 Elizabeth 25 G 7
George 7 15 25 29 39 40 42 45
George Jr 25 Honour 25 J 174
James 37 40 111 171 John 92
141 154 200 Joseph 111 193
Sarah 25 William 92
WHEATLY, Dianah 14 George 14
James 72 John 174 William 92
WHITE, Alex 109 Elizabeth 169
James 201 Nathan Skipweth 43
Thomas 182
WHITECOTTON, Axton 51
WHITING, Betty 108 Fran 63
Fran's 198 Francis 36 54 57
108 109 114 169 John 36 Matthew 36 63
WHITLEDGE, John 45 108
WHITLEY, 153 George 64 Joseph
192
WIATT, Lettice 173 William 173
WICKLIFE, Mary 176
WICKLIFFE, Charles 176 David
190 Lidia 176 Nathaniel 29
Robert 176
WIGENTON, Samuel 161
WILBORN, Edward 52
WILBURN, Edward 27
WILCOX, John 16
WILIAMS, David 14
WILL, William 177
WILLBOURN, Edward 57
WILLIAM, 11 Evan 5
WILLIAMS, 172 Alice 17 Benj'n
44 Betty 26 Charles 75 165 196
197 Chas 177 207 David 26 29
42 Elizabeth 37 42 61 Evan 88
89 106 151 186 Frances 61
George 17 39 44 46 71 75 103
154 196 197 200 Honour 25
James 15 45 75 76 190 Jesse
75 196 207 John 12 63 87 John
P 196 197 John Pope 75 196
206 Jonas 23 45 57 111 Jos 37

WILLIAMS (continued)
81 Jos'h 16 Joseph 3 4 8 37 61
71 77 81 93 99 133 144 181 182
Lewis 196 197 Margaret 44
Mary 4 99 196 Nathaniel 44
196 197 206 207 Paul 25 31 57
72 88 111 Pope 207 Sarah 25
Thomas 154 William 169
Winnefred 206 Winnifred 206
Wm 103
WILLIAMSON, Alexander 153
Compton 135
WILLOUGHBY, Benjamin 49
John 4 54 156
WILLSON, Cumberland 94 James
16 Judith 16
WILSON, Cumberland 89 98
Jeremiah 140 143 170 186 Mr
65 Wm 79
WIMBISH, John 92
WINN, 99 Dorothy 41 48 Hannah
203 James 56 61 72 81 92 102
132 171 177 203 John 40 41 48
61 81 Margaret 48 132 Minor
40 41 48 63 81 106 131 132 170
171 177 203 Minor Jr 157 177
Minor Sr 48 Richard 56 Sarah
203 W 177
WISELEY, Edward 171
WISELY, Edward 163 172
WISLY, Edward 171 172 Mary 171
WITHERS, Catharine 117
Catherine 117 James 39 41 44
104 117 191 James Sr 203 John
19 31 44 191 203 206 Mr 110
Thomas 17 19 25 42 44 80 119
Thos 133 180 William 31 39
William Sr 185 Wm 44 104
Wm Jr 75 Wm Sr 203
WODROW, A 168 Alex'r 73 147
Alexander 49 52 135
WOOD, Abisha 186 Abishai 186
Benjamin 58 Catharine 4 7
Cathe 7 Dickerson 133 Edward
156 184 Elias 4 Elizabeth 185
Gideon 46 Henry Machen 96
James 11 96 97 99 104 105 116
172 Jas 96 John 96 97 104 128
160 186 195 198 Joseph 6 190
198 Joshua 37 70 71 Lettice 96
Lewis 58 Mary 116 133
Nathaniel 4 Nehemiah 185 186

WOOD (continued)
Peter 104 156 158 Samuel 77
Sarah 77 Thos 22 Tobias 153
201 W 142 William 7 70 97
142 160 172 William Jr 96 97
142 185 Wm the Older 186
Wm the Younger 186
WOODBURN, James 76 98 101
WOODFORD, C 124 Catesby 124
125 140 143 170 186
WOODROW, Alexander 41
WOODSIDE, Alander 50 Alex 50
Alex'r 84 Alexander 93 John 34
62 John Jr 98 John Sr 98 99
WOODSIDES, John 63
WOODYARD, 85 86 James 86
Lewis 86 Nessy 86
WRIGHT, 131 Ann 39 170 171
George 115 J 161 James 51 52
63 72 101 111 John 11 20 33 38
39 51 63 72 89 113 132 144 171
179 John Jr 38 39 112 113 170
171 John Lee 118 Joseph 93
112 Mary 11 23 26 192 200
Reuben 200 Reubin 192 Wil-
liam 5 11 23 26 35 36 77 152
174 193 197 Winfield 33 51
Winkfield 52
WROUGHTON, Mary 175 177
WYAT, James 72
WYATT, 167 Lettice 173 Wil-
liam 4 139 173
YATES, George 93 William 131
186
YEATES, Joshua 103
YOUNG, 17 Bryant 158 Christian
104 Francis 52 James 46 69
106 111 115 170 182 195 196
198 John 97 105 116 160 170
Margaret 97 116 160 O 156 158
Original 6 29 55 72 84 90 94 95
98 99 104 106 108 156 158
Originald 156 Richard 55 187
Sennett 22 Sinet 62 Sinit 84
Sinnet 84 William 97 141 158
Wm 160 204